UNIX for People

A Modular Guide to the UNIX Operating System:

Visual Editing, Document Preparation, & Other Resources

UNIX* for People

A Modular Guide to the UNIX Operating System:

Visual Editing, Document Preparation, & Other Resources

Peter M. Birns

Patrick B. Brown

John C. C. Muster

Prentice-Hall, Inc., Englewood Cliffs, N.J. 07632

* UNIX is a trademark of Bell Laboratories

Library of Congress Cataloging in Publication Data

Birns, Peter.
  UNIX for people.

  Includes index.
  1. UNIX (Computer operating system) I. Brown,
Patrick B. II. Muster, John C. III. Title. IV. Title:
U.N.I.X. for people.
QA76.6.B5725 1984   001.64'2   84-10678
ISBN 0-13-937459-0
ISBN 0-13-937442-6 (pbk.)

UNIX is a trademark of Bell Laboratories

Editorial / production supervision: Barbara H. Palumbo
Cover design: Celine Brandes, Photo Plus Art
Manufacturing buyer: Anthony Caruso
Page layout: Peggy Finnerty, Jill Packard, Toni Sterling
Photographers: John C.C. Muster, Patrick B. Brown, Peter M. Birns
Typesetting: Patrick B. Brown, Peter M. Birns, John C.C. Muster
Illustrations: Kevin Daly and Dana Cuff

Printed in the United States of America

10 9 8 7 6 5 4 3 2 1

ISBN: 0-13-937459-0
         0-13-937442-6 {PBK.}   01

PRENTICE-HALL INTERNATIONAL, INC., *London*
PRENTICE-HALL OF AUSTRALIA PTY. LIMITED, *Sydney*
EDITORA PRENTICE-HALL DO BRASIL, LTDA., *Rio de Janeiro*
PRENTICE-HALL CANADA INC., *Toronto*
PRENTICE-HALL OF INDIA PRIVATE LIMITED, *New Delhi*
PRENTICE-HALL OF JAPAN, INC., *Tokyo*
PRENTICE-HALL OF SOUTHEAST ASIA PTE. LTD., *Singapore*
WHITEHALL BOOKS LIMITED, *Wellington, New Zealand*

Contents

Modules

Command Summary Section

Location of Material within the Book

Foreword

**Why Does Anyone Need a Book to Help Them Learn to Use
UNIX?** The UNIX computing environment enhances *human* productivity. No other single reason can explain its growing popular-
ity. Yet some would—be users have considerable difficulty learning how to use it, and others never learn to tap its power
effectively. Why is this so? The following bit of Bell Laboratories
apocrypha nicely captures this paradox:

> UNIX is so complicated the secretaries
> have to teach the engineers how to use it!

We have observed similar activities in our own environments, so
even if the quote is not a literal truth (and is a disservice to both
secretaries and engineers), it is a useful illustration of the importance of the *method* by which one learns how to use UNIX, and
learns how to use it effectively. The key here is that secretaries,
and other people who need to use computers to get their work
done, have the luxury of learning *experientially* — often in a supportive environment full of other users who have learned what
they know in similar fashion.

But there are problems with learning to use UNIX experientially.
First, in the absence of a book like this, one must have access to
the right kind of supportive environment, something difficult to
find outside certain institutions. And second, the experiential
learning tends, eventually, to be self—limiting. It is hard to
develop, unilaterally, the requisite conceptual models which unlock
the real power of the UNIX environment.

Both experiential learning and conceptual models are necessary.
One reason analytically inclined would—be users (our maligned
engineers) have difficulty getting started is that "analysis" is a ter-
ribly inefficient way of discovering the *skills* necessary to be an

effective user. And it's not much fun. The problem with *too much* experiential learning is that, eventually, UNIX users come to the point where they enter a mere line of text and *"mountains move"!* If it wasn't the right collection of mountains, or they didn't go to the right place, experience rarely provides the explanation. It's here that an (analytical) model can help a user probe the process UNIX uses to execute his or her command, to reveal the source of the error. Lest the reader be intimidated by this, simple diagrams or a repertoire of well chosen examples can provide much of what is needed.

So most would—be UNIX users, especially ones who are learning how to use computers for the first time, need a good book — one that provides sufficient guidance for the experiential learning, and one which also helps consolidate the experience via the timely introduction of conceptual models.

Why This Book? This book addresses both barriers to learning UNIX. It provides guidance sufficient to allow computer—naive users to learn how to use UNIX experientially, even if they must do so on their own, *and* it provides some of the requisite models of how UNIX works, models necessary for consolidation of the experientially acquired material. The user "experiences" laid out by the authors are fun and efficient. The experiences convey a wealth of material, without seeming burdensome. Similarly, the models of *editor—states,* of the UNIX *command interpreter,* and of the *hierarchical file system* are clear, carefully pictorial, and essential! They give the reader the confidence to engage in mountain—moving with reasonable expectations for success.

What Can Readers Expect To Be Able To Do Once They Complete It? Users who complete this book will be well on their way to enhancing their computing productivity. As the early focus is on word—processing and document preparation, readers begin getting real work done as soon as possible; and the exposition is sufficiently tool—oriented (again, tools are what one uses to get work done) so that readers will be able to learn to work in other arenas, such as program development and maintenance. The tool—building techniques illustrated are very general and are among the most powerful activities that UNIX facilitates.

Ultimately, the real power of UNIX lies in the methods it enables for getting work done with a computer. These methods are hard to articulate, computer scientists are struggling with them as we write, but they can be learned from examples. One of the strengths of this book is that its authors had to learn these methods, unconsciously, to complete their book. The book was a group effort resulting from the focus of different backgrounds on a single topic — how to teach people how to use UNIX. It has been field tested by students and staff, gone through numerous revisions and might never have been completed had it not been done using UNIX. Thus, the UNIX methodology is implicit in what the authors have done, and their real success is that they have communicated this experience to their readers.

Mark S. Tuttle
Charles Woodson
Michael J. Clancy

Computer Science Division — EECS
University of California, Berkeley
March, 1984

Preface

This book is a creature of UNIX. It was written over the span of two years, using a UNIX system. We began with the modest intention of providing our friends with some introductory, English language materials on how to text process with UNIX. It is a comment about the ability of the system to foster evolving group projects that our five page introduction grew into this book. One of us wrote a few pages explaining how to. . . Another modified and expanded the ideas. More was written, revised, combined, thrown out, synthesized, and rewritten—with the entire process taking place in one set of files in one UNIX account.

Our desire is that the reader quickly, efficiently, and with a minimum of frustration learn how to do what took us collectively over 10 years to discover concerning how to use UNIX. An understanding of the information presented here would allow you to create a product matching the detail and complexity of this book.

UNIX is a seductive beast. We thought we had the text finished several times, only to discover some additional ideas, a new command, or a different way of looking at the whole thing that just had to be included. Because revisions are so easily accomplished with UNIX, we made the changes.

What was originally intended as an introductory book on text processing and the visual editor (perhaps 200 pages at most) has grown into a more complete introduction to the entire UNIX Operating System. The expansion of our task was due largely to the feedback we received from students using drafts of the text in workshops and classes. Each group of students identified aspects of the system they wanted to know more about.

We are not computer scientists. We like to consider ourselves educators. We selected and ordered the topics, wrote explanations, and created conceptual maps with the goal of providing educationally sound, accessible material. Our objective was to remain truthful about how the system works and to present this information in an educationally effective way.

Three people—our respective partners—have made enormous contributions to this project. We are profoundly in their debt. Without their support we could not have completed this book.

Finally, we offer a sincere thanks to the cast of thousands who used this book in its various unpublished stages and gave us a chance to explore firsthand which parts of our efforts were effective and which needed additional work.

Peter M. Birns
Patrick B. Brown
John C. C. Muster

University of California
Berkeley

Module One
How to Use This Book

Introduction

The UNIX operating system provides an effective and efficient way to compose papers, write computer programs, enter data, and maintain records. UNIX is a powerful system: there is virtually no limit to what can be accomplished using its variety of commands and programs. Because it can do so much it is rather complicated.

Due to its complexity people have often found learning to use UNIX a frustrating and at times overwhelming experience. As a direct result of interacting with people as they learned UNIX and text processing we developed this *modular*, *self-paced*, "*low-jargon*" handbook.

Prerequisites

None. It is assumed that the reader has no knowledge of computers, UNIX, or text processing.

Objectives

The objective of this Module is to introduce you to the essential conventions and the modular format used in this book so you can effectively learn UNIX and text processing.

The objectives of this book are the following:

(a) Completion of Modules One through Ten will allow you to use the visual editor to prepare most research papers or reports and to enter and edit computer programs;

(b) Mastery of the individual Modules Eleven to Twenty-Nine will allow you to complete more advanced specific tasks, such as use special characters for searches and substitutions, send electronic messages to other UNIX users, create and easily move among several levels of directories, generate typeset documents, access the UNIX preformatters which exist to help with bibliographies, equations, and tables, and write your own formatting commands (macros); and

(c) Completion of Modules One through Twenty-Nine will prepare you to format a document or written project similar in complexity to this book.

Procedure

(1) **Establishing an Account:** Make arrangements through your supervisor, department, or system administrator for a UNIX account. Depending upon your location, you will need to obtain two or three pieces of information about your account:

(a) If you are located in a large organization in which there is a "network" of UNIX machines, you will be assigned to one of them and given a *system name.* You will need to know the name of the machine you are assigned. This information consists of a system *name, letter,* or *number;*

(b) Your account *login name;* and

(c) Your account *password.*

Be certain you obtain the appropriate information about your account. Without this information you will not be able to gain access to UNIX.

(2) **How People Learn:** It has been our experience teaching courses and workshops in text processing that people:

(a) Learn at different speeds;

(b) Learn best when they can try out each process as they read about it;

(c)   Grasp ideas better in self-contained units;

(d)   Remember more effectively if they practice commands and procedures;

(e)   Master complicated material most easily when led through in a "step by step" way; and

(f)   Better retain information when given opportunities to review recently learned material in *self-diagnostic* "quizzes."

(3)   **Using These Modules:** Although we are firm believers in the educational value of getting lost and finding your way back home, UNIX can be a very unfriendly universe for someone who is off the path and unfamiliar with the rules. We suggest you allow us to hold your hand and lead you step by step through the basic procedures of the first ten Modules. Hundreds of people learning UNIX guided our design and revisions of the modular sequence and content of this book. You will find learning UNIX least frustrating if you study each section in order. Don't skim over paragraphs, and be sure to try each procedure at least once. Avoid the pressure to hurry—relax and master each part.

(a)   Each Module starts with a brief *Introduction* to set the stage.

(b)   Following the *Introduction* is a list of *Prerequisites.* Make sure you satisfy each prerequisite before proceeding.

(c)   The *Objectives* section lets you know what you will be able to do after completing each Module.

(d)   The *Procedure* section is a step by step list of actions you should take and explanations you should read.

(e)   Exercises, reviews and self-check questions are an integral part of the procedures. Taking the time to perform or answer them will improve your ability to remember the material (and you may surprise yourself with what you know how to do).

(f)   You will be asked to type in text as you proceed through the book. Don't begin learning text processing with a paper or other written material that is important to you! Practice with something you can afford to lose.

(g)   The following conventions are used throughout this book. All UNIX commands are in **boldface** type. When you are to supply information to a command sequence (such as your own password) the requested $\boxed{word}$ will be put inside a $\boxed{box}$.

(h)   Be patient with yourself. There is a lot to learn about UNIX—it can be frustrating, but it can be mastered. You are better off taking a few extra moments reviewing each section than rushing through the process.

(i)   (This is for the technical "types" in the crowd.) This book was written to be used with Bell Lab's UNIX Version 7 with Berkeley enhancements (BSD UNIX). This material should be of use for instruction about any UNIX system that supports the visual editor "vi." Due to the many versions of UNIX currently available—in addition to the many local variations in implementation—there may be some slight differences between the procedures you should use and those presented in this book. These variations will be most pronounced when getting started or accessing the UNIX system. If so, ask for help getting "logged in."

(j)   We have made every effort to insure that all suggestions are appropriate and command sequences correct. We have been through several drafts of these materials—and thousands of students have worked with many of the Modules—to eliminate errors and problems. Please be aware, however, that the sophistication and complexity of the UNIX Operating System—coupled with the various versions in use—make the task of completely "bomb proofing" your experience essentially impossible. Before attempting to use a new procedure with your version of the Great American Novel or Nobel Prize-winning report you should first experiment with a practice file. Only then can you feel comfortable that the command or procedure will do what you want it to do.

(4)   It might be helpful (but is not necessary) to identify an experienced UNIX user (most college campuses have paid computer consultants, while in a business or office setting there will be someone familiar with the local UNIX system). Inform this individual of your intention to learn UNIX with the help of this book, and ask which logging in steps outlined in the first few pages of Module Two are appropriate for your location.

(5) Modules One through Ten comprise the foundational core of the book and should be studied in the order presented. Each builds upon skills mastered in prior Modules. Modules Eleven to Twenty-Nine can be taken in any order, as long as all prerequisites are satisfied.

(6) Proceed to Module Two and enjoy the learning process.

Module Two
Accessing the UNIX System

Introduction

In this Module you will learn how to access (logon) and finish work (logout) on your UNIX account. Four commands will be used to illustrate the kind of resources available on UNIX.

Prerequisites

You need to have a UNIX account. An account can be established through contacting your supervisor, department, or system administrator. Depending upon your location you will receive one, two, or three pieces of information about your account. If you are in a large organization in which there are several UNIX systems you will be assigned to one of them and given (a) a *system name*. At all locations you will be given (b) a *login*, a short name that the computer and you will use to identify your work. Most locations will also provide you with (c) a secret code *password*, which is used to protect access to your account. Before beginning this Module enter this information *in pencil* in the spaces provided here:

(a) My system is: _____

(b) My login is: _____

(c) My password is: _____

Although your login name will be available to anyone interested, your password should remain secret so that only you can access your account. Your password is like your instant cash bank card "secret" code number which is known only to you and the bank.

Objectives

After completing this Module you should be able to:

(1)   Identify yourself to UNIX and inform it you are beginning work (logon);

(2)   Inform UNIX you are quitting work (logout); and

(3)   Make use of the UNIX commands which:

   (a)   Present a list of who is currently logged in;

   (b)   Give today's date and time;

   (c)   Provide a list of correctly spelled words; and

   (d)   Change the password to your account.

Procedure

Module Two contains four sections. First you will learn how to logon and logout of your UNIX account. In the second section the Conceptual Map of the logging on and out process is discussed. Four basic commands will be used in the third section to illustrate the kind of resources available in UNIX. The final section consists of a review of the material presented in this Module.

Logging onto UNIX:

Gaining Access to the System

Many people have found that logging onto UNIX for the first time can be a very frustrating experience. If you have not already done so, it might be useful to identify an experienced UNIX user in your institution and ask which parts of the logging in procedures outlined in this Module are appropriate for your location.

Additionally, you may find it helpful to put a check next to the number of each activity once you've completed it.

(1) **START, Turning the Terminal ON:**

    (a) ___ Turn on the power to the terminal. On many terminals this switch is located on the back, lower right. The terminal may answer with a beep. Wait a few seconds.

    (b) ___ Find the brightness dial—usually located either just above the top right of the keyboard *or* on the back, lower right near the power switch. Adjust the brightness of the screen to a comfortable level.

    (c) If you are in a location with several UNIX systems (and you were given a system name) you might have a small box with a switch or button attached to your terminal.

    ___ If your terminal has such a switch or button, push it—if it is without a button, skip this Step and proceed.

If you make an error at any point in the logging in procedure you should turn the power to your terminal off and then back on and begin again.

(2) ___ Locate Map A at the end of this Module. Two copies are included in this text. We suggest you remove one copy to place next to your terminal for easy reference as you proceed through this material. We will refer to Map A throughout the next few pages.

The objective of logging in—as pictured in Map A—is to get to the box labeled *Shell Mode*. Once you are there, you can enter commands to perform such activities as edit text, look up spellings, and print material.

In the process of getting to the Shell you may be stopped and asked for from one to four different pieces of information, depending on how your system is organized. You may be asked only for your login (account name), or you may be asked for login, password, system name and even for the name of the type of terminal you are using.

Map A is a sketch of the trip from turning the terminal on to arrival in the Shell. Consider yourself to be at the beginning of

Map A at the place labeled *Start*. Now imagine yourself traveling down the path toward the Shell. On Map A we have indicated the four stations that lie between turning the terminal on and the Shell. If your system needs information corresponding to one of the stations, you are stopped at that station and asked for the appropriate information. Once you type in the needed information you are allowed to go on. If information at a station is not needed, you are not stopped but passed on to the next station.

(3) **Station 1, System Name:** If the word *Request:* appears on the screen, you have been stopped at Station 1. The printing of *Request:* indicates that you have the machine's attention and it needs to be told your *system* name, letter, or number.

___ Type the number, letter, or name (lower case) of the UNIX system you were assigned [Item (a) entered by you in the *Prerequisites* section above]. Press the **RETURN** key.

If your system name does not appear on the screen as you type it, you should push the button or turn the power to the terminal off and back on. Once *Request:* reappears, re-type your system name. You must enter the letter(s) of your assigned system within 15 seconds of the appearance of the word *Request:* or else the computer will not attend to your response.

Feeling Depressed? If the machine is presenting all upper case characters check that the **ALPHALOCK** key is not locked on. Make certain that this key is not depressed (perhaps administer .5 mg of lithium) by pressing the **ALPHALOCK** key to release it. Next re-start the logging in sequence by pressing the button or turning the power to your terminal off and back on.

(4) **Station 2, Login Name:** The printing of *login:* indicates that you have been stopped at Station 2, and the machine is ready to receive your login name.

___ Type your login name [Item (b) in *Prerequisites.]* Be certain to use *all lower case* letters or numbers, with *no spaces.* Press the **RETURN** key.

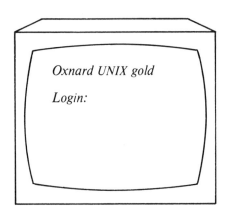

Oxnard UNIX gold

Login:

(5) **Station 3, Secret Password:** If the word *Password:* appears on the screen, you have been stopped at Station 4. You will not be allowed to go any further without entering the password that is associated with your account.

___ Enter your password (again, leave no spaces), and press **RETURN**.

As you type your *password* it will *not* appear on the screen, so that no one else can see what it is. It is, however, being registered by the computer. (A few seconds will now pass.)

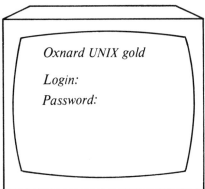

Oxnard UNIX gold

Login:

Password:

Error in Logging On: If *either* your **login** or **password** was entered incorrectly the terminal says *login incorrect* and repeats the word *login:.* You must then re-enter both the *login* and *password.* Be very careful to enter both *exactly* as provided you. Remember to use all lower case letters or numbers with no spaces, and to press **RETURN** after entering each. (Note that if you make a mistake entering the *password,* you will be told *login incorrect* and you must properly enter *both* the login and password.)

If both the login and password were correctly typed and match with the computer's list of accounts, you are permitted to continue down the path. Depending on how your local system is managed, the screen may or may not begin filling with dated news items.

(6) **Station 4, Terminal Type:** If your terminal displays the words *TERM* = [*Terminal Type:*] you have been stopped at Station 4. UNIX must be informed what type of terminal you are using. This will allow UNIX and your terminal to communicate without any misunderstandings. (Pardon my dialect, but I'm from the Bronx.) In the most straightforward case UNIX will be informed automatically about what type of terminal you are using, and you will pass by this Station.

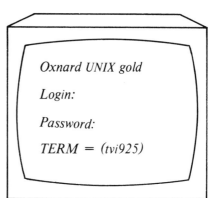

If you are stopped at Station 4, your screen will probably display a line that looks something like one of the following:

$$TERM = (tvi925):$$

or:

$$TERM = (z29):$$

The letters in parentheses are an abbreviation for the most common terminal at your location (e.g., *tvi925* for *Televideo 925* or *z29* for *Zenith 29*. You will need to determine whether you are using the type of terminal mentioned in the above line (inspect the terminal for a nameplate and/or ask someone near you).

___ If the terminal is of the displayed type you need only press the **RETURN** key.

___ If the terminal is a different type, determine the appropriate abbreviation and carefully enter it then press **RETURN**. UNIX now knows what type of terminal you are using.

(7) **The Shell Mode:** If you entered a terminal type that UNIX recognized, a Shell *Prompt* % appears on the screen (this should take a few seconds). Note: Alternate versions of UNIX use different characters (%, $, or #) Whenever we display a Shell prompt in this book we will use the % sign. When the terminal displays the Shell Prompt, you have made it to the Shell.

(8) **Logging Out:** The appearance of the prompt means you have completed the login procedure and the computer is waiting for your next instructions.

You now know how to log onto UNIX. Logging out (ending communication with UNIX) is much simpler.

___ Logout of UNIX by typing the command

logout

and press **RETURN**. This command tells UNIX you are finished working on your account and want to terminate this session.

If you were successful, one of several things probably occurred. Either the screen went blank or the screen displayed a written message like "logout complete."

If you are not logged out and the terminal displays the words *Command not found* you probably mistyped the word **logout**. Retype the command **logout** and press the **RETURN** key.

Conceptual Map

As an aid to your understanding of how the UNIX system operates, we will be introducing a series of "Conceptual Maps." Each Map will visually present those segments and paths of the system with which you are working. You have been using Map A to logon to the system.

(1) **Map Symbols:** To utilize the rest of Map A and the other Maps in later Modules, you need to know what the various symbols mean:

(a) The boxes and circles are "locations" in UNIX and contain both a descriptive label for the part of the UNIX system being accessed and the function performed by that part of the system.

(b) The arrows reflect commands used to move from one place to another.

(c) The symbol ® is used to indicate when you are to *press the*

RETURN *key* (right-middle of most keyboards). The ⓡ notation will be used throughout this book to indicate *Press the* RETURN *key*.

(2) ___ Now that you have logged out, log back in following your path on the Conceptual Map. Notice how the information you type (system, login, password) moves you from one location (Station) to the next.

Once fully logged on, logout. Repeat the logging in and logging out procedure until you feel comfortable with both processes.

(3) ___ Logout of your UNIX account and continue reading this Module.

> *Do not forget to logout* whenever you are finished with a UNIX session—if you neglect to logout, your account will continue to accrue the hourly connection charge. In addition, some unscrupulous, dastardly, or generally ornery critter may discover your oversight and proceed to first use your account to perform his/her own UNIX tasks, then delete all your files and send nasty notes to your friends, thereby causing you untold grief and probably leaving you little choice but to leave town on the first freight train if you are even remotely honorable.
>
> In summary: be certain you logout after each UNIX session.

Four Shell Commands

The appearance of the Shell Prompt % indicates that you are in the "Shell Mode," the main command center of the UNIX system. (Find the box marked *Shell* on Map A.) Being *in* the Shell means that you can issue a specific set of commands which the machine is programmed to respond to. The following procedure steps introduce four of these commands.

Each of these four resources can be accessed *only* from the Shell Mode (with the % or $ or # prompt). This is because the Shell Mode is programmed to perform a specific function in response to your entering each of these commands. The appropriate command is typed in and then the **RETURN** key ⑧ is pressed. *Until you press the ⑧ the machine does not process what you have typed.* Rather, it sits quietly waiting for you to indicate that you are finished typing instructions (which you do by pressing the **RETURN** key). Within the Shell Mode, pressing the ⑧ key is interpreted to mean "process this line."

(1) ___ Follow the Conceptual Map and log onto your account. If necessary, review the steps indicated in the prior section. Once you are logged in, and the Shell prompt is displayed, proceed to the next step.

Note: if after entering one of the next commands you receive the note "Command not found" you probably mistyped the command. Try it again.

(2) **Who is on the System?** You can request of UNIX a list of who (what logins) are currently logged onto the system.

___ To access this command from the Shell type:

who   ⑧

Remember: ⑧ as used above means *press the* **RETURN** *key.*

A list of current users allows you to see if any of your friends are on the system and what terminal locations they are using. This will later prove useful once you learn how to communicate with them via UNIX. Notice that your login is included among the several that are presented.

Two-Way Commands: Find the Shell on Map A. Locate the **who** command just used. Note that it is attached to an arrow that has heads on both ends (a two-way arrow). A *two-way arrow* with a command next to it indicates that by typing in the command you cause the computer to execute that command and then *automatically* return you to the original mode. For instance, the command **who** is given from the Shell and will access the *who* system file. After performing its function (listing the logins of everyone logged onto the system) it will return you to the Shell Mode (your originating mode).

(3) **What Time Is It?** Should you awake one day, forget to strap on your $7900 Rolex day-date wristwatch, log onto your UNIX account, and desire to know the current time and date, UNIX can provide this information.

___ To determine today's date and time type:

date   ®

(4) **How Do You Spell . . . ?** UNIX maintains an on-line spelling dictionary with a word volume somewhere between Webster's elementary school version and the New Oxford Dictionary.

___ As an example of how to access this dictionary try the following. When the Shell prompt % appears type:

look *egg*   ®

A list of *egg, egghead, eggplant,* etc. will be displayed. In most cases the word you might like to know how to *spell* is contained in the display (the UNIX dictionary does not contain definitions to words, only the spellings).

look egg

You enter the first few letters of a word and UNIX displays all the words contained in its dictionary which begin with these first few letters. Another example probably best explains how this works. The command

look *psych*   ®

will produce a whole flock of words like *psychologist,* and *psychology.* Try this command again, using the first few letters of a word that amuses you.

The words will parade by at a rapid rate. If you would like to temporarily halt the presentation of words press the **CTRL-S** key (hold down the key marked **CTRL** and press the **s** key one time). Scrolling resumes when you press the **SPACEBAR**.

CTRL-S

(5) **Change My Password:** We have noted the importance of keeping your password a secret. One solution is to never write it down. The only problem with not having it written down anywhere is that it can be forgotten, especially if the password assigned to your account is a nonsense collection of random letters.

You can easily change your password (or, if one was not provided you, create one) to a "word" that does hold meaning to you. Your new password must be between five (5) and eight (8) characters in length, and should contain at least one letter and one number. Be careful to select a password that is not obvious: computer theft occurs with disturbing frequency. An obvious password provides no protection from any *account snoopers* who may inhabit your system. For instance, your birth date or the name of a spouse may not be good choices. A better choice would be some combination of several meaningful words (*ml8ml8* if you like rabbits, or *10sne1* if tennis is your hobby).

To change your *password* type (from the Shell):

passwd   ®

After typing the **passwd** command UNIX will ask you:

(a)   To supply your old password;

(b)   To type a new password; and

(c)   To repeat your new password.

Be sure to remember the new password, as it will be your UNIX password from now until the next time you change it.

A Note on Making Corrections

It is easy to make corrections *within a single line* because the Shell does not process the line until you press the **RETURN** key. If you make an error in a line you may back up one or more characters by using the **CONTROL-H** key. Hold down the **CTRL** key and press the **h** key one time for every space you want to back up. If your terminal has a **BACKSPACE** key it may be used to accomplish the same thing. The characters can then be retyped.

Once you press **RETURN** the line is "processed." If you mistype a command and then press ® UNIX will reply "Command not found" and display another Shell prompt.

(1) ___ Type the "word" *dote* (typed incorrectly), then backspace and retype the correct Shell command *date*.

If you experience difficulty using the **CTRL-H** or **BACKSPACE** keys (perhaps the cursor does not backspace or the terminal *beeps* whenever you press these keys) you probably made an error when informing UNIX of the type of terminal you are using. Please see the section of Module Twenty-Eight: *Trouble Shooting* entitled *Specifying Your Terminal Type*.

The Finale

Without referring to prior sections of this Module or the Map perform the following actions:

(a) Logout of your account and turn the terminal off.

(b) Log back onto your account.

(c) Ask UNIX to look up the spelling of all words starting with the following letters: *electr*

(d) Logout of your account and turn the power to the terminal off.

When you can perform the above actions without referring to sections of this Module you have mastered the ability to access your UNIX account. You are now ready to learn how to create your own files, which just conveniently happens to be the content of Module Three.

A PDP 11-70; UNIX was originally designed to run on this machine.

Map A

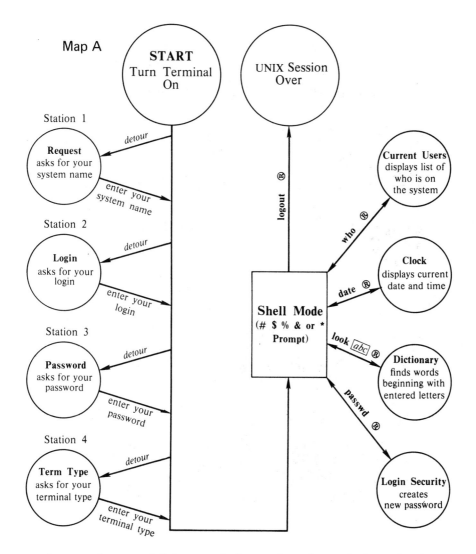

A second copy of this map is located at the end of the book.

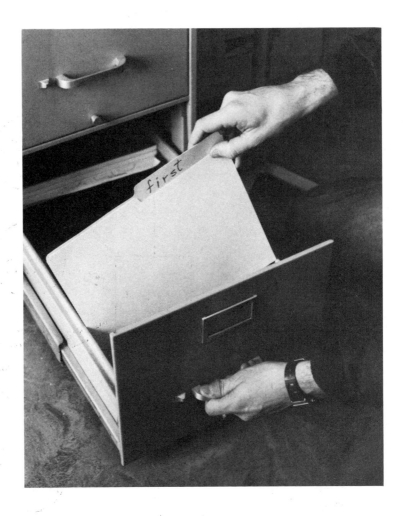

Module Three
Your First File

Introduction

In this Module you will be using two important components of the UNIX system—the *Shell* and the *Visual Text Editor vi*—to create a "file." A *file* is the term used for a collection of characters that is stored together, such as the words in a letter or a paper, a computer program, or a listing of data. This information is kept together so you and UNIX can work on it.

The file generating process is often confusing at first meeting. Take heart: You are not expected to know all about the Shell and *vi* when you finish this Module. Rather, it is intended that you will gain experience you can build on in later Modules to understand the UNIX system.

His first file.

Prerequisites

You need to know how to access your account (logon) and terminate work on the account (logout). If you are not sure how to accomplish these procedures, review Module Two.

Objectives

Upon completion of this Module you should be able to:

(1) Create a file for visual editing;

(2) Append text to the file;

(3) Escape from Text Append Mode;

(4) Quit working on a file, save the changes made in the file, and return to the Shell;

(5) Display a list of all files in your account; and

(6) Have a copy of your file sent to the printer.

Procedure

The Procedure section of this Module is in two parts. The first section leads you through the process of creating and appending text to a file. The second section introduces the Shell commands to list the filenames in your account and to print a file. A brief self-quiz and a comprehensive command summary are placed at the end of this Module. A second Conceptual Map is included to help you chart your course through the paths of UNIX.

Creating a File, Appending Text, and

Returning to the Shell

(1) ___ Locate Map B at the end of this Module—two copies have again been included. You should remove one and place it next to your terminal to review as you complete your activities.

(2) ___ Logon to your UNIX account following the procedure you learned in Module Two. Once fully logged on you are in the *Shell* Mode (which usually has a % prompt). Find this Mode on Map B; it is your home base in the UNIX game of Hide and Seek.

(3) **Starting Your First File:** There are two steps to beginning your first file:

(a) From the Shell enter the following two words (which must be separated by a space):

$$\textbf{vi } \textit{first}$$
$$\uparrow \text{ space}$$

(b) Press the **RETURN** key.

Once you have entered the command sequence **vi** *first* and pressed the **RETURN** key the screen will clear and a note will appear at the bottom of the screen saying either *"first" No such file or directory* or *"first" New file.* Tildes (~) will parade in a column down the left, and the cursor will appear at the top left of the screen. Line numbers may also appear along the left border of the screen. This translates as: "OK, you've called for the file with the name *first*. It did not exist but is now being created and, at this moment, contains no text."

Let's take a look at what you have just done. The command sequence **vi** *first* is in two parts:

(a) **vi** means that you wish to employ the UNIX **vi**sual *text editor,* and

(b) *first* is the *name* of the file to be worked on.

The *filename* can be any single word you choose, within some limitations that will be discussed later. (We are suggesting you title this file *first* because, curiously, it is your first file.)

Locate the **vi** [*filename*] ® command on Map B. The *filename* is in a box to indicate that you can substitute the name of whatever file you want for [*filename*] . In this instance, you have named this file *first.* Recall also that ® included at the end of a command means *press the* **RETURN** *key* after you enter the command sequence.

From Map B note that the command sequence **vi** [*filename*] ® moves you from the Shell to the *vi* Command Mode.

(4) **Appending Text:** "How can I add text to this file?" you ask. Although there are several ways to add text, we'd like to initially introduce one of the most useful commands.

You are in the Visual Editor Command Mode. To inform the editor that you want to enter text, press this key a **single** time (and *do not* press the **RETURN** key):

a

What happened? Nothing. How come this **a** didn't appear on the screen? Because in the Command Mode, pressing the **a** key tells *vi* that you want to add or append text to the file. *After pressing the* **a** *key the visual editor will add anything you type to the file and at the same time display it on the screen.* You are now in what is called *Append Mode*, because everything you type will be entered as text.

(5) ___ Type the following sentence:

I anticipate a long and harmonious relationship with UNIX.

(6) **Typing Suggestions:**
___ PLEASE read this BEFORE you begin any more typing, as we'd like to offer a couple of very important hints.

Short lines are most easily
worked with when using UNIX.
You should press the **RETURN** key
after each main idea
or 5-8 words, and
always after the end of each sentence.
(Just like these lines.)
It will make editing much easier.
Your text should look like this section:
short lines, with all sentences starting
on a new line.
After your text is formatted
(Module Five),
the short lines will be joined together
to form lines of uniform length.
(Like the remainder of this text.)

(7) ___ Now type the 16 short lines of text contained in Procedure Step 6 above. This is for *practice,* so don't worry about mistakes.

Leave the typing errors alone—in a later Module you'll learn how to easily correct them. Just blast in the text. *Don't bother with corrections*—just type a line, press ®, then type in another line, press ® . . . .

Finished? Note how all lines of text began at the left margin. You did not indent paragraphs or try to center lines or double space while typing in the text. UNIX possesses a set of *formatting* commands which you will meet in Module Five. At that time you will insert specific commands to indent paragraphs, double space, and center lines. Whenever you enter text you should not attempt to format the material yourself—let UNIX do it for you.

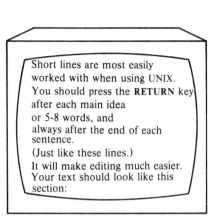

Short lines are most easily worked with when using UNIX. You should press the **RETURN** key after each main idea or 5-8 words, and always after the end of each sentence. (Just like these lines.) It will make editing much easier. Your text should look like this section:

(8) **Leaving the Append Mode:** At this point you should now have 15 to 20 lines of text displayed on the screen before you. How do you now tell UNIX that you are finished *adding* text and want to do something else?

___ Try typing these words:

stop, finish, getmeoutofhere, and *pleaseletgoofmeiwantoutofthisthing*

None of these words will move you out of the Append Mode (which you entered when you pressed the **a** key). You are finished, but everything you type continues to be entered into the file. What you must do is tell the visual editor editor to move you *out of* Append Mode and *back to* Command Mode.

stop, finish, getmeoutofhere,

pleaseletgoofmeiwantoutofthisthing

(9) ___ Look at Map B. What is the command written on the arrow that moves you *from* Append Mode *back* to *vi* Command Mode?

THE WAY OUT OF APPEND MODE IS THROUGH
PRESSING THE ESCAPE ESC *KEY*

The ESC key is your best *vi* friend—find it on the keyboard (usually near the top on the left), introduce yourself, and then gently, lovingly press it. Anything happen? Nothing appeared to happen, but *you are now out of Append Mode* and back in the Command Mode. To be certain, press the ESC key a second time. If a *beep* sounds, *vi* is simply telling you that you are already in Command Mode. Let us stress this point. In your trials and tribulations experienced while learning to use the visual editor you may find yourself a bit lost. While in the midst of entering text into a file you may not be sure whether you are in Command or Append Mode.

The **ESCAPE** *key is your path out of this confusion.*

When in doubt about whether you are in *vi* Command or Append Mode press the ESC key. Within the Append Mode the ESC key means, "Move me into Command Mode." Within the Command Mode the ESC key means, "Please beep." When using the visual editor pressing the ESC key will always leave you in Command Mode. You can decide from that point what it is you want to do. Trace the action you just now completed on Map B. Notice that the **ESCAPE** ESC key moved you *out* of Append Mode and *back* to Command Mode.

Please review the information presented above. Knowing when to use the ESC *key is the single most critical factor leading to successful editing with the visual editor.*

(10) ___ To insure you are in the Command Mode, press the ESC key. Did it *beep* at you? The beep translates as, "But Captain, you are already in Command Mode."

(11) ___ From the Command Mode type this word:

duty

What happened? The terminal should have beeped at you; several times, in fact. (If it did not beep and the word *duty* appeared on the screen, press ESC and repeat this step.)

(12) ___ Type the following:

aduty

This time the word *duty* should appear on the screen. It appears because the first letter of the "word" *aduty* was **a** and this **a** is the **a**ppend command. Therefore the **a** was interpreted to mean, "Move me from Command Mode into the Append Mode." Thus, when you typed the next four letters *d u t y* they were entered into your file as text.

(13) ___ Press the ESC key. You are returned to the Command Mode. You have just had another real-life encounter with the **a** (**a**ppend) and ESC (ESCAPE) commands.

> Summary: the **a** command permits you to start entering text; the ESC stops the append process and returns you to Command Mode.

(14) **Returning to the Shell:** The text you have entered is now sitting on the screen staring at you and waiting for you to do something with it. Suppose you want to finish working on the file for now—leaving any typing mistakes you made in composing it uncorrected until later. You need a command which will tell the visual editor "I'm finished—save this text in a file for another time and bring me back to the Shell." Looking at the Conceptual Map, what command moves you from *vi* Command Mode back to the Shell?

___ Go ahead now and type (Upper Case):

ZZ

If the letters **ZZ** appear on the screen you are still in the Append Mode. You must first move to Command Mode for this command to be properly interpreted. Press ESC to move to the Command Mode and then type the **ZZ** command (hold the **SHIFT** key down and press the **Z** key two times).

What happened? At the bottom of the screen appears the note something like:

"first" 20 lines, 568 characters.

Below this is the Shell prompt % which indicates you are back in the Shell Mode and that the system is awaiting your next Shell command (remember the Shell commands **who, date, look,** and **passwd** practiced in Module Two?).

> Examine Map B. If you are in the Shell and enter the command **vi** [*filename*] ® you are moved *into* the Command Mode. The **ZZ** command moves you *out* of Command Mode and *back to* the Shell, and can *only* be executed when you are in the Command Mode (and *not* Append or Shell Mode).

So far you've written 15-20 lines of text and saved this material as a file named *first* (where it will wait patiently for your return.)

(15) **A Second File:** It would now be useful to practice the procedures through which you created your *first* file.

___ From the Shell type the following:

vi [*second*]   ®
     ↑ space

As before, we put *second* in a box to indicate that you need not call this new file by the name *second*, but can use whatever name you want.

Trace the action you just completed on Map B. Note that the arrow leading into the *vi* Command Mode is a one-way arrow. This indicates that, from the time you enter the command **vi** [*filename*] until you return to the Shell Mode, you are in a "different world" where a different "language" is spoken. The commands that the Shell can interpret cannot be understood by the visual editor, nor can the Shell properly interpret commands meant for the visual editor. The commands that are properly interpreted by the Shell will be either misinterpreted or entirely not understood by the visual editor. Each Mode has its own commands.

(a) In what UNIX Mode must you be to use the **vi** *second* command? _____

(b) After you enter the **vi** *second* command, in what mode are you located? _____

(c) What will be the name of this new file you are creating? _____

Answers: (a) Shell   (b) Command Mode   (c) second

(16) ___ To append (add) text to the file called *second* what command must you enter? Press this key (lower case):

a

Again look at the Conceptual Map. Pressing the **a** key moves you to what mode? _____

Answer: You are in the Append Mode, so text can now be added to the file.

(17) ___ Now that you are in the Append Mode, type 6 to 8 short lines of text. Write anything you want, *but remember to keep your lines short* and *start all new sentences on new lines.*

Once you have entered these 6 to 8 lines, you should tell *vi* you are finished appending text, want this text saved in a file, and want to return to the Shell. Refer to Map B; is there a command to move *directly* from Append Mode to the Shell? No. In order to reach the Shell you need to move in two steps:

(a) From Append Mode to Command Mode; and then

(b) From the Command Mode to the Shell.

You have been adding text, so at the moment you are in the Append Mode. Map B shows the command to move out of Append Mode and into Command Mode. It is the ESCAPE [ESC] key. Press:

[ESC]

You are now in the Command Mode.

(18) ___ How do you move from Command Mode to the Shell? Again, Map B indicates that **ZZ** is the appropriate command. Type:

ZZ

You should now be back at the Shell. (If the **ZZ** appeared on the screen, you forgot to press the ESC key before the **ZZ** was entered.)

Listing and Printing Files

Two more commands and you're finished with Module Three.

(1) **Listing Files:** Suppose you want to know the names of the files in your UNIX account. The command **ls** will call forth a list (*ls →* list) of the names of your files.

___ Type the Shell command:

ls   ®

Did the filenames *first* and *second* appear? The names of other files will also appear if you have created any others, or if your account is used by other people. The *list* command will work only from the Shell.

(2) **Line Printing Files:** You might now like to produce a printed copy of one of your files. Look at Map B. What command is on the arrow from the Shell to the printer? The [filename] in the command **lpr** [filename] ® means that you can substitute the name of any file you want printed.

___ To print out the file *first* you should type:

lpr [first]   ®
↑ space

The *line printer* (*lpr →* line **pr**inter) command is only understood by the Shell. For the terminally curious, the term *line printer* is derived from the fact that most early high speed printers printed one *line* of output at a time.

You can also send the file *second* to be printed with the command:

lpr $\boxed{second}$ ®

(This next point is relevant only if your printer is located away from your terminal.) Several moments after you have entered the **lpr** $\boxed{filename}$ ® command sequence a message may appear on the screen informing you *where* your printed output (here, a copy of your file *first*) may be found.

(3) ___ (If appropriate) Write down the name of the building, room number, and the box number displayed on the screen, as you may need each to identify the location of your printout.

(4) ___ You are now finished with the on-line activities contained in Module Three. Logout of UNIX (from the Shell type the word **logout**) and continue reading the last section.

You've Made It (Puff-Puff)

With the knowledge gained in this Module you are now text processing. Certainly there is much more to learn (otherwise we wouldn't have written the next 400+ pages). Still, the fundamentals are contained in this section, and you'll build on them in later Modules.

A summary list of the commands you have practiced follows the text of this Module.

A Quick Self-Quiz: Consider yourself finished with this Module when you can answer these questions:

(a) In what mode must you be to start a new file? _____

(b) What must you type to start a new file to be named *bonzo*? _____

(c) What is the command to add (append) text to a file? _____

(d) What is the command to leave Append Mode and return to Command Mode? _____

(e) What is the command to quit an editing session, save the additions and changes you made in that session, and return to the Shell? _____

(f)   What is the command to display a list of the filenames in your account? _____

(g)   What is the command to have a copy of a file printed on the line printer? _____

Answers: (a) Shell   (b) **vi** *bonzo*   (c) **a**   (d) ESC   (e) **ZZ**   (f) **ls**
(g) **lpr** *filename*

Note: If you correctly answered question (d) you are awarded the *Houdini* ESCAPE *Artist Award.* Please turn to the last page of this Module for your extravagant certificate, suitable for framing.

Command Summary

Visual Text Editing Commands

Command	Function
a	Moves you into Append Mode, where you can **a**dd text to a file.
ESC	Escapes from Append Mode and returns to **vi** Command Mode.
ZZ	Quits working on the file, writes changes made in an editing session, and returns you to the Shell.

Shell Commands

Command	Function
vi filename	Starts a file or retrieves an existing file named *filename* for visual editing.
ls	Displays a l*is*t of file names in your account (**ls** → l*is*t.
lpr filename	*Has a copy of filename* printed on the l*ine* **pr***inter* (**lpr** → l*ine* **pr***inter*).
who	Presents a list of **who** is currently logged onto your UNIX system.
date	Displays today's **date** and time.
look abc	**Look***s* in dictionary for correctly spelled words beginning with *abc*.
passwd	Changes the **passw***ord* assigned to your UNIX account. (Remember your new password!)

Map B

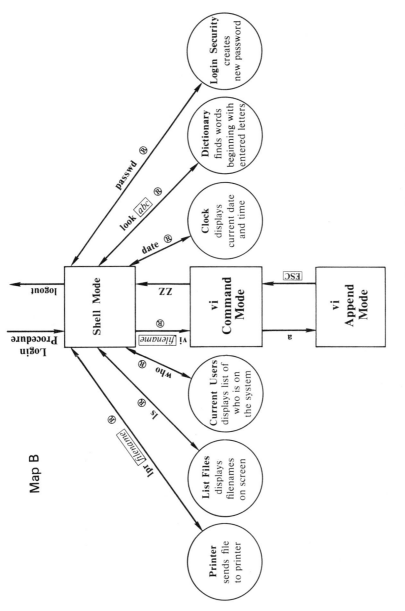

A second copy of this map is located at the end of the book.

35

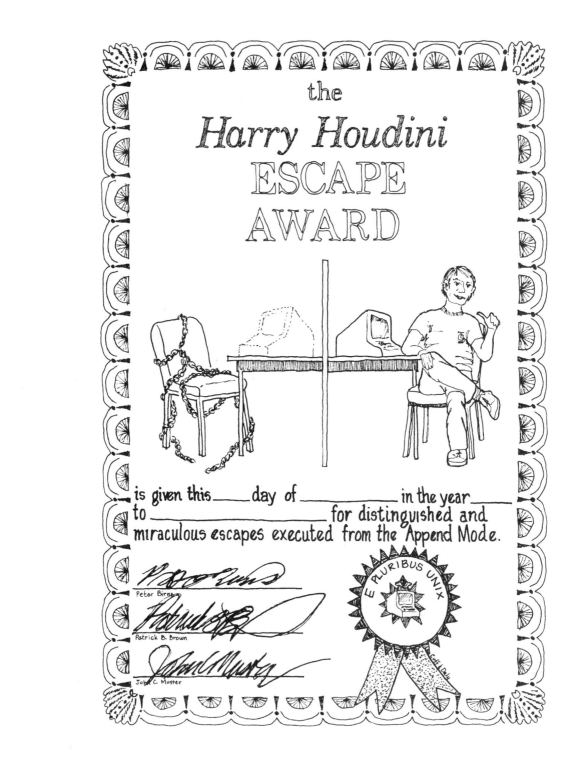

the

Harry Houdini
ESCAPE
AWARD

is given this _____ day of _____ in the year _____
to _____ for distinguished and
miraculous escapes executed from the Append Mode.

Peter Birns

Patrick B. Brown

John C. Muster

E PLURIBUS UNIX

Module Four
Editing Files Using the Visual Editor

Introduction

We seldom express ourselves precisely in first drafts of written work. As a result good writing involves revising, editing, and adding to our first attempts. An advantage of text processing with UNIX is the precision and ease with which changes and additions can be made. Letters, words and paragraphs can easily be replaced, expanded, or moved around. A copy of the paper (with all revisions) can then be printed, without having to retype the entire manuscript.

Although there are dozens of UNIX commands available for editing text, only an introductory set of essential and very versatile commands will be used at this time. More specialized procedures will be included in later Modules.

One approach to the editing process

Prerequisites

To employ this Module you should be able to use the following commands introduced in Module Three:

Command	Function
vi $\boxed{\textit{filename}}$	Starts or retrieves a file for visual editing and moves you from the Shell to *vi* Command Mode.
a	Allows you to start appending text to the file. (Moves you from Command to Append Mode.)
$\boxed{\text{ESC}}$	Signals that you no longer want to add text to a file. (Moves you from Append to Command Mode.)
ZZ	Saves changes made during an editing session, quits work on the file, and returns you to the Shell.

Objectives

After completing this Module you should be able to:

(1) Access an existing file for editing;

(2) Position the cursor on desired lines and words within a file;

(3) Delete letters, words or lines;

(4) Replace letters or change words;

(5) Undo the effect of the last text change command entered; and

(6) Add more text wherever you want in the body of a file.

Procedure

This Module contains five sections. Files and filenames are considered in section one. Section two introduces several cursor moving commands, while text changing commands are discussed in section three. Additional text appending commands appear in section four. The fifth section asks you to practice your text editing skills. Self-check quizzes appear at several points throughout the Module.

Log onto your UNIX account following the procedure you learned in Module Two. After the Shell prompt is displayed, proceed to the first section.

Files and Filenames

(1) ___ From the Shell Mode, type the command

ls   ®

which causes the Shell to display the names of the files you have in your account. (The ® means *press the* **RETURN** *key* and is necessary to let the Shell know you are finished typing a command.)

The screen will display the names of the files in your account, including the files you began in Module Three (*first* and *second*). The Shell prompt is then displayed, indicating that the system is awaiting your next Shell command.

(2) **Recalling an Existing File for Editing:** In Module Three you used the command **vi** *filename* to begin creating a new file. The *filename* you assign to the file (for instance, *first* or *second*) becomes the identification label used to let UNIX know which file you want to work with. Once the filename is assigned, you must use the *same* filename to recall the file for further editing.

___ We suggest you edit the file *first* which you began in Module Three. To call the file up for visual editing you must type the following command sequence (two words):

vi *first*   ®
↑ space

The beginning lines of the file will appear on the screen (perhaps all of the file, depending on its length). The *cursor* will be positioned at the start of the first line.

Yes, the command to reenter a file is exactly the same as the command used to start the file in the first place:

vi *filename*   ®

where you supply the *filename.*

Once you type **vi** *filename* and press the ® key one of two things will happen:

(a) If the *filename* you type after the **vi** is the name of an already existing file, the Shell recalls that file for you to edit; or

(b) If the *filename* you type is *not* the name of an existing file, the process of starting a new file with that name begins.

What happens if you want to work on an existing file, but incorrectly type the name? The Shell will search for a file with the filename *exactly as you typed it.* Because the name of the file is typed incorrectly, the Shell won't be able to find a file with that name. Therefore, it will start a new file with the misspelled *fylename* as its name. To stop the process of setting up a new file and return to the Shell, type the (upper case) **ZZ** command.

(3)   ___ Locate Map C at the end of this Module, and find the box marked:

Shell

Locate the arrow leading downward from the Shell with the label **vi** |*filename*| ® (where *filename* is the name of the file you want to edit: in this instance it is the file named *first*). According to Map C, if you are in the Shell Mode and enter the command **vi** *filename* you are moved into what Mode?

The command **vi** *filename* moves you from the Shell to *vi* Command Mode. It is only from *vi* Command Mode that you can begin editing a file. Make sure you find that transition on Map C.

When editing a file you often need to correct the spelling of particular words, remove specific lines of text, or insert additional text at a particular point. With the screen full of lines of type, how can you tell *vi* which specific word or line you want to change or where you want to add more text?

The cursor, or moving light rectangle, is central to communicating with the visual editor and must be moved to the word or line you want to alter.

Cursor Moving Commands

The Arrow Keys: The basic method for moving the cursor through a file is by using the *arrow keys*. These are separate keys on some terminals ⬅ ⬇ ⬆ and ➡ and the **h, j, k,** and **l** keys on others.

(1) Once you have called up a file for editing with the **vi** *filename* command, the cursor should be at the first line of the file. If this line does not contain text, press the *down arrow* key until the cursor is on a line of text.

___ Locate the key with the arrow pointing to the *right* ➡ and press it. If you did not see the cursor move when you pressed it, press the arrow key again while carefully watching the cursor on the screen. The cursor should move to the right one character. If the cursor does not move immediately wait a few seconds. UNIX is a time sharing system, which means that it shares its brain among you and the other users. UNIX may not be able to follow your every command as soon as you issue it. (If the cursor still does not move, depress the key marked ESC and then try again.)

(2) ___ Try each of the four *arrow keys*. What happens when you try to move the cursor too far to the left? Beyond the text to the right?

You should be able to move the cursor up, down, right and left through the text. NOTE: If the four *arrow keys* don't move the cursor, you may have made a mistake during the *logging in process* when you told UNIX what type of terminal you were using. If the cursor is not behaving properly, see the section of Module Twenty-Eight: *Trouble Shooting* entitled *Specifying Your Terminal Type*.

(3) ___ Select a word in the middle of the second line of text and, using the arrow keys, move the cursor to the beginning of that word.

(4) ___ Press the *right arrow* →| key four more times. The cursor should move four spaces to the right.

(5) **Augmenting the Arrow Keys:** You can include the number keys (**1 - 9**) as part of *arrow* commands. The result is to move the cursor several lines or characters at once.

___ For instance, try pressing the **4** key and then pressing the *down arrow* ⬇| key. Did the cursor move down four lines?

___ Now press the number **3** key followed by the *down arrow* ⬇| key. Again, the cursor should move down 3 lines.

> **Warning:** Many terminals have an extra row of keys located directly above the number keys. These keys may be labeled **F1**, **F2**, **F3**, etc. These are called *Function Keys* and do not have the same action as the conventional number keys. Instead, they will cause much grief if unintentionally struck. Avoid them for now.

(6) ___ Try the **2** key followed by the *up arrow,* then **4** →| **3** ⬇| and **4** ←| .

Rather than repeatedly pressing keys it is usually easier (but not as tension releasing) to include numbers preceding arrow keys when you want to move the cursor several spaces or lines at once.

Note that when you press the arrow keys the editor does what you request (moves the cursor) and then waits for your next command. You can issue cursor-moving command after cursor-moving command without leaving the Command Mode. Find the arrow key commands in Map C. Are they single or double-headed?

These double-headed arrows represent the actions of two-way commands. These commands do not move you into another Mode, and do not require that you use the **RETURN** or |ESC| keys. They take effect immediately upon being typed, and you remain in the originating Mode.

You have probably noticed that there are limits to where you can move the cursor on the screen. If you try to move the cursor past the left margin or to the right beyond the last character of your text, it does not move but instead you hear a *beep*. You cannot go beyond the text which you have added. (Remember that blank spaces, whether between words or accidentally placed at the end of a line, are characters.)

(7) ___ Select another word near the bottom of the text. Use number keys followed by arrow keys to place the cursor at the beginning of the word.

(8) **The Search Command:** An easier way to move the cursor to a specific word in the text is with the *search* command. When you type (from Command Mode) /*specific* the cursor will move to the word *specific* in the text.

(9) ___ Select a word somewhere near the top of the your screen of text. Move the cursor to the word you selected by typing

$$/ \boxed{word} \quad \circledR$$

where $\boxed{word}$ is the *word* that you want the cursor to find.

As you enter the *slash* and the target *word* the terminal displays what you type in the lower left corner of the screen. You are *not* moved to Append Mode (and this display is *not* entered into your text). After you press the $\circledR$ key, the cursor moves to the specified *word* in the text. If it does not, press $\boxed{ESC}$ and try again. (Why press **ESCAPE**? The *slash-search* command is a *vi* Command Mode process and $\boxed{ESC}$ makes sure you are in the Command—and not Append—Mode.)

(10) ___ Select another word and use the *slash-search* command to move the cursor to that word. The *slash-search* command is a powerful way to locate a word in your text. It is a two-way command—you are always returned to Command Mode.

(11) **Finding Clones:** If the *word* you select in this exercise is found more than once in your file, the *search* command can go to only one of them at a time. Pressing the **n** key (for **n***ext*) will send the cursor to the *next* identical *word* in your file. Repeat this process and you will locate the next . . . and the next . . . instance of the *word.* When the editor has reached the end of a file it will loop back to the beginning of the file and continue the search.

(12) ___ No doubt you used the word *the* more than once in your file. Type

$$/\textit{the} \qquad ®$$

and move to the next *the* by pressing the **n** key. The **n** command is a two-way command.

Two-Way Text Changing Commands

(1) **Deleting Lines:** Lines of text are easily deleted. To delete an entire line of text, position the cursor on *any* character on that line and type:

$$\textbf{dd}$$

Blank lines (as well as text lines) can be removed with the **dd** command.

Note: You do *not* press the ® key. As soon as the second *d* is struck, the machine does what is requested . . . and ZAP!! The line is removed. The **dd** command is a two-way command.

(2) **Undoing an Editor Command:** It is possible to *undo* the effect of the most recent text changing command using another command, the *undo* command.

___ Type the **u***ndo*, or "I goofed" command:

$$\textbf{u}$$

The just removed line should reappear on your screen. The **u***ndo* command allows you to go back *only one* text changing command. You can only issue the **u***ndo* command from the Command Mode of the visual editor.

(3) ___ Press **u** again. What happened? Because **u** undoes the preceding command, pressing the **u** key a second time will have the interesting effect of undoing the previous **u***ndo*. This will return your file to the condition it was in before you issued the first *undo* command.

(4) ___ Type

3dd

which will delete three lines starting with the line on which the cursor is located.

___ Bring the lines back with the *undo* command.

(5) **Time to Fill in the Blanks!** Consider the following questions:

(a) What is the command to delete one line of text? _____

(b) Where must the cursor be positioned to delete a line of text?

_____

(c) What is the command to delete eight lines of text? _____

Answers: (a) **dd**   (b) anywhere on the line   (c) *8dd*

(6) **Deleting a Single Word:** It is possible to remove *single* words from the text.

___ Move the cursor to the first letter of any word and type:

dw

The **dw** command stands for **d**elete **w**ord. Nice disappearing act, isn't it?

___ Now bring the word back with the **u** command.

(7) ___ Place the cursor in the middle of a word and try the **dw** command. Does it delete the whole word?

(8) ___ Position the cursor on the first letter of another word and press these keys:

3dw

As with most *vi* Command Mode commands, numbers can be used preceding the **dw** command to increase the effect of the command.

(9) **Deleting Specific Characters:** Select a letter someplace in the text and move the cursor to that letter. Delete it with the command (lower case):

x

The **x** command deletes only the single character under the cursor. It is the *delete one character at a time* command. (Now you can place an **x** over a character, and instead of leaving a smudge, the character disappears.)

(10) ___ What do you expect **6x** will do? Try it.

The space between words on a line is a character just as are letters or numbers. Thus, the **x** can be used to delete unwanted spaces between words.

(11) **Another Quick Review:**

(a) What is the command to delete an entire line of your file?
_____

(b) What command deletes one word? _____

(c) What command deletes the one character under the cursor?
_____

(d) Without referring to the commands, return to your current file and remove one more line, one more word and one specific letter.

Answers: (a) **dd**　(b) **dw**　(c) **x**

(12) **Replacing a Single Character:** The *vi* commands **dd**, **dw**, and **x** allow you to selectively *delete* lines, words and characters. At times what is needed is the *substitution* of one character for another. The **r** command **r**eplaces the one character located under the cursor with the *very next character that you type*. For instance, imagine the cursor is located at the *w* in the word *two*. If the **r** command were typed, followed by the letter *o*, then the *w* in the word *two* will be replaced by an *o*. The word *two* becomes *too*. This may seem confusing, but the action we're describing is not.

___ Move the cursor to a particular letter and replace it by typing the command

r

followed by the replacement character. Practice the **r** command with several other characters in your file.

That *☺*!' dogcatcher's back --
Now there's a character I'd like to replace......

(13) **Breaking Up a Long Line:** One of the handy uses of the *replace* command is to break one long line into two lines. If a line is too long what is really needed is for a **RETURN** to be placed in the middle, making it two lines, right?

___ Select a long line in your text. Move the cursor to the space between two words near the middle of the line. Type the *replace* **r** command and then press the ® key. You are replacing the "space" character between the two words with a ® . As a result, the second part of the line should move to a new line. This action works because the ® is just another character to the visual editor.

One-Way Text Changing Commands

(14) **Substituting for a Single Character:** The **r** command allows you to *replace* a single character with *one* other character. Often an author or programmer needs to substitute several characters for a single character. The **s** command will **s**ubstitute for the *one character* under the cursor whatever you type until you press the ESC key.

Select a word in your file that you might like to alter. Position the cursor over a letter in that word and type (lower case):

s

Type one or more characters, then press ESC . Unlike the **r** command, the **s** command must be followed by ESC when you are finished entering text.

The difference between the **r** and **s** commands is important. Each command removes a single character in your text. The **r** will *replace* the one character with a single new character. The **r** command makes the single substitution and returns you automatically to the Command Mode (**r** is a two-way command). You are not left in Append; you do not use the ESC key. In contrast, the **s** command allows you to *substitute* as many characters as you wish for the one removed character. The **s** command moves you from Command Mode to Append Mode and leaves you there until you use the ESC to return to Command Mode (**s** is a one-way command).

(15) **Substituting for a Word:** It is also possible to exchange a specific word in your text for other words. Position the cursor on the first letter of a word. Type the command:

cw

The **cw** stands for *change word* . A dollar sign ($) will now appear at the end of the word being replaced. You then can type the replacement text. Although the command removed only one word, you can replace that one word with several words, entire sentences, or pages. Typing the **cw** command removes the one word and moves you into the Append Mode; therefore everything you type will be entered as text until you press the ESC key.

(16) **Weird Characters on the Screen:** A common mistake is to try to move the cursor, thinking you are in Command Mode, when you are actually in the Append Mode. A series of weird characters (^K^K^L^L^H^H or ^[A^[B^[D^[D) will appear on the screen (not unlike a *Monty Python* movie). If this happens, you are in the Append Mode, and those ^K or ^[A type characters are the *control characters* associated with the arrow keys. The visual editor is following your instructions and happily adding control characters to your file. Should this happen you need to press ESC and use the **x** command to delete the control characters.

(17) **Substituting for Lines:** The **s** and **cw** commands allow you to substitute text for a single character and for specific words, respectively. You can also substitute for entire lines in your file.

___ Place the cursor on any character in a line that is a likely candidate for substitution and enter the command (lower case):

cc

Whatever you now type will be entered into the file in place of the one line that went *poof!* You are not limited to entering only one line, but can append any number of lines at this point.

(18) **Append Mode/Command Mode:** It is important that the function of the various commands be understood. Look again at Map C. Whenever you leave the Shell and enter the visual editor you are always placed in *Command Mode*. All this means is that the machine is programmed to understand and act on a limited number of specific commands. These result in moving the cursor, deleting or changing text, or moving into Append Mode.

When an append command is given (such as **a** to **a***ppend* text or **cw** to **c***hange a* **w***ord*) the machine is programmed to move you out of Command Mode and into Append Mode. Once in Append Mode, virtually every character you type will be put in the file as text and displayed on the screen. You remain in Append Mode *until you press the* ESCAPE ⏄ESC⏄ *key.* This means you must tell the editor when you are finished adding text and want to return to the Command Mode, *regardless* of which particular command you may have used to enter the Append Mode. The ESCAPE key is the way back to Command Mode!

> When in doubt about what mode you are in, press the ⏄ESC⏄ key. If you are in Append Mode (adding text) you will be moved to the Command Mode. If you are already in Command Mode, pressing the ⏄ESC⏄ key will do no harm. It will inform you that you are already in Command Mode by harmlessly "beeping."

Appending Text to a File

(1) In Module Three you used the **a** command to append text when you initially started a file. The **a** can be used any time you want to add text to the *right* of the cursor.

___ Pick a place in the text where you could add more text and move the cursor to the last letter of the word *just before* where you want to make the addition. Then press the **a** key. You are moved to Append Mode and whatever you type will be entered as text. Add several words and then press ⏄ESC⏄ to return to Command Mode.

The **a** command allows you to start adding text to the *right* of the cursor. But what if you need to add text to the *left* of the cursor (as the first character on a line, for example)?

(2) **Inserting Text:** Select a place to add some text (such as the beginning of a line). Move the cursor to that place and use the

i

command to insert (**i** → **i**nsert) text. The **i** moves you from Command Mode to Append Mode. Every character you type *after* typing the **i** command will be entered as text in your file starting with the space to the left of the cursor.

(3) ___ Add several words or lines of text. The way to indicate that you want to stop adding text and return to *vi* Command Mode is, not surprisingly, with the ESC key.

i **|** a

Figure 1

Figure 1 indicates where the various *Text Appending Commands* start adding text relative to the position of the cursor: **a** **a***ppends* text to the right of the cursor, and **i** **i***nserts* to the left.

Practice using both the the **a** and **i** keys. Position the cursor on the first letter of a word in your file, press either key, add a word of text, and note where the new word is placed.

(4) **Opening a Line Below:** It is also possible to add text *between* two already existing lines. Select a line, move the cursor to some place on that line and type (lower case):

o

The **o** stands for **o***pen* a new line *below* the cursor line. A space opens up for a new line between the line where the cursor is located and the next line in your file. [When you enter the **o** command on dumb terminals the line below appears to be removed. Panic not—it will reappear when you press ESC and the screen is "redrawn." The next line is not deleted, just temporarily "covered over" to make room for the new one (or ones).]

___ Add some new text. You can continue typing as long as you wish; you are not limited to that one line. As with all Append Commands, you must use ESC to let the machine know when you are finished adding text and want to return to Command Mode.

(5) **Opening a Line Above:** In addition, you can open up a new line *above* the line in which the cursor is located. Move the cursor to any character on the *first line* of text in your file and type the command (Upper Case):

O

The **O** stands for **O***pen* a line *above* the cursor line. A new line *above* the cursor should open up and whatever you type will be added at that point. Again, if the first line "disappears" it has not been removed. The **O** (Upper Case O) command is the easiest way to add text to the top of a file. As you have now discovered, it can be used to open a line for text above the first line.

As with the **o** (lower case o) command, you can continue typing as long as you wish; you are not limited to that one line. Because these two *open a new line* commands move you from Command to Append Mode, you must use the [ESC] key to signal when you are ready to stop adding text and return to Command Mode.

(6) **Summary of Append Commands:** You now know how to append text on all four sides of the cursor. This ability is summarized in Figure 2: with the cursor as your starting point, **i** *i*nserts to the left; **a** *a*ppends to the right; **O** *O*pens the line above; and **o** *o*pens the line below.

$$\text{O}$$

$$\text{i} \mid \text{a}$$

$$\text{o}$$

Figure 2

(7) ___ To make sure you are in *vi* Command Mode press the [ESC] key. You can save the file as it now is written and return to the Shell by typing the command:

ZZ

(8) **Time to Fill in the Blanks:** Look at Map C and follow the path from Shell to *vi* Command Mode to Append Mode, then back to Command and finally back to the Shell. Locate answers to the following questions on Map C.

(a) What is the command to move from the Shell to *vi* Command Mode? _____

(b) What are four commands to move from *vi* Command Mode to the Mode where text can be added? _____

_____ _____ _____

(c) In what mode must you be to employ the cursor moving arrows? _____

(d) After entering an **o** or **O** command, what Mode are you in?

_____

(e) What is the command to let the editor know you are finished appending text and want to return to *vi* Command Mode?

_____

(f) What command saves the new (and improved) version of your file in the memory of UNIX and returns you to the Shell?

_____

(g) What is the command to begin starting a new file?

_____

(h) What is the command to leave the Shell, terminate the UNIX session, and return to Reality Mode, where a new set of commands is understood? _____

(i) What command do you use to add text to the line below the cursor line? _____

(j) How would you add text after a particular word?

_____

Answers: (a) **vi** *filename*   (b) **a, i, o, O**   (c) Command Mode of the visual editor   (d) Append Mode   (e) ESC   (f) **ZZ**   (g) **vi** *filename* (h) **logout**   (i) **o** (lower case)   (j) place cursor on the last letter of the word and enter the **a** command

Another Practice File

(1) You should still be in the Shell Mode. If you logged out, log back into your UNIX account. Once the Shell prompt appears you should start a new file which we will call *experience*. From the Shell type:

vi *experience*   ®

In this new file we'd like you to describe how the process of learning text processing is going. Summarize what you have learned so far, whether or not you are enjoying the process, and what suggestions you'd make about improving these Instructional Modules. Keep the lines short, don't correct mistakes as you are entering the text, and just type away. Attempt to enter as much text as quickly as you can.

(2) ___ Enter *at least 30 short lines.* Forty lines will make the activities practiced in later Modules more useful to you.

(3) ___ Now go back and make corrections to this text using the commands that were introduced earlier (the *slash-search* /*word* command, *arrow keys* ⬅ ⬇ ⬆ ➡ , change word **cw** command, etc.). A summary of the commands you have used is included as the final pages of this Module. Be sure to try each of them several times as you write your new *experience* file.

(4) ___ Examine what you have written. Move the cursor to the first line; open up a line above that line and enter an introduction.

(5) ___ Find several places to add more text and do so.

(6) ___ Change one word into another word.

(7) ___ Delete one line and add new text in its place.

(8) ___ Remove the period at the end of a sentence and make that sentence longer with the **s** command.

(9) ___ Return to the Shell and save the file using the **ZZ** command.

(10) ___ Make a paper (line printed) copy of the file *experience* using the Shell command sequence:

        lpr   *experience*   ®

(11) **Round Four of "Filling Blanks":**

  (a) Consider the rectangle in the diagram at right to be the cursor. What commands append text to the cursor's left, right, above, and below?

  (b) You have now practiced the commands that delete characters, words and lines. You have also used the commands that substitute or change characters, words and lines. The command that substitutes text for one character is **s** and is printed in the appropriate box in the following chart. Fill in the other five commands.

	Character	Word	Line
Substitute	s		
Delete			

Answers: (a)

O

i a

o

(b)

	Character	Word	Line
Substitute	s	cw	cc
Delete	x	dw	dd

(12) Your *experience* file will be useful as you complete the next Modules; add as much to it as you can.

(13) Please read the following command summary before beginning Module Five.

Command Summary

Shell Commands

Command	Function
vi *filename*	Starts or retrieves a file named *filename* for **vi**sual editing.
ls	Displays a l*ist* of file names in your account.
lpr *filename*	Has a copy of the specified *filename* printed on the l*ine* **pr***inter*.
who	Presents a list of **who** is currently logged into your UNIX system.
date	Provides today's **date** and time.
look *abc*	**Look**s in dictionary and displays a list of correctly spelled words beginning with the letters *abc*.
passwd	Changes the **passwo***rd* assigned to your UNIX account. (Don't forget your new password!)

Vi Text Editing Commands

Cursor Moving Commands

⬅️⬇️⬆️➡️	(**h,j,k,l** keys) Moves cursor one line up/down or one space right and left.
arrows	Moves cursor number # of lines or characters.
/	Moves cursor forward through text to *word*.
n	Moves to next *word*. (Used with **/***word* command.)

Text Changing Commands

Two-Way Commands

(Automatic Return to Command Mode)

Command | Function

dd   Deletes cursor line of text.

#| **dd**   Deletes number # of lines of text.

dw   Deletes one word from text.

#| **dw**   Deletes number # of words from text.

x   Deletes the one character under the cursor.

#| **x**   Deletes number # of characters from text.

r |c| Replaces the one character under the cursor with the next character typed *c*.

u   Undo: Reverses last text change action.

Append Mode Commands

One-Way Commands

(Leave You in Append Mode)

a   Appends (adds) text to a file to the right of cursor.

i   Inserts (adds) text to a file to the left of cursor.

o   (lower case o) Opens a line below cursor line for appending text.

O   (Upper Case O) Opens a line above cursor line for appending text.

cw   Change word: exchanges new text for one word in text that it removes.

cc   Change line: exchanges new text for one line in text that it removes.

S   Substitution: exchanges new text for one line in text that it removes (same as **cc** command).

Mode Changing Commands

Command   Function

ESC   Escapes from text Append Mode and returns to *vi* Command Mode.

ZZ   Quits work on a file, writes changes made during that editing session into the memory of UNIX, and returns to the Shell Mode.

Map C

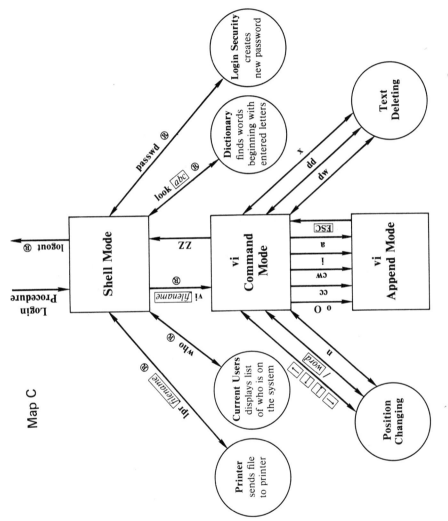

A second copy of this map is located at the end of the book.

Module Five
Nroff Formatting Commands

```
.ce
Example Text
.sp
.ti 5
The lines of text
you are now reading demonstrate the
function of formatting commands.
The upper chunk of text
has formatting commands
inserted in it (like .ce and .sp).
The lower chunk is the
.ul
same text
after it has been sent to the formatter.
```

Example Text

    The lines of text you are now reading demonstrate the function of formatting commands. The upper chunk of text has formatting commands inserted in it (like .ce and .sp). The lower chunk is the <u>same text</u> after it has been sent to the formatter.

Introduction

In the first Four Modules you learned how to use the UNIX system to create, edit and print files. With these skills you could produce your programs, reports, or papers on UNIX. Considering the extensive capabilities of the system, however, this would be similar to using your new Porsche as a go-cart to roll down hills. The UNIX text processing system contains features which both save time and make for a more attractive finished product. The features that you will meet in this Module are a set of formatting commands (that you embed in your text) and a Shell command that sends your file to be formatted. *By placing a few simple commands into your paper* you can tell the machine when to start paragraphs, double space, underline, center, adjust line length, and many more of your favorite things.

Nroff is the basic formatting package available on UNIX systems. Several additional formatting packages (called *macro* packages) exist on UNIX. These macro packages are used with *nroff.* They allow you to easily achieve complicated formatting effects that would be tedious and time consuming to format with *nroff* alone. We introduce *nroff* at this time in advance of your meeting macros in *Module Nine,* for two reasons. The *nroff* commands (called *requests*) are the basic building blocks of macro packages. Second, regardless of which macros you ultimately use to assist with your formatting tasks, you will continue to use many of the *nroff* commands.

Prerequisites

Before starting this Module you should be able to:
(1) Log onto your UNIX account;
(2) Create a file; and
(3) Edit a file using the visual editor.

Objectives

After completing this Module you should be able to:
(1) Place formatting commands in your file;

(2) Use commands to double space, make paragraphs, skip lines, underline words, and center text in a paper; and

(3) Send your file to the formatter and have the formatted file printed on the line printer.

Procedure

This Module begins with a brief introduction to the *nroff* formatting process. Section two discusses where formatting commands should be inserted in text files and describes how these commands work. Section three demonstrates how to obtain formatted output. Page management commands are considered in section four. This final section discusses the process of writing with UNIX.

(1) ___ Logon to your UNIX account.

(2) ___ From the Shell type:

vi *experience*   ®

(Remember, ® means that you should *press the* **RETURN** *key.*)

This command will cause the contents of the file *experience* you created in Module Four to appear on your screen. The beginning few lines of your file should appear, with a line that looks something like the following at the bottom:

"experience" 35 lines, 870 characters

Use the ⬆ arrow key you met in Module Four to move the cursor through your entire file (if the whole text is not now on the screen). As you view the file, note the shortness of the lines and the jagged right edge of the text.

(3) ___ Once you have completed scanning your file use the (upper case)

ZZ

command to return to the Shell. (If you left Command Mode

while looking at the file and entered some text you will need to press ESC before you type **ZZ**.)

(4)   **Having Your File Formatted:** You will soon be introduced to a command that will send your file to be formatted. When this process is complete the formatted version will be displayed on your screen. This command may take a few seconds or as long as several minutes to be executed.

___ Enter the following command sequence to have your file *experience* formatted and displayed in approximately page-length chunks on your terminal:

↓ space

nroff *experience* | **page**   ®

The | is called the *pipe* and on some terminals appears as a ¦ To have more text displayed, press the **SPACEBAR**. To return to the Shell you can continue pressing the **SPACEBAR** until the entire file has passed, or if you want to end the show and tell, press the **DELETE** DEL or **RUBOUT** RUB key to immediately return to the Shell.

Note that the formatted *experience* file displayed on your screen no longer has a jagged right margin. The lines have been joined and spaces were added to produce a formatted version that has a straight right margin. It is "filled" and "left-right justified." (Don't worry; your file named *experience* still exists in its nonformatted form.)

For another demonstration of the actions of the *nroff* formatter see the *Example Text* at the beginning of this Module. The short lines have been joined in the formatted version to create lines of consistent length. Your formatted *experience* file should be quite similar.

Inserting Formatting Commands

(1)   ___ From the Shell call up your *experience* file for visual editing. Use the command:

vi *experience*   ®

Once again the beginning of your file should appear on the screen with a line that looks something like this at the bottom:

"experience" 35 lines, 870 characters.

(2) **Conventions for Formatting Commands:** Formatting commands are placed in a file just like text. How does the formatter recognize a command? For the formatter to interpret the commands as instructions *and not text* all *nroff* commands *must:*

(a) Be at the beginning of a line;

(b) Begin with a period; and

(c) Be the only characters on the line.

(3) **Skipping lines:** If you want to leave several blank lines in your formatted paper (perhaps for a drawing or graph) you must indicate the number of lines you want skipped. The command **.sp 2** (**.sp** → sp*ace down*) causes the formatter to leave two blank lines at that point in the text. The command **.sp 8** will result in eight blank lines . . . . The following 4 lines of blank space are brought to you by the **.sp 4** command.

___ Find a place in your *experience* file where it might be fun to include a drawing of a glassy-eyed UNIX text-processing student and insert the appropriate command so that there will be room for it in the formatted paper.

(4) **When Do Formatting Commands Take Effect?** Refer to the two versions of the sample text found at the end of this Module. Note that all Formatting Commands were *inserted* in the file with the text. (They were entered in the same way as text—through the Append Mode.)

Formatting Commands *do not* have an immediate effect. They *are not* interpreted until the file is later sent to the formatter. For example, the **.sp 2** command *does not* cause two blank lines to appear on the terminal *immediately* while you are editing the file. The visual editor does not interpret this command. To *vi* the **.sp 2** command is just a series of characters to be placed in the file. Later, when the file is sent to the formatter, the **.sp 2** command will be interpreted by the formatter to mean *skip two lines.*

(5) **Centering Text:** One of the most painful aspects of typing any paper is figuring out how to center a line. Much easier on UNIX! If you insert the command **.ce** above the line you want centered, (**.ce** → **ce***nter*) the formatter will count the number of characters in the text to be centered, divide . . . and presto!

A centered line of text!

___ Find a place in the file where a centered title or line would be, if not interesting, at least instructive. Above the line, insert the command

.ce

What if you wanted to center several lines of text? Yes, **.ce 12** will center the next 12 lines of text that you enter in your unformatted file.

Did you remember to press the ESC key? A common mistake is to add formatting commands someplace in the text and then forget to press the ESC key. When the person then tries to move the cursor to the next place of interest, a collection of control characters (such as ^K^K^H^L^L) is added to the text. The weird characters are the control characters associated with the arrow keys. You are in effect appending arrow keys to the file, because you are still in Append Mode. You will have to press ESC , delete the weird characters, and move on.

(6) **Standard Paragraphs:** Return to the Sample Paper at the end of the Module. Notice that the paragraphs were formatted by putting the **.sp** and **.ti 5** commands *on separate lines* and *above* the start of the new paragraphs. When the commands **.sp** and **.ti 5** are encountered the formatter interprets them to mean *space down* one line (**.sp**) and *indent* five spaces (**.ti 5**). *Nroff* then reads in the

text that follows. You have already met the **.sp** command, but the **.ti 5** command is new. This command tells *nroff* to *temporarily* i*ndent* the left margin of the next line of text 5 spaces to the right. The combination of both commands formats the beginning of a paragraph. The text for the paragraph begins with the next line of the file.

___ Find a line in your file that could be the start of a paragraph. Move the cursor to that line and open the line above it using the (Upper Case) **O** command. Now enter the paragraph formatting commands **.sp** and **.ti 5** *on separate lines.* Again, don't forget ESC when finished.

(7) **Block Paragraphs:** If you do not want the standard, five space indented paragraph that the **.sp** and **.ti 5** commands will provide, perhaps a non-indented (Left Block Style) paragraph would be appropriate.

___ Enter the command

.sp

somewhere in your file, by itself, to produce this formatting effect. *Nroff* reads the **.sp** command, spaces down one line, and resumes filling text to the left and right margins with the next line.

(8) **Underlining Text:** A time-honored way of placing emphasis in papers is with underlining. *Nroff* readily accommodates your requests for underlining.

___ Find a line of text in your file that you would like to underline. Open up a line above it and insert the command:

.ul

When the formatter comes to the **.ul** (**.ul** → u*nderline*) command it will underline the next line of text in your file. Note that it underlines the next line of text that is *in your file,* and not the next filled and justified line in the final paper. This command can be used to underline a single word or a whole flock of words, depending on the number of words you place on the line in your file following the **.ul** command. The Sample Paper contains another example of the effect of the **.ul** command.

(9) ___ Go back and add another of each of the *nroff* requests you have met thus far (**.sp**, **.ce**, **.ti**, and **.ul**) to your file.

(10) ___ When you have used each of the mentioned commands at least twice use the **ZZ** command to save your *experience* file in the memory of the beast, quit working on the file, and return to the Shell. (If **ZZ** appears on your screen instead of the Shell prompt, press ESC , remove the **ZZ** with a *delete* command, and try the **ZZ** again.)

Producing Printed Copies of Your File

(1) ___ After you have been returned to the Shell use the

lpr *experience* ®

command to get a line printed copy of your unformatted file (the file *experience* as you entered it into UNIX). The formatting commands embedded in the text will appear on this copy.

(2) ___ When the Shell prompt reappears use the

nroff *experience* | **lpr** ®

command sequence to get a printed copy of the *formatted* version of your paper. (Again, the | is called the *pipe* command and is located at the top right of the keyboard on most terminals.)

(3) ___ Pick up the line printed copies you made in Steps 1 and 2 (they may take from 5 minutes to 3 hours to be printed, depending upon conditions at your location) and compare them to see how each formatting command works. Note that the version you sent *directly* to the line printer (with the **lpr** *experience* command) contains the "input" text including formatting commands while the version that was formatted *before* line printing (with the **nroff** *experience* | **lpr** command sequence) is formatted according to the commands you embedded in the file. The commands themselves have been removed from this version.

One-Way Page Management Commands

As you examine your printed version of the file *experience,* notice that several formatting decisions were made for you. The lines of type are 6.5 inches, with one inch margins on each side. The paper is single spaced, and the right margin is straight. All of these formatting decisions are set *by default* but each can be changed. This section will describe these default values and how to modify them.

(1) **Line Length:** The default line length is 6.5 inches (to fit on 8.5 inch paper with one inch margins.) A change in l*ine length* is made with the **.ll** command.

___ To instruct the *nroff* formatter to start formatting lines of 4.0 inches, you would include the following command in the file immediately preceding the text you want set in 4.0 inch lines:

.ll 4i

The **i** is for i*nches* and is therefore quite important. (Neglect to include the **i** and the line length will be 4 *characters* . . . a trifle narrow for most purposes.)

Consider a portion of a file which includes the following lines:

.ll 4i
Text will then be set in four inch lines
until you instruct the formatter to set
a new line length.
You would set the new line
length with the nroff request: **.ll** *number.*

After sending the file to *nroff* the following formatted text results.

Text will then be set in four inch lines until you instruct the formatter to set a new line length. You would set the new line length with the nroff request: **.ll** *number.*

The line length nroff request is a *one-way* command. Once you establish the line length in *nroff,* that line length remains in effect until you specify a new length.

(2) **Page Length:** You now know how to instruct *nroff* to create lines of a specified length. As you select the line length, you are also establishing the margins at the sides of the printed page. But what about page length and top and bottom margins? This is a more difficult issue. Informing *nroff* of your intention to create pages of a specified length is a simple matter. The **.pl** command instructs *nroff* as to **p**age *length*. The page length command only identifies the boundary between pages, it does not tell *nroff* what to do at the beginning and end of each page. In other words, you can easily instruct *nroff* to format text for eleven inch pages (the command **.pl 11i** will do this). But *nroff* will not automatically leave margins at the top and bottom of the page. Instead, *nroff* will run one page into the next. This leads to the curious effect that no one (except you and *nroff*) knows where an old page ends and a new one begins. *Nroff* will generate one long stream of text, with no apparent page breaks. This is seldom a satisfactory state.

The *nroff* instructions to create top and bottom margins identifying the pages require the use of *macros*. Macros are essentially bundles of *nroff* requests. They are discussed later in the book in the two macro Modules (Modules Nine and Twenty). In those Modules several additional *nroff* commands related to page length will also be discussed.

The inability of *nroff* to adequately create identifiable pages demonstrates that using *nroff* requests alone to format your text is very difficult. This is why most people either use an available macro package or write their own macros and why after this introduction to the basic *nroff* requests you will meet the *-ms macros*.

(3) **Line Spacing:** The *nroff* formatter will automatically *single* space your file unless you specify otherwise. When the formatter comes to an input line consisting only of the command **.ls 2** (**ls** → **l**ine **s**pace) it begins to double space with the next line of

text in your unformatted file. Like right here. The machine will

continue double spacing the text until it comes to the line spacing

command which resets the spacing to single space. To single space, the nroff request is **.ls 1** and Surprise! the command **.ls 3** will cause triple spaced output. And then there are **.ls 4** and **.ls 5** and . . . .

If you want to double space the entire paper, the **.ls 2** command must be among the very first commands in the beginning of your file.

___ Double space all of the text in your *experience* file. Move the cursor to the first line of text and press (Upper Case):

O

___ Insert the **.ls 2** command *by itself* on the first line. When finished press ESC .

(4) Now that the **.ls 2** instruction is included in the file, let's have the file formatted again. Return to the Shell and then enter:

nroff *experience* | **page**   ®

Filled and Unfilled Text: The creation of straight right margins is a two step process: *filling* and *justifying*.

Lines from File
Neither Filled nor Justified

These two versions of this paragraph
are placed here to demonstrate
how filling and justifying work.
The version on page 71,
set in italics,
is neither filled nor justified.
The version on page 72,
set in bold type,
is filled*, but not justified.*
Note how words from the second and third lines
are added to the first to fill *it*
close to the margin in the filled version.
The remainder of this book, with its
even right margin, is both filled and justified.
Spaces were added to the filled *lines*
until the right margin was straight.

Lines Filled, not Justified

These two versions of this paragraph are placed here to demon-strate how filling and justifying work. The version on page 71, set in italics, is neither filled nor justified. The version on page 72, set in bold type, is filled, but not justified. Note how words from the second and third lines are added to the first to fill it close to the margin in the filled version. The remainder of this book, with its even right margin, is both filled and justified. Spaces were added to the filled lines until the right margin was straight.

(5) **Stopping the Filling Process:** On occasion it is desirable to leave text in an *unfilled* condition. You have seen how one of the UNIX formatter's basic functions is to join short lines of text together to form lines of approximately equal length (filling).

While this process is normally appropriate,
there will be
times when you wish to leave text
exactly
as you typed it—short lines of uneven length.
Like this.
The **no** f*ill*
command
.nf
tells UNIX
not to fill the text which follows.

Filling resumes with the **.fi** command (**.fi** → **fi**/*l*.) The **.nf** and **.fi** commands must be used *as a pair*, as without the **.fi** all of your text following the **.nf** will appear unfilled. Both are one-way commands.

___ Isolate a passage of unfilled text in your paper with the **.nf** and **.fi** commands.

(6) **Justified Text:** You may also direct *nroff* to fill but not justify your text. The one-way command

.na

stops the adjusting process (**.na** → **no a**d*just*) and leaves the right margin ragged. The lines are of about equal length, but not quite.

The adjustment process can be turned back on with the

.ad

(**.ad** → ad*just*) command. Similar to the **.nf** and **.fi** commands, you must also use the **.na** and **.ad** commands *as a pair*. They are one-way commands, leaving you in *adjusts* or *no adjust* until you specify otherwise.

___ Isolate a passage of non-justified text in your paper with the appropriate commands.

(7) **Print Offset:** If your printer uses wide paper you probably find that the formatted version of your file is printed very close to the left margin of the paper. Fortunately it is possible to instruct the formatter to offset the printing from the left margin of the page.

___ Insert the command

.po 2i

as the first line in your file. The **p**rint *offset* command instructs the formatter, in this instance, to offset the printed output 2 inches. Any reasonable offset (from 1 space to 4-5 inches) will be followed. For example, **.po 10** will have the printing offset 10 spaces.

(8) Time to have *nroff* interpret the commands you have now entered in you *experience* file and format the output.

___ Return to the Shell and enter:

nroff experience | page   ®

(9) **One-Way** *Nroff* **Requests:** Recall that all one-way commands remain in effect until superceded by a new command. While formatting your paper *nroff* keeps track of requested line length, spacing, filling, justifying and several other one-way commands that determine the formatting of your text. Every time *nroff* starts formatting a line of text, it checks its memory for the specified instructions about line length, whether the material is to be filled and justified, etc. *Nroff* begins with a "default" value for each of the variables (line length = 6.5 inches, single spacing etc.) which it will use unless or until you specify otherwise.

When you enter an instruction to change one of these formatting variables, *nroff* stores the information in its memory. Then, when *nroff* checks for the latest instruction as it begins formatting the next line in your file, it finds the new specifications. The new instructions are followed as it formats the line.

The following table presents several of the most frequently used *nroff* requests. The column labeled *Default* contains the initial instructions which *nroff* will use if no others are provided.

Nroff Requests and Default Values		
Command	Default	What it Governs
.po #	0 inches	Page offset
.ll #	6.5 inches	Line length
.ls #	Single space	Line spacing
.nf	Text filled	Causes filling to be stopped. **.fi** resumes filling.
.na	Text adjusted	Causes adjustment to be stopped. **.ad** resumes adjustment

Note: The # symbol is *never* used in the commands. You substitute an appropriate value in inches (3.5**i**), points (38**p**), centimeters (11**c**), picas (22**P**), or Em's (3**m**) for the # symbol. The values you set for any of the above variables will remain in force until you specify a new value to *nroff* (this will not be the case when you use the *-ms* macros).

(10) ___ Call up another file (perhaps *first*) for visual editing. Enter the appropriate text and *nroff* format instructions to:

(a)   Have the formatter construct lines 9 inches long.

(b)   Have the printer offset the output 2 inches.

(c)   Display a centered title: *Sideways Page*

(d)   Underline the title.

(e)   Format two paragraphs.

(f)   Fill but not justify one paragraph of text.

Note: The line length information given in this exercise will print on 8½ by 11 inch paper held sideways (11 by 8½).

(11) **That's Just About It For Module Five:** Go on to Module Six when you feel comfortable using:

(a)   The eleven formatting commands presented in this Module (**.ls**, **.ce**, **.ti**, **.sp**, **.ul**, **.nf**, **.fi**, **.na**, **.ad**, **.po**, and **.ll**); and

(b)   The following Shell command sequences:

lpr |*filename*| ®

nroff |*filename*| | **page**   ®

nroff |*filename*| | **lpr**   ®

The Writing Process

During the course of producing any finished written document most people progress through the following sequence of steps:

(a)   Use the Append Mode of the visual editor to enter text and basic formatting commands into a file.

(b)   From the Shell use the **nroff** *filename* | **lpr** command to have the file formatted and printed.

(c)   Use a pencil (or *quill and ink,* if you prefer) to make corrections and additions to the formatted paper.

(d) From within the Append Mode enter these corrections into the original file (the file with the formatting commands in it—called the "input file").

(e) Repeat steps (b) through (d) until you are satisfied with the end product, or the "powers that be" demand a finished product, or your UNIX account is terminated, or you are terminated, or . . . .

A cursory (how punny can we get?) review of steps (a) through (e) reveals that text processing on UNIX involves a cyclical (and not linear) experience. With a text processing system papers are no longer static entities (or beasts). Even after a copy of your paper has been formatted and printed the original file lies awaiting further revisions, always ready to be modified (when inspiration strikes) or printed again. To demonstrate: some of the Modules in this book underwent 9 major revisions and countless less drastic editing sessions. As we encountered problems or hit upon an idea, we revised and reprinted. The problem—and it is not trivial—is to determine when to quit revising a written work. Since it is now difficult to "finish" writing a piece, a conscious decision to "abandon" a project must often be made.

You have now completed Module Five. A list of the formatting commands presented in this Module follows on the next page. A complete list of *nroff* formatting commands is located in the *Command Summary Section* at the end of the Book.

"I promise, just a few more changes and I'll quit!"

Command Summary

Formatting Commands

Command	Function
.ls #	(lower case l) Controls the spacing of the paper. The command **.ls** *2* will double space.
.ti #	Temporarily indents # spaces, beginning with the following line of text.
.sp #	Skips the next # number of lines (leaves them blank).
.ce #	Centers the next # of lines.
.ul #	Underlines the next # number of lines.
.nf	Stops filling of text. Must have a **.fi** to resume filling.
.fi	Resume filling text (normal *nroff* mode).
.na	Stops the adjustment of lines, leaving right margin ragged.
.ad	Starts the adjustment of lines, resulting in straight right margin.
.ll #	Establishes line length. For instance **.ll**5*i* will result in 5.0 inch lines in the formatted output.

Note: In the above commands, the # symbol stands for a number which you must supply.

Shell Commands

Command	Function
lpr $\boxed{filename}$	Sends *filename* to the line printer for printing.
nroff $\boxed{filename}$ | page	Formats *filename* and displays it on the screen.
nroff $\boxed{filename}$ | lpr	Formats *filename* and sends it to the line printer for printing.

```
.ls 2
.ce
SAMPLE PAPER
.sp
.ti 5
```
Note that all formatting commands
are inserted in your file
in a fashion similar to
the text you are writing.
These formatting commands DO NOT have
an immediate effect.
They ARE NOT executed until
the file is sent to the formatter.
For example,
the .ce command does not cause
the next line of text to be
formatted while you are editing the file.
But when the file is sent
to the formatter,
the .ce command will cause the following
line of text to be centered,
while also suppressing the
printing of the .ce command itself.
```
.sp
.ti 5
```
In order for the formatter
to recognize them as commands and
not text,
```
.ul 2
```
they must be at the beginning of a line
and begin with a period.
Remember, it is
```
.ul
```
essential
that a formatting command
be on a line by itself.
Note also that the command
will function on the
```
.ul
```
following line
of text.

SAMPLE PAPER

Note that all formatting commands are inserted in your file in a fashion similar to the text you are writing. These formatting commands DO NOT have an immediate effect. They ARE NOT executed until the file is sent to the formatter. For example, the .ce command does not cause the next line of text to be formatted while you are editing the file. But when the file is sent to the formatter, the .ce command will cause the following line of text to be centered, while also suppressing the printing of the .ce command itself.

In order for the formatter to recognize them as commands and not text, they must be at the beginning of a line and begin with a period. Remember, it is essential that a formatting command be on a line by itself. Note also that the command will function on the following line of text.

Module Six
File Management with Shell Commands

Introduction

The Shell is the Mode you originally meet upon logging onto your UNIX account. From the Shell you enter commands which allow you to work with, or manage, *entire files*. This Module will introduce several file management commands.

Prerequisites

Before starting this Module you should be able to:

(1) Edit files using the commands introduced in Modules Three and Four;

(2) Send your text files to be formatted (or, for programmers who are not currently learning text processing, send files containing programs to be compiled and executed); and

(3) Produce a printed copy of a file.

Objectives

After finishing this Module you will be able to:

(1) Creatively name your files;

(2) Copy or rename an existing file;

(3) Remove files from your account;

81

(4) View the contents of a file without entering text edit mode;

(5) Run a Shell process in the background;

(6) Analyze a text file for proper diction, and check for spelling errors;

(7) Describe the structure of Shell command lines;

(8) Use Shell modification commands to reroute output to files or other Shell commands.

(9) Combine Shell commands to effect several actions with one command line; and

(10) Access the on-line *UNIX Programmer's Manual;*

Procedure

These procedure steps are grouped into eight sections. The first section discusses the topic of naming files, while the second presents commands which allow you to copy, move, or remove files from your account. The third section introduces four Shell commands which allow you to view the contents of a file without entering text edit mode. Three UNIX programs that assist with the analysis of file content are considered in section four. Section five introduces the concept of backgrounding a process, while section six discusses the structure of Shell command lines. Section seven describes the process of combining Shell commands. The final section looks at two ways to access the on-line *UNIX Programmer's Manual.*

How to Name a File

A *file* is the term used for a collection of characters that are stored together. For instance, the words in a letter or a paper, a list of addresses, and a listing of data are all collections of characters that can be stored together as files. This information is kept together so that you and UNIX can work on it as one entity. Because you will have several files in your account, each file needs to be given a separate, identifiable name. The filename allows UNIX to locate the file for you when you want to return and work with it. The name you select for each file is up to you and is used only to identify the file. The name selected does not become part of the file; it is just its "identifier."

To this point we have told you what names to give to files (*first*, *second* and *experience*) so that we can refer to them easily. You will normally have the luxury of dreaming up your own filenames. You should be aware of the following rules about naming files.

(a) The name selected must be all one "word" or "string of characters." No spaces are allowed and the "word" should be fourteen characters or less (less is better). Be certain to include sufficient information so that it is obvious what the file contains.

Why can't a file have the name *letter to mom*? Spaces are used by UNIX (and other operating systems) to identify the discrete "pieces" of a command line in the same way they are used in regular language. Thus, this phrase makes sense, while th isphr asema keslittles ense. If you enter

vi   letter to mom   ®

the Shell would interpret this to mean "edit the three separate files named *letter*, *to*, and *mom*.

(b) Don't begin a file name with a character that is not a letter or number. *Never* use the characters !, ", *, >, <, |, $, @, or ?, as these have special meanings to the Shell and are thus not good choices for filenames. For example:

Acceptable Filenames	Not Acceptable
ozzie	ozzie nelson
why-me	why-me?
bonzo-4	president.bonzo
english190	english 190
great	great!
letter.mom	letter to mom
prog1	*prog1
bfido.nerfball	bfido nerfball

Finally, we would like to offer two suggestions to help you avoid the problem of forgetting what contents are associated with which filename.

(a) You might use a word from the actual title of the paper contained in the file. A report on *War and Peace* could become any of the following:

> peace
> war
> war-peace

(b) You can draw on the purpose of the file to create the name (the paper for English 1A becomes *english1A*, Module Six becomes mod6, and a program that plays chess becomes *chess.prog*).

Copying, Removing, and Renaming Files

(1) ___ Log onto your UNIX account.

(2) ___ From the Shell type:

> **ls**   ®

A listing of your file names should appear on the screen.

(3) **Copying a File:** From the Shell the contents of any file can be copied into a second file.

___ To make a copy of the file *experience* and have it named *temp*, enter:

> **cp** *experience* *temp*   ®
> ↑ space   ↑ space

In general, the **cp** command is entered:

> **cp** $\boxed{file1}$ $\boxed{file2}$ ®

This command line creates a **copy** of the first file listed (*file1*) and gives it the name you list next (*file2*).

(4) ___ Use the **ls** command to see whether you now have a file called
temp.

(5) **Removing a File:** Once a file has been created, it remains in
storage until you remove it.

___ Let's remove a file. Since *experience* and *temp* are identical
copies of the same file, shall we remove your cloned file called
temp? From the Shell type:

$$\textbf{rm} \quad \textit{temp} \qquad ®$$

The Shell prompt reappears, and it looks like nothing really happened. Did this command do its job?

___ Use the **ls** command to list your files again. The file *temp*
should no longer be listed, indicating that you did indeed remove
it. *It is now gone forever.* There is no *undo* command for actions
performed in the Shell Mode, so you should be *very careful* when
removing files. (In a later section of this Module you will learn
how to modify the system so that you are asked whether you *really*
want a file removed.)

(6) **Changing the Name of a File:** From the Shell you can also change
the name (rename) a file.

___ Type the following:

$$\textbf{mv} \quad \textit{first newfirst} \qquad ®$$
$$\uparrow \text{space} \uparrow$$

By changing the name of the file the Shell command

$$\textbf{mv} \quad \boxed{\textit{file1}} \quad \boxed{\textit{file2}} \qquad ®$$

in effect **m**oves *file1* into *file2*.

(7) ___ Once the prompt reappears, ask the Shell to again list the
names of your files (**ls**). The contents of your *first* file now exist
under the filename *newfirst*.

(8) ___ From the Shell type

$$\textbf{vi} \quad \textit{newfirst} \qquad ®$$

and see for yourself that this is the material you knew previously as *first*. (The name has been changed to protect the innocent but the malady lingers on.) When finished viewing the material you should type **ZZ** and return to the Shell.

(9) ___ Use the following Shell Command line to move the contents of *newfirst* back into the filename *first*:

$$\textbf{mv} \quad \textit{newfirst first} \qquad ®$$
↑ space ↑

Your *first* file has now returned; use the **ls** command to make sure.

(10) **Round One of "Fill in the Blanks":**

    (a)   You can change the name of a file from what Mode?

    _____

    (b)   What would you type to change the name of the file *paper1* to the name *catherine*? _____

    (c)   What is the Shell command to remove the file named *dust*?

    _____

Answers: (a) Shell   (b) **mv** *paper1 catherine*   (c) **rm** *dust*

Viewing the Contents of a File

UNIX offers several ways (indeed, there tend to be several ways to do anything with UNIX) to view the contents of a file. Each of the following methods displays some portion of a file on the screen. These displays are for viewing only—a file *cannot* be edited with these commands. To edit a file you must be in a text edit mode, such as the visual editor *vi*.

(1) **The Page (or More) Command:** Perhaps the easiest way to view the contents of a file is to use the **page** (or **more**) command. (Note: **page** and **more** are equivalent commands available on different UNIX versions. We suggest that you first try **page**. If the Shell responds *"Command not found"*, you will need to use the **more** command. From now on when we refer to the **page** command you will need to substitute the command that works at your

location.) The commands **page** and **more** will *display* the contents of a file on the screen in chunks of about twenty lines.

___ Select one of your files for viewing and enter the command:

$$\textbf{page} \quad \boxed{\textit{filename}} \qquad ®$$

The first screenful of your file should now be displayed with a line that looks something like this presented at the bottom of your screen:

--More-- (75%)

At this point you have two choices:

(1)   To see the next screenful of text press the SPACEBAR.

(2)   If after viewing any screen of text you wish to return to the Shell, just press the DELETE key.

Browse through your file and, when you are back at the Shell, proceed to the next step.

(2)   **The Cat Command:** While **page** will display text one screenful at a time, the **cat** command will scroll through your text at a truly alarming rate. You can halt the scrolling process with a CTRL-S (depress the key marked CTRL and press the S key one time). Scrolling resumes when you press the SPACEBAR.

___ Select another file for viewing and type:

$$\textbf{cat} \quad \boxed{\textit{filename}} \qquad ®$$

Halt the scrolling process with a CTRL-S, then resume with the SPACEBAR. The **cat** command is nerve wracking compared to the controlled **page** command, but **cat** is a good way to quickly scan large amounts of text.

(3)   **The Head Command:** Once you work with UNIX for a period of time you will probably begin to collect quite a few files. While the *names* ascribed to these files give you some indication of their contents, you may remain uncertain about just what they hold. Perhaps a glimpse of the first few lines of a file will help you match filenames with file contents.

___ Select a file for viewing and type:

head [*filename*]   ®

The **head** command will display the first ten lines of a file, giving you a brief insight into the contents of the file.

(4) **The Tail Command:** If the **head** command doesn't seem to jar your memory, perhaps a look at the final few lines of the file will help. The task of displaying the final ten lines of a file falls to the **tail** command.

___ Select a file for viewing and type:

tail [*filename*]   ®

Ways to Analyze Text

UNIX supports several programs which will help you become a more effective writer by examing your text for errors of spelling and diction. It helps us to think of these programs as a microprocessed *Mrs. Zak*, a regionally famous 8th grade English teacher.

Note that all programs are not available at all locations. The few introduced here are among the most widely available, however. Additional text analyses programs are noted in the *Writer's Workbench* section of Module Twenty-Nine: *Where to Now?*

(1) **The Spell Program:** You met the first half of the UNIX dictionary (**look**) in Module Two. The remaining member of the pair is the **spell** program. To demonstrate this program we suggest you use your *experience* file. This command will take several moments to run, so you can read the next paragraph while waiting for UNIX to finish.

___ From the Shell type:

spell *experience*   ®
↑ space

Note that this command consists of two parts separated by a space:

the Shell command **spell** and the name of a file (*experience*) that you want **spell** to examine. (In this case **spell** is the Shell command and *experience* is the file to be sent to **spell**. Hence, the file *experience* is the input.) The one thing that is not specified here is what **spell** should do with the output. That is, after the **spell** program has compared each word in your file to its dictionary and created a list of words present in your file but not in its dictionary, what should happen to the list? Because you did not tell UNIX what to do with the list it will *automatically* (by *default*) print the result on your screen. Wait until this list is displayed. When the Shell prompt reappears go on to the next step.

(2) **Redirecting the Output:** Now let's see what happens if you specify what to do with this output. Type

spell *experience* > *newname*   ®

where *newname* is a new file created to accept the list generated from the **spell** program. In this case you have specified that the **spell** program should find misspellings in the file *experience* and that the output of this process should be put into the new file called *newname* instead of being displayed on your terminal (the default). The > (greater than symbol) is the command used to take the output from one Shell process and put it into a new file, and is called the *redirect* symbol. It can be used with most Shell commands. Note: if you already had a file called *newname* the above command line will either erase that material and replace it with the new spelling list or respond "*File exists*" and ignore your command.

(3) ___ Use the following command line to inspect the contents of this file:

page *newname*   ®

(4) **The Diction Program:** The **diction** program will read through any text file you select and note instances where the diction appears fuzzy.

___ Select a text file and type:

diction |*filename*| > |*anothername*| ®
    ↑ space

When the program is completed and the terminal displays a Shell prompt, look at the new file *anothername*. The bracketed words and/or phrases were identified by *Mrs. Zak* as being cumbersome or awkward. Note: If the Shell responds, *"diction: Command not found"*, neither the **diction** nor the **suggest** program is available on your system.

(5) **The Suggest Program:** Now that you have a detailed list of words and phrases in your text that appear suspect to *Mrs. Zak*, what are you going to do about them? Notice any instances that look particularly appropriate for further inspection? The **suggest** program awaits your call.

___ Select a word or phrase from the list generated by **diction**. For instance, if you used the phrase *in order to* in your file, **diction** identified the phrase and put brackets around it. To have **suggest** suggest an alternative, enter:

> **suggest** *in order to*   ®
> ↑   ↑   ↑ space

In general, the process is to enter:

> **suggest** |*word or phrase*| ®

where *word or phrase* is the word or phrase that *Mrs. Zak* bracketed (fancier then a red pencil). *Mrs. Zak,* through the **suggest** program, will cheerfully provide alternatives to the *word(s)* entered in the above sequence. After providing alternative phrases **suggest** will prompt you for additional troublesome expressions. If you want additional advice, enter another phrase; otherwise enter CTRL-D to end this process and return to the Shell.

Backgrounding a Process

It is occasionally desirable to run a Shell process "in the background." This allows you to perform some other UNIX operation while the backgrounded process is being executed. We will introduce one component of this aspect of the UNIX system at this time. Module Seventeen: *Backgrounding a Process* explores this topic in greater detail.

(1) **The & Backgrounding Character:** The **&** character can be used at the end of a Shell command line to signal the Shell to run the job in the background.

___ Type the command:

spell *first* > *sfirst* **&**   ®

The **&** tells the Shell to continue working on the assigned process in the background and to immediately give you a new Shell prompt. You are free to attend to other UNIX tasks while the machine performs the *backgrounded* Shell command.

On some systems the Shell will notify you when the process you have requested (in this case, a spelling check of the file *first*) is complete. Versions without a notification service require that you check to see if the job is finished. This can most easily be done by using the **page** command to view the file designated to hold the output when the job is completed. *Do not* logout before determining that the process is completed. The process may be terminated if you do logout.

(2) ___ Use the command

page *sfirst*   ®

to have UNIX display the contents of the *sfirst* file.

If this file has not yet been filled with the output from the *spell* program continue reading this Module. When you receive a note from UNIX indicating your backgrounded process is finished, (or alternatively, when you feel like checking to see if this process has been completed) repeat this step.

All of the Shell programs you have met in this Module can be put in the background (**&**) as well as have their output placed in a new file using the > redirect symbol (although doing this with the **page** command makes little sense).

Commands, Options, and Arguments:

The Verbs, Adverbs, and Nouns of
UNIX Command Sequences

You have used several different Shell command sequences (e.g. **ls**, **cp** *file1 file2*, **page** *file1*, etc.) to perform a variety of functions. In this section you will learn about the *structure* of UNIX command lines—*command syntax*. This information will give you greater control over the way Shell commands function.

(1) ___ Use the **ls** command to get a listing of your files.

(2) **File Names as Arguments:** In general an *argument* is anything used in a command line that is not part of the command itself. An argument to a Shell Command will normally tell the command *what to act upon*. For example, you have been using the command line **vi** *filename* to edit files. The *filename* in this sequence is the argument and tells the Shell what file you want to edit.

The **ls** command can be used with a filename as its argument. This command is useful in more complicated sequences as will be demonstrated in later procedure steps.

___ For now, enter the command

ls [filename]   ®

where *filename* is the name of one of your files. The Shell will respond be listing your file *filename*.

(3) **Shell Commands with Multiple Arguments:** The **head** command (like most Shell commands) can also be used with more then one filename as an argument.

___ Try the following command sequence with the names of two of your files (you could use *first, second,* or *experience*):

head [file1] [file2]   ®

(4) **A Shell Command that Requires Two Arguments:** Let's use the **m**ove command to rename one of your files.

___ Enter the command line

mv $\boxed{file1}$ $\boxed{file2}$ **®**

↑ spaces ↑

where *file1* is the name of one of your files and *file2* is the new name you have chosen. In this example the command (**mv**) tells UNIX what to do (the verb of the command line) while the argument tells UNIX *what to act on* (the direct object of the command line).

Defaults: It would be helpful to compare the actions of the **ls** and the **mv** commands. Note that, whereas the *move* command requires two file names as arguments, the **ls** command—without any additional instructions—"knows" what to function on. The **ls** command, when used without an argument, will *default* to listing all of your filenames.

A *default* is simply the way a command is programmed to function in the absence of any modifiers. You have already used Shell commands both with arguments (**vi** *filename*) and without (**ls**). Arguments *must* be separated from each other and from commands by spaces so that the Shell can decide where each part of the command line ends and the next begins. Shell command arguments always follow the command and are either filenames, options or both. What's an option? The following procedures will demonstrate the nature of these beasts.

(5) **Options as Arguments:** Options can be used to specify variations in how a command "does its thing." For instance, the **ls** command can be used with an option to give you additional information about *filename*.

___ Enter the command (and leave a space between the command **ls** and the option **-l**)

ls **-l** $\boxed{filename}$ **®**

space ↑

where *filename* is the name of one of your files. Here **ls** has two arguments. One is the option **-l** and the other is the *filename*. The **-l** option for the **ls** command gives you a *long listing* for the specified file(s). Something like the following should now appear on your screen:

-rw------- 1 3people   2729 May 16 21:44 mod6

The meaning of *-rw-------* and *2729* is explored in Module Twenty-Two: *Commands, Files, and Directories.* For now focus your attention on the date (*May 16*) and time (*21:44*) on the right side of the above line. This is the time the file was last modified. The name of the file (which can be a fairly useful bit of information) is the final entry on the line.

(6) The **ls** command can also be used with the **-l** option as its only argument. Enter the command:

ls -l   ®
    ↑ space

The Shell command **ls -l** calls up a long listing of all of your files.

(7) You have used the **ls** command both with and without a filename as an argument, and both with and without an option as an argument. You have used the **mv** command with two filenames as arguments. In this next step you will use your old friend **rm** (*remove* a file) with an *option* as one of the arguments.

___ Enter (and don't forget the space before the **-i**)

rm -i [*file1*] [*file2*]   ®
    ↑ space

where *file1* and *file2* are any two of your practice files' names. This particular *option* (the **-i**) added to the **rm** command informs the Shell to question your attempt to remove the specified file(s). (Some UNIX installations set up their accounts so that this option is automatically part of the **rm** command.)

The Shell will now individually present each of the two filenames you specified. If you really do want to remove the file you answer *yes* by typing **y** and pressing the ® key. If you've changed your mind and wish to keep the file, answer *no* by just pressing the ® key. Remember: once you have entered the letter *y* and pressed ® the file is a goner. *And, hey, let's be careful out there!*

A Second Quick Review: Time for some thought questions:

(a)   What two types of things can be used as arguments to Shell commands? _____ and _____

(b)   What happens when the **mv** command is used without an argument? _____

(c)   What is the default action for the **rm** command when no option is specified and only one filename is given as an argument? _____

Answers: (a) filenames and options   (b) the Shell cannot carry out the **mv** command without an argument (two files to act upon)   (c) on most systems the file is removed; no questions asked, no apology offered.

Combining Shell Commands

(1)   Shell commands can be combined in helpful or interesting ways. Consider the following command line:

nroff *experience* | **lpr**   ®

This command will send the file *experience* to the formatter. The output of this process (the formatted file) will then be routed to the line print program which prepares the file for printing and sends it to the line printer. The | is the *pipe reroute* command. Whereas the > sends the output from a Shell command to a new file, the pipe | sends the output to another *Shell* process.

Another example of a pipe reroute command line is:

spell *filename* | *lpr*   ®

This sequence will send the output of the **spell** program to the lineprinter.

(2)   ___ Now, for a lengthy command line. Enter the following:

nroff *experience* > *n.experience* ; **lpr** *n.experience* **&**   ®

The semicolon (;) permits you to enter more than one command *on the same line* and specifies the order of execution. This command will:

(a) Format the file *experience*;

(b) Route the formatted output into a new file *n.experience*;

(c) Once (a) and (b) are completed, line print the file *n.experience*; and

(d) Perform all the above in the background.

(3) Here is an additional example of the use of the semicolon:

spell *filename* > *sfilename* ; **lpr** *sfilename* **&** ®

This command will:

(a) Check *filename* for spelling errors;

(b) Route the output of the spelling check to *sfilename*;

(c) Once (a) and (b) are completed line print the file *sfilename*; and

(d) Perform all the above in the background.

(4) ___ Practice using the Shell commands and Shell command modifiers presented in the Command Summary section at the end of this Module. The summary contains the commands introduced in this Module as well as a review of Shell commands presented in prior Modules. First practice each command individually, and then try using them in various reasonable combinations. Try to use every command at least a couple of times. (You might check them off as each is used.) In practicing these commands do not attach the **&** to the command sequences, as it is easy to forget about a backgrounded process during this exercise. Should you logout without cancelling a backgrounded process the process may continue running (costing you money and the computer needless effort).

If at any time you get lost and want to return to the Shell press the **DELETE** [DEL] or **RUBOUT** [RUB] keys (one or the other key will normally be located on the far right hand side of keyboard). Pressing one of these keys should cause any incomplete process *not in the background* to terminate, and you will be given a Shell prompt. Because this will cause any incomplete process to terminate you should not make pressing this key a regular habit. (For information about how to terminate a backgrounded process refer to Module Seventeen: *Backgrounding a Process*.)

Another Module Six Quiz:

(1) What action would each of the following Shell commands perform?

(a) **nroff** *first* > *nfirst* ®

_____

(b) **nroff** *first* > *nfirst* **&**   ®

_____

(c) **nroff** *first* > *nfirst* **;** **spell** *first* > *sfirst* **&**   ®

_____

(2) Write a command line that will accomplish each of the following:

(d) Format the file *vacation* and send it to the lineprinter, but have the computer do all that in the background so you can proceed to other UNIX operations.

_____

(e) Have the computer examine the file *report2* for spelling errors, place the misspelled words in a new file called *errors,* print a copy of the *errors* file and return you immediately to the Shell.

_____

Answers:

(a) Format the file named *first* and place this formatted text into a file named *nfirst.*

(b) Format the file named *first,* place this formatted text into a file named *nfirst,* and perform these tasks in the background.

(c) Initially format the file named *first* and place this formatted text into a file named *nfirst,* then have the **spell** program examine the file named *first* and place the contents of this examination into a file named *sfirst.* The entire sequence will be performed in the background.

(d) **nroff** *vacation* | **lpr &**   (e) **spell** *report2* > *errors*; **lpr** *errors* **&**

The UNIX Programmer's Manual

The most complete reference source for the UNIX Operating System is the *UNIX Programmers' Manual.* This very dense and terse piece of documentation can be almost impossible to read, yet it is often the only place to turn when you need to have certain questions answered. Because of its importance, we offer a 30 second discussion titled:

Reading The UPM
or
How to Become a UNIX Snob

(1) **Accessing the Manual:** To use this resource type:

man *look* ®

This command asks UNIX to search its on-line "how to do it" manual for entries relating to the **look** command. The output of this search will be displayed on your screen. Information about almost all commands can be gained with the **man** $\boxed{command}$ line. It is not always possible to understand the information provided, however, due to the technical jargon and references to concepts known only to advanced UNIX programmers.

While we cannot offer any sure fire methods of conquering this beast we can offer the following suggestions:

(a) **Persevere:** Because this type of writing is difficult to read, you may need to read it several times. If after two or three readings you still don't understand something, skip the confusing part and trudge onward.

(b) **Be Selective:** If you want to know the format for some command, check the Synopsis. Optional components are in square brackets [ ]: don't be discouraged if the Description section (or any other section for that matter) is baffling.

(c) **Options:** The list of available options for each command is often the most important piece of information. Read these sections carefully.

(d) **Be Patient with Yourself:** Learning to productively access *The Manual* is a skill that takes time to develop. Don't worry if you're unable to understand something on first or second reading. There are passages which continue to baffle UNIX programmers.

(2) **Apropos:** If you have questions you'd like to ask the *Manual,* but don't know where to start, the **apropos** command is for you. The **apropos** command will generate a list of *UNIX Programmers' Manual* entries related to the keyword you specify.

(3) To demonstrate this process, type

> **apropos** *copy* ®

and feast your eyes on the list of Manual entries generated. There should be enough material there to keep even the most adept UNIX user busy for a couple of nights.

Command Summary

Command	Function
|	Routes output from a prior Shell command to the next Shell command.
>	Routes output from a prior Shell command to a file.
&	Returns you to the Shell after beginning process, without waiting until that command has been executed. No more waiting until UNIX completes one task before going on to another.
;	Allows you to type several Shell commands on one line. UNIX will progress through each command in the order written.
apropos *topic*	Displays a list of manual entries that relate to the specified *topic*.
cat *filename*	Scrolls through your file without stopping. Press DEL to terminate.
cp *file* *newname*	Creates a second co**p**y of *file* called *newname*.
date	Displays today's **date** and time.
diction *filename*	Reads through *filename* and notes instances of questionable **diction**.
head *filename*	Displays the first ten lines (**head**) of *filename*.
logout	Ends communication with UNIX.

Command	Function
look $\boxed{word}$	**Look**s in dictionary for specific *word*.
lpr $\boxed{filename}$	Has a copy of *filename* printed on the **l**ine **pr***inter*.
ls	Displays a **l**i**s**t of all filenames in your account.
man $\boxed{command}$	Displays the UNIX **man***ual* information about whatever *command* you specify.
mv $\boxed{file}$ $\boxed{newname}$	Changes name of *file* to *newname*.
nroff $\boxed{filename}$	Will cause a formatted (**nroff***ed*) version of *filename* to be displayed on the screen.
page $\boxed{filename}$	Displays *filename* on your screen one **page** at a time (file cannot be edited, only viewed).
passwd	Changes your **passwo***rd*.
rm $\boxed{filename}$	**R***em*oves *filename* from your directory. (Be Careful!)
spell $\boxed{filename}$	Compares **spell***ing* of words in *filename* to words in its dictionary and reports all those in *filename* but not in dictionary.
suggest $\boxed{word(s)}$	**Suggest**s replacements for target *word(s)*.
tail $\boxed{filename}$	Dispays the last ten lines (**tail**) of *filename*.
vi $\boxed{filename}$	Creates a file or retrieves an existing file for **vi***sual* editing.
who	Presents a list of **who** is currently logged into your UNIX system.

Map D

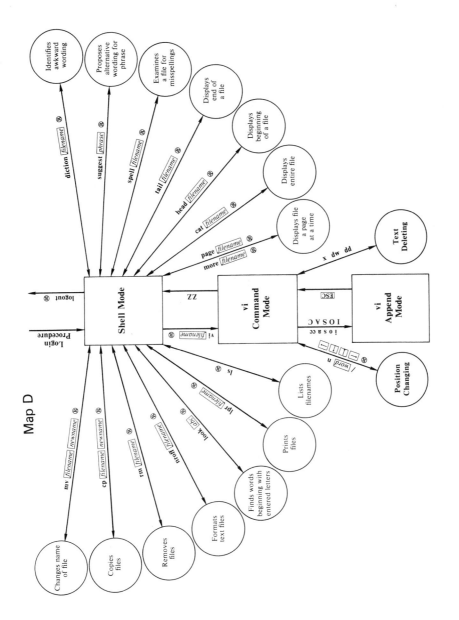

A second copy of this map is located at the end of the book.

103

Module Seven
Conceptual Overview

Introduction

Through the first six Modules the emphasis has been on *doing* things with UNIX. In this Module we will shift from the "activity" focus and instead offer a *conceptual overview* of text processing on the UNIX operating system. Our hope is that this discussion will help you tie some of the loose ends together by answering such questions as:

What does it mean to be "in" the Shell?

How can I throw away the mess I have made of this file and go back to how it was before I started this editing session?

How is nroff different from the Shell?

Prerequisites

Before starting this Module you should be able to:

(1) Append text to a file;

(2) Edit text;

(3) Append formatting commands to a file (for text processors only);

105

(4) Send a file to be formatted (or, for programmers, send a program to be compiled and executed); and

(5) Produce a printed version of both the formatted and nonformatted versions of your file (for text processors only).

Objectives

With the completion of this Module you should be able to:

(1) Describe the roles of the buffer and the disk;

(2) Return to the Shell without writing changes made to a file;

(3) Write changes made to a file without returning to the Shell;

(4) Comfortably move from one Mode of the UNIX system to another (Shell, vi Command, and vi Append);

(5) Describe the role of Command Interpreters in UNIX;

(6) Identify which commands you can execute from within each Mode; and

(7) Be able to anticipate *when* your commands will be executed.

Explanation

This overview is presented in four sections. The first part describes how the memory of UNIX is used in file editing. The second section describes the four sets of UNIX commands and the Modes that recognize and act on them. The third section reviews the concept of one- and two-way commands. The role of command interpreters is described in the final section.

The Buffer and the Disk: A Short Story

All files which you create in your UNIX account are stored on a memory device known as a "disk." This relatively permanent version of each file is referred to as the *disk copy*. When you call up a file for editing using the **vi** *filename* command, a *copy* of the *permanent* (disk) version of the file is made for you to edit. This cloned version of your file—the one you work with and make changes on during your editing session—is in fact a *temporary* copy (sometimes called the *buffer* copy) of the file. Thus while you are in the process of editing, two copies of your file actually exist:

(a) The *disk* copy, containing your file *as it was* when you started the editing session, and

(b) The *buffer* copy on which you are currently making changes.

You have used the **ZZ** command as a way to end an editing session (leave *vi* Command Mode and return to the Shell). This command actually has several functions, however. For our purposes the most important of these are:

(a) *Overwrite* the permanent (disk) copy of your file with the temporary (buffer) copy containing all changes you made during the current editing session (in effect substituting the new version for the old), and

(b) *Return* you to the Shell Mode.

Abandoning an Editing Session: All too often individuals accidentally copy lines into the wrong place, delete an unknown portion of text, or generally make a word salad of a file, and then think, "I wish I could return to the way this file was before I started messing it up." It is possible to return to the Shell and leave your file the way it was *before* you began editing, because both a buffer and disk version of your file exist. This involves returning to the Shell *without* having the temporary  copy overwrite the disk (permanent) copy of your file. Thus it requires a command other than the **ZZ** command.

To return to the Shell *without writing the buffer onto the disk,* you must be in the *vi* Command Mode and enter the following command (the colon and exclamation point are essential):

$$\text{:q!} \qquad ®$$

This is the command you will use when you have ruined a file and want to jettison the changes made during an editing session. Your file will remain in the memory of UNIX the way it was before you called it up for visual editing. The file will be *untouched* by whatever destructive changes you effected during your current editing session, and you will be returned to the Shell. The **:q!** command can protect you from your own unintentional actions. (Now, if we can only develop a **:q!** command to use after the New Year's Eve party.)

Writing and Remaining in a File: The **:q!** command returns you to the Shell without overwriting the disk copy of your file. You can also replace the current disk copy with the buffer copy *without* returning to the Shell. In this instance you are left in the visual editor to continue editing, but the permanent disk copy of your file is "updated" to reflect the work just completed. To write the buffer onto the disk, but remain in the vi Command Mode, you enter the following command:

:w!   ®

This command is similar to the **ZZ** except that you *do not* return to the Shell and are instead left to continue working on the file.

The existence of both a buffer and a disk version of your file during an editing session is a mixed blessing. On the one hand it can protect you from accidentally destroying the file as you edit it, since you are really only editing a copy and the "permanent" version remains untouched in the memory of UNIX. On the other hand, it means that any changes made during the editing session will not appear on the permanent copy until you enter a command to have this done (**ZZ** or **:w!**).

An Alternative to the ZZ Command: The **:wq** will also write the changes you have made while editing *and* return you to the Shell. The **:wq** functions the same as the **ZZ** command.

The Four Sets of Commands

The Shell Mode, visual editor Command Mode, visual editor Append Mode, and *nroff* each have their own sets of commands. In the prior Modules you have used a large number of UNIX commands, and in the next series of Modules you will meet many more. Remembering this information is easiest if you can organize it in some fashion. This section outlines a structural framework or method for grouping the commands. This framework should help you to recall when and how to use each command.

> **A Review:** A significant benefit of working with UNIX is the ability to efficiently format files, move around within the text, check spelling, shift blocks of text, delete words or lines, and quickly print files. These processes are achieved by entering the appropriate commands from: the Shell, the visual editor Command Mode, or the visual editor Append Mode. The keys which you press to move the cursor (**$**, **G**) or delete text (**dd**, **x**) are the very same keys you press to put *$*'s, *G*'s *d*'s, and *x*'s in the text itself. When in the text Append Mode, an a is an a, b is b, etc. The multiple functions ascribed to most keys require that UNIX have some systematic and consistent way of knowing when you press a key whether you are entering text, giving a Shell command, or giving an editor command. The way to tell them apart is built into the UNIX system: the Mode changing commands such as ESC **ZZ**, or **vi** *filename*.

The Shell and its Commands: When you log onto UNIX you are initially greeted by the Shell. You can tell you are *in* the Shell when the Shell prompt is displayed. Being *in* the Shell means that a limited set of commands is available which will have UNIX perform a specific set of actions.

When you are in the Shell you enter a command and the Shell acts on it as soon as you press ®. When the Shell is finished doing whatever you requested, it informs you (with the prompt) and awaits your next command. This is the way you interact with the Shell:

Command . . . *Response* . . . Command . . . *Response.*

The interactive nature of communicating with the Shell is why: (1) you are said to be "in" the Shell, and (2) the Shell is called a Mode.

The Visual Editor Command Mode: An essential aspect of UNIX consists of editing a file using a set of specific commands executed from the *vi* Command Mode. You can reposition the cursor in your text, delete lines, move paragraphs, delete characters, and move to the Append Mode *only* if you are in the Command Mode.

Like the Shell, the visual editor Command Mode is also interactive. You enter one command and it is interpreted and followed immediately. The commands to delete a word, move to the next line, or move text are all accomplished as they are requested. You can be "in" the visual editor Command Mode.

Visual Editor Append Mode Commands: As you press each of the keys **s m i l e** the appropriate symbols *s m i l e* are entered into your file and are displayed on the terminal. Nearly every Append Mode command consists of pressing a key which says: "Enter the character represented by the key pressed, but do not take me out of Append Mode." Each character is entered, and because their *order* has meaning to the humans involved in the process, text or programs are created.

Upon pressing each key a character is entered into the buffer version of your file, and UNIX awaits your next command (pressing the next character key). The only keys you have used which do not mean "enter the appropriate symbol in the file" are the ESC , **BACKSPACE** and **DELETE** keys. ESC and **DELETE** return you to the Command Mode, while **BACKSPACE** moves the cursor back one character.

Formatting Commands: The specific instructions you insert in your file (such as **.sp 2** or **.ce**) are interpreted not by the visual editor or the Shell, but by the formatter *nroff* when the file is sent for formatting. With *nroff* commands (also called *nroff requests*) you tell the formatter to double space, begin paragraphs, underline, center lines, and left and right justify the margins of your paper. When you give these instructions they *are not* carried out immediately. *First* you place the commands in your paper at the appropriate points, *then* at some later time you send your paper to the formatter and it obeys your every command. The process is not interactive. The formatter has no information about a file until you send the entire file to the formatter. After it receives the file, the formatter follows all the *nroff* requests in the file by going through the file from the top, formatting it line-by-line. You do not interact in a command-by-command sequence with the formatter, so it is not a Mode. You cannot be *in* the *nroff* Mode. (Programmers Note: Most compilers are also noninteractive command interpreters. You are not *in* the compiler mode.)

One-Way and Two-Way Commands

Thus far we have discussed one approach to categorizing commands—as *Shell, Visual Editor Command Mode, Visual Editor Append Mode,* or *Formatting* Commands. Another distinction illustrated in Conceptual Map D is the difference between two-way and one-way commands. You will recall that we introduced the concept of two-way commands earlier in the book. Both one-way and two-way commands exist in all four of the command groups.

Shell Commands: When you type the **ls** command UNIX displays a *list* of all the files in your current directory. Once it has completed this task, it *automatically* returns you to the Shell Mode. The command is executed and you are returned to the Mode from which you started. The **ls** command is a two-way command, as are most Shell commands.

This two-way process contrasts with what occurs when you use a one-way command. For example, when you type the command sequence **vi** *filename*, you *leave* the Shell and move into *vi* Command Mode where you remain until you choose to return to the Shell. The sequence **vi** *filename* is a one-way command. This command, when executed, moves you to a different Mode within UNIX and *you* must do something (in this case, type **ZZ**) to return to the Mode from which you started. Another one-way Shell command is **logout** which returns you to the world.

Visual Editor Command Mode: When you press the **x** key, the **x** command is immediately executed (delete the character under the cursor) and you are automatically returned to the *vi* Command Mode. The **x** command is a two-way command. This contrasts with the **a** and **cw** commands which are one-way commands that move you from Command Mode to Append Mode. The **ZZ** is another one-way command and returns you to the Shell.

Visual Editor Append Mode: Nearly all of the keys are two-way commands instructing the editor to enter a specific character in the file as text. BACKSPACE moves the cursor back one character and removes it from the temporary version of the file. The ESC and the DEL keys are the one-way tickets back to Command Mode.

Formatting Commands: The actions of one- and two-way commands can also be seen in the way formatting commands function. For example, the **.sp** command is a two-way formatting command. When *nroff* is formatting your file it reads the **.sp** command, spaces one line (**.sp** → **sp***ace one line*), and returns to normal formatting. This contrasts with **.ls 2** which is an example of a one-way formatting command. With the **.ls 2** command placed in your file the line spacing of your formatted paper is set at double spacing (**.ls** *2* → **l***ine* **sp***ace 2*). All text will be double spaced *until* you tell *nroff* differently.

Which of the following commands are two-way: (circle them)

lpr *filename*	**vi** *filename*	**.nf**
date	**ls**	**.ls** *1*
cw	*/ word*	**O**
.ce	**.ti** *5*	**x**
r	**.PP**	**i**

UNIX *Command Interpreters*

The following discussion will help explain why commands only work properly in the Mode for which they were designed (e.g., the **who** command will call up a list of who is on the system only if you are in Shell Mode and *not* if you are in *vi* Command or Append Modes).

Commands are understood only if you are in the Mode that is programmed to recognize (interpret) the command. The Shell has not been given instructions about how to interpret two Capital Z's (**ZZ**). Thus, should you type **ZZ** while in the Shell Mode it responds *Command not found*. The Command Mode of the visual editor *is* programmed to respond to **ZZ** and writes the buffer onto the disk and transfers you back to the Shell. Entering **O** in the

Shell results in another *Command not found* message. If you are in the *vi* Command Mode, entering the same character will open a new line for text and move you into *vi* Append Mode. Once in Append Mode, the **O** is treated like any other character and is entered as text. The ESC key is understood only when pressed in the Append Mode of the visual editor. It beeps harmlessly at you if you are in Command Mode. It is not understood by the Shell. The ESC has only one function: to move you from the Append Mode to the Command Mode of the visual editor.

While logged onto UNIX you are constantly issuing commands which are interpreted. You are in communication with one of several *command interpreters.* The command interpreters you deal with regularly are *nroff,* the Shell, *vi* Command Mode, and *vi* Append Mode. (Programmer's note: compilers and translators are also command interpreters.) Each possesses a set of instructions telling it what strings of characters (words) it will respond to and how it will respond. For instance, the **O** key can be pressed at any time, but the effect will be quite different depending upon the command interpreter you are dealing with.

As another example, if you enter **who** while you are in the Shell Mode, the Shell *interprets* the command to mean "please let me know who is logged onto the system at the moment." If you are in the *vi* Command Mode, **w h o** means something quite different. (You will soon learn that **w** is interpreted to mean "move the cursor to the next word." The **h** is the arrow key meaning "move the cursor left one space." The **o** results in the opening of a new line and transition to Append Mode.) In Append Mode **who** is simply three characters which will be placed as text in your file and appear on the screen. *Nroff* will treat *who* as three characters to be placed in a line of output, (unless **who** is preceded with a period and at the start of a line. In this case, *nroff* will not recognize, and therefore not respond to, the "command.")

As you move from one Mode to the next you are moved from one command interpreter to another. For instance, the command **vi** *filename* moves you from Shell Mode to *vi* Command Mode. Once this transition is made, you are no longer in communication with the Shell, and the *vi* Command Mode interpreter takes over. Commands which were recognized by the Shell no longer work. A new set of commands which the *vi* Command Mode interpreter understands must now be used. Commands (such as **look**) which

the Shell would recognize and act upon will receive a very different response from the *vi* Command Mode: they are either no longer interpreted, or will be interpreted in a different way. For example, the Shell interprets **ls** to mean "list my filenames," whereas the *vi* Command Mode interprets **ls** to mean "move the cursor one space to the right (**l**) and start a substitution (**s**)." To *nroff* **.ls** means "single space the output."

Interactive and Noninteractive Command Interpreters: There are two types of command interpreters within the UNIX operating system. *Interactive* command interpreters execute commands at the time you issue them (Shell, *vi* Command Mode, *vi* Append Mode). *Noninteractive* command interpreters execute an entire sequence of commands only after these commands are sent, as a unit, to the interpreter (*nroff* or, for programmers, most compilers).

How Each Interpreter Spends Its Time:

(a)   The **Shell** is an interactive command interpreter that understands commands that *manage* your files. With Shell commands the entire file is dealt with at one time (such as sending it to the line printer, searching the entire file for misspelled words, and changing the name of the file).

(b)   The **vi Command Mode** interpreter is also interactive. It understands commands which *move* the cursor through your file and *modify* your text (such as delete lines or move text). All *vi* Command Mode commands affect *only the file you are currently editing.* You can move the cursor, delete words, delete lines and move to Append Mode only from vi Command Mode.

(c)   The **vi Append Mode** is also an interactive command interpreter. Within the *vi* Append Mode nearly all characters are interpreted to mean "append this character to the file at the location of the cursor."

(d)   **Nroff** is a noninteractive command interpreter. *Nroff* commands are inserted into your file in the same way as text. When you send your file to the formatter (via the Shell command **nroff** *filename*) the formatting commands embedded in your file are read and executed and your text is formatted in accordance with them.

Standard Input and Output

Most UNIX users take for granted the ability to link Shell commands. For example, consider the command line **nroff** *filename* | **lpr**. The output of one command (**nroff**) becomes the input to the next command (**lpr**) through the use of the | pipe. The output of the first command becomes the input of the second command; the output of the second becomes the input of the third . . . . Such linkages are made possible by the *standard input* and *output*.

The Reserved File Descriptors: When some programs (such as **spell**) are running there are various points in the process where the program places information in temporary files to be accessed later in the program. Each of the temporary files that a program uses has a specific *file descriptor* associated with it. These file descriptors are used by the program to identify its temporary files in much the same way as the Shell uses filenames to locate and identify regular files. One of several possible file descriptors is attached to each temporary file as it is created. After all intermediary steps are finished, the information (in the case of **spell**, this is a list of misspelled words) is placed in a file with an assigned file descriptor. It is not given just any file descriptor, however (as was the case in the intermediary steps of the **spell** process). Rather, it is given a specific descriptor that is reserved specifically for final output. While the (**spell**) program is running it will select any one of several file descriptors for temporary storage, *except three descriptors which are reserved*. One is reserved for the final output of the program. The second reserved file descriptor is assigned to the temporary file that a program reads its input from. The program uses the third for writing error messages. The input, output, and error message files are given agreed upon file descriptors, and are thus called *standard output*, *standard input*, and *standard error*, respectively.

The Connecting Pipe: Consider what takes place when you enter the command line **spell** *filename* | **lpr**. A pipe or connector is placed between the standard output of the **spell** program and the standard input of the **lpr** program. When the **spell** program has done its duty and written the unidentified words into its standard output file, the pipe transfers the information to the standard input of the **lpr** program. The **lpr** program then has the list printed.

The fact that most UNIX programs use standard input and standard output makes it possible to connect command programs together with the pipe | acting as the connector between the inputs and outputs.

It may be helpful to think of the standard input and output as streams of information leading into, and coming out of, command programs. Information can be sent into Shell programs using the standard input stream. After the program has completed its task, the output comes out as the standard output stream. These streams of information can be connected together by using the pipe | so that the output stream of one program is connected to the stream leading into the next program. Additionally, standard output can be directed into named, permanent files in your directory by using the > redirect symbol.

Files as Input: How do Shell commands receive their input (the material upon which they act)? Most Shell commands have been programmed to accept input from one of two sources: (1) a file named as an argument to the command, or if no files are specified, (2) the standard input. These two sources can be contrasted in a UNIX activity you regularly perform—viewing the contents of a file. To view the contents of a file named *tuttle* you could enter the Shell command **page** *tuttle*. This corresponds to source (1): a filename (*tuttle*) is named as an argument to the command. Alternately, you could enter the command line **page** < *tuttle*. Here you use the < redirect symbol to connect the file named *tuttle* to the standard input of the **page** command.

Likewise, consider what happens when you enter the command line: **nroff** *filename* . The Shell program **nroff** takes as input the file named as an argument. If, however, you just entered **nroff** and pressed the ® key, a different result would occur. Not finding a specified file, **nroff** would look to its standard input for material to format. Because the standard input is connected to the terminal, whatever you typed until you entered a **CTRL-D** would be formatted.

The < redirect symbol is most useful for commands and/or situations where you can not use a filename as a simple argument within the command line. You will encounter several examples of the use of this symbol in later Modules (in producing form letters or sending files as electronic mail to other UNIX users).

When you enter the command **spell** *filename*, misspelled words in *filename* are identified and, once the whole list is completed, placed in the standard output by the **spell** program. Because you have not specified otherwise, the standard output of **spell** is connected, by default, to your terminal. Thus when the completed output arrives at the standard output file, it is transferred to your terminal (and is displayed on your screen). This action compares with the sequence **spell** *filename* | **lpr**. Here the pipe connects the standard output from **spell** to the standard input of the **lpr** program. The information is then sent to the printer.

The standard input and output are not default values for the device or file that input will be read from or output will be sent to (i.e. your terminal is not the standard output). There are, however, default settings for the standard input, output, and error of most command programs. By default the standard input is usually attached to your keyboard and both the standard output and standard error are normally attached to your screen.

Review Questions for Module Seven: Locate Map D and answer the following questions which relate to UNIX commands and their interpreters:

(a) List several *vi* Command Mode commands that *automatically* return you to *vi* Command Mode after they are executed. _____

(b) List several *vi* Append Mode commands that leave you in Append Mode until you press the ESC key. _____

(c) What are two *vi* Append Mode Commands that do not place a character on the screen (and in your file)? _____

(d) List several *vi* Command Mode commands that can be used to move through your file. _____

(e) Commands that manage entire files are executed in which Mode? _____

(f) The ESC key has meaning to which command interpreter? _____

(g) The relatively permanent copy of your file is called the _____ copy.

(h) The temporary copy made during an editing session is called the _____ copy.

(i) What Command Mode command will allow you to terminate an editing session and return to the Shell without affecting the file? _____

(j) What Command Mode command will write changes made during an editing session into the permanent copy of your file, but leave you in the editor to continue working? _____

(k) In the command **spell** *sweetie* | **lpr** what is the standard input to the line printer? _____

Answers: (a) **D, dw, dd, arrow keys,** /*word*, **S, x**   (b) **a b c d e f g**. . .**x y z**
(c) Ⓡ   BACKSPACE ESC DEL   (d) **arrow keys,** /*word* (with the **n** key), Ⓡ
(e) **Shell**   (f) *vi* Append Mode   (g) disk   (h) buffer   (i) **:q!**   (j) **:w!**
(k) the standard output of the **spell** program.

Module Eight
Advanced Visual Editor Commands

Introduction

In prior Modules you learned how to use the UNIX system to create, edit, and format text. Module Four introduced a set of basic visual editing commands (such as **a**, **dw**, **dd**, and /*word*) which are available to create and modify text. In Module Five you inserted formatting commands (such as **.ul**, **.ls 2**, or **.ce**) at appropriate points in the body of your paper. With the commands you already know you *could* write all your papers and computer programs. However, there exists a substantially larger body of commands which can make your text processing and program writing experiences more effective and less time consuming.

At this point we will introduce a greatly enlarged set of visual editing commands: a set which, when mastered, will make you much more proficient at using the UNIX visual editor. This Module does not present a *comprehensive* list: a more complete *vi* Command Summary is included in the *Command Summary Section* near the end of this book. In addition, Module Thirteen: *Truly Advanced Visual Editing* describes in some detail more sophisticated *vi* commands.

Prerequisites

To employ the commands presented in this Module you should:

(1) Feel comfortable using the visual editing commands practiced in Module Four; and

(2) Have created a file with at least 40 lines of text. You will soon be introduced to commands which allow you to quickly move about in your file. A minimum amount of text (40 or more lines) is required if these exercises are to be useful. (You can't learn to run when confined to your bedroom.) Check to see that your file *experience* contains at least 40 lines. If it does not, you should expand it to at least that length using the append commands presented in the prior Modules. You will find your experience with the present Module even more useful if your file contains substantially more text: 60 or more lines would be ideal.

Objectives

Upon completion of this Module you should be able to easily and skillfully employ the commands which:

(1) Adjust the screen's visual display of the text in your file;

(2) Move the cursor through your file;

(3) Add text to your file at desired locations;

(4) Alter or make corrections to existing text; and

(5) Undo the changes you have just made in the text.

Procedure

The commands you will use in this Module have been grouped according to their functions. The first is the set of *Moving Commands*, which allow you to move to particular locations of your file. They will cause the terminal to display different sections of your file and position the cursor on a desired line. The second is the set of *Text Changing Commands*, which allow you to change the contents of your file or add to it. The introductory visual editor commands you met in Module Four have been incorporated in this Module at appropriate places.

There are two sets of Moving Commands in the visual editor: *Cursor Moving Commands,* which allow you to re-position the cursor throughout your file (such as the **arrows** and */ word*), and *Display Adjusting Commands,* which cause the terminal to display different sections of your file.

Moving the Cursor

(1) **Getting Started:** An extensive assortment of commands exists which will allow you to quickly position the cursor at a desired location in your text.

___ Log onto your UNIX account.

___ Have a list of the files in your account displayed on the screen (use the **ls** command).

___ Call up for visual editing your pre-existing file named *experience* (with the **vi** *experience* command).

If there are less than 40 lines of text in your file (the number of lines in your file will appear at the bottom of the screen), turn back to Module Four and begin using the commands presented there to expand your file to at least 40 (and preferably 50) lines length. Once you have enlarged this file to a sufficient length, return to this Module and continue working.

(2) **Moving Forward:** You can move one character at a time with the [→] *arrow* key, and to a specific *word* using the slash-search */word* command. It is also possible to move forward one word at a time.

___ Position the cursor on any line of text in your file. Press the following key:

w

What happened? Press it several more times. The **w** command is used to move the cursor *forward* through your text to the next beginning of a **w***ord.*

___ Place a number ahead of the **w** command to move forward several words. Try **3w**.

___ Type the command (lower case):

e

What happened? The letter **e** was chosen for e*nd* of word. With each **e** pressed the cursor moves to the next e*nd* of a word. Press this **e** key several times. What happens at the end of a line? Try it. Compare **e** and **w**.

___ Now place a number before the **e** key. Type:

5e

The **w** and **e** commands—like all of the *Moving Commands*—take effect immediately and are two-way commands. (Recall the distinction between one and two-way commands discussed in prior Modules?) Each of the moving commands is accessed only from the Command Mode, and once each is performed you *remain* in the Command Mode. They *do not* move you to another Mode (Shell or Append) and *do not* require that you use the **RETURN** or the ESC keys. They take effect immediately upon being typed.

(3) **Moving Backward:** You can move backward through your text with the **b** key.

___ Position the cursor near the middle of any line in your file and press this key:

b

What happened? Press this key several times. With each **b** that you press, the cursor moves **b**ackward through your text to the previous beginning of a word.

Now place a number before the key. Type **3b**.

The **w** and **e** keys move you *forward* through your text, while the **b** key moves you *backward* through your text. With these keys you can quickly position the cursor on a word within any line (and even move from one line to the next).

(4) **Cursor Moving Commands:** As you read the following list of *Cursor Moving Commands,* try each one several times.

> Note: Most of the *Cursor Moving Commands* (the **arrow** keys, **e, w,** and **b**) can be made to move more than one character, word or line by typing a number as an argument *before* the command. For example, the command **3b** moves the cursor to the beginning of the third word back, while **5** ⬇ (or **j** key) moves the cursor down 5 lines. This is in contrast to the modifications made to Formatting Commands (i.e., where **.ce 2** means center the next two lines typed into the file).

Cursor Moving Commands

Command	Function
⬅⬇⬆➡	**(h,j,k,l)** Moves cursor one line up/down or one space right or left.
0	(zero) Moves cursor to the beginning of whatever line it is on.
$	Moves cursor to the end of the line.
*42***G**	Moves cursor to line 42 (or any number).
G	Moves cursor to the last line in your file.
w	Moves cursor forward to the first letter of the next word.
e	Moves cursor forward to the next end of a word.
b	Moves cursor backward to the previous beginning of a word in your file.

L	Positions cursor at lowest line displayed on the screen.
M	Positions cursor at mid-point on the screen.
H	Positions cursor at the highest line on the screen.
f $\boxed{b}$	Moves cursor forward through text to next *b* in the line (**f***j* moves cursor to next *j*).
F $\boxed{b}$	Moves cursor backward through text to previous *b* in the line (**F***m* moves cursor to the previous *m*).
/ $\boxed{word}$	Moves cursor forward through text to next instance of *word*.
? $\boxed{word}$	Moves cursor backward through text to prior instance of *word*.
n	Moves to the next pattern identified in a **?***word* or **/** *word* search.

(5) **Cursor Moving Exercises:** Perform each of the following actions. The commands which will accomplish each task are contained in the previous Cursor Moving Command Summary and are also noted below.

(a) Move the cursor to line 14 in your text using the **G** command.

(b) Move to the end of the line.

(c) Move to the last line in your file.

(d) Move backward three words.

(e) Put the cursor to the top line that is presently displayed on the terminal.

(f) Move to the middle line that is displayed.

(g) Move to the lowest displayed line.

(h) Move the cursor forward to the beginning of the fourth word.

(i) Move the cursor to line 18.

(j)   Move to the next letter *a* in the line.

(k)   Move forward to the end of the fourth word.

(l)   Move backward to the previous letter *o* on the line.

Answers: (a) *14G*   (b) **$**   (c) **G**   (d) *3***b**   (e) **H**   (f) **M**   (g) **L**
(h) *4***w**   (i) *18G*   (j) f*a*   (k) *4***e**   (l) **F***o*

Changing the Terminal Display

With the previous commands the cursor was relocated but the part of your text displayed generally remained the same. The following commands adjust the terminal's display of text.

(1)   **Display Adjusting Commands:** As you read through the *Display Adjusting Commands* try each of them several times. Note those commands which seem particularly helpful. Remember that the commands indicated **CTRL-D** or **CTRL-U** (for example) mean that you hold down the **CTRL** key while you press the **d** or **u** key.

Display Adjusting Commands

Command	Function
CTRL-D	Scrolls down or moves on to more text in file.
CTRL-U	Scrolls up or moves back to prior text in file.
CTRL-F	Brings up next block or window of text.
CTRL-B	Goes back a window of text.
z#.	Makes screen show only # lines of text, with the cursor line at the middle of the display. (**z4.** will display only 4 lines at a time; the number can be 1 to 23.)
z.	Redraws screen, with cursor line in center of the window.

(2) The command **z#.** specifies the number of lines that are displayed when the screen is drawn. For instance, the command **z3.** results in 3 lines displayed. The **z#.** command can save you time when editing, because it takes less time for the terminal to display a smaller screenful of text. This is particularly helpful when using the *slash-search* command to find certain words.

(3) The amount of text which appears with each **CTRL-D** or **CTRL-U** can be modified by placing a number before the command. For example, *15***CTRL-D** will scroll down through 15 lines of text. From that point on each **CTRL-D** or **CTRL-U** will scroll 15 lines.

(4) Practice each of the above *Display Adjusting Commands* until its actions seem familiar. These commands will allow you to quickly move to a desired section of your text.

(5) ___ Each of the following display or cursor moves is often needed in text processing. Perform each of them. If you are not certain which command is appropriate, you may refer to the answers which follow.

(a) Redraw the screen, with the cursor line as the center line.

(b) Have the text which follows the display scroll up onto the screen.

(c) Bring up the next "block" of text.

(d) Have the screen display only 3 lines of text.

(e) Go back to text which precedes the display.

Answers: (a) **z.**   (b) **CTRL-D**   (c) **CTRL-F**   (d) **z3.**   (e) **CTRL-B**

Another Brief Quiz: To help you remember the *Moving Commands* answer the following questions:

(a) What is a command which will scroll down or move onto more text in your file? _____

(b) What is the command which will make the screen display only 6 lines of text? _____

(c) What is the command which will move the cursor to line 17 of your file? _____

(d) What is the command which will move the cursor to the beginning of the line? _____

(e) What is the command which will move the cursor *forward* to the next end of a word? _____

(f) What is the command which will move the cursor *backward* to the previous beginning of a word? _____

(g) What is the command which will move *forward* in the line to the first instance of the character *m*? _____

Answers: (a) **CTRL-D** (b) z6. (c) *17*G (d) **0** (zero) (e) **e** (f) **b** (g) **f***m*

Text Changing Commands

Once you have correctly positioned the cursor in the text you can employ one of several commands for adding or changing text. In Module Four you met the **i** and **a** commands for appending to the left (**i**) and right (**a**) of the cursor, plus the **o** and **O** which open lines below (**o**) and above (**O**).

Append commands let the computer know two things: (1) that you want to start *adding* characters to the file and (2) *where* you want the addition. Hence anything you type *after* one of these commands will be *entered* appropriately as text and will *appear* on the screen until you press the ESC key.

As with the *Moving Commands*, each of the following *Text Changing Commands* is interpreted in the intended way only if you are in the Command Mode of the visual editor. There are both *one-way* and *two-way* Text Changing Commands. Recall that a defining property of the one-way command is that by entering it you are moved *out* of one Mode and *into* another Mode, until you give the appropriate command to return. The following one-way commands move you out of Command Mode and into Text Append Mode. With all one-way Text Changing Commands the way back to *vi* Command Mode (once you complete typing whatever text you want) is by pressing the ESC key.

One-Way Commands for Adding Text

Inserting Text: Module Four introduced the four append commands **i**, **a**, **o**, and **O**. Figure 1 is a representation of where text is added relative to the position of the cursor with each of these append commands.

O

i | a

o

Figure 1

You are not limited to those four append commands, however.

(1) ___ Place the cursor in the middle of any line of text in your file and press this key (Upper Case):

I

Notice that the cursor moved to the *beginning* of the line. You are now in Append Mode. Everything you type will be **I***nserted* before the first character of the line. Type a couple of words, then press the [ESC] key.

This command allows you to quickly move to the *beginning* of a line and **I***nsert* additional text.

(2) **Appending Text to the End of a Line:** It is possible to **A***ppend* text to the *end* of a line without first moving the cursor to the end. Place the cursor near the middle of a text line and, from the Command Mode, enter:

A

The cursor moves to the end of the line and you are now in Append Mode. Add some text and return to Command Mode.

All append commands move you into the Append Mode. What is different is *where in your file* the text you type will be added. The "where" of the six general append commands is illustrated in Figure 2.

Figure 2

The black rectangle represents the cursor location. **I** will **I**nsert text at the beginning of the line, and **A** will **A**ppend text at the end of the line.

Substitution Commands: The role of *substitution* commands was introduced in Module Four, where you learned to substitute for characters, words, and lines. First, a review of the **s** and **cc** commands.

(3) ___ Position the cursor on any letter of a word in your file and press this key (lower case):

s

The character under the cursor disappears, and you are now in Append Mode. Whatever you type (one character or several lines of text) will take the place of that single character that disappeared. Type a few words. When you finish, press the ESC key.

(4) ___ Position the cursor anywhere on a line in your file and press:

cc

The cursor line disappears, and you are now in Append Mode. Whatever you type (until you press the ESC key) will be substituted for the one line of text that was removed. Type a few lines of text. Yes, you can substitute any number of words or lines for the line you just caused to disappear. When you finish, press the ESC key. Note: the (upper case) **S** command is equivalent to the **cc** command. Try it with another line of text in your file.

(5) **Changing the Rest of a Line:** The **cc** (and **S**) command **cc**changes an entire line (the **S** command **S**ubstitutes). There is another text changing command: upper case **C**.

___ Place the cursor in the *middle* of a line of text and enter (Upper Case):

C

The **C** command **C**hanges that part of a line from the cursor location to the end of the line. It leaves the part of the line up to the cursor unchanged. You are now in Append Mode and whatever you type (one character or pages), will take the place of the remainder of the line. Type a few words, then press ESC . Try the **C** command on a different line of text.

(6) ___ Practice each of the following commands a couple of times, again noting the action each performs.

One-Way Text Changing Commands

(Leave You In Append Mode)

Command	Function
a	Inserts text one space to the *right* of the cursor.
A	(Upper Case) Starts adding text at the end of the line.
i	Starts adding text to the *left* of the cursor.
I	(Upper Case) Inserts text at the beginning of the line.
o	Opens a line (or inserts) before the next line of text.
O	(Upper Case) Opens the line above (inserts above the cursor line).

cw	Replaces only the one word under the cursor.
s	(Lower Case) Substitutes for a single character.
S	(Upper Case) Substitutes for an entire line.
cc	Substitutes for an entire line (same as **S**).
C	Changes the rest of the line (from the cursor position forward).

Because *all* of the above commands move you into the Append Mode, each requires the ESC key to move you out of Append Mode and back to Command Mode.

Modifying Text with Two-Way Commands:

The previous append commands were one-way commands: you moved from Command Mode to Append Mode, where you remained until you pressed the ESC key. The following Commands perform their duties and then immediately return you to the *vi* Command Mode. They are *two-way* commands. You do not use the ESC key. The visual editor is programmed to execute each of these commands and then return you to Command Mode.

(7) ___ Read through and try out the following commands. Several will be recognized from earlier Modules. An explanation of how to use the *Yank* and *Put* commands, and the commands prefaced with a colon (:), follows this listing.

Two-Way Text Changing Commands

(Return You To Command Mode)

Command	Function
x	Erases (**x** *out*) only the letter under the cursor.
dw	Deletes only the word under the cursor.

dd	Deletes the entire line.
D	Deletes the rest of the line (from the cursor position on).
r $\boxed{b}$	Replaces the letter under the cursor with the letter *b* (**rw** replaces character under cursor with the letter *w*).
J	Joins cursor line with the next line in your text.
yy	Yanks the cursor line.
$\boxed{\#}$ **yy**	Yanks # lines. For instance, **6yy** is the "make a copy of the next 6 lines, remember them, and put them where I tell you to" command (See *put* commands).
P	(Upper Case P) Puts the yanked or deleted line(s) just above the cursor line.
p	(lower case p) Puts the yanked (or deleted) text just below the cursor line.
:1,26 **m** *82*	Moves lines 1 to 26 to after line 82. (You select the line numbers.)
:1,26 **co** *82*	Copies lines 1 to 26 and places them after line 82. (You select the line numbers.)
:1,26 **d**	Deletes lines 1 to 26. (You select the line numbers.)

Shifting Blocks of Text Within a File

Yanking and Deleting Text: These commands offer one method for moving text or paragraphs around in your file—they are the *cut* and *paste* action of UNIX. Because of the importance of the *yank* and *put* commands we'd like to walk you through an exercise using them.

(8) ___ Place the cursor on a line you would like to copy and place somewhere else in your text. Press:

yy

Now move the cursor to a different line in your text, one where you would like this **yy**anked line of text to be **p**ut. Press this key (lower case):

p

What happened? A copy of the *yanked* line of text should now appear as the line *below* the cursor line. (If you do not want this text to remain in this location, press the **u** key.)

(9) ___ Try the *yank* and *put* commands several times. If you do not want the yanked and put text to appear in *both places* in your file you must return to where the lines were originally *yanked* and delete them.

(10) ___ Try both the (Upper Case) **P** and the (lower case) **p** with the same portion of *yanked* text. Press first the **P** and then the **p** and notice where this text is placed with each command.

(11) **Deleting and Putting Lines:** The *put* commands will also work with the **dd**elete line **dd** command, in a fashion quite similar to the *yank* command. You can *delete* a line of text, move the cursor to a different location in your text, and use the *put* command to re-place this deleted text.

Select a line that you might like placed somewhere else in your text. You may position the cursor on any character on the line and press:

dd

(12) ___ Then move the cursor to another line of the file where you want this text re-placed and use a *put* command. Press this key:

p

Note: You can use only cursor moving commands between the *yank* or *delete line* command and the *put* command. You cannot save text in "yanked" or "deleted" form while you alter some other part of the text. If you delete text and then perform an additional *text changing* activity before replacing the deleted text, the original text is lost. This means you cannot *first* delete a line, add text, replace a character, change the spelling of a word, and *then* try to have the editor put the deleted line into another part of your text. Get into the habit of *yanking* or *deleting* the text, moving the cursor to the new section of your text (where you wish to reposition this *yanked* text), and then using the *put* command.

The visual editor also maintains a set of *lettered* (a - z) buffers in which you can place yanked or deleted blocks of text. Text blocks placed in these buffers will remain there during the entire editing session, and can be accessed at any time through the use of the appropriate command sequence. The use of these buffers is described in Module Thirteen: *Truly Advanced Visual Editing.*

(13) **Deleting and Putting Words and Characters:** The **P** and **p** commands can also be used to *put* deleted characters or words in a different location in your file.

___ Move the cursor to the beginning of a word and delete the word with the **dw** command. Now move the cursor to the space between two other words and press the (lower case) **p** key.

___ The (lower case) *put* command allows you to quickly transpose characters in your text. Place the cursor on the first letter of any word in your text and press the **x** key. Now press the **p** key, and the two letters are transposed.

The Next Brief Quiz:

(a) What is the command which will allow you to substitute new text for an entire line of old text? _____

(b) What is the command which will allow you to substitute new text for a single character of old text? _____

(c) What is the command which will allow you to insert new text at the beginning of a line of old text? _____

(d) What is the command which will open up a line for appending text above the cursor line? _____

(e) What is the command which will delete the word under the cursor? _____

(f) What is the command which will put a portion of deleted text just below the cursor line? _____

(g) What is the command which will scroll down or move onto more text in your file? _____

(h) What is the command which will move the cursor to the first letter of the next word in your file? _____

(i) What is the command which allows you to substitute text for a single word? _____

(j) What is the command which places deleted text just above the cursor line? _____

Answers: (a) **cc** or **S**   (b) **s**   (c) **I**   (d) **O**   (e) **dw**   (f) **p**
(g) CTRL-D   (h) **w**   (i) **cw**   (j) **P**

Moving Text with Colon Commands

You now have some experience with the *Yank* and *Put* procedure for copying lines of text in a file. For files of even moderate length this is a cumbersome process, however. Ever aware of our needs, UNIX has provided a more efficient method for moving or making copies of blocks of text: the *colon* (:) commands. A subset of the *colon* commands allows you to include the line numbers associated with the target lines to assist with the movement of text blocks.

To use these commands you need to have *numbers* displayed on the screen next to each line in your file. If you do not already have this editing convenience, you should request it with the following *vi* Command Mode sequence:

:set nu*mber*   ®

(1) **Copying Text Within a File:** From *vi* Command Mode enter the command (and don't forget the colon):

:2 **copy** *4*   ®

A copy of line 2 was made and placed after line 4 in your file.

With the **copy** command the first number following the colon is the line number of the text *to be copied*. The number following the word **copy** is the line number *after* which the copied line *should be placed*.

___ What command would make a copy of line 15 and place it after the third line of the text in a file? _____

Answer: *:15* **copy** *3*

Did you remember to start the command with a colon? Note that all colon commands (such as *:15***copy** *3*) are given from the Command Mode of the visual editor. As usual, if you are not sure of your location, press ESC .

(2) ___ You can remove the change made in Step (1) with the undo command:

u

The copy of line 2 which is now line 5 should disappear.

(3) ___ Try copying some other line in the text and placing it at a new location.

(4) You do not have to limit yourself to cloning text one line at a time. Several lines can be "xeroxed" and placed at a specific location in a single operation.

___ Enter the command

:1,4 **copy** *7*   ®

A copy of the lines 1 through 4 is placed after line 7. The original lines remained in place, but a copy was added to your text after line 7.

Line Addresses: The editing commands which start with a colon (such as the **:copy** command) allow a block of text to be identified *by its beginning and ending line numbers*, each separated with a comma. Hence, *1,4* refers to lines 1,2,3, and 4. Likewise, *57,62* refers to the lines starting with line 57, up to and including line 62.

Be sure to enter the lower number first; UNIX does not understand such line address sequences as *62,57* or *9,2.*

The format for the **copy** command which was used above is:

(a) Colon (:);

(b) Followed by the line numbers which identify the block of text *to be copied,* separated by a comma;

(c) The **copy** command; and

(d) The line number *after which* the block *should be placed.*

(5) ___ Regarding the command sequence:

$$:4,8 \textbf{ copy } 10 \quad ®$$

(a) Which lines will be copied? _____

(b) Where will the copies be placed? _____

Answers: (a) lines 4 through 8   (b) placed after line 10

The **co**py command can be abbreviated to the letters **co.** For instance:

$$:10 \textbf{ co } 4 \quad ®$$

makes a copy of line 10 and places it after 4. Likewise:

$$:10,14 \textbf{ co } 4 \quad ®$$

copies the entire block of text from lines 10 through 14 and places it after line 4.

(6) ___ Try copying lines near the end of your text and placing them near the beginning.

(7) **Moving Text in a File:** What if you do not want to make *copies* of lines for inclusion in different locations in a file but rather want simply to *move* lines from one place to another? The **move** command makes this possible.

___ Enter (don't forget the colon):

$$:1 \textbf{ move } 4 \qquad ®$$

Line 1 now follows line 4.

(8) The same address procedure used with the **:copy** command is also used with the **:move** command. Try:

$$:1,6 \textbf{ move } 10 \qquad ®$$

(9) ___ How would you move lines 1,2,3,4, and 5 to a new location following line 15? Since the editor accepts the abbreviation **m** for **m**ove, the following works:

$$:1,5 \textbf{ m } 15 \qquad ®$$

(10) ___ Sometimes an author wants to move text to the very beginning line of a file. The following command sequence will work, because line 1 (the first line in your file) follows the "zero" line (yes, computers are extremely logical, if not particularly creative). Try (the last character is a zero):

$$:10,15 \textbf{ m } 0 \qquad ®$$

___ The dollar sign (**$**) is the editor symbol that, when used in line addresses, means *the last line in the file.* Hence to move lines 3,4,5 and 6 to the end of the file—regardless of the file's length—enter:

$$:3,6 \textbf{ m } \$ \qquad ®$$

(11) **Deleting Blocks of Text:** When deleting blocks of text you have a couple of choices. To delete the first 10 lines from a file you could move the cursor to the first line and type:

$$10\textbf{dd}$$

Or, *regardless of the cursor location,* you could type:

$$:1,10 \textbf{ d } \qquad ®$$

This command says "find lines 1 through 10, then delete the little critters."

___ Select one of the *delete text* commands listed above and delete lines 1 through 10 of your current file.

(12) **The Undo Commands:** You met (lower case) **u** in Module Four and saw how, for instance, **u** would bring back a deleted line. If you add a line of text, move to some other location, and then press **u** the added line is removed. The **u** command goes back one append or delete command only.

There is a second *undo* command, however, which undoes several changes that you made to the *one line where the cursor is located*: the upper case **U** command.

___ Select a line of your text. Delete one word and change another word in that one line. Then, *without moving the cursor away from the line*, enter:

U

The removed word will come back, and the altered word will return to its original state.

If, however, you move the cursor away from the line where you made the changes, only the last change can be undone, and only with the lower case **u** command. (There are also ways to go back a greater number of changes using *numbered buffers*. Accessing these buffers is described in detail in Module Thirteen: *Truly Advanced Visual Editing*. The appropriate command sequence is also listed in the Command Summary Section at the end of the book.)

(13) In the Conceptual Overview you met the "return to Shell without writing changes" command **:q!** After the exercises practiced in this Module your *experience* file may look a trifle distorted. This might be a good time to use the **:q!** so that your file can remain in its pre-Module Eight state.

The Undo Commands

Command	Function
u	(Lower Case) Undo the effect of the last command given.
U	(Upper Case) Undo the effect of all changes made to the line, providing cursor is still on the line.

The Final Module Eight Quiz: When you feel comfortable using most of the commands in this Module (and have used each of the commands at least twice) proceed to the self-check questions which follow.

(a)   What Mode must you be in to use the colon commands?

_____

(b)   What command do you enter to move lines 17 to 93 of your file to the end of the file? _____

(c)   What colon command would allow you to delete everything in a file following line 117? _____

(d)   How could you move a paragraph beginning on line 32 and ending on line 57 to the beginning of your file?

_____

Answers: (a) *vi* Command Mode   (b) *:17,93* **move** *$*   (c) *:118,$* **d**
(d) *:32,57* **move** 0

A complete *vi* Command Summary is located in the *Command Summary Section* at the end of the book.

Module Nine
Advanced Formatting Commands
The -ms Macros

Introduction

In Module Five you learned how to use several formatting commands (**.ce**, **.ul**, **.ti 5**, **.sp**, **.ls 2**, **.nf**, **.fi**, **.ll**, **.na**) which give directions to the UNIX formatter. These commands serve as instructions to *nroff* about how you want your file formatted. The formatting commands introduced in Module Five are known (in Uni-Jargon) as *nroff requests*. There exists another large set of formatting commands: the *-ms macro package*. A macro is a bundle of several *nroff* commands. This bundling allows a macro to handle complex formatting problems (such as numbered section headings or indented paragraphs) with a single command.

The *nroff* requests, which you already use, are available on all UNIX systems. The *-ms* macro package is the most widely distributed set of *nroff* macros, but is not available (or used) in some settings. It is possible to create a set of your own macros to be used *in place* of the *-ms* package. Some locations have taken advantage of this feature of *nroff* to develop their own macros.

For this reason it is advisable to determine whether the *-ms* macro package is available on your system before you begin the Procedure section of this Module. The two easiest ways to find out if the *-ms* macros are available are: (1) Check with an experienced UNIX user at your location; or (2) If you have the on-line UNIX manual, enter the **man ms** command from the Shell. If you are greeted with information about the *-ms* macros, then you have them on your system.

If your UNIX location does offer the *-ms* macro package (most sites with *vi* do) then *welcome to Module Nine!* If you use a different set of macros you may want to skim the material presented in this Module and then move directly to Module Ten. After completing Module Ten, all readers are referred to Module Twenty: *Macro Construction* for more information about how macros are built and how they operate.

Prerequisites

To employ this Module you should:

(1) Determine whether the *-ms* macro package is available at your location;

(2) Have at least 30 lines of text—and *no* formatting commands—in a file. Forty or more lines of text would be even better. The file *second* should be empty of formatting requests and easily increased to that size;

(3) Be able to employ the visual editor commands which you learned in Modules Four and Eight to insert text, add text, open lines, move the cursor, and scroll the text; and

(4) Be able to employ the *nroff requests* introduced in Module Five.

Objectives

Upon completion of this Module you should be able to:

(1) Direct *nroff* and the *-ms* macro package to format a paper, controlling such basic features as the indentation, margins, and centered headings;

(2) Add emphasis to a paper using labeled paragraphs, headers and footers;

(3) Use *nroff* and *-ms* commands together with some degree of success; and

(4) Format footnotes, quoted paragraphs, and displays.

Procedure

The procedure steps of this Module are presented in five sections. The first section briefly describes the action of the *-ms* paragraph macros. The second section illustrates how to produce numbered and unnumbered section headings. Section three demonstrates how to alter the way pages are set up. The fourth section illustrates how to mix and match *nroff* requests and *-ms* macro calls. The final section presents additional *-ms* commands which can be used to format text files.

The -ms Paragraph Macros

Each of the *-ms* macros is actually a collection of *nroff requests* packaged together in a "bundle" and given a special name.

For example, if you were limited to using only *nroff* requests, a standard paragraph would require the use of *two* requests (**.sp** and **.ti 5**). The *-ms* macro that contains these two *nroff* requests (along with several other *nroff* requests) is called **.PP** (as in **P**aragra**P**h).

The actual "bundles" of *nroff* requests that make up commands such as the standard paragraph or left paragraph are known as the *macro definitions*. The names of the commands (in this case **.PP** or **.LP**) are known as *macro calls*. When the formatter meets a *macro call* within a text file (encounters a **.PP**, for example), it interprets the call to mean, "perform the specific *nroff* requests that are contained in the macro definition." Thus, with a **.PP** the **.sp** and **.ti 5** calls are performed, resulting in a blank line and a five space indent.

(1) **Compatibility of** *nroff* **and** *-ms* **Commands:** It is not always possible to mix *nroff* and *-ms* formatting commands and have them perform as expected. For this reason we suggest that you first practice using the *-ms* macro calls by themselves, and for now include no *nroff* requests. We will discuss the ways that *nroff* and *-ms* commands can be used together at a later point in this Module.

   ___ Call up for visual editing a file that is at least 30 lines long and contains *no formatting commands*. The very dusty and musty file named *second* (created in Module Three) should be about right.

(2) **Paragraph Macros:** Read through the following examples of paragraph macros. The unformatted text—as it would appear in a file—will first be presented. This is followed by the formatted version of the same text.

Paragraph Macro Examples

(3) **Standard Paragraphs:**

.PP
This is a standard indented ParagraPh.
As usual, the -ms request .PP must be on a line by
itself and begin at the very first space.
The .PP paragraph is probably the most used
macro in the system.

      This is a standard indented ParagraPh. As usual, the *-ms* request .PP must be on a line by itself and begin with the very first space. The .PP paragraph is probably the most used macro in the system.

___ Enter a .PP as the *first line* in your file. Make certain it is the very first line. (Place the cursor on what is presently the first line and enter the Command Mode command **O** to open a line above the cursor line, and then enter the .PP macro.)

(4) **Left Block Paragraph:**

.LP
The Left block Paragraph skips a line,
but does not indent five spaces.
The first word begins
at the left margin.
Notice in these -ms macros that two
upper case letters are used, in contrast
with the two lower case letters in *nroff.*

The Left block Paragraph skips a line, but does not indent five spaces. The first word begins at left margin. Notice in these *-ms* macros that two upper case letters are used, in contrast with the two lower case letters in *nroff.*

___ Enter a call for a left block paragraph somewhere in your file.

(5) **Indented Paragraph:**

.IP
Indented Paragraphs are spaced down,
and not only the first line, but all
lines are indented.
The useful thing about indented paragraphs is
that they can be labeled.
Any new paragraph call will conclude
the indented paragraph.

> Indented Paragraphs are spaced down, and not only the first line, but all lines are indented. The useful thing about indented paragraphs is that they can be labeled. Any new paragraph call will conclude the indented paragraph.

___ Select a group of lines that you would like to be formatted as an indented paragraph and precede them with the appropriate command.

(6) **Labeled Indented Paragraph:**

.IP *(A)*
For instance this paragraph is labeled with an
(A) because the (A) follows the **.IP**
in the *-ms* request.
The labels can be letters,
numbers, symbols
or whatever you place after the **.IP**.
You must leave *one* space between the **.IP**
and the label.

(A) For instance this paragraph is labeled with an (A) because the (A) follows the **.IP** in the *-ms* request. The labels can be letters, numbers, symbols or whatever you place after the **.IP**. You must leave *one* space between the **.IP** and the label.

___ Place the call for a labeled, indented paragraph somewhere in your file.

(7) **Longer Labels:**

.IP *Example* **9**
If the label you want to use is more than 5 characters
long, the standard indented paragraph indent will
not be enough.
You must include
a number *following* the label.
(In this case, the number 9.)
The number will be read by
the formatter as the number of spaces to indent.

Example If the label you want to use is more than 5 characters
long, the standard indented paragraph indent will not be
enough. You must include a number *following* the label.
(In this case, the number 9.) The number will be read by
the formatter as the number of spaces to indent.

____ Place the call for a long labeled indented paragraph in your file.

(8) **Two Part Labels:**

.IP *Example\\0 -3-* **12**
The label can have no spaces in it.
If you want the formatter to print a space,
you must include a **\\0** where you want the
space included.
The **\\0** is not interpreted by the formatter
as a *backslash* and a *zero*,
but rather as an instruction to include a space the size
of a zero at that location.
This allows the number *-3-* to appear
independent of the word *Example*.

Example -3- The label can have no spaces in it. If you want the
formatter to print a space, you must include a **\\0**
where you want the space included. The **\\0** is not
interpreted by the formatter as a *backslash* and a *zero*,
but rather as an instruction to include a space the size
of a zero at that location. This allows the number *-3-*
to appear independent of the word *Example*.

___ Try labeling a paragraph with a space in the label. An alternate way to include two part labels in an **.IP** macro call is to enclose the label within double quote marks (for example, "*Example -3-*").

(9) **Quote Paragraph:**

.QP
The **Q**uote **P**aragraph is indented
from both the left *and* right margins.
There is no macro for the end
of the quoted paragraph.
The quoted paragraph will end
with the next paragraph macro.

> The **Q**uote **P**aragraph is indented from both the left *and* right margins. There is no macro for the end of the quoted paragraph. The quoted paragraph will end with the next paragraph macro.

___ Set off a few lines of text as a quoted paragraph. Note: The quote paragraph command will not automatically single-space the material.

(10) **Exdented Paragraph:**

.XP
The *e***X***dented* **P***aragraph*
is an inverted standard paragraph.
It leaves the first line at the left margin
and indents the remainder of the lines.
Many people use exdented paragraphs for
bibliographic entries when they are constructing
a bibliography by hand (rather than using
the *refer* package.)

The *e***X***dented* **P***aragraph* is an inverted standard paragraph. It leaves the first line at the left margin and indents the remainder of the lines. Many people use exdented paragraphs for bibliographic entries when they are constructing a bibliography by hand (rather than using the *refer* package.)

___ Go ahead and exdent a paragraph in your file.

Section Headings

The *-ms* system provides an easy way of formatting and ordering section headings. Five sample section headings are presented below. Each instance demonstrates both the input lines and the formatted section heading.

(1) **An Ordinary Section Heading:**

.SH
This is a Section Heading of some
substantial and generally unnecessary length.
.LP
Standard S*ection* H*eadings*
are left justified and underlined (bolded by *troff*).
One blank line will precede the heading.
Section headings can be one word
or several lines.
The end to the section heading is indicated by
the next paragraph or section heading macro.

This is a Section Heading of some substantial and generally unnecessary length.

Standard S*ection* H*eadings* are left justified and underlined (bolded by *troff*). One blank line will precede the heading. Section headings can be one word or several lines. The end to the section heading is indicated by the next paragraph or section heading.

___ Enter a section heading command in your file.

(2) **Numbered Headings:**

.NH
This is a Numbered Section Heading
.LP
A N*umbered* S*ection* H*eading* is identical
to a regular section heading, except that
numbering is automatically provided.
The numbers will automatically increase
with each subsequent section heading.

1. This is a Numbered Section Heading

A *Numbered Section Heading* is identical to a regular section heading, except that numbering is provided. The numbers will automatically increase with each subsequent section heading.

___ Enter a numbered section heading at an appropriate location in your file.

(3) **Multiple Levels of Numbered Section Headings:**

.NH 2
Second Level Heading
.LP
You are not limited to one level of
Numbered Section *Headings.*
Multiple levels of numbering can be
created by specifying (as an argument
to the section heading macro)
the level of the numbering.
The .NH 2 means that this is a
second level heading, and results in
the addition of a decimal point and number.

1.1. Second Level Heading

You are not limited to one level of *Numbered* Section *Headings.* Multiple levels of numbering can be created by specifying (as an argument to the section heading macro) the level of the numbering. The .NH 2 means that this is a second level heading, and results in the addition of a decimal point and number.

___ Place a second level section heading before some appropriate text in your file.

(4) **Ascending Numbers for the Headings:**

.NH 2
Another Second Level Heading
.LP
As each new section heading is entered,
the number for its level is increased by one.

Because this is the second instance of a
section heading of the 2 level,
the number for that level is
increased by one.
Hence this paragraph will be
numbered 1.2.

1.2. Another Second Level Heading

As each new section heading is entered, the number for its level is
increased by one. Because this is the second instance of a section
heading of the 2 level, the number for that level is increased by
one. Hence this paragraph will be numbered 1.2.

(5) **Even Higher Levels:**

.NH 3
A Third Level Header
.LP
This is an example of a third level heading.
Since it is the first entry of the third
level, it is called **1.2.1**;
the next third level header would be **1.2.2** and
the next **1.2.3** etc.
There are five levels available for
numbering section headings.
The formatter will keep track of
which numbers have been used
on all levels.

1.2.1. A Third Level Header

This is an example of a third level heading. Since it is the first
entry of the third level, it is called **1.2.1**; the next third level
header would be **1.2.2** and the next **1.2.3** etc. There are five levels
available for numbering section headings. The formatter will keep
track of which numbers have been used on all levels.

___ Enter at least two second or third level numbered section
headings in your file.

(6) **Obtaining Formatted Output:** At this point it would be useful for you to have your *second* file formatted so that you can examine the effects of the several paragraph and section header macros entered. You will also have a chance to view the unrequested (uncalled for) formatting additions that *-ms* has made.

___ Return to the Shell and enter the following command (leave a space between *nroff* and *-ms*.

nroff -ms [*filename*] | **lpr**   ®
↑ space

___ If you do not have immediate access to a printer and want to examine the formatted file on the terminal, enter the following command to have the file formatted and displayed on your screen:

nroff -ms [*filename*] | **page**   ®

It is essential when using the *-ms* macros to let UNIX know you have done so. You must include the notation **-ms** after **nroff** and before the *filename* to have the *-ms* macros read by the formatter. Without the **-ms** in its proper location *nroff* will not know how to interpret the *-ms* macro calls, and your file will not appear formatted as you wish.

(7) ___ Compare your output to the previously presented examples of paragraphs and section headings. Can you remember which macro call was used to create each paragraph?

(8) **Volunteer Formatting by** *nroff -ms*: Examine the formatted version of *second*. Note that, along with the paragraphs and section headings being formatted in accordance with your instructions, many additional formatting decisions were automatically made for you by *-ms*:

(a) Each line is 6 inches long.

(b) The page length is 11 inches.

(c) The header and footer margins are 1 inch.

(d) The pages are numbered.

(e) The date is included on the bottom of each page.

(f)   The indent for paragraphs is 5 spaces.

(g)   The distance between paragraphs is one space.

(h)   The output is single spaced.

(i)   The text is filled and justified.

Although you did not specify values for each of the above, *default* values were assumed and the text was formatted in accordance with these values. In the next section we will explore how to make changes in the default values.

Page Control

One of the important functions of the *-ms* package is to take care of formatting details that affect each page of your output. As you noticed in your formatted *second* file, the *-ms* macro package automatically made several decisions about the layout of pages. You have the option of modifying these decisions, however, by supplying alternate *page management* instructions. Because these instructions affect every page in your paper they are usually entered as *the very first commands* in your file.

There are three kinds of page management instructions: *nroff* requests that control when new pages are started or the line spacing is changed, *number registers*, and *string definitions*. Each of these will be considered over the next few pages.

(1)   **Beginning a New Page:** You may find it occasionally necessary to instruct *nroff* when to begin a new page of formatted text. The *nroff* request to **b**reak **p**age is **.bp** . This command can be used, for example, to start a new page following a title page.

   ___ Find a place in your text where a new page could begin. Place the **.bp** command at this point. Remember to place the command on a line by itself, and don't forget the period.

(2)   **Needs:** The **.bp** command is useful when you are sure of where you would like the page to break, regardless of how much of the page has been used. But what about the opposite situation? Perhaps you know where you *don't* want a page break to occur (such as in the middle of a list), but otherwise do not care where the break falls. Whenever you have some meaningful unit of text

that you do not want to be broken across pages (such as a column of data or a table) you can specify that these lines stay together with a **ne**ed. If there is sufficient room on the current page, the lines will be printed on that page. If there is not enough room left on the page, *all* specified lines will be placed on the next page.

Needs are often placed before centered headings because a centered heading at the bottom of a page—with no text following— looks rather peculiar. You can avoid having a head separated from its body (an unfortunate state that should be avoided at all costs) by placing a **ne**ed command before the heading. To demonstrate, consider the following lines placed in a text file:

```
.ne 5
.ce
Heading Text
.sp
Text for the paper continues . . . .
```

The **.ne** *5* command placed before the heading will request that the centered header (*Heading Text*) and the space (**.sp**) appear on the same page with at least three *output* lines of text. If, when *nroff* arrives at the **.ne**5 command, there are five output lines available on the current formatting page, the header and the text will be printed on that page. If less than 5 lines remain on the page, the entire set will be moved to the next page.

___ Find an appropriate place for a **ne**ed command in your file.

(3) **Page Length:** Module Five stated that the **.pl** request can be used to specify the page length used by *nroff* to format your page. At that time we noted the fact that it is not possible to convince *nroff* to do anything at the top or bottom of a page without using the services of macros. As you have just seen, the -*ms* macro package takes care of this problem by setting up default values for page length and includes top (*header*) and bottom (*footer*) margins.

The *default* for both -*ms* and *nroff* is to create output that will fit paper that is 11 inches long. If you require a different page length this information must be specified.

___ To have the formatter produce output to fit on 14 inch paper with one inch header and footer margins, enter the command:

.pl *14i*

If the **.pl** $\boxed{Number}$ command precedes *all* text in your file, the entire file will be printed with the specified page length. If you insert the command after beginning the text, it will take effect at the start of the next page.

(4) **Using nroff Requests with -ms Macro Calls:** Strange things can go on when you precede a *-ms* paragraph macro with a *nroff* command.

Your *second* file presently has a **.PP** as the first *-ms* macro call. Open a line *following* this macro call and enter the following two command lines:

> **.ll 4i**
> **.ul**

The **.ll 4i** command is the *nroff* request for formatting lines 4 inches long, and the **.ul** is your old friend the **u***nder* **l***ine* request. The file should now have **.PP** as the first *-ms* macro call, followed by a **.ll 4i** and a **.ul**, followed by text.

___ Now locate the third paragraph macro call in your file. Place a **.ll 2i** and a **.ul** *nroff* request just *before* this third paragraph macro call. When finished, use the **ZZ** command to save the changes made to the file and return to the Shell.

(5) ___ Send the file to the formatter using one of the Shell command lines listed at the end of the last section:

> **nroff   -ms $\boxed{filename}$ | lpr   ®**

> **nroff   -ms $\boxed{filename}$ | page   ®**

When you have retrieved your output, continue with this Module.

Was the first line of text underlined? Yes. Is the text set in lines which are four inches long? Yes. But this line length remained in effect only for a while, until the start of the next paragraph. When the next paragraph began—regardless of whether it was standard, left block, indented or exdented (**.PP**, **.LP**, **.IP**, **.XP**)—the line length was reset to 6 inches.

You placed a second request for an underlined line and a line length (of 2 inches) before the third paragraph macro in your file. How did these commands affect the formatted version? Not one bit. Hmmm. . . .

You have just met two of the -ms paragraph resets. At the start of this Module we stated that the **.PP** consisted of a **.sp** and a **.ti 5** "along with other *nroff* requests." These other requests (included in all *-ms* paragraph macros) consist of instructions to *reset* several of the *nroff* one-way (line length, page offset, etc.) commands. In addition, instructions are included which will turn on filling and turn off underlining, centering, and assorted other *nroff* functions. For this reason two-way *nroff* requests (underlining and centering are two examples) should not be used directly preceding *-ms* paragraph macros. If you wish to underline or perform any other two-way nroff action *within a paragraph*, the *nroff* request should follow the paragraph macro call. Otherwise the macro call will defeat your formatting request.

(6) **Resetting Number Registers:** It is clear from the experience with your *second* file that the paragraph macros (**.PP, .LP, .IP, .XP, .QP**) reset the *number registers* (memory) associated with certain *nroff* one-way commands (line length, for example). Where do the paragraph macros get the values used in resetting? This action requires the use of two sets of number registers: (a) the *-ms* macro set of number registers, and (b) the *nroff* set of one-way command number registers. In most cases, the *nroff* memories are reset by each *-ms* paragraph macro to specific values that are stored in the set of *-ms number registers.* Whenever a paragraph macro is encountered the value in each *-ms* number register is checked and assigned to the corresponding *nroff* number register.

This action can be viewed in the formatting of your *second* file. You initially instructed the formatter to construct lines 4 inches long (**.ll 4i**). It followed your request. . . for a while. The formatter complied with this *nroff* instruction, starting with the next line in your file. But this specified line length ended as soon as the next paragraph macro was encountered. Because all *-ms* paragraph macros reset the line length to the value specified in the *-ms* number register—and you did not make a change to the line length number register—the next paragraph macro in your file reset the line length.

Why was it reset to 6 inches? The default value in the *-ms* **LL** (**L***ine* **L***ength*) number register is 6 inches. Unless you tell the formatter otherwise, lines are set 6 inches long. Thus, when the next paragraph macro reset the line length, the formatter read the Line Length number register and set the length to the default 6 inches.

Just before the third paragraph macro call in your file you included a request for lines to be 2 inches long (**.ll** *2i*). No lines were formatted to that specification. The formatter did read your instruction, however, and the line length was set to be 2 inches. Immediately afterward (before reading any text) the formatter came to the *-ms* paragraph macro. This macro called for the line length to be reset to the value residing in the number register—6 inches. Since there was no text between your *nroff* request and the *-ms* paragraph macro's resetting, no text was set at 2 inches.

(7) **Changing the Number Register's Value:** What if you want to have *all* text set at a specific line length (such as 6.5 inches)? Entering the *nroff* command **.ll** *6.5i* would work only until a paragraph macro appeared in your file. At that point the line length would be reset to the (default) value in the *-ms* number register. The key is to change the value of the *-ms* number register associated with line length. Once you have changed the register to whatever value you want, the paragraph macros will reset to the value you specified in the number register (the default value no longer applies).

The command to change the **n***umber* **r***egister* for the **L***ine* **L***ength* to 6.5 inches is:

    .nr LL *6.5*i

Likewise,

    .nr PO *2*i

is another "change the number register" command. It tells *nroff* to reset the **n***umber* **r***egister* (**nr**) that controls the **P***age* **O***ffset* (**PO**) to the value of 2 inches (*2i*). As a result there will be a 2 inch space to the left of the formatted page. You can ask *-ms* to offset the page 1 inch (*1i*), 6 centimeters (*6c*), or whatever distance suits your needs and will fit on the paper.

Whenever you use a paragraph macro—and in effect call for a resetting of the *nroff* one-way number registers—the value you specified in a **n***umber* **r***egister* will be used for the reset. This is why, if you want every page to reflect the values you select for these page set up number registers, you must specify the values *before* the *first* paragraph macro call.

In summary, one-way *nroff* requests (such as line length **.ll** *6.5i*) may be used to alter formatting within paragraphs, *if the nroff request follows the paragraph macro.* If you want to affect several paragraphs you must use the *-ms* number registers (**.nr LL** *6.5i*)

___ A complete list of *-ms macro* number registers and their default values is included with the Summary of Formatting Commands located on page **517**. Locate this summary and read through the list of number registers and their functions. These number register commands are normally used at the very beginning of a file (so they can affect the entire paper), but they can also be used within the body of a paper. The **PO, HM,** and **FM** number registers take effect at the beginning of the next page. The remaining number registers (**LL, FL, PI, QI,** and **PD**) take effect at the start of the next paragraph.

(8) **Initializing for -ms Use:** Whenever the *-ms* macros are included in a file, *nroff* must be informed of their use. As was noted earlier, this information is conveyed by appending the **-ms** argument to the Shell command line (**nroff -ms** *filename*). One additional action is necessary, however. Within your file the various **nroff** one-way formatting commands (such as those which affect the line length and header and footer margins) must be given their initial values. This *initializing of nroff* is done by including one of the *-ms paragraph* commands before any text in your file.

Earlier in this Module you placed the **.PP** as the first formatting command in your file *second.* While the **.PP** command formatted a regular paragraph, it also served to initialize *nroff*—it had the formatter read the number registers and establish the *nroff* one-way command values. Whenever you use the *-ms* macros you need to include a paragraph macro before the text of your file. Even if your initial formatting objective is to center a line of text, you must begin the file with a *-ms* paragraph macro.

(9) **Changing the Header and Footer Space:** The default settings for the header and footer margins are one inch. They can be changed by changing the header and footer number registers.

___ Enter the following formatting commands as the first two lines in your file, *preceeding* the initializing paragraph macro call.

> **.nr HM** *1.5i*
> **.nr FM** *1.5i*

These commands have the following meanings to *nroff* and the *-ms* macro package:

.nr HM *1.5i*   leave a one and one-half inch **H**eader **M**argin at the top of each page,

.nr FM *1.5i*   set the **F**ooter **M**argin to one and one-half inch.

Why are these commands placed at the beginning of your paper? They set the values in the two number registers. When the first (initializing) *-ms* paragraph macro is read the values you specified for header and footer margins will be used, instead of the default values.

(10) **Header and Footer Title Lines:** With the *-ms* macros it is possible to have three part title lines inserted in the middle of your header and footer margins.

___ Enter the following six lines directly following the header and footer margin **n**umber **r**egister commands entered in the previous step and before the initializing paragraph macro call.

> **.ds LH** *left top*
> **.ds CH**
> **.ds RH** *%*
> **.ds LF** *left foot*
> **.ds CF** *center foot*
> **.ds RF** *right foot*

These commands will have the following effect when used with the *-ms* macros:

.ds **LH** *left top*	print *left top* in the left position within the header margin,
.ds **CH**	print nothing in the center position (default is to print the page number in this position),
.ds **RH** *%*	print the current page number in the right position of the header margin (the % can be used in any of the six positions to indicate, "print the page number here"),
.ds **LF** *left foot*	print the phrase, *left foot* in the left position of the footer margin,
.ds **CF** *center foot*	print *center foot* in the center footer position, (Default is date in this position.)
.ds **RF** *right foot*	print *right foot* in the right footer position.

(11) ___ Return to the Shell and have a copy of the file formatted as you did in the previous step 5. Examine the effects of the **ds** string definition requests.

(12) **Review Time:** Consider the following questions:

(a) What formatting command would label a paragraph (1) ?

_____

(b) What command would label a paragraph *Objective 4*?

_____

(c) What formatting instruction would result in paragraphs indented 10 spaces? _____

(d) What instruction would result in footer margins of 1.5 inches? _____

(e) What formatting instruction would result in two spaces between all paragraphs instead of one? _____

(f) What Shell command line will have the formatter properly interpret the previous commands? _____

Answers: (a) **.IP (1)**   (b) **.IP** *Objective\04 15* or **.IP** *"Objective 4" 15*
(c) **.nr PI** *10*   (d) **.nr FM** *1.5i*   (e) **.nr PD** *2v*   (f) **nroff -ms** *filename*

(1) **The Order of Commands Using -ms:** The resetting of number registers makes it essential that the commands be placed in correct order at the beginning of the file.

___ Locate the *unformatted* version of the *Second Sample Paper* at the end of this Module.

___ As you examine this paper take note of several points:

(a)   As usual, the text lines are short;

(b)   The formatting commands are placed within the body of the text;

(c)   Each command is on a line of its own;

(d)   The number register specifications are first (**.nr LL**);

(e)   String definitions are second (**.ds CH**);

(f)   Third should be the one-way *nroff* commands not reset by **-ms** (line spacing and page length).

(g)   An initializing paragraph macro (**.LP**) is next;

(h)   Followed by the text.

(2) ___ Positioned after the unformatted version of the *Second Sample Paper* is the same file after it was formatted by **nroff -ms**. Locate this version and notice how the *-ms* formatting commands were followed and removed from the text.

(3) ___ Read and compare the two versions, noting the effect of each command.

(4) ___ Locate the *-ms Command Summary* on page **511** in the *Command Summary Section*. Read through the list of *-ms* commands and note those that seem most helpful to you.

It is certainly not necessary to "memorize" the summary. Keep it handy for reference and with experience you will be able to remember most of the commands.

After you have read through the Command Summary, complete the following exercises with your *experience* file.

(5)   **Exercises:** The following procedures are designed to help you "get your feet wet" in the formatting puddle (or muddle). Read each direction, locate the mentioned command in the Command Summary, and then insert it in the appropriate place in your *experience* file.

Do not forget that several of the *-ms* formatting commands are one-way commands. This means they require a complementary command to return paper formatting to the prior state. For example, the command **.RS** will indent the left margin 5 spaces. This indentation will remain in effect until you place a **.RE** command in the file. In fact, all *-ms* formatting commands that begin with the same letter and end with the letters **S** (for **S***tart*) or **E** (for **E***nd*) must be paired.

Remember our warnings about mixing and matching *nroff* and *-ms* format commands. If you find that your format commands do not work as you think they should, it is possible that an unappreciated *-ms* number register is at fault.

(a)   ___   Underline 3 lines of text with the **.I** command. Remember to use the **.R** to return to normal (non-underlining) formatting.

(b)   ___   Indent the left margin of part of your text 5 spaces with the **.RS** command. Remember to use the **.RE** command to return to normal (non-indented) formatting.

(c)   ___   Select two paragraphs of text to place as footnotes in your paper. [1]

(d)   ___   Want to fool your friends into thinking you wrote this paper several weeks (or years) ago? On the line following the two **.ds** commands place the **.DA** *date* (replace *date* with the desired *date*).

---

[1] Use the .FS and .FE commands to surround the text you would like to appear in each footnote. See example on page 165.

(e) ___ Experiment with 2 or 3 of the *number register* commands.

(f) ___ Finally, add as many more formatting commands as you can find an excuse to use. If possible, we suggest you try each command at least once.

(g) ___ Examine your file to be certain that the number register commands are first, string definitions second, followed by a paragraph macro, then text. If you are satisfied that all is well, save the file with the **ZZ** command.

(6) **Checking for Errors:** When you have completed a file and think you are ready to have it formatted, you can have it checked for common formatting errors. The Shell program **checknr** will examine a file and report on unrecognized or unbalanced instructions. For example, it will check to make sure that each **.RS** command has a corresponding **.RE** command.

___ To have your file examined by **checknr** enter the following Shell command:

checknr $\boxed{\textit{filename}}$ ®

A list of objections or possible problems will be displayed on your screen. The program is not foolproof, however, so even though no problems are reported by the **checknr** program, there could still be problems in the output. Conversely, not all instances reported by **checknr** will actually interfere with your output.

(7) **Obtaining Output:** When your *experience* file is ready to be formatted ask *nroff* (with a little help from its friend *-ms*) to format and line print the file.

___ From the Shell enter the command:

nroff -ms *experience* | **lpr**   ®

Remember: When using the *-ms* macros you need to let *nroff* know. Including the argument **-ms** *after* the *nroff* and before the *filename* in the Shell command line will do this. The *-ms* commands will now be understood by the formatter.

(8)   ___ Request a line printed copy of the unformatted (input) file (**lpr** *experience*) so that you can compare it with the formatted version.

(9)   **A Final Review:** And now a review of the formatting commands you learned in both Module Five and this Module:

(a)   What is the command to center two lines of text? _____

(b)   What command will underline the next line of text? _____

(c)   What command will have page numbers printed in the lower left corner of each page in your paper? _____

(d)   What command will cause a standard, five space indented paragraph to be started with the next line of text? _____

(e)   Name both the *nroff* and the -*ms* commands which will indent the left margin 10 spaces. _____

(f)   Name the *nroff* and the -*ms* command(s) which return the left margin to its normal setting. _____

(g)   What command starts a new page with the following line of text? _____

(h)   What command indents both the left and right margins for a quoted paragraph? _____

(i)   What set of commands is used to set off a footnote in your text? _____

(j)   Where would you place the **.ul** command if you want the first line of a paragraph to be underlined? _____

(k)   What is the order that the initializing macro, one-way nroff requests, number register changes, and string definitions should be placed in the beginning of a file for formatting using the -**ms** macros with **nroff**?

_____

Answers: (a) **.ce** *2*   (b) **.ul** or **.I** |text| **.R**   (c) **.ds LF %**   (d) **.PP**
(e) **.in** *10* or **.RS** and **.RS**   (f) **.in** *0* or **.RE** and **.RE**   (g) **.bp**
(h) **.QP**   (i) **.FS** and **.FE**   (j) After the paragraph request   (k) number registers, string definitions, one-way nroff requests and then the initializing macro.

A summary list of both *nroff* and -*ms* formatting commands is included in the *Command Summary Section* located on page **507**.

```
.pl 8i
.nr HM .6i
.nr FM .6i
.nr LL 4i
.nr FL 4i
.ds CH
.ds CF Example Page
.LP
.ce
```
Example Page
```
.sp 3
.PP
```
This page is an example of a file
which was formatted using the -ms macros.
Our objective is to give the reader a chance to
see a text file in which the initial page management
commands are correctly ordered.
```
.FS
```
This is a footnote; notice where the text and
commands are located in the unformatted version.
```
.FE
.PP
```
Several section headings
of different levels
are included.
Examine how each command works.
```
.PP
```
The various page dimensions are marked on the
formatted page.
```
.NH
```
Page Setup
```
.PP
```
The first eight lines of this file are the nroff and -ms
macro formatting commands that control page dimensions.
Notice that the number register commands and string
definitions are placed before the initializing macro.
```
.NH 2
```
Nroff Request
```
.PP
```
The first command (.pl 8i) is the nroff
request that sets page length to 8 inches.
```
.NH 2
```

Number Registers
.PP
The next four commands reset the number registers
that control the header margin (.nr HM .6i),
footer margin (.nr FM .6i), line length (.nr LL 4i),
and footnote length (.nr FL 4i).
.NH 2
String Definitions
.PP
The next command (.ds CH) instructs
the formatter to leave the center
of the header margin blank (the default is
to print the page number in that position).
The following string definition (.ds CF Example Page)
causes the formatter to place the
string ''Example Page'' in the center
of the footer margin.
This last command overrides the default printing
of the date in this position.
.PP
The two string definition commands result
in footers beginning on page one and
headers beginning on page two.
.NH 2
Initialization
.PP
The next command (.LP) serves as the initializing macro.
It prepares the formatter to format the text that follows
in accordance with the -ms formatting commands.
.NH 1
Using Nroff Requests
.na
.PP
Note how the .ce command is used immediately preceding
the centered heading (Example Page)
and centers the next input line.
Blank lines are included
where the .sp command is used.
This section is filled but not adjusted because the .na
command precedes it.
.ad

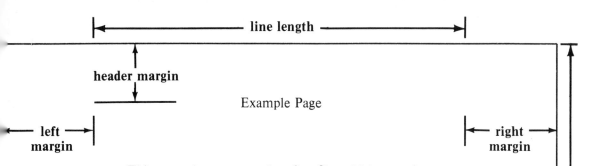

Example Page

This page is an example of a file which was formatted using the -ms macros. Our objective is to give the reader a chance to see a text file in which the initial page management commands are correctly ordered.

Several section headings of different levels are included. Examine how each command works.

The various page dimensions are marked on the formatted page.

1. Page Setup

The first eight lines of this file are the nroff and -ms macro formatting commands that control page dimensions. Notice that the number register commands and string definitions are placed before the initializing macro.

1.1. Nroff Request

The first command (.pl 8i) is the nroff request that sets page length to 8 inches.

1.2. Number Registers

The next four commands reset the number registers that control the header margin (.nr HM .6i), footer margin (.nr FM .6i), line length (.nr LL 4i), and footnote length (.nr FL 4i).

1.3. String Definitions

The next command (.ds CH) instructs the formatter to leave the center of the header margin blank (the default is to print the page number in that position). The following string definition (.ds CF Example Page) causes the formatter to place the string "Example Page" in the center of the footer margin. This last command overrides the default printing of the date in this position.

This is a footnote; notice where the text and commands are located in the un-formatted version.

Example Page

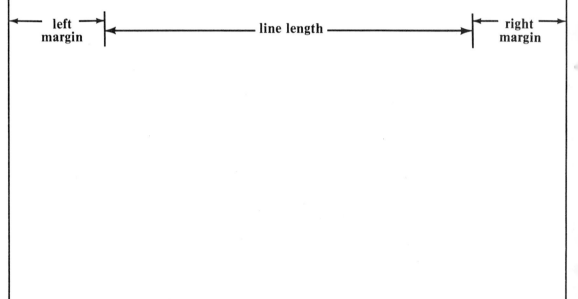

header margin

The two string definition commands result in footers beginning on page one and headers beginning on page two.

1.4. Initialization

The next command (.LP) serves as the initializing macro. It prepares the formatter to format the text that follows in accordance with the -ms formatting commands.

2. Using Nroff Requests

Note how the .ce command is used immediately preceding the centered heading (Example Paper) and centers the next input line. Blank lines are included where the .sp command is used. This section is filled but not adjusted because the .na command precedes it.

left margin ← **line length** → **right margin**

footer margin

Example Page

Module Ten
A Stroll Through a Full Production Number

Introduction

The first part of this book introduced the basic procedures that are prerequisite to using the text processing component of the UNIX operating system. The procedures were introduced in a systematic step-by-step fashion appropriate for UNIX beginners. This Module marks the transition to the second half of this book, which consists of a series of Special Topic Modules explaining the applications of various advanced UNIX features. Understanding these features will make you a stylish—as well as a skillful—text processer (and the world needs more stylish UNIX users).

The purpose of this Module is to provide guidance concerning the production of a "full scale" paper of substantial length and complexity. Over the course of "stepping through" this process we will introduce a large number of new UNIX features. We will not in this Module offer a detailed explanation of how to use the new features, but will instead indicate where in the remaining Modules information about each new command or procedure is located.

Prerequisites

Before starting this Module you should be able to use:

(1) The visual editor with wit and diplomacy;

(2) Formatting commands to perform such standard functions as start paragraphs, emphasize text, and control line spacing; and

(3) Shell commands to format, correct misspellings, and print copies of your paper.

Objectives

Upon completion of this Module you should be able to locate the resources which will help you produce your own full scale paper.

Procedure

The process of conceptualizing, researching, writing, editing, and printing a written document can take a variety of directions. In most cases this is not a linear but rather a cyclical process, in which you shift across activities during the life of the project and re-cycle through each step several times. In presenting the material in this Module we will consider the paper production process to involve three principal phases. While these phases are not rigidly sequential, any written project would seem to involve working through these general steps:

(a) *Advance work*, which includes the topical planning phase, researching the area, and UNIX account housekeeping activities;

(b) The *grind-it-out* writing and editing sessions which produce the content of the paper, including the insertion of both prose (content) and formatting commands; and

(c) *Final production issues*, such as adjusting the appearance and producing the final formatted version of your paper.

These general phases will be discussed separately. A large number of possible steps involved with each phase will be introduced, along with references to additional book material more fully describing each step.

UNIX **Topics Worthy of Consideration at Any Time:** The Modules comprising the remaining sections of this book contain detailed information about a variety of topics pertinent to effectively using the UNIX editors and account management programs. While an understanding of all of this material is not critical to your being able to use this system, six Modules contain information which may be particularly helpful to all users:

(a) Module Eleven: *The Line Editor Ex*

(b) Module Twelve: *Special Search and Substitution Characters*

(c)   Module Thirteen: *Truly Advanced Visual Editing*

(d)   Module Fifteen: *The UNIX Directory Structure*

(e)   Module Sixteen: *Account Management Activities*

(f)   Module Seventeen: *Backgrounding a Process*

These Modules contain information which can make your text processing experience more productive and less time consuming. You are encouraged to study them at any time.

Problems with UNIX: What, Me Worry? Problems encountered while using UNIX are both frustrating and not uncommon, owing in part to the complexity and power of the system (and the vagaries and moods of any electronic beast). In Module Twenty-Eight: *Troubleshooting* we have attempted to address some of the more common problems encountered by us and the UNIX users we have known.

Advance Work

The activities comprising this section can be performed while researching and considering the actual content of the paper. These are primarily account management and initial file creation tasks. In preparation for these activities you need to have a general idea as to:

(a)   What the topic of your paper will be;

(b)   The approximate length of the paper (5, 15, 50, or 500 pages);

(c)   What form the final, formatted version of the paper will take (*nroffed* and lineprinted or *troffed* and phototypeset); and

(d)   Whether you will utilize special UNIX packages such as *refer*, *eqn*, or *tbl* to assist with reference materials, equations, and tables, respectively.

(1) **Customizing Your Account:** General account management is often the first task. Module Sixteen: *Account Management Activities* considers a variety of Shell Commands which will make the task of keystroking and editing your paper much easier.

(2) **Creating Directories:** From your Home directory you should create a new directory (with a name reflecting this new project) to accept all the files generated over the course of the project. See the *Better Living Through File Relocation* section of Module Fifteen: *The UNIX Directory Structure.*

(3) **A Title Page?** Move into this new directory and create a file to accept the formatting instructions for a title page. Enter text to create the title page. See the section on *Formatting a Title Page* in Module Twenty-Four: *Special Formatting Topics.*

(4) **A Table of Contents or Index?** Do you anticipate including a Table of Contents and/or an Index with your work? UNIX would like to help with either. See the sections on *Formatting a Table of Contents* and *Formatting an Index* in Module Twenty-Four: *Special Formatting Topics.*

(5) **Sections as Files:** Is the paper going to be of substantial length? If so, it will be useful to break it up into component parts (perhaps along chapter divisions) and place each part into a separate file. You can later format these separate files together so that the paging comes out correctly. This procedure is described in Module Eighteen: *Parts and Wholes.*

(6) **A Bibliographic Package:** Have you made the acquaintance of the UNIX bibliographic package entitled *refer*? If not, introduce yourself and decide whether it offers a service you would like to engage. See Module Twenty-Five: *Bibliographies and Footnotes.*

(7) **Formatting Tables:** Anticipate needing to include tables in the paper? The *tbl* preprocessor will make you life much easier. Take a look at Module Twenty-Six: *Setting Tables: A Busboy's Nightmare.*

(8) **Formatting Equations:** If your paper will contain scientific equations you may wish to use the UNIX formatting packages specifically designed to help with this task: *eqn* prepares equations for *troff*, while *neqn* prepares equations for *nroff*. This preprocessor package is described in Module Twenty-Seven: *Equalizing Equations.*

(9) **Utility Programs:** Regardless of topic or anticipated needs you would be well advised to glance at Module Twenty-One: *Utility Programs* and note any packages that appear interesting or useful for your current task.

(10) **Quality of Final Output:** Pause for a moment and consider how you want the final paper to appear: lineprinted or typewriter quality will require the use of *nroff* (and possibly *-ms* macro) commands while phototypesetting (highest quality, used to produce this book, and costs mucho dollars) requires the use of *troff* (and *-ms*) formatting commands. If you want to go the typeset route, read up on the *troff* commands relating to type-size, font selection, and text emphasis options in Module Nineteen: *Phototypesetting with Troff and Troff -ms.*

The above activities can be completed at any time during the conceptualizing and researching phases of your project. Your UNIX decisions at this point are *not* cast in stone: you will most probably wish to modify the layout of your title page or the directory structure created to house the paper.

Grinding-It-Out

The *grinding-it-out* phase includes researching, reviewing, writing, and editing your paper. The actual structure of your paper may take any number of forms, and the commands which will perform the desired formatting effects have been introduced throughout this text.

(1) **Moving Text within a File:** You will probably want to move blocks of text around *within* your file as you edit your material. See the section on *Moving Text in a File* located in Module Eight.

(2) **Moving Text across Files:** You may need to shift blocks of text *out of* your current file and *into* new files during your editing sessions. See the section on *Writing Material Into Another File* in Module Eighteen: *Parts and Wholes.* You may also want to read text *from* other files *into* your current file. See the section on *Copying Another File Into the Current File* in that same Module.

(3) **Facilitating Your Editing Tasks:** If you anticipate using a certain phrase or sequence of commands repeatedly, your efforts keystroking these characters can be minimized by any of four options:

(a) Read into your file at the appropriate points the contents of a second file which contains only the desired phrase. See the section on *Copying Another File Into the Current File* in Module Eighteen: *Parts and Wholes*;

(b) Devise a two character (perhaps the letters *zz*) ''word'' which the editor will recognize as an abbreviation for a complete phrase and automatically expand into the phrase. See the section on *abbreviations* in Module Thirteen: *Truly Advanced Visual Editing*;

(c) Create your own formatting macros to assist with your writing. See Module Twenty: *Macro Construction*; and

(d) Create your own *vi* Command Mode commands which can then represent a sequence of commands. See Module Thirteen: *Truly Advanced Visual Editing* for the section on *mapping*.

(4) **Pattern Searching:** While editing you may need to search for certain words or phrases in your file. Use the *slash-search* commands (*/word or ?word*) described in Module Eight or the global search and substitution commands presented in Module Twelve: *Special Search and Substitution Characters.*

(5) **Improved Editing:** The visual editor commands for addressing text and modifying text can be combined in a wide variety of ways. Also, when quickly working through your file (during an editing session) you may want to reduce the size of the display screen, thereby equally reducing the time required of UNIX to redraw a screenful of text. See the sections titled *Text and Operators* and *Display Adjusting Commands* in Module Thirteen: *Truly Advanced Visual Editing.*

(6) **Special Formatting Tasks:** The three UNIX support packages mentioned earlier which can make your writing more effective and infinitely less time consuming are:

(a) **refer**, which is described in Module Twenty-Five: *Bibliographies and Footnotes*;

(b) **tbl,** which provides a welcomed assist with formatting tables. See Module Twenty-Six: *Setting Tables:A Busboy's Nightmare*; and

(c) **eqn** and **neqn,** packages of commands which will help you to format scientific formulas and equations. See Module Twenty-Seven: *Equalizing Equations.*

(7) **Write Your Own Macros:** Do you have an unusual, difficult, or repetitive formatting task that existing macro calls handle poorly or not at all? No problem; just write your own macro(s)! This process is described in Module Twenty: *Macro Construction.*

(8) **Bored with the Project?** Or perhaps you feel an irrepressible need to learn all you can about the UNIX system. Module Twenty-Two leads you on a tour through the *Paths, Bins, and Yellow Brick Modes* of UNIX. Your conceptual map of UNIX cannot be completed without this trek.

(9) **Checking for Errors:** A couple of Shell Commands introduced in earlier Modules are very helpful with text editing. The Shell Commands **spell** and **look** provide an on-line dictionary to help correct spelling errors. (**Spell** is described in Module Six, while **look** is considered in Module Two.) The *Writer's Workbench* series of programs exist to help you write more effectively. Two of the more widely available programs are **diction** and **suggest** (described in Module Six: *File Management*). Several special purpose Shell commands are introduced in Module Twenty-One: *Utility Programs.*

(10) **Input from Others:** Would you like to have your colleagues review drafts of your work? Their comments on an advance copy can be invaluable. Use the electronic mail capabilities of UNIX to forward a draft to these individuals. See Module Fourteen: *Communicating with Others.*

Production Issues

There are two sections to this phase: (1) Previewing your final draft for typesetting and formatting errors; and (2) Selecting the type of printer to use.

(1) **Reassemble the Files:** The various files created at the beginning of the process to hold individual chapters or sections can now be combined or sequenced for printing. Strategies for these actions are discussed in Module Eighteen: *Parts and Wholes*.

(2) **Previewing your Formatted Paper:** Once your paper contains the desired content you are ready to begin the final process of customizing the output to reflect just how you want your paper to appear:

    (a) **Widows and Orphans:** As you look through the semi-final draft of the paper, be on the look out for *widows* (the first line of a paragraph sitting alone at the bottom of a page) and *orphans* (the last line of a paragraph sitting alone at the top of a page). Also check for words which have been incorrectly hyphenated across two lines (Note: if the hyphenation crosses state boundaries this is a federal offense).

    (b) **Checking for Format Errors:** The UNIX program known as **checknr** exists to examine your file for *nroff* formatting errors. It is described in Module Six—give it a fling.

(3) **What Printer?:** Once the content of the file is complete and appears formatted correctly on a line printed copy, you may want to produce a better quality copy of your paper. Letter quality printers are widely available and easy to use—check around for one. (This topic is touched upon in the section entitled *nroff Options* in Module Eighteen: *Parts and Wholes*.)

(4) **Work in the Background:** When printing copies of your paper, consider doing this in the background. This has two advantages: (1) The terminal is free to attend to other UNIX tasks; and (2) If you send your jobs with the *batch* command the cost is considerably less. Review this method in Module Seventeen: *Backgrounding a Process*.

Finally, the Finished Product

You should now hold in your hands the fruits of your diligent UNIX labors. Present a copy of the paper to whomever you deem appropriate, then head for the: (a) hills, (b) ocean, or (c) river of your choice and relax.

Module Eleven
The Line Editor Ex

Introduction

You are now able to skillfully employ the visual editor (affectionately known as *vi*) to create and edit files. This Module will present some new commands, accessible from the visual editor, which may be used to "cut and paste" a file. Each of these important procedures makes use of an alternate set of editing commands available on the UNIX system: the line editor *ex*. Fear not, *ex* commands are not strangers. You met several of them in Module Eight as "Colon Commands."

Prerequisites

To begin the activities in this Module you should be able to:

(1)   Use the visual editor commands presented in Modules Three, Four, and Eight; and

(2)   Employ the six colon (:) commands introduced in Module Eight:

:*1,6* **co** *8*	**Co**pies lines *1* through *6* and places them after line *8*
:*1,6* **m** *8*	**M**oves lines *1* through *6* to after line *8*
:*1,6* **d**	**D**eletes lines *1* through *6*

:w	Writes the current file onto disk without returning you to the Shell
:q!	Returns you to the Shell without writing changes you made in current file onto disk (**q**uits!)
:wq	Writes current file onto disk and returns you to the Shell (**w**rites and **q**uits)

Objectives

Upon completion of this Module you should be able to:

(1) Read the contents of a different file into the file you are currently editing;

(2) Save a part of your current file in a new file (with a new *filename*);

(3) Append a selected portion of your current file to an old file;

(4) Save both the permanent copy and the edited copy of a file;

(5) Relate the read and write operations to the buffer and the disk;

(6) Use the line editor to create and edit files;

(7) Use line addresses within the line editor to perform the above operations as well as move and copy text in a file; and

(8) Shift from employing the visual editor to the line editor and back.

Procedure

The procedure steps in this Module are presented in three sections. The first reviews the function of the buffer and the disk and introduces several new commands for saving and overwriting files. The second section introduces the line editor *ex* and relates the colon commands to the *ex* editor. The final section describes how to quickly transfer from the visual editor to the line editor and back.

The Buffer and the Disk Revisited

(1) ___ Log onto your UNIX account.

(2) **Creating a Junk File:** In a moment you will be asked to call up one of your files for visual editing. The file you select should be one that is *at least 20 lines long and one that you don't mind mucking up.* (Don't use *experience*; you will need it later.)

___ If you don't have a file to sacrifice, you can make a second copy of one of your present files using the **copy** command:

cp *filename junk*   ®

As usual, ® means *press the* **RETURN** *key.* For ease of communication we suggest you name this new file *junk* because *junk* is how we'll refer to it from now on. Use the *junk* file for the rest of this Module.

(3) ___ From the Shell type:

vi *junk*   ®

Line Numbers for Editing a File: You are now in the Command Mode in the visual editor. *Important:* Do you have line numbers on the left margin of the screen? If not, enter the command:

:set number   ®

The editor will now display line numbers on your screen. These numbers will not become part of your file. They appear on the screen for your convenience only. Note: If, in the future, you want line numbers while editing some other file, you will need to enter the **:set number** command as you begin editing. If you want to have line numbers included automatically whenever you edit a file, see Module Sixteen: *Account Management.*

(4) Module Seven introduced the concepts of the *buffer* and the *disk.* Recall that, while editing any file, two copies of the file actually exist.

(a)   The relatively permanent *disk* copy, containing the contents of your file as it was before you started the editing session, and

(b)   The temporary *buffer* copy on which you are currently making changes.

When you give the **ZZ** command from *vi* Command Mode you are telling the editor:

(a)   Overwrite the relatively permanent *disk* copy of your file with the temporary *buffer* copy containing all changes you made during the current editing session, and

(b)   *Return* you to the Shell so you can do even more wonderful things.

(5)   **The Two-Step Return to Shell:** You have used the **ZZ** command to return to the Shell and write the edited version of the file onto the disk. It is possible to accomplish each action separately.

___ Delete 2 or 3 lines of text in your *junk* file.

(6)   **The Write Command:** The **:write** command, which you met in Module Seven, tells the editor to save the current buffer version of your file as the new disk copy but *does not* return you to the Shell. The **:w** can be used as an abbreviation for the **:w**rite command.

___ From the Command Mode type:

:w   ®

Even though you have written the buffer onto the disk, you are still in *vi* Command Mode. This command is actually the first half of the **ZZ** command. Now for the second half.

(7)   **Returning to the Shell:** The **:quit** command performs the second part of the **ZZ** command and tells the editor to return you to the Shell. The abbreviation **:q** can also be used.

___ From the Command Mode now type:

:q   ®

If you have not altered *junk* since you typed the :w command, you will be returned to the Shell. If any changes have been made, you must first type :w and then :q.

Summary: You can indicate to the editor that are finished editing a file in two ways:

(a) From the visual editor Command Mode enter :**write** and write the buffer onto the disk, and then enter :**quit** to return to the Shell; or

(b) Accomplish both operations at once with the familiar **ZZ** command (or the colon command :**wq** that is the same).

(8) **Quiting without Writing:** In order to examine the way the :w*rite* and :q*uit* commands work let's turn again to your *junk* file. Call up *junk* for visual editing.

___ Now add some text to the file (perhaps the line *Still crazy after all these Modules*). When you have entered a line, return to the Command Mode by pressing the ESC key. Do not go on to the Shell. Remain in Command Mode.

(9) ___ From the Command Mode type:

:w   ®

This command permanently saves the change you just made to the file by overwriting the disk copy of *junk* with the buffer copy of *junk* you just edited.

(10) ___ Move the cursor to the first line of your *junk* file and remove the first 10 lines by typing:

10dd

(11) Recall that you added one line of text to your file in Step 8 and then wrote the file by using the *write* command (:w) in Step 9. You then made an additional change to your file in Step 10. If this last change (*delete lines 1 - 10*) was undesirable, what could you do to make sure that change was not saved (and made a permanent alteration of your disk copy)?

___ Among other options you could try typing the **:q** (**q**uit) command. Do this now. Type:

$$:q \quad \circledR$$

Did this command work? Probably not. Most likely the editor told you something to the effect of *"No write since last change (use q! to override)."* But you don't want to write this new copy to your disk; you want to quit and trash the buffer copy, right? OK, so now type:

$$:q! \quad \circledR$$

The exclamation mark (!) after the **:q** tells the editor *Yes, I really do want to quit this file* without writing it, even though I have made changes since my last write. The **:q!** command is the emergency exit which leaves the file as it was when you last wrote it. It is the emergency hatch—but *all changes* made since the last **w**rite are lost, even those you might want to save.

(12) ___ From the Shell, enter the command sequence **page** *junk* and examine the file to be certain that it is the original version, unaffected by the 10 line deletion effected in Step 10.

Writing for Safety: We suggest that, as a safeguard, you use the **:w** command every fifteen minutes or so when you are editing. When you use the quit (**:q!**) command you void all changes you have made to your file since the last *write* (**ZZ** or **:w** or **:wq**) command was given. All editing work done between the last *write* and the **q!** is lost. If you *write* the file every fifteen minutes or so, you remain in the Command Mode, editing the file, but with each **:w** you update the disk version to reflect the changes you have made. Thus, you are risking less.

To make this suggestion more poignant imagine that you have been editing the same valuable file for two straight hours *without* entering a *write* command. You are in the middle of deleting a line of text when a momentary power surge causes a system crash. Yikes!!! Was UNIX kind enough to save your buffer copy of the file at the moment the system went down? Perhaps. But if you were not so lucky, you have lost all work performed over the past two hours. Anger, panic, resentment, cheated . . . take your pick. If, on the other hand, you had been "doing a *write*" every fifteen minutes, you could only suffer the loss of those changes made since your last *write* (and at most 15 minutes of work would be lost).

(13) **Saving Both the Buffer and Disk Copies:** Sometimes it is convenient to save both the version you are editing and the original that is on the disk. For instance, suppose you are editing a file named *novel*. After making several changes you decide that you might like it better the way it was before you started but you are not sure. It occurs to you that you would like to print out *both* versions to compare them. To use the command **ZZ** is to destroy the disk version; and to enter **:q!** says goodbye to the buffer and its changes.

Fortunately, it is possible to write the buffer copy of *novel* onto the disk under a *new* file name and keep the disk copy of the original file unscathed.

___ For example, to write the present version of *junk* onto the disk under a new name, enter the command:

:w junk2 ®

The buffer copy will be saved with a new filename: *junk2*.

The original *junk* file is unaffected. You remain in the Command Mode of the visual editor, working on the buffer copy of the file, however. Since you do not want to overwrite the (original) disk copy of the file with this buffer copy, you must return to the Shell without using the usual **ZZ** command. You already have *both* versions of the file on the disk, so the buffer should be discarded.

___ Enter the **:q!** command.

In summary, you can write the buffer onto the disk with a new filename using the command:

:w 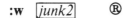 ®

which saves the *new* version. You must then return to the Shell without destroying the disk or old version, using the **q!** command. Note that *newfilename* can not be the name of an existing file.

If you use an existing filename, this command will at best not work, and you will receive an error message. At worst it will *overwrite* (replace) the existing file with the new material.

(14) **Writing Material Into Another File:** Sometimes a section of one file is needed for inclusion in some other file. Other times a paragraph no longer fits, but you may want to "save it" rather than just delete it. The editor offers a procedure which can be used to make *new files* by copying parts of other files. The **w** command (which you already know can be used to write whole files onto the disk) can also be used to save only *part* of your file under a *new* name.

___ Call up your *junk* file for visual editing. When it appears on the screen, from the Command Mode enter:

:1,8 w junkout   ®

This command sequence follows the same format as the earlier colon commands and tells UNIX to copy lines 1 through 8 of your current file into a new file named *junkout.* Any block of text (identified by two line numbers separated by a comma) can be written out into a new file. The *write* command does not, however, delete the lines from your current file. A *copy* has been made and is placed in a separate file. In this instance, this new file is named *junkout.*

The general form for the command to write out part of a file is:

:#,# write   <u>newfilename</u>   ®

where the line address #,# identifies the text to be written into the new file *newfilename.* Note that *newfilename* can not be the name of an existing file. If you use an existing filename, either you will receive an error message or you will *overwrite* (replace) the existing file with the new material, *and you can kiss the existing file goodbye!*

(15) Since a copy of these 8 lines now exists in a separate file, you can delete lines 1 - 8. In Module Nine you found out that this can be accomplished with either a **vi** or **ex** command.

The two ways to remove the eight lines are:

(a)   You can move the cursor to the first line of text and type:

8dd

(b)   Or, *regardless of the cursor's location* you can type:

:1,8 d   ®

The second command sequence says *find lines 1 through 8 and delete them.*

___ Select one of the two methods and delete lines 1 through 8 in your *junk* file.

(16) ___ It's time once again to save all changes and return to the Shell. Enter the **ZZ** command.

(17) ___ Check that the file *junkout* was actually created by using the Shell command **ls** to get a listing of all your current files.

(18) ___ To view the contents of *junkout* type the command:

page *junkout*   ®

(19) **Writing Material into an Existing File:** The **:1,8 write** *newfilename* command sequence you have just learned allows you to create a *new* file containing material designated from your current file. It *will not* allow you to write material into a pre-existing file.

It is useful at times to write material into an *existing* file. This process is accomplished with a modification to the **w** command you just used.

___ First call up a practice file for visual editing. Do *not* select the file *junkout*.

___ Scan the contents of this file and select several lines to copy and write *into* the file *junkout* (will lines 10 - 20 work?). Type (be sure to use the colon and the double arrow heads >>):

:*10,20* write >> *junkout*   ®

___ Return to the Shell (use the **ZZ** command) and view the contents of *junkout* with the **page** command. Does a copy of the lines you just wrote in (lines 10 to 20) appear at the end of this file?

The two arrow heads >> are interpreted to mean, "append to the end of the existing file, without destroying the file."

(20) **Reading Another File into the Current File:** It is also possible to have the contents of another file *read into* the file you are currently editing.

___ Call up the file *junk* for visual editing. Note that the text that you deleted from the file *junk* and saved as the file *junkout* is gone from the file.

___ Move the cursor to the last line of text (using the **G** command) in your file and enter the following (don't forget the colon):

$$:\textbf{read} \quad junkout \qquad ®$$

With this command the contents of *junkout* will once again be with you. (This may not be as useful as having *the Force* with you, but . . . .)

The file that you *read* from is not altered. The command **:read** *filename,* which can be abbreviated as **:r** *filename,* makes a *copy* of the file *filename* and places it following the cursor line in whatever file you are currently editing.

(21) **Reading in a File at a Specified Location:** You may designate the placement of this new material in your file without using the cursor. For instance,

$$:\textbf{5 r} \quad junkout \qquad ®$$

will place the contents of *junkout* following line 5, regardless of where in the file the cursor happens to be located.

___ How is another file read into the *beginning* of the current file? From the *vi* Command Mode type:

$$:\textbf{0 r} \quad junkout \qquad ®$$

This command places a copy of the contents of the file *junkout* in your current file following the zero line (therefore before line 1).

___ Write your file onto the disk and return to the Shell (use the **ZZ** command).

Occasionally after repeatedly using the **:r***ead* command the editor becomes confused. When you attempt to use the **ZZ** command to store the file in permanent memory the editor responds with the note:

"filename" file exists - use "w !" to overwrite

Should this happen you should go ahead and follow the editors sage and thymely advice (as Rosemary would say) and use the **:w!** command to definitely write the buffer onto the disk. You can then use the **ZZ** (or **:q**) command to return to the Shell.

(22) ___ To find out if the file *junkout* still exists as an independent entity use the Shell command **ls** to get a listing of all your current files.

(23) ___ OK, *junkout* is still there. It is of no use, so you can get rid of it. Use the Shell Command:

rm *junkout* ®

(24) **Reading a Spelling Check into your File:** In Module Six we described how to have UNIX check for misspelled words in a file. You enter the command line **spell** *filename* > *newname*. The program **spell** then examines *filename* and enters all words that it does not recognize in a new file called *newname*.

After **spell** has completed its job you could examine the file *newname*, write each misspelled word down, and then visually edit *filename* to make corrections. Another solution is to **read** the contents of the **spell** check (the file *newname*) into the top of the original *filename*, then use the */word* command to locate the instances of misspelled words.

___ Select one of your files and follow the steps listed on the top of the next page.

Spelling Check Procedure:

(a) ___ From the Shell type

$$\textbf{spell} \quad \boxed{\textit{filename}} \quad > \quad \boxed{\textit{newfilename}} \quad ®$$

where *filename* is your subject file and *newfilename* is (curiously) a name for a new file. The word list generated by the **spell** program will be entered in *newfilename*.

(b) ___ When the Shell prompt reappears, call up for visual editing the file that was examined by **spell** (the file *filename*).

(c) ___ Once you are in the *vi* Command Mode type:

$$\textbf{:0 r} \quad \textit{newfilename} \qquad ®$$

The list of all misspelled (or unidentified) words in *filename* is read into the top of the file (following line zero).

(d) ___ The first misspelled word can be located in your text using the *slash-search* (/*word*) command.

(e) ___ Correct that instance of the word.

(f) ___ Move to the *next* location of the misspelled *word* with the **n** (for **n**ext word) command.

(g) ___ Once UNIX takes you back to line 1 in your text, you have corrected all examples of the misspelled word. You can then delete this first *word* and move on to the second *word*.

(h) ___ Repeat this process until all words have been corrected and the misspelled words are removed from the top of the file. When finished, use the **ZZ** command to return to the Shell.

(25) A Quick Review:

(a) What command saves changes you have made to a file without returning you to the Shell? _____

(b) What command returns you to the Shell without saving the changes you have made? _____

(c)   What command both saves changes you have made to a file and returns you to the Shell? _____

(d)   What command would save the first five lines of your current file as a separate file entitled *wisesayings*?

_____

(e)   What command could you use to read the file named *candy* into your current file after line ten? _____

(f)   What command sequence would write out the lines 20-50 of your current file and append them to the existing *jerry* file?

_____

(g)   What command allows you to save both the disk version of the file *report* and the buffer copy that you have been editing (under a new name)? _____

Answers: (a) **:w**   (b) **:q!**   (c) **:wq!** or **ZZ**   (d) *:1,5* **w** *wisesayings*
(e) *:10* **read** *candy*   (f) *:20,50* **write** >> *jerry*   (g) **:w** *newname* followed by **:q!**

The Line Editor Ex

You have been using a set of commands which we have called "colon" commands because from the visual editor they all are preceded with a colon (e.g. **:r**, **:w**, **:1,20d**, etc.). These commands are part of a larger set of *ex line editor* commands.

The line editor works much like the visual editor. Both can be used to edit the same old files or to create new ones, both have Command and Append Modes, and both are accessed from the Shell. The significant difference is that the visual editor possesses, in general, the more powerful Command Mode, because it allows you to move the cursor around the screen making changes at any place in any line. The Command Mode of the line editor *ex* is restricted to giving directions for changes only on the current line (or on sets of lines referenced by line numbers—e.g., *1,6* represents lines *1 - 6*). You cannot move the cursor to a word and issue the delete word command using the line editor. Instead you first ask the editor to locate the line with the word in question, then to substitute nothing for the word. In this way the word is deleted.

Transitions between the visual and line editor Command Modes are easily made because both sets of commands are actually subsets of the same editor. For example, the command **w** is the *line editor* command for **w**rite. By adding a colon as the first character in the command we can use it from the *vi* Command Mode (**:w**). The visual editor reads the colon to mean "temporarily put me into the line editor Command Mode and execute the following command, then return me to the *vi* Command Mode."

This section will demonstrate how to directly access the *ex* line editor so that you can use the line editor in place of the visual editor. You might need to use *ex* for one of four reasons: (a) You may find yourself logged onto a UNIX system without the Berkeley enhancements (which, among other things, might mean that *vi* would not be available to you); (b) Some terminals are not "smart" enough to handle *vi*; (c) A visual editor will not work on hard copy terminals (terminals without a video screen); and (d) The *ex* editor is less expensive, both in computer time and dollars, to operate.

(1) **Editing a File Using the Line Editor:** The line editor is called into action in a manner similar to the visual editor.

___ Call up a file for line editing by typing

ex [*filename*]   ®

where *filename* is any one of your existing practice files. The sequence **ex** *filename* is the command used to call up a file for line editing just as **vi** *filename* is used to call up a file for visual editing.

Note the presence of a colon (**:**) on your screen. This creature indicates that you are now *in* the Command Mode of the *ex* line editor. It is the *ex* Command Mode prompt.

When you call up a file using the *visual* editor, the first part of your file is automatically displayed on the screen. That is not the case with *ex*.

(2) **Viewing Lines:** To view a particular section of your file within the Command Mode of *ex* you must specify the line numbers you would like to view.

___ For example, to see lines 1 through 10 you type:

1,10   ®

The first ten lines of your file should now appear on your screen.

This file is the *identical* file you have worked with in the past. In prior Modules you told UNIX that you wanted to *visually edit* (*vi*) this file. Here you have asked for the *line editor* (*ex*) to work on the same file.

(3) **Line Addresses:** Within the line editor *ex* line numbers perform a function analogous to that of the cursor within the visual editor. The line numbers tell the editor *where* and *on what portion of text* commands should function. The line editor usually functions only on the *current line.* You have been specifying the line numbers for all *ex* commands.

___ From the *ex* Command Mode type:

8   ®

Line 8 is now on the screen. Line 8 is not only displayed, but it is now the *current line.*

(4) **Deleting a Line:** When you enter an *ex* command such as **d** to delete, or **a** to append, the editor will follow your instructions. Unless explicitly stated, the editor assumes that your instructions are to affect the current line. Thus the following *ex* Command Mode *deletion* command removes line 8, the current line:

d   ®

(5) ___ Press **u** to *undo* the deletion and bring back the line.

(6) **Command and Append Modes of the Line Editor:** Yes, Authoritarians Also Rule Ex. As is the case with the visual editor *vi*, there are two Modes (Command and Append) within the line editor *ex*. The process of going from one Mode to the other is different in *ex*, but not difficult. Examine Map E at the end of this Module. To move from the Command Mode of the *ex* editor to the Append Mode, you must enter a one-way command.

___ Now press the *append* command:

a   ®

A blank line *after* line 8 should be opened and you are now in the *ex* Append Mode.

___ Now type the following line:

This is my first ex append line.

At this point you must make a decision. If you want to add more text you simply continue typing. To return to Command Mode you perform the following actions:

(a) Press ® to have the cursor at the start of a new line.

(b) Enter a single period (.) and then

(c) Press the ® key again.

Enter that three-step sequence now. You are back (safe and sound) at the Command Mode of the line editor.

(7) **Quick Review Number Two:**

(a) What command puts you in the Command Mode of the *ex* line editor? _____

(b) What *ex* command would display line 17? _____

(c) Once you entered the command requested in question (b), then entered the letter d, what line would be deleted?

_____

(d) What *ex* command would display lines 17 to 30? _____

(e) You have just finished entering several lines of text. What three steps must you take to return to the *ex* Command Mode?

(1) _____

(2) _____

(3) _____

Answers: (a) **ex** *filename*   (b) **17**   (c) line 17   (d) **17, 30**
(e) (Step 1) ®   (Step 2) dot   (Step 3) ®

(8) **Adding Text Using Line Addresses:** You should still be in the Command Mode of the *ex* line editor. If you are in the Shell, recall your file *junk* for line editing with the Shell command:

ex junk   ®

(9) You now know that **1,10** ® tells UNIX to display lines 1 though 10 on the screen. The command also tells *ex* to make line number 10 your *current line*. This means that if you next typed the **a** command *ex* would assume you wanted to add text *after line ten*. Note that the colon is the prompt, and that each of the line editor commands does *not* have a colon in the command itself.

(10) ___ From the *ex* Command Mode press:

1,10   ®

___ Enter the Append mode with:

a   ®

___ Type several lines of text.

(11) Where did the editor place the text you just entered? Why? Return to the *ex* Command Mode (® dot ®).

(12) There are two ways to enter text at a particular place in your file:

(a) You can type the desired line number, press ® and then press the **a** key, or

(b) You can name both the line and the command as one statement (**14a**).

To perform this second action you should, from the *ex* Command Mode, type:

16a   ®

A line after line 16 should be opened for text. You are in the *ex* Append Mode.

___ Enter 3 or 4 more lines of text and then return to the *ex* Command Mode (press ® , enter a dot on a line by itself, and press ® again).

___ To move from the *ex* Command Mode to the *ex* Append Mode and add text above the existing line 1, type (Zero a):

0a   ®

The **0** tells the editor to move to the zero line of your file (or before the first line, if you prefer to think of it that way). The **a** tells the editor to open a new line following the cursor for additional text.

___ Enter 2 or 3 lines of text and then return to the *ex* Command Mode.

(13) **Inserting Above Current Line:** The command **a** appends text as the next line of the file. On Map E, examine the arrows between the *ex* Command Mode and *ex* Append Mode.

___ If you want to insert text above the current line, enter the command:

i   ®

Note the content of the current line, then enter the **i** command and add some text. When finished return to *ex* Command Mode.

(14) **Changing the Current Line:** The *ex* editor also permits changing a line. Note which line is the current line and enter (lower case):

c   ®

The current line is deleted, you are in Append Mode, and whatever text you enter is added to the file taking the place of the **c**hanged line. Add a few lines of text, then when finished return to *ex* Command Mode.

(15) ___ To view the first twenty lines of your file (replete with the splendid modifications you have just entered) type:

1,20 ®

(16) **Returning to the Shell:** If you were in the visual editor you would type either **ZZ** or **:wq** to write and return to the Shell. You are not in *vi*, you are in *ex*—and the colon is already there as the prompt—so to write and quit you need only enter:

wq ®

The file is placed back into the memory of the Beast, and you are returned to the Shell.

Moving Between the Ex and Vi Editors

(1) **Moving from Vi to Ex:** Select one of your files (pick a file, any file) to use with the next exercises. From the Shell enter the command:

vi *filename* ®

Each of the line editor's commands can be used while you are in the visual editor by placing a colon before the desired command. This ability is particularly helpful when shifting blocks of text within a file (**:1,6 move 8**) or across files (**:1,6 write** >> *debby*). If you have a series of *ex* commands that you want to execute, it may be useful to move into the *ex* Command Mode and stay there.

(2) To move into *ex* Command Mode you could return to the Shell and call the file up for line editing (**ex** *filename*), or you can change from the *vi* Command Mode editor to the *ex* editor in mid-stream. Enter the command:

Q

You are no longer in *vi* but are in *ex* Command Mode. You could now perform any *ex* commands (without colons) as though you had initiated the editing session using the **ex** *filename* command sequence.

(3) ___ Once you are in *ex* Command Mode try moving lines 8, 9, and 10 to after line 16. Enter:

8,10 m 16 ®

Again, you do not enter a colon when using *ex* commands in the *ex* editor. A colon appears automatically—you do not have to provide it.

(4) **Moving from Ex to Vi:** To return to *vi*, from the *ex* Command Mode, enter the command:

vi ®

You are now back in *vi* Command Mode.

Figure 1 and Map E show the relationship between the *vi* and *ex* Command Modes. From within the visual editor the colon (:) can be used to *temporarily* visit the *ex* Command Mode *for one action only*. It is a two-way command. You are automatically returned to the *vi* Command Mode once the *ex* command is executed. The **Q** command is a one-way command which leaves you in the *ex* Command Mode. You may perform any number of editing actions. You remain in the *ex* editor until you enter the command **vi** to exit the line editor and return to the visual editor.

Figure 1

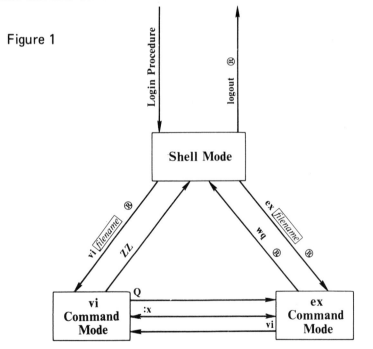

(5) **Returning to the Shell:** With the command **vi** you are moved into the *vi* Command Mode. To place the file into the memory of the Beast from *vi* Command Mode and return to the Shell you have three choices:

(a) Enter the command **ZZ**,

(b) Temporarily invoke the *ex* editor and return to the Shell with **:wq**, or

(c) Transfer into the *ex* editor with **Q** and return to the Shell with **wq**.

Make certain that all three of these paths to the Shell are clear to you from Map E. Select one method for returning to the Shell and perform that action.

(6) **The Final Review:** Consider the following questions:

(a) What command calls up a file named *sarah* for line editing?

_____

(b) From the *ex* Command Mode what command would move lines 415 to 493 and place them after line 300?

_____

(c) From the visual editor Command Mode what "colon" command would move lines 415 to 493 and locate them after line 300? _____

(d) What command will move you from the line editor to the visual editor? _____

(e) What command would move you from the visual editor to the line editor? _____

Answers: (a) **ex** *sarah*   (b) *415,493* **m** *300*   (c) *:415,493* **m** *300*
(d) **vi**   (e) **Q**

A summary of the *ex* commands you have met —along with a few which will be new to you—follows. These commands are also included among the *vi* commands in the command summary at the end of the book.

Ex Line Editor Command Summary

Command	Function
a	Appends text as line after current line (*33***a** appends text following line 33)
c	Changes (substitutes) text for current line (*21***c** changes text on line 21)
1, 6 **co** *9*	Copies text lines 1 to 6 and places them after line 9
d	Deletes current line (*1,6* **d** deletes lines 1 to 6)
f	Prints name of current file
g/*word*/*action*	Performs global search for *word* and initiates indicated *actiion*
i	Inserts text as line before current line (*33***i** inserts text before line 33)
1,6 **p**	Prints lines 1 to 6 on screen (**p** can be omitted on most systems)
1,6 **m** *44*	Moves lines 1 to 6 to after line 44
q	Quits an editing session and returns to Shell
r *file1*	Reads a copy of *file1* into current file after current line (*55***r** *file1* places material after line 55)
w	Writes copy of buffer onto disk; remains in *ex* Command Mode
set *option*	Changes setting of editor *option*

Command	Function
s/*word1*/*word2*	Substitutes *word2* for *word1* on current line
u	Undoes last editor change command
/*word*/	Searches forward for next instance of /*word*/
?*word*?	Searches backward for next instance of /*word*/
//	Repeats last // or ?? search command

Map E

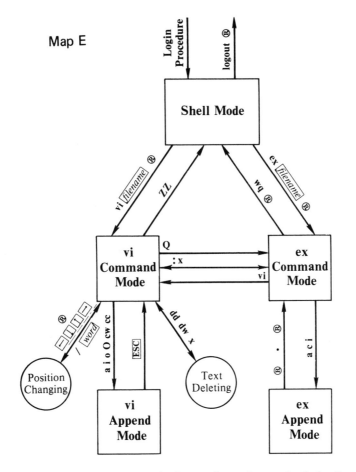

A second copy of this map is located at the end of the book.

Module Twelve
Special Search & Substitution Characters

Introduction

The slash-search (*/word*) command that you use to locate specific words has additional properties. It can team with special characters to locate and make substitutions for a wide variety of *patterns* in addition to words. For instance, you can locate words beginning with any upper case letter. The special characters and procedures introduced in this Module are available from the Command Mode of either the visual or line editor.

Prerequisites

For this Module you should be able to use editing commands in both the visual editor *vi* (Modules Four and Eight) and the line editor *ex* (Module Eleven).

Objectives

Upon completion of this Module you should be able to:

(1) Locate numbers, upper and lower case of the same letters, multiple letters, beginning or ending of lines, and periods;

(2) Locate characters by exclusion;

(3) Have located lines displayed on the screen;

(4) Substitute characters for specific characters on a line; and

(5) Change every occurrence of some word (*mispell*) to a different word (*misspell*) in one easy step (global substitutions).

Procedure

The procedure steps in this Module are presented in four sections. The first section introduces several special characters which are used with the slash-search command. Section two presents search and substitute commands which you can use to correct typos and misspellings throughout a file. The next section describes the use of special characters in these global search and substitutions. The final section demonstrates how these operations can be performed "hands off" with simple editor scripts.

Special Characters
For Searches and Substitutions

You have used the /*word* command to locate words in your text as you move from place to place making additions or corrections. How would you use the slash-search command to find a word whether it is capitalized or not? How can words with one or two *t*'s be found? This section introduces a set of special *meta-characters* that can greatly enhance the power of the editor's search commands.

The following steps show visual editor commands. Note that those *vi* command sequences that are prefaced with a colon (:) can be executed from the *ex* editor by dropping the colon and using the rest of the sequence.

(1) ___ Call up for visual editing your largest *practice* file. This file needs to be in excess of 200 lines. If it is not of that length you will need to copy the file one or more times until this minimum size has been reached. To copy the lines of the file use this command sequence from the visual editor Command Mode:

:1,$ copy $ ®

The $, when used in a line address, is the symbol for the last line in a file. The previous command requests that the editor copy the first through the last line of your file and place these lines after the last line in your file.

(2) **Patterns vs. Words:**

___ From the *vi* Command Mode enter the command:

/*he*   ®

As you recall from prior Modules, the slash-search command tells the editor to "go to the first line containing the following word." But does the cursor find the first instance of the "word" *he*? Maybe, but *shepherd*, *the*, *their*, *mother*, or any ot*he*r word containing the characters *he* may have been found instead. This is because the *slash-search* command, in its simplest form, does not actually look for "words" but instead looks for a sequence or "string" of characters. S*he*pherd, t*he*, t*he*ir, and mot*he*r all contain the character string *he* and are thus all valid objects for this search.

This example demonstrates an important aspect to all search commands. In any search the editor scans the text looking for the target character pattern ("*word*"). So long as it contains the target pattern, discrete words ("*he*") are treated no differently than parts of words ("t*he*ory").

A Word of Caution: The ability of the editor's scanning property to isolate all instances of a sequence of characters—regardless of whether they exist as discrete words—has presented little problem *up to this point*. In the next section of this Module you will, however, learn several methods for expanding the power of the slash-search command. These new methods will allow you to affect systematic changes to several parts of your text—often with quite dramatic results. Because of this care should be exercised in attempting these sequences. (This is why we have asked you to work through the exercises in this Module with a *practice* file.) Extensive—and occasionally quite destructive—changes can be affected. Remember that you can always *undo* the effect of any single editor action with the **u** command, or you can jettison all of the modifications made during an editing session with the **:q!** command.

(3) **Beginnings and Endings of Words:** What if you want to find the specific word *he*? Enter the command:

$$/\backslash < he\backslash >\qquad ®$$

The $\backslash <$ signifies the beginning of a word and the $\backslash >$ signifies the end of a word. Thus this command will find only the word *he*. (Note: the $\backslash <$ and $\backslash >$ characters do not work on some UNIX systems. Fear not if this is the case at your location—you simply place a space both before and after the target pattern to indicate a discrete "word." Unfortunately, this trick will not work if the target word occurs at the beginning or end of a line, or is directly followed by a punctuation mark.)

As another example, the following will move the cursor to the next letter *a* in your file that is at the *beginning* of a word (not embedded within a word):

$$/\backslash < a\qquad ®$$

(4) **Beginning of a Line Character:** You now know how to locate characters at the beginning and end of words. What if you want to search for characters at the beginning or ending of a line?

___ Try the following search command:

$$/\char`^\qquad ®$$

Press the **n** several time to move to the next instance of what the command locates.

The ˆ caret is the symbol for the beginning of a line. The ˆ symbol can be used to find lines that begin with a specified sequence of characters. Enter the command:

$$/\char`^The\qquad ®$$

The next line that starts with the characters *The* will be found.

(5) **End of Line Character:** The editor reads the dollar sign **$**, when *not* in a line address, to signify the end of a line. For example, the

next command will locate lines in the file that end with the word *werewolf:*

/*werewolf*$ ®

(6) **Finding Blank Lines:** The beginning and end of line characters can be used together to locate blank lines. Enter the command:

/^$ ®

The above command will locate the next line containing a beginning ^ and an ending $ with nothing in between (in *Unijargon* these are referred to as a "blank lines").

(7) **Upper and Lower Case Searches:** Perhaps you would like to locate a word in your file, but do not remember whether it was spelled with an upper or lower case first letter. This command

/[*Ff*]*ormatting*   ®

will find the first example of a string of characters that begins with an *F* or an *f* followed by the letters *ormatting.*

___ Try the brackets several times, substituting a word that interests you. Next try the brackets with the **?** instead of the **/** to search backward through your text for a word.

(8) **Locating a Range of Characters:** Interested in locating the next occurrence of a number in your file? The following command will do just that:

/[*0-9*]   ®

The dash between the *0* and *9* instructs UNIX to look for all numbers from zero up to and including nine. The cursor will move to the first instance of any number.

___ The next line containing an upper case letter can be found with the command:

/[*A-Z*]   ®

___ Create your own command that will search for places in your text that have the numbers 3,4,5,6 or 7.

(9) **Excluding Characters from a Search:** The following command will find the first instance of a character which is *not* a lower case letter:

$$/[\char94 a\text{-}z]$$ ®

The ^ when placed as the first character *inside* brackets asks the editor to locate characters that *are not* any of the characters specified within the brackets. The ^ allows you to specify what you do *not* want located.

As another example, the command to locate any characters that are not numbers is:

$$/[\char94 0\text{-}9]$$ ®

(10) **Including Several Identifiers:** You are not limited to one identification scheme inside the brackets. For instance:

$$/[\char94 0\text{-}9a\text{-}zA\text{-}Z]$$ ®

will go to those characters *not* numbers 1 through 9, nor upper or lower case letters. What characters will the above command locate? Try it and see.

(11) **Any Character:** Enter the command:

$$/.$$ ®

Does the editor find the next dot in your file? No, the dot (.) is a special character within the editor that stands for *any single character*. The cursor will find the next instance of any character in your file. Thus /.*he* would locate the next instance any character followed by the letters *he*.

___ To find the next example of a three-letter word ending in *he* enter the command:

$$/\backslash<.he\backslash>$$ ®

(12) **Repeated Characters:** The following command will find all words that have an *o* followed by zero or more *l*'s:

$$/ol* \quad ®$$

The ***** means "any possible number of the previous characters." This gives the ***** the unusual ability to match none, one, two, or fifty instances of the prior character. The following sequence would locate upper and lower case versions of the word *formatting* spelled with one or more *t*'s:

$$/[Ff]ormatt*ing \quad ®$$

To use the star to locate sets of two or more characters in your file you need to include *two identical characters* before the ***** .

(13) **Any Number of Any Characters:** The **.** and the ***** characters can be used together to match any sequence of characters.

___ Enter the command

$$/s.*s \quad ®$$

to locate the next line containing an *s* followed by any sequence of characters followed by another *s*. Note that the identified sequence may be a single word or cut across a series of words.

What command would locate the next instance of a sequence of characters starting with the letter *M* and ending with the letter *p*?

Answer: $/\<M.*p\>$

(14) **Removing Magic:** The ability of the dot to match any single character is all well and good, but what if you want to find a string of characters (such as a format command) that actually does start with a dot (or you are looking for a dot by itself).

___ Enter the command:

$$/\. \quad ®$$

The backslash \ is the *Kryptonite* of special characters. It takes away special powers and turns them into ordinary mortal characters. Thus the above command should find the next example of a dot (period) in your file.

(15) **Lines that Start with Periods:** To find the next line containing a period (dot) as the first character you would type:

$$/^\backslash . \qquad ®$$

This command will check the first character of each line (the ^ means *the beginning of a line*) and find the next line that starts with a period (a formatting command). This sequence can be used to locate all *nroff* and *-ms* formatting commands in your file.

(16) ___ Create and test a command that will find lines containing *only* a dot followed by any two other characters.

Review Exercises:

(a) What command would locate the word *I* but ignore words beginning with the letter *I*? _____

(b) What command will locate the word *absurd* regardless of whether it begins with an upper or lower case *a*?

_____

(c) What command would locate the next character that is not a letter, number or period? _____

(d) What command would locate the next instance of a sequence of characters (hopefully but not necessarily a word) starting with *psy* and ending with *y* or *t*? _____

(e) What command would locate the next instance of the formatting command **.ce**? _____

Answers: (a) /\<*I*\>   (b) /[aA]bsurd   (c) /[^a-zA-Z0-9\.]
(d) /psy.*[yt]\>   (e) /^\.ce

Global Searches and Substitutions

The visual editor's slash-search command will help you locate any *word* in a file. General patterns—in addition to regular words—can be located with the special characters just introduced.

This section demonstrates how the *substitution* command can be used in conjunction with the search command to make changes in your text. In addition, we will introduce an alternate *search* command which will find all instances of a specific *word* and simultaneously change each. Just think: with one command sequence you can change every occurrence of a word or phrase in your file (*scoop of ice cream*) into a new pattern (*hot fudge sundae*).

The following steps will build upon the slash-search command to create more powerful commands. You will recognize these as line editor commands which have been accessed from the visual editor through placing a colon before the command sequence. You could as easily enter *ex* Command Mode and use these commands without the colon.

(1) **Substitutions within the Current Line:** Select one of your practice files for use in these exercises. Call up the file for visual editing.

(2) ___ To locate the next occurrence of the word *the* type:

> :/*the*   ®

(3) ___ From within the *vi* Command Mode type (and don't forget the colon):

> :s/*the*/*some*   ®

This command will change the next occurrence of the word *the* on the current line into the word *some* (this substitution command is how the *change word* process takes place in the *ex* editor). This command can be used to change one word to a different word *if and only if* the line where the word is located is the current line.

(4) **Substitution on a Specified Line:** If you know the number of the line that contains the "to-be-substituted-for" word you can specify this in the substitution command. The command

> :7s/*the*/*some*   ®

will make line number 7 the "current line" and then look for the word *the*. If *the* is found, it will be replaced by the word *some*.

(5) **Substitution for the Next Occurrence:** What if you are not sure of the number of the line that contains the word to be substituted? Fortunately, the slash-search and the substitute commands can be combined so that you can simultaneously find the next occurrence of the word *the* and also change it into the word *some*.

___ From the *vi* Command Mode type:

$$:/the/s/the/some \qquad ®$$

The reason the word *the* was mentioned twice in the above command can be made clear by examining the command sequence. Reading left to right:

The **:**/*the*/ means "find the next line containing the word *the* and make that line the current line;"

The **s**/*the*/*some* means "*substitute* for the word *the* the word *some.*"

Having to type the *target word* (*the*) twice presents no problem when that word is short. But what if the target word were *Massachusetts?* Rather a pain to type once, let alone a second time. Fortunately, UNIX has a way of avoiding rewriting the *to-be-substituted-for* word.

(6) **The Easier Way to Substitute for the Next Occurrence:** From the *vi* Command Mode type:

$$:/the/s//some \qquad ®$$

This statement will have the same effect as the command sequence presented in the previous step. From left to right this statement reads, "find the next line containing the word *the* and make it the current line, then *substitute* for the *last string of characters mentioned in this search* (the word *the*) another word *some*." The // indicates "the last string of characters mentioned."

Note that so far substitutions have been made for *only the next occurrence* of the target word(s) found in the file.

(7) **Substitution on All Lines:** There is an easy way to have *search and substitute* actions carried out on the first occurrence of the specified word in *every line* in your file instead of only on the first occurrence encountered. For example, type:

:g/the/s// mutate   ®

The **g** is for **g**lobal, and has the command apply to *all* lines.

(8) ___ Examine the contents of your current file and note that many of the occurrences of the word *the* have been changed to the word *mutate*. However, if you had a line in your file containing more than one instance of *the* only the first occurrence was modified.

Substitution for All Occurrences: The above command sequence will only substitute for the *first* occurrence of the target word in each line. What if there are several instances of it on a line? This problem is eliminated with the next command.

___ To insure that *all* occurrences of the word *and* are replaced by the word *or* in the file, type:

:g/and/s//or/g   ®

The difference between this command sequence and the previous one is the second **g** placed at the *end* of the command line. The **g** at the beginning of this sequence tells the substitution to function on all lines in the file; the **g** at the end requests the substitution to function on *all* occurrences of the word within each line.

You may have noticed how this command sequence changed *all* occurrences of the "word" *and* into the "word" *or*, including those instances where the *and* was part of another word. Thus, the word *command* becomes *commor*. This is not such a good idea.

You need a way to have a command work *only* on the intended word and not all instances where the word appears within another word. Thankfully, such a beast exists, and was met in the previous section on *special characters*. The following command sequence will affect only the word *and* and not instances where the characters *and* appear within another word:

<p style="text-align:center">:g/\<<i>and</i>\>/s//<i>or</i>/g   ®</p>

An alternate command sequence which will have the identical result in most cases is:

$$:g/ \; and \; /s// \; or \; /g \quad \textcircled{R}$$

↑ space ↑   ↑   ↑

(9) ___ Finally, return to the Shell, using either **:q!** to jettison the changes, or **ZZ** to save the somewhat bizarre changes you have made to this file.

Summary of Substitution Commands

Command	Function
:/*word*/**s**//*newword*	Changes first occurrence in first line.
:**g**/*word*/**s**//*newword*	Changes first occurrence in all lines.
:**g**/*word*/**s**//*newword*/**g**	Changes all occurrences in all lines.

A Quick Review: Consider the following questions:

(a) What command will find the next occurrence of the word *spud* in your current file? _____

(b) What command will change *spud* to *tater* but will only work if used immediately following the above command?

_____

(c) What command will find every example of *nematode* in your current file and change it into *worm*? _____

Answers: (a) /*spud*   (b) :**s**/*spud*/*tater*   (c) :**g**/*nematode*/**s**//*worm*/**g**

Using Special Characters for Global
Searches and Substitutions

(1) **Print a Display of Identified Lines:** It is possible to locate all lines that fit a search description and have the identified lines displayed on the terminal. For example, if you enter the following

$$\text{:g/}\textit{Formatted}\text{/p} \qquad ®$$

all lines containing the word *Formatted* will be displayed.

The **/p** at the end of the command line tells the editor to **p**rint a list of all target lines on the terminal. You can temporarily halt the scrolling of the lines with the **CTRL-S** key. Scrolling resumes when you press the **SPACEBAR**.

To offer another example, the command

$$\text{:g/}^\wedge\backslash\text{./p} \qquad ®$$

will locate and print every line containing an *nroff* or *-ms* command.

___ Make up your own search scheme and have the located lines displayed on the terminal.

(2) **Removing Multiple Spaces:** The following sequence will locate every occurrence of multiple spaces between words and substitute a single space in each instance. Be certain to leave two spaces between the first / and the *, and one space between the fourth / and the last / character:

$$\text{:g/}\quad\text{*/s//} \ \text{/g} \qquad ®$$

2 spaces ↑   ↑ 1 space

This command will find every place where there are two or more spaces (note that you entered two spaces before the *) and substitute just one space. Excess spaces between words are unnecessary and can cause unwanted formatting results. You can use this command to rid your file of such nuisances.

(3) **Removing Spaces at the Beginning of Lines:** All lines of text in your files should begin at the first position in the line. There should be no spaces at the start of lines. (A blank space at the beginning of a line will be interpreted by the formatter as "start a new line."

___ The following command will find every line that begins with any number of spaces and substitute *nothing* for the spaces, in effect removing the spaces. Be certain to leave two spaces between the ˆ and the * characters):

$$:g/ˆ \ */s/// \quad ®$$

2 spaces ↑

(4) **Removing Spaces at the End of Lines:** Trailing blanks can be very problematic to some pre-formatters, especially *tbl* and *refer*.

___ The following command will find every line that has blanks following the last character and remove the blank space(s). Enter (make sure to leave two spaces between the first / and the *):

$$:g/ \ */s/// \quad ®$$

2 spaces ↑

In this case, the **$** stands for "end of line."

(5) **Removing Blank Lines:** The following command finds all lines with a beginning (ˆ) and an end (**$**) but no middle (ie., blank lines) and deletes them:

$$:g/ˆ$/d \quad ®$$

Note the use of the trailing **d**, which stands for **d***elete* and can be used to delete characters or phrases in any global search.

(6) **Adding to Words:** Suppose you had the following lines of text somewhere in your current file:

The longest English word is antidisestablishmentarian.

You subsequently recall that the letters "ism" can be added to this word to make it even longer. You can use the following search and substitute command to make the appropriate change *and* display the changed line on the screen:

$$\text{/}mentarian\text{\\}>\text{/s/}/\text{\&}ism\text{/p} \qquad \circledR$$

Note the **&** placed before the characters *ism*. Without the **&** this command would substitute the characters *ism* for the partial word *mentarian*. The **&** stands for *the last pattern found*, so the *ism* will be appended to the character pattern matching *mentarian\>* (*antidisestablishmentarian*). The **p** at the end causes the changed line to be displayed on the terminal.

The **&** character can also be used to *pre*pend characters to the beginning of words. This is demonstrated in the following example, where the letters *extra* are prepended to the word *terrestrial*:

$$\text{:g/}\text{\\}<terre.*\text{/s//}extra\text{\&/g} \qquad \circledR$$

(7) **Rethink Time:**

    (a) What command would have all lines containing the word *micron* displayed on the screen? _____

    (b) What command would remove all two character *nroff* and *-ms* command lines? _____

    (c) What command would find all instances of *.pp* and change them to *.PP*? _____

    (d) How could you, in a fit of depression, locate all instances of the word *possible* and add the characters *im* so that it read *impossible*? _____

        Answers: (a) **g/***micron***/p**   (b) **g/^\...$/d**   (c) **g/^\ .pp/s//.PP/g**
        (d) **g/\\<***possible***\\>//***im***&/g**

Editor Scripts

One of the useful aspects of the *ex* editor is its ability to perform an entire series of commands on a file at one time. In the prior section you met several command sequences which can make desired changes throughout a file. In this section we will discuss how to use an *editor script*. An editor script is a file of these commands that *ex* will apply one at a time to a specified file.

(1) To demonstrate the action of an editor script, you should first create a file called *script1* containing the following two lines:

g/ [0-9]/d
g/ *Bill*/s// *William*/g

Return to the Shell and select one of your *practice* files for the next step. Enter the following Shell command sequence:

ex [*filename*] < *script1*   ®

The editor will apply the contents of *script1* to the selected *filename*. Hence all lines in the file containing numbers will be deleted and all instances of *Bill* will be changed to *William*.

The Care and Feeding of Editor Scripts: Because an editor script can perform several editing functions "behind the scenes" and without giving you a chance to observe the process as it occurs, you need to be very careful with them. An incorrectly written script will at best have no effect on your file and at worst make bizarre changes. Your best procedure is to first use the individual script commands as editor commands with a practice file. Once you are certain that each script command will have the desired effect, you can then feel confident that, as a script, the command(s) will perform the function(s) you want.

(2) **A Clean-Up Script:** We have prepared a multi-purpose *clean-up* script which can be used to painlessly remove unwanted spaces and blank lines from a file. If you would like to use it you should place the following five lines in a separate file (you might name this file *clean-up*). Be certain you *carefully* read our descriptions of each command sequence before using the script, however. You would also be prudent to use each command separately within an editor to insure that you have correctly typed it:

g/^ */s///
g/ *$/s///
g/^$/d
g/ */s// /g
wq

To explain the action of each line:

(a) **g/^ */s///** will find all lines which begin with a blank space and remove the space (when typing this line be certain to leave two blank spaces before the *);

(b) **g/ *$/s///** will find all lines which end with a blank space and remove the space (when typing this line be certain to leave two blank spaces before the *);

(c) **g/^$/d** will find all lines which are empty (ie., no text) and delete them;

(d) **g/ */s// /g** will find all lines which contain two or more blank spaces and substitute a single space (when typing this line be certain to leave three blank spaces before the *, and one blank space between the fourth / and the final /); and

(e) **wq** is the usual line editor command to write changes made to the file into the memory of UNIX and return to the Shell.

(3) Select one of your *practice* files to test the effect of your new *clean-up* script. Then enter the following Shell command sequence:

$$\text{ex} \quad \boxed{filename} < clean\text{-}up \qquad \circledR$$

where *filename* is the file to be serviced by the *clean-up* script. The clean up script removes the unwanted spaces and blanks, then writes the file back onto the disk. It is just the same as if you had called up the file for editing, personally made each of the specific changes, and then wrote the file back onto the disk.

(4) **One Final Problem:** Create a script file which would do each of the following actions:

(a) Remove all requests to change line spacing so the entire document is single spaced.

(b) Change all instances of **.sp** to **.sp 2**.

(c) Whenever prices were mentioned (such as $138.00) remove the zeros after the decimal point.

Answers:

(a) **g/\ .ls [2-9]/d** (b) **g/\ .sp$/s//\ .sp 2/** (c) **g/\ .00/s//\ ./g**

Search and Substitute Summary Table

Meta-Characters

Command	Function
^	Match beginning of line.
$	Match end of line.
.	Match any single character.
*	Match any number (including 0) of occurrences of previous character.
[ ]	Match any characters (or range of characters) enclosed within the brackets.
[^]	Match any character (or range of characters) not enclosed within the brackets.
\<	Match beginning of a word or phrase.
\>	Match ending of a word or phrase.
&	Replace "target character(s)" with last character pattern encountered.
\	Remove "magic" of Special Characters (Kryptonite).
//	Match last pattern in search.

Regular Characters

Command	Function
g	If placed at the beginning of a search will address all lines in the file. If at end of search statement will function on all cases of pattern within specified lines only. (May be used in both places to function on all cases of pattern within current file.)
s	Substitute for last pattern found.
p	When placed at end of search will display pattern found on your screen.
d	When placed at end of search will delete pattern found.

Module Thirteen
Truly Advanced Visual Editing

Introduction

Mastery of the material presented in Modules Four and Eight will allow you to be a competent, effective user of the visual editor. Should you desire or need to acquire additional skills, however, mastery of the material contained in this Module will make you an even-more-effective and ever-so-fashionable editor. You have seen how UNIX often provides several ways—with varying degrees of efficiency—to perform the same task. Here we present more direct, yet more sophisticated ways to prepare your electronic work.

Prerequisites

To utilize the information in this Module you should have completed Modules One through Ten. Familiarity with the material in Modules Eleven and Twelve would also be helpful.

Objectives

Upon completion of this Module you should be able to:

(1) Initiate a visual editing session in several ways;

(2) Utilize new Append Mode special characters;

(3) Utilize several new methods to redraw the screen or reposition the cursor;

(4) Describe the relationship between the delete and substitute characters and the text upon which they act;

(5) Access multiple blocks of deleted and yanked material;

(6) Customize your editing environment with the **set** commands; and

(7) Create your own *vi* commands with the **map** and **abbreviation** commands.

Procedure

This Module is presented in seven sections. The first section presents several alternate ways to begin visually editing a file, such as beginning on a specified line. Section two describes the complete set of Append Mode Special Characters. The third section considers a series of commands which assist in cursor relocation and adjustment of the screen display. Section four introduces mixing and matching specific commands in the visual editor Command Mode. Section five describes the text storage buffers available to hold blocks of yanked and deleted text during an editing session. A method for customizing your editing environment is introduced in section six. The final section considers two ways to create your own editor commands.

Additional Ways to Call up a File for Editing

Several ways exist to call up a file for visual editing. A number of these allow you to begin the file editing process at a point other than the first line of the file. The list of the approaches available to you is presented at the top of the next page.

Note that with each of these commands you leave *one space* after the command **vi** and before the *filename*. For example, with the command sequence **vi** +*200 file1* you leave a single space between the **vi** and the +*200* and another space between the +*200* and the *file1*.

M
O
D
U
L
E

13

Each of the following commands moves you from the Shell Mode to the Command Mode of the visual editor.

Commands to Enter the Visual Editor

Command	Function
vi $\boxed{filename}$	Starts a file or retrieves an existing file for visual editing.
vi $+200$ $\boxed{file1}$	Places cursor at line 200 of file *file1* (leave no spaces within the $+200$ string).
vi $+$ $\boxed{file1}$	Places cursor at last line of file *file1*.
vi $+/word$ $\boxed{file1}$	Places cursor at first instance of *word* in file *file1* (leave no spaces within the $+/word$ string).
vi **-r** $\boxed{file1}$	Recalls (recovers) *file1* which was saved for you by UNIX when the system crashed.
vi ®	Accesses a buffer for visual editing without assigning a filename. Material must be given a *filename* (using the **:w** *filename* command) to be saved when the editing session is terminated.

Additional Append Mode Special Characters

The Conceptual Overview Module stated that almost all keys hold face value when pressed in the Append Mode. This means that, from the Append Mode, pressing the *a* key will result in an *a* character being placed in your file (and appearing on your screen). Only a few keys have special or magic powers. The exceptions noted at that time were the $\boxed{\text{ESC}}$ key and **CTRL-H** or **BACKSPACE** keys. In addition, there are five more special keys available to you when in the Append Mode. A complete list of the Append Mode special characters is presented at the top of the next page.

Append Mode Special Characters

Command	Function
CTRL-H	Backspaces one character.
BACKSPACE	Backspaces one character.
CTRL-W	Backspaces one word.
CTRL-V	Allows input of **RETURN** or **CONTROL** characters.
CTRL-I	**TAB** character (moves 8 spaces right).
ESC	Escapes to Command Mode.
DEL	Escapes to Command Mode.
@	Erases all input on the current line.

Practice Session: Select one of your practice files for use with the next set of activities.

(a) ___ Call up the file using the command that will place you at the first instance of the word *the* in the file.

(b) ___ Place the file back in storage; then call it up a second time in such a way that you are located at the end of the file.

(c) ___ Append a line of text; then, without leaving Append Mode, backspace two words using the **CTRL-W** command.

(d) ___ Enter a second line of text; then, without leaving Append Mode, remove the entire line and type a different line.

Answers: (a) **vi** **+**/*the* $\boxed{filename}$ (b) **vi** **+** $\boxed{filename}$ (d) @

Cursor Relocation and Display Adjusting Commands

This section describes three additional sets of Command Mode resources. These are commands which will: (a) move the cursor through large blocks of text; (b) "mark" the position of your cursor in a file; and (c) clear and redraw the display of text on the screen.

(1) **Moving the Cursor:** You are presently able to use a variety of cursor moving commands which will reposition the cursor from character to character, word to word, to the end or beginning of a line, or to a specific word in the text. It is also possible to move the cursor forward and backward through larger blocks of text. A list of these commands follows.

Note: The commands presented below do not work with *nroff* formatting commands. They are designed to locate paragraph or section header format commands available in the most common macro packages. If they do not work for you it is because your editing environment is not configured appropriately. You will learn more about set*ting* your editing environment later in this Module.

Additional Cursor Moving Commands

Command	Function
}	Move cursor forward through text to beginning of next paragraph (locates next paragraph macro).
{	Move cursor backward to beginning of previous paragraph (locates next prior paragraph macro).
]]	Move cursor forward through text to beginning of next section (locates next section heading macro).
[[	Move cursor backward to beginning of previous section (locates next prior section heading macro).

(2) ___ Call up one of your practice files for editing using the Shell command which puts the cursor on line 12:

$$\text{vi} \quad +12 \quad \boxed{filename} \qquad ®$$

(3) ___ Try the paragraph to paragraph moving commands { and } several times.

(4) **Returning to a Marked Spot:** First note the line number where the cursor is currently located. Then reposition the cursor at some other line in your file (perhaps enter a command such as *45***G**).

___ Now enter two single quotation marks:

' '

Often while editing you need to move to a distant corner of the file to check on some specific concern. Once the task is completed, you must return to the prior line to continue editing. Relocating your prior position can be a minor irritant, particularly if you neglected to note the correct line number. The two single quote marks is a useful command that will return you to your previous location in a file.

(5) **Marking Your Place in a File:** Suppose you are editing a file, and wish to quickly locate a particular line (such as the start of a table) regardless of its line number? The **m**_ark_ command can help with this task. Several positions in a file may be marked, each with a different letter (a - z). Once this is done you can easily return to each, even though the line numbers associated with each line may have changed during the editing session. Your markings will last only for the one editing session, however.

The sequence of steps necessary to use the **m**_ark_ command is:

(a) Select a location in the text where you would like to pay a return visit. With the cursor on that line type:

m_b_

You may select any letter a through z.

(b) Reposition the cursor at some other location in your text. You may perform any tasks that occur to you while located at this new position.

(c) To return to the location you _marked_ in step (a) you type (single quote followed by the letter you used, in this case the letter _b_):

'_b_

The cursor should be repositioned at your original location.

(6) **Adjusting the Display of Text:** Several commands are available to redraw the screen's display of text. You met one of them in Module Eight: the **z#.** command. The following commands are useful for reducing screen size (thereby reducing the time it takes to draw a screenful of text—a tedious process on slow terminals).

In addition, the following can be used to clear and redraw the screen if for any reason the display appears distorted (as will occur should UNIX send you a message).

Following the table of *Display Adjusting Commands* is a second table summarizing each of these actions.

Display Adjusting Commands

Command	Function
z.	Redraw screen with current line at middle of the window.
z4.	Have screen show only 4 lines of text. The number can be 1-23 (and don't forget the period). Current line at middle of the window.
z-	Redraw screen; current line at bottom of window.
z4-	Request that screen show only 4 lines of text. The number can be 1-23. Current line at bottom of window.
z ⓡ	Redraw screen; current line at top of window.
z4 ⓡ	Make screen show only 4 lines of text. Redraw screen, with current line at top of window.
CTRL-R	Redraw screen, current line unchanged.

Summary of Commands

cursor position on screen	same size window	4 line window
Top	z ⓡ	z4 ⓡ
Middle	z.	z4.
Bottom	z-	z4-
Unchanged	CTRL-R	—

Text and Operators

In Module Eight: *Advanced Visual Editing* you met several text modifying commands. Included among these were:

dw which deletes one word,

cw used to append text in place of one word,

dd which deletes a complete line,

cc changes one complete line into whatever text you enter (same as the **S** command), and

yy which will yank a complete line of text (same as the **Y** command).

These commands can be arranged in the following table of *Text Changing Commands*:

Text Changing Commands

	delete	change	yank
Affects One Word	**dw**	**cw**	
Affects One Line	**dd**	**cc**	**yy**

(1) One cell of the table of Text Changing Commands has been left unfilled. Your task is to enter the command which you expect could be used to yank *one word* of text. The correct command is noted later in this Module.

Various Ways to Delete Text: You have used the Command Mode command **b** to move backward through your text one word at a time.

___ If you have used the **b** only infrequently, try it a few times now before proceding.

___ Next, place the cursor on the space *after* the last letter of a word in your file and enter:

db

What happened? The **db** deletes from the cursor position *backward* to the next prior space character—the reverse effect of the **dw** command.

In Module Eight you used the **f***x* command to move forward through your text to the next *x*. For example, the command **f***z* will move the cursor to the first instance of the letter *z* (provided the *z* exists on the same line as the cursor).

(2) Given what you now know about how the delete command **d** works and how to "address" a character on a line with the **f***x* command, how could you delete from where the cursor is located to the first instance of the letter *t*?

(3) ___ Select a character (such as the letter *t*) on the line to the right of the cursor and enter:

df*t*

The text from the cursor to and including the letter *t* should have been removed as soon as you completed the command.

Changing Text: You have used the **cc** to change a complete line of text, the **cw** to change one word, and the **db** command to delete the one word before (to the left) of the cursor.

(4) How could you *change* the one word to the *left* of the cursor?

___ Place the cursor on the space after the last character of a word and enter:

cb

The cursor moves to the first letter of the to-be-removed word, while the last letter of the word is changed to a **$**. You are placed in Append Mode. The space between the cursor and the **$** (the to-be-removed word) will now be filled with whatever text you type. Enter three new words, then press the ESC key.

(5) How could you *change* text from the cursor position forward to a specific character on the line? To delete text from the cursor position forward up to and including the letter *s* you would use **df***s*.

So, to change text from the cursor position forward to the letter *s* you would use the **cf***s* command. (This command can be thought of as meaning *change forward* through the letter *s*.)

Variations on the Theme of Yanking Text: The last few minutes were spent describing how the *change* and *delete* text commands work. New combinations of old commands have been demonstrated. We now describe two new ways to use the *yank* command.

(6) On the prior page you were asked to supply the missing yank command in the table of *Text Changing Commands*. The answer is the **yw** command, which will **y***ank* a single **w***ord* of text. The **db** command will delete the word to the left of the cursor. What yank command would you expect to use to yank the one word to the left of the cursor?

(7) Similarly, what command would yank from the cursor position forward up to and including a specific letter in the line?

Mixing and Matching Text Operators: The following *Summary of Text Operators* indicates how the various command pieces can be mixed and matched to achieve a whole variety of changes, deletions, and yanks. Several of these combinations will be new. You should practice each of them a couple of times before continuing with the material that follows. (Note: the *g* represents any character in the text.)

Summary of Text Operators

Affected Text	move to	delete	change	yank
lines	®	dd	cc	yy
word to right	w	dw	cw	yw
word to left	b	db	cb	yb
right to *g*	t*g*	dt*g*	ct*g*	yt*g*
left to *g*	T*g*	dT*g*	cT*g*	yT*g*
right including *g*	f*g*	df*g*	cf*g*	yf*g*
left including *g*	F*g*	dF*g*	cF*g*	yF*g*

It is impossible to memorize a table of commands such as the *Summary of Text Operators*. However, if you remember the basic addresses (**w**, **b**, **t**, **T**, **f**, **F**) and operators (**d**, **c**, **y**) you can put them together as needed.

(8) **Review Question Set Number One:** Consider the following questions relating to material presented in the last few pages:

(a) What Command Mode command will move the cursor forward through the text to the beginning of the next paragraph?
_____

(b) What text changing command will yank the three words to the right of the cursor? _____

(c) What text changing command will allow you to change forward through the first instance of the letter *s*? _____

(d) What text changing command will delete backward up to the first instance of the letter *j*? _____

(e) What moving command will place the cursor on the first prior instance of the letter I? _____

Answers: (a) }   (b) **3yw**   (c) **cfs**   (d) **dT***j*   (e) **F***Y*

Text Storage Buffers

Up to now you have been somewhat restricted in how you use the text deletion and relocation commands. Module Eight stated that when you *Yank* a line of text you must move to the new position within your file and *put* it without making any text changes between these two actions. If you do make a text change between these two actions the yanked text is no longer available to you.

Similarly, once you deleted a block of text you could recover the material only until you made an additional text change. At that point the deleted text was no longer available to you.

In this section you will learn several new commands which will increase your ability to recover deleted text and work with yanked text.

Numbered Buffers: The editor conveniently saves the last nine (9) *text block deletions* affected during an editing session and places them in a set of *numbered* (1 - 9) buffers. Whenever you delete a block (one or more lines) of text the material is *automatically* placed in buffer number 1. Note: Individual word or character deletions are *not* saved. With each text block deletion the new material is placed in buffer 1, and the old buffer 1 material is shifted into buffer 2. This process of "bumping" deleted blocks of text from buffer to buffer continues up to buffer 9. Through this process your last 9 text deletions exist in buffers numbered 1 to 9.

(1) To demonstrate the way the buffers work, perform the following actions in a *practice* file:

(a) Delete one line of text;

(b) Reposition the cursor on a new line and delete two lines of text;

(c) Reposition the cursor on a new line and delete three lines of text; and

(d) Finally, delete a single word of text.

(2) Now that three text blocks (of one, two, and three lines length) and a single word have been deleted, how can they be retrieved?

To access the deleted material held in buffer 2 you would type:

"*2***p**

The deleted text held in buffer 2 will appear below the cursor. If no text existed in buffer 2 you would receive a note stating "*Nothing in Register 2.*"

You access a numbered buffer with the following command sequence:

"#**P**

In this sequence, the " is the double quotation marks, the # is the desired buffer number (1 - 9), and **P** is the *Put* command. You may use either the lower case or upper case P depending on your needs.

___ You deleted a single word of text in procedure step 1 (d) a few moments ago. Was this word saved for you in a numbered buffer? Access the numbered buffers and see.

Searching Through the Buffers: Because deleted material keeps being bumped from buffer to buffer, you often will not know in which buffer the material you want is presently residing. This presents no problem, however, as you can explore and discard until you find what you want.

(3) For example, suppose you want to recover the single line of text you deleted in procedure step 1 (a). You do not remember that it was the first of three text block deletions (and hence should be in the third buffer).

You could locate the missing text by employing the following sequence of commands:

"1p

u

.

u

.

In this example the **"1p** command instructs the editor to copy the material from buffer number 1 into your file and onto the screen. Since the recalled text is not correct, the **u** command is typed which will *undo* the first text recovery—in effect removing the text. The dot (.) is next typed (dot means *repeat the last text change action*) and the material in buffer 2 is automatically recalled. Since buffer 2 does not hold the desired material, another **u** is typed, followed by another dot. The material in buffer 3 is next presented. In this instance buffer 3 holds the desired text.

The editor *automatically* ascends through the numbered buffers when you follow the command sequence outlined above. You may continue through the sequence until you've accessed all 9 numbered buffers.

Lettered Buffers: The visual editor also maintains a set of lettered (a - z) buffers where you can place *yanked* or *deleted* text. Unlike the numbered buffers—where deleted text is *automatically* deposited—you must direct the editor to save material in a lettered buffer.

Yanking Text into a Lettered Buffer: Text is yanked and placed into a lettered buffer with the following command sequence:

$$"a\mathbf{yy}$$

Here, " is the double quotation marks, *a* refers to lettered buffer *a*, and **yy** means yank a line of text.

(4) ___ Place the cursor on a line of text and have a copy of that line yanked and placed in the *b* buffer.

Five lines of text are yanked and placed in lettered buffer *q* with the following command sequence:

$$"q5\mathbf{yy}$$

Deleting Text into a Buffer: A line of text is deleted and placed in lettered buffer *b* with the following command sequence:

$$"b\mathbf{dd}$$

Here, " are the double quotation marks, *b* refers to lettered buffer *b*, and **dd** means delete a line of text. You would delete five lines of text and place them in lettered buffer *g* with the following:

$$"g5\mathbf{dd}$$

(5) ___ Delete four line of text and place them in the *z* buffer.

Accessing a Lettered Buffer: You access the material placed in lettered buffer *a* with the following command sequence:

$$"a\mathbf{p}$$

As another example, you would place the material contained in lettered buffer *z* before the cursor with the following sequence:

$$"z\mathbf{P}$$

(6) ___ Call back the material you placed in buffer *z*.

You may undo an action with the *undo* command. There is no way to automatically access ascending lettered buffers (as there is with the numbered buffers), however.

(7) **Review Question Set Number Two:** Consider the following questions relating to material presented in the last few pages:

(a) What command will access the deleted material residing in buffer number 5 *and place it after the cursor line?* _____

(b) What command will place a copy of 6 lines of text in lettered buffer *r*? _____

(c) What command will access the yanked material residing in lettered buffer *r* and place it before the cursor line? _____

(d) What command will place 4 deleted lines of text into lettered buffer **b**? _____

(e) What command will access the deleted material residing in lettered buffer *b* and place it after the cursor? _____

Answers: (a) "*5*p   (b) "*r6*yy   (c) "*r*P   (d) "*b4*dd   (e) "*b*p

Customizing Your Editor Environment

The visual editor possesses a set of options that can make your editing experience both more exciting and effective. You met one of these options in Module Eight: the **:set nu** command which causes the editor to affix line numbers to each line during the editing session. (The command to "turn the numbers off" is **:set nonu**, which stands for **no nu***mber*.)

A listing of the settings of editing environment variables currently in effect for your account can be found with the Command Mode command:

:set all

Selected Editing Environment Variables

Name	Default Value	Description
ignorecase	noignorecase	Ignore upper or lower case during a search
list	nolist	**TAB** characters appear as ^I and ends of lines marked with **$**
magic	magic	The characters **. [*** are given special meaning in searches sequences
number	nonumber	Attach line numbers in editor environment
paragraphs	pars=IPLPPP	Paragraph macros denoted; default macros are **IP LP & PP**
redraw	redraw	A dumb terminal will simulate a smart terminal (Useful only at high baud rates)
sections	secs=NHSH	Section header macros denoted; default macros are **NH & SH**
shiftwidth	sw=8	Set distance of > & < shift
slowopen	slowopen	Do not redraw screen during each text change
term	dumb	Establish terminal type used

There are two kinds of editing variables: options that are either on or off, and those that allow you to indicate a value. Options without values (**list** or **number**, for example) are set with the following command line:

:set *option*

Options without values can be unset with the command line:

:set no*option*

For example, the command

$$:\text{set ignorecase}$$

will have the editor ignore upper and lower case information when conducting a search. Conversely, to have the editor consider the case of letters while searching, the following command must be entered:

$$:\text{set noignorecase}$$

Editing options which allow you to indicate a value are set with the following general sequence:

$$:\textbf{set } option = value$$

Creating Your Own Editor Commands

The visual editor allows you to create your own Command Mode commands: in effect, generate your own *magic keys*. You can create your own complex editing command sequences (**map**) or have a few characters represent an entire phrase (**abbreviation**).

The Map Command: You can "program" the editor such that pressing a single key will perform a series of editing actions.

(1) ___ From the Command Mode of the visual editor, enter the following:

$$:\textbf{map } \% \textbf{ ohello}$$

Now whenever you press the % key from the Command Mode the editor will open a line below the cursor (**o**), and place you in Append Mode. The word *hello* will appear on that new line. You will be left in Append Mode.

When creating your own **map** command be certain to leave a single space between the word **:map** and the character which will stand for your map (in the above example this is the % character). Leave another space between that character and the program (**ohello**).

If you are beginning a program or entering data such that the same information must be repeated, programming a seldom used key to enter the information and leave you in Append Mode can be very helpful.

(2) A more useful **map** would be the following. See if you can interpret what it will do before reading the explanation:

:map ! o.PP^V^M.ul^V^M

Note: The ^V character is a CTRL-V; it allows you to input a SPACE, BACKSPACE, [ESC] (CTRL-[or ^[character) or ® (CTRL-M or ^M character).

To interpret: Pressing the ! key will open a line below the cursor (**o**), moving you into Append Mode. It will then enter the *-ms* macro indented paragraph format command **.PP**, ® , enter the *nroff* command to underline the next line of text, and ® a second time. You will be left in Append Mode. This **map** would be useful if you were going to underline the first line of each indented paragraph in a file.

(3) Now, for a more sophisticated example. Should you decide to devote your life to the pursuit of television science fiction, you may have some use for this next example:

:map + O*Status*^V *Report*^V^M*Mr.*^V *Spock*^V^M^V^M*Yes,*^V *Captain*^[

Pressing the **+** character will now produce:

> *Status Report,*
> *Mr. Spock*
>
> *Yes, Captain.*

You can remove your **+** map command with the Command Mode line:

:unmap +

The Abbreviation Command: Abbreviation commands allow you to type a short word or series of characters and have them *automatically* expand into a larger word or phrase.

(4) ___ For example, consider the sequence:

:ab sta *Star Trek Addicts*

Now, whenever you type the letters *sta* they will be replaced with the entire phrase *Star Trek Addicts*. Conveniently, only the abbreviation (*sta*) and not words in which the letters of the abbreviation appear (no*sta*lgia) will be affected.

You can remove your **sta** abbreviation with the command:

:unab sta

(5) **Review Question Set Number Three:** Consider the following questions relating to material presented in the last few pages:

(a) What editor command will cause numbers to appear appended to each line of text in your file? _____

(b) What editor command will cause the TAB characters in your file to appear as ˆ*I*? _____

(c) What editor command will remove the ˆI characters which appear in place of the TAB character in your file? _____

(d) Describe the action of the following editor Map command: **:map $ O.sp**

_____

(e) Describe the action of the following editor command: **:ab pl President Lincoln**

_____

Answers: (a) **:set nu**　(b) **:set list**　(c) **:set nolist**　(d) Pressing the **$** key from the Command Mode will open a new line above the cursor line, move you into Append Mode, and place a **.sp** command on that line. You will remain in Append Mode. (e) The "word" **pl**, when typed from the Append Mode, will be replaced with the name *President Lincoln.*

This completes the material in Module Thirteen. It would be helpful to you to take a few minutes and review the eight Command Summaries presented in this Module. Practice working with those commands which appear most useful.

Module Fourteen
Communicating with Others

Introduction

UNIX maintains two services which enable you to communicate with others on the system. *Electronic Mail* allows you to send and receive messages (including files) to and from other UNIX users, *whether they are logged on or not*. The Shell command **write** will place you into *immediate contact* with another login, but *only when this individual is currently logged on*. Additional reference material about how each works at your location is available in the *UNIX Programmer's Manual*, accessible through the **man mail** or **man write** Shell commands.

Prerequisites

To use this Module you should be able to edit files and issue Shell commands (have completed the material through Module Six).

Objectives

After completing this Module you should be able to:

(1) Receive messages from other UNIX users; and

(2) Send messages or a file to other UNIX users.

Procedure

You must be in the Shell to send and receive **Mail** or use the **write** command. The **Mail** service will be discussed first. The **write** command is described in the second section.

Electronic Mail

Two versions of the UNIX **Mail** program are currently in use. To the user their differences are not extensive, and your system will support either **Mail** (Upper Case *M*) or **mail** (lower case *m*). Numerous locations support both programs. **Mail** is the more recent widely available version, and will be the one demonstrated here. Most of what is included is also applicable to **mail**. The discussion of the UNIX **Mail** program will consist of two sections: receiving and sending mail.

Receiving Mail

Accessing Your Mail: Immediately upon logging in, should you have mail, you will see a message indicating:

You have mail.

When this note is displayed you have the option not to read your mail (and instead attend to other tasks) or you can decide to take a look at what people have sent to you. If you want to view your messages enter the Shell command:

Mail   ®

A brief pause will occur, followed by a response from the machine indicating (as an example):

Mail version 2.0 January 19, 1984 . . . .

2 messages:

1 tigger: Fri Jan 16 14:36 27/432 "lawn bugs"
2 ozzie: Thu Jan 15 17:55 14/200 "dinner time"

Examine the line beginning "*1 tigger: . . .*" in the example:

(a) The number *1* prefacing the line reflects the sequence in which the mail messages are available to you. This is message number 1, while the next is message 2.

(b) *tigger* is the login of the person who sent you that message.

(c) The date the message was sent (Fri Jan 16, 14:36) follows.

(d) The notation *27/432* tells you that the message contains 27 lines of text and 432 characters.

(e) Finally, *lawn bugs* is a subject header, reflecting the content of the note.

Reading Your Mail: To read your messages in the sequence they have arrived simply press the ® (RETURN) key. With each ® a new message will be displayed. The messages will automatically appear in the sequence they were listed when you first called for your *Mail.*

As each message scrolls across the screen you may use the CTRL-S key (depress the key marked CTRL and press the S key one time) to halt the text motion. Pressing the SPACEBAR resumes scrolling. You can terminate the *Mail* session at any time with a CTRL-D.

There are several options when dealing with *Mail*, in addition to just reading it as it goes by. You can place a message into a file with the **w** *filename*, read in a selected order using the numbers, and write return messages (**r**). The principal options are presented in the summary table at the end of this Module.

In most instances a message, once read, is placed in your *mbox* file. UNIX will automatically create this *mbox* file to hold your once-viewed messages. You can access this file in the same way you would any other file (**vi** *mbox* or **page** *mbox*, for example).

Sending Mail

Mailing a Note: You can easily send messages or files to other UNIX users (and even yourself). From the Shell you type:

Mail $\boxed{login}$ ®

The machine *may* next come back with a request for a message header. If it does, insert a short descriptive title, and press the ®️ key. In any case, you may now begin the text of the electronic letter you wish to send. Note that whatever you type on the screen (and do not erase with the **BACKSPACE** key) will be included in your message and sent. You can make corrections on the current line only—once the ®️ key is pressed the line is "processed" and cannot be edited without using an editor, which will be explained shortly.

When finished with your communication, press ®️ and then type **CTRL-D.** A message reading *EOT* (for *end of transmission*) will appear, followed by the Shell prompt (the prompt may take a few seconds to appear). This tells you that your message has been sent.

Sending a File: You also have the ability to send someone (including yourself) a copy of one of your files. This is accomplished with the following command sequence (leave one space between the word **Mail** and the *login*):

$$\textbf{Mail} \quad \boxed{login} \quad < \quad \boxed{filename} \quad \text{®️}$$

Note that following the person's *login* you place the < (less than) character, located on most keyboards above the comma (,).

As an example, should you wish to send a file entitled *tritesayings* to someone with the login *rreagan* you would type (from the Shell):

$$\textbf{Mail} \; rreagan \; < \; tritesayings \quad \text{®️}$$

Finally, if the *login* you wish to communicate with is on another UNIX system, you must include this (system) information in your address. In some locations the various UNIX machines in the "network" are given names (such as *UNIX monet, UNIX populi,* and *UNIX ruby*). For example, suppose you want to send the file *tuna* to the login *tigger* which lives on UNIX system *monet*. The appropriate Mail address would be:

$$\textbf{Mail} \quad tigger@monet \; < \; tuna \quad \text{®️}$$

Remember: the system name or letter *follows* the login and is separated from it with an *at* (@). Note that the *at* is also the *kill* character on a number of terminals. To type an *at* on one of these terminals you need to precede it with a backslash character (\@). In general the command sequence to send **Mail** across systems is (leave no spaces between the *login*, @ and system name):

Mail $\boxed{login}$ @ $\boxed{system}$ < $\boxed{filename}$ ®

Note: On some systems the *at* character is replaced with the \! characters. Try using the @ in your **Mail** sequence first, and if it does not work, try the alternate.

Using the Visual Editor with Mail: It is possible on many systems to shift into the visual editor Command Mode when sending mail. This allows you to edit your note before mailing it—a process unavailable with the usual **Mail** service. After you have practiced using the regular Mail process a few times (go ahead and send yourself a couple of notes), try the following:

(a) Enter the usual **Mail** *login* procedure.

(b) When you are presented with the first blank line to start your message, enter (*tilde vi*):

~**vi** ®

The screen will clear and you are in Command Mode of the visual editor.

(c) Type whatever text you wish, making corrections or additions as you usually do with the visual editor.

(d) When you are finished with the text of the communication, type **ZZ**. You are not returned to the Shell but to **Mail**.

(e) You must still enter CTRL-D to send the message and return to the Shell.

Other Possibilities: An incredibly large number of options exists to modify your sending and receiving Mail. For instance, you can place certain commands in your *.mailrc* file to permanently affect how your *Electronic Mail* is handled. (Your *.mailrc* file is one of your *housekeeping* files. These files are discussed in Module

Sixteen: *Account Management.*) For complete information about these options you should access the on-line manual sections dealing with **Mail** (use the **man mail** Shell command).

The Write Command

You may send and receive messages to and from another *currently logged on* UNIX user through the Shell command sequence described below.

From the Shell type **who** (or **whom**) to elicit a list of users (logins) currently logged onto their UNIX accounts. Once you have determined that someone you wish to *write* to is on board, enter (leave one space between the *write* and the *login*)

write ⌷*login*⌷   ®

which will put you in *immediate* contact with *login*. You may then type your message, and at each ® the line just finished will be sent to *login*.

Most probably *login* will wish to return the favor of your message and you will receive a response from this person (initiated in a fashion identical to that which you employed to send your message). To coordinate your conversation it is helpful to employ the "pilot's trick" of using *o* (small o, for "over") at the end of each exchange. Complete your dialogue with an *o/o* (over and out). You press **CTRL-D** to terminate your conversation and return to the Shell.

Options: This type of message is usually disruptive (though often a welcome diversion from some tedious task). If you do not want to receive messages while working on UNIX you must type the Shell command

mesg n   ®

which means *"I don't wish to be disturbed at this time."* You can change your message status at any time with the **mesg y** Shell command.

Terminal Location: You may need to include the terminal location code along with the *login* when addressing your message, particularly if *login* is on the system at more than one terminal location. The terminal location code (normally a 5 character sequence beginning with the letters *tty*) is the **who** Shell command. As an example, the form of a **write** message to login *debby* at terminal location *ttyic* would be:

write debby ttyic   ®

Note: Sending **write** messages across UNIX systems is not possible.

This book was created using a machine like this.

Command Summary

Selected Electronic Mail Options

Command	Function
?	Provides a summary of Mail commands.
t1	Displays 1st message on screen.
t2	Displays 2nd message on screen.
®	Displays next message on screen.
d1	Deletes 1st message.
d1-3	Deletes 1st to 3rd messages.
w1 file1	Writes 1st message into a file called *file1*.
w1-3 file1	Writes 1st to 3rd messages into a file called *file1*.
f1	Requests "who is first message from?"
h	Print message headers.
top	Requests first few lines of each message.
q or CTRL-D	Quits Mail and places you back at the Shell.
x	Leaves Mail in original condition (ignores deletions) and places you back at the Shell.
r	Replies to sender of message you are now reading.

Module Fifteen
The UNIX Directory Structure

Introduction

All UNIX files are located within directories, in the same way that files are kept in file cabinets in an office. For most of you all the files you have created thus far have been in your "Home" directory. In this Module you will create new directories within your Home directory (called "sub-directories") and you will explore how to move from one directory to another. The liberal use of directories can help keep your account manageable.

Prerequisites

Before you begin this Module you should be able to easily create, edit, and remove files (have completed the first ten Modules of this book).

Objectives

Upon completing this Module you should be able to:

(1) Create multiple levels of directories originating from your Home directory;

(2) Move into directories located above or below your current directory;

(3) Move files into and out of directories; and

(4) Use the full pathname of a file to perform various UNIX functions on the file.

Procedure

The procedure steps of this Module are presented in five sections. The first section introduces the UNIX directory structure, while the second includes multi-level directories and the concept of pathnames. The third section describes how pathnames can be used to work on files from a distance. Section four presents commands which are useful if you become lost within directories or forget in which directory a file resides. The final section introduces some special characters used when moving between multi-level directories.

Directories: Order from Chaos

(1) ___ Log onto your UNIX account, and ask UNIX to provide a list of all files located in the *Home directory* of your account. To do this use the **ls** Shell command.

The names of the files that you have created while working through this book should now appear on the screen. Perhaps you have only a few files; if so, this listing is quite brief. Imagine what will happen in 6 months, however, after you have used UNIX to write several papers, programs, letters, or records. Your account *could* begin to look like ours (this is not meant as a curse). At last count we had 288 *different files*. What a mess to keep track of, right?! Well, it used to be, until we discovered:

Better Living Through File Re-Location

The key to maintaining a manageable UNIX account is the liberal use of *directories*. It is helpful to group those files which pertain to the same topic or issue together. UNIX provides the "housing" for several files in what is called a *directory*.

(2) **Creating Directories:** We are going to walk through the creation of a new directory to be housed in your Home directory. A directory located within another is called a *sub-directory*.

(3) ___ From the Shell type:

mkdir *Study* ®

(**mkdir** →m*ake* dir*ectory*) We are suggesting you use the name *Study* for your first sub-directory because that is what we will call it in the following instructions. (You may wish to call a future directory *C.S.Programs* or *Poetry* or *Letters* or *History* or . . . .) The **mkdir** *Study* command made a new sub-directory with the name *Study*. This new sub-directory now exists *within* your Home directory. But what is the character of this new beast?

(4) ___ List the contents of your Home directory (with the **ls** command). The name *Study* should now appear. Note that when you get a listing of the contents of your Home directory, there is no immediately *apparent* way to tell the difference between the rest of your files and the directory you have just created. Thus, it is helpful to adopt a convention when naming files and directories that will readily distinguish between them. Our favorite convention (besides the *Annual Berkeley Garlic Convention*) is to begin all file names with lower case letters and all Directory names with Upper Case Letters. Hence *Study* would be a directory, and *study* would be a file.

(5) **Changing Directories:**

___ You can "move into" the directory you just created by typing:

cd *Study* ®

The command **cd** stands for **c***hange* **d***irectory.*

(6) ___ You are no longer in your Home directory but are "in" your new *Study* directory. What that means will become apparent as you enter the **ls** command to request a listing of the contents of the directory. Type:

ls ®

Nothing. Zip. What happened to the files that appeared with your last **ls** command? They still exist, but *in your Home directory.* You have moved into your new *Study* directory by entering the

cd *Study* ® command: *Study* exists below your Home directory. At the moment you have no files in your new *Study* directory; it is a clean space where files can be placed.

(7) ___ Let's create a junk file in the *Study* directory, just to make it feel needed. Type

vi *first* ®

where *first* will be the name of this junk file. Type a few lines of text, and when finished ESC to Command Mode and then enter the **ZZ** command to return to the Shell.

(8) **Listing the Contents of a New Directory:** You are now located at the level of your *Study* directory (but note that you are still in the Shell Mode—the Shell commands still work in this new directory).

___ Again list the names of the files located in this directory (use the **ls** command). The name *first* should appear, indicating that the file *first* resides in your *Study* directory.

(9) **Changing Directory Home:** You used the command **cd** *sub-directory* (in this case **cd** *Study*) to move into the *Study* sub-directory located within your Home directory. How do you move back to the Home directory?

___ The ~ (tilde) means "Home directory" to the Shell. Thus you are moved back to the Home directory when you type:

cd ~ ®

In addition, the **cd** command, when used without any directory name, will place you back at your Home directory. This occurs because the **cd** command with no directory name following it (the default) returns you to your Home directory.

(10) ___ Now that you are back in your Home directory, call up a listing of the names of the files (use the **ls** command). *Study* appears, along with your other files, including (probably) a file named *first*.

(11) ___ You are now back in your Home directory. Use the Shell command

page *first*   ®

to have a copy of *first* displayed on the screen. (If the **page** command does not work on your system you should use the **more** command.) Is this the file named *first* you just created? No, this *first* is the file you created several Modules back. This demonstrates one important aspect of directories: you may store many files with identical names in your account so long as the files are kept in different directories.

Although the names of subdirectories appear in listings of the contents of the Home directory, the names of the files *inside* the subdirectories do not.

(12) **Listing Files and Directories:** You were told in step (4) that one way to distinguish between Directories and files was to use upper case first letters for names of directories. You can also use the **ls** command with the **-F** *option* to differentiate files and directories.

___From the Shell, enter the command:

ls   -F   ®

This command will bring forth a list (to be listed in the normal fashion) of all file names in the directory where you are presently located. Directory names will be listed with a / appended to the end of their names. The / indicates that they are indeed directory names. (For programmers, object files will be followed by an * .)

Time Out for an Attempt
at Conceptual Clarity

Consider your UNIX account to be a large filing cabinet. All the files you own are in the cabinet. If you have only a few files, you can place all of them in one drawer and they'll be easily accessible. However, as your collection of files expands, you may wish to organize your files around specific topics, projects, or events.

For example, our account—while we were writing this book—had five sub-directories: *Modules, Minis, Pat, Peter,* and *John.* The first contained files relating to the first ten *Modules* of this book, the second (*Minis*) contained files relating to the Modules 11 through 29, and the last three contained each of our *personal* files. When we logon, a listing (**ls**) of the contents of our Home directory displays the names of those five sub-directories. We then change directories to the specific sub-directory which contains the file on which we want to work.

These *sub-directories* serve the same purpose as file drawers. It is as though we have a five drawer file cabinet, with the drawers labeled: *Modules, Minis, Pat, Peter,* and *John.* When we create a file, we do so from within whatever directory is appropriate. This organization helps to minimize our confusion (which is a never ending source of amusement to our friends), particularly when we possess a large number of files and have a need for more than one file with the same *filename.*

At the moment your directory structure should look something like Figure A, where directories are symbolized by large D's and files by rectangles.

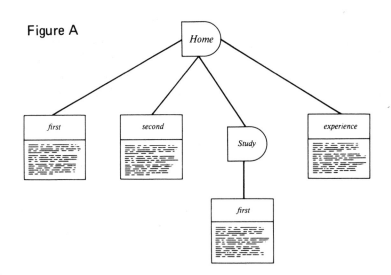

Figure A

(13) **Moving Files into a Sub-Directory:** To impose order on the chaos of an untamed Home directory you will need to be able to move some of your files out of your Home directory into a sub-directory.

___ For the next exercise you must be in your Home directory. To insure that you are, type:

cd ®

Select one of the practice files in your Home directory to move into your *Study* directory. (Don't use your *first* file. You already have a file with this name in your *Study* sub-directory, and if you shift a new file *with the identical name* into this directory you will either electronically vaporize the file that is already there, or be told no and sent to your room.)

___ From the Shell of your Home directory type:

mv *filename Study* ®

(14) ___ List your files in the Home directory to see if *filename* is still there (**ls -F**). Not found? Then move into your *Study* directory by entering:

cd *Study* ®

(15) ___ Now let's see if *filename* was moved into your *Study* directory: type the **ls -F** command. Your files *first* and the *filename* you just sent should be listed.

The command to move a file from the current directory into a sub-directory is:

mv *filename subdirectoryname* ®

(16) **Moving Files into a Parent Directory:** To move *filename* back into your Home directory type:

mv *filename* ~ ®

Remember: the ~ (*tilde*) is located on the top right of most keyboards, and is the Shell's name for your Home directory.

(17) ___ Now return to the Home directory and see if the file was properly "beamed back up." How do you get back to the Home directory?

cd ®

(18) ___ To see if *filename* was moved back into your Home directory you should type the **ls -F** command. All of your old files—including *filename*—should be listed. (Thomas Wolfe was wrong—you can go home again.)

This concludes your first encounter with *directories*.

(19) **Review Questions:** Because there is a lot of material in this Module we are including several chances for you to review the content. Here is the first:

(a) What is the command to make a directory named *Proposals*?
_____

(b) What command will move you into the *Proposals* directory?
_____

(c) What are two commands that move you back to the Home directory? _____ and _____

(d) What list command will distinguish the files from the directories? _____

(e) You are in the Home directory and enter the command line **cd** *Study*. You then start a file named *confused*. In what directory will the *confused* file be located? _____

(f) How is it possible to have two files with the same filename in your account? _____

(g) You are in the Home directory. What command will move a file named *florence* to a directory named *Proposals* which is a sub-directory of the Home directory? _____

(h) You are in the *Proposals* directory. What command would move the file *eakins* back up to the Home directory?
_____

Answers: (a) **mkdir** *Proposals*   (b) **cd** *Proposals*   (c) **cd**   and   **cd** ~
(d) **ls -F**   (e) *Study*   (f) the files exist in different directories
(g) **mv** *florence Proposals*   (h) **mv** *eakins* ~

Directories and Pathnames

Directories within Directories: To demonstrate how pathnames work you need to have a directory structure that includes several files and directories on several levels. The following steps will create such a structure.

Begin in your Home directory. From the Shell type the **cd** command.

(1) ___ Your first task is to move into your *Study* directory which you created earlier in this Module. Enter the command:

cd   *Study*   ®

You are no longer in your Home directory, but have moved into *Study*, a sub-directory below your main directory.

(2) Now let's create a sub-directory *within* your *Study* directory. Enter the Shell command sequence

mkdir   *Cabinet*   ®

to create a sub-directory named *Cabinet* (which is inside the *Study* directory, which is inside the *Home* directory).

(3) To leave the *Study* directory and move into your new *Cabinet* directory enter the command:

cd   *Cabinet*   ®

(4) ___ Put a file called *report3* in your *Cabinet* directory by entering the command:

vi   *report3*   ®

(5) ___ Type a few lines of text, then write this file and return to the Shell with the **ZZ** command. You are returned to the Shell Mode but are still located in your *Cabinet* directory.

You now have the file named *report3* in your *Cabinet* directory that is within your *Study* directory that is within your *Home* directory. (*There was an old lady that swallowed a fly . . . .*) At this point your directory structure should look something like the accompanying Figure B.

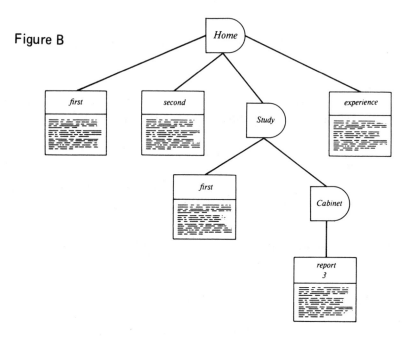

Figure B

(6) To move back to the level of your *Home* directory enter the command:

cd   ®

(7) Now enter the command:

ls -F   ®

Pathnames: The directory named *Study* should appear on your screen along with a complete listing of all your files and directories located in your main or Home directory. But what about the *Cabinet* directory and the file *report3*? This directory and the *report3* file are not listed because they are not located in your main or Home directory. Instead they are located in directories one or more levels beneath the Home directory. To move down the UNIX ladder to the *Cabinet* directory (in order to view your *report3* file) you should enter the follow sequence of commands:

(a) **cd**   *Study*

(b) **cd**   *Cabinet*

(c) **page**   *report3*

You are in your *Cabinet* directory.

(8) ___ Enter the command **cd** to move all the way back up to Home. The **cd** command's direct access "secret passage" back to your Home directory is nice, but moving down into one directory in order to move into the next in order to . . . is a pain. Fortunately there exists a shortcut which will allow you to move *directly* from your current position (your Home directory) into your *Cabinet* directory.

___ Be sure you are in the Home directory (by entering the command **cd**). To zip from home into the Cabinet directory enter the following command sequence (leave no spaces between the directory names and the /):

cd *Study/Cabinet*   ®

This command is the efficient way to move through a sub-directory (*Study*) directly into it's sub-directory (*Cabinet*).

(9) ___ Now type the list command:

ls   ®

And there it is again, your *report3* file. You must now be in your *Cabinet* directory.

Using Pathnames: Now let's take a closer look at the command sequence you entered in Step 8 (**cd** *Study/Cabinet*). This action consists of two parts: (1) Moving out of your *Home* directory and into your *Study* directory, and (2) out of your *Study* directory and into your *Cabinet* directory. The **cd** *Study/Cabinet* command sequence makes use of a UNIX feature known, in Unijargon, as a *pathname*. A pathname is (among other things) a way of specifying the full address of a file or directory.

Imagine that you have a real (non UNIX) file in a cabinet, in your study, in your house. A friend is trying to find it for you. Your friend asks, "Where did you say I could find that file?" If your friend is already in your study you would say, "It's in the cabinet" (analogous to **cd** *Cabinet*). However, if your friend is in another room of your house you might answer, "Go into the study and look in the cabinet" (analogous to **cd** *Study/Cabinet*).

And if your friend is calling you from a pay phone in Cincinnati? The full pathname for the *Cabinet* directory might then read:

Cincinnatiairport/Chicagoairport/Oaklandairport/AirportBARTStation /BerkeleyBARTStation/12642MonroeStreet/Study/Cabinet

(10) ___ Return to your Home directory by typing the **cd** command.

Action at a Distance

Pathnames can also be used to make Shell commands function on files that are not located in your current directory.

(1) **Editing a File:** At the moment you are in the Home directory (if in doubt, type **cd**). You created a file in the *Cabinet* directory called *report3*. Assume you want to work on *report3*. A question: if from the Home directory you enter the standard **vi** *report3*, would the file be called up?

___ Try it. From your Home directory type the command:

vi *report3* ®

This command will either (1) begin the process of creating a new file called *report3* in your Home directory or, (2) if you already have a *report3* in the Home directory, it will access that file. In any case, you cannot reach the *report3* file located in your *Cabinet* directory with the usual Shell command sequence entered from your Home directory. Use the **ZZ** command to leave this unwanted file and return to the Shell.

To get to the desired *report3* file you could change directories into your *Cabinet* directory and then edit it, or you can use the following procedure.

(2) ___ To visually edit the *report3* in your *Cabinet* directory *without leaving your Home directory* enter the command (and leave no spaces between the words and the /):

vi *Study/Cabinet/report3* ⓡ

By using the full pathname of a file you can have any UNIX Shell command "reach down through" the directories to work on a file not in your current directory. This is the "beam me aboard, Scotty" method of working on a file not located in your current directory.

(3) ___ Make some changes or additions to the file and use the **ZZ** command to leave *report3* and return to the Shell. What directory are you in? You are still in your Home directory. You worked in the file located in a lower directory, but you remained in your Home directory.

(4) **Copying Files into Another Directory:** Full pathnames are particularly useful with the **cp** and **mv** commands. You can copy or move files from one directory to another.

For instance, the following will: (a) make a copy of the Home directory *experience* file, (b) have the copy placed in the Cabinet directory, and (c) give the new copy the name *experience2.*

___ From your current position within your Home directory enter the command (leave no spaces between the words and the /):

cp *experience* *Study/Cabinet/experience2* ⓡ

The general form of the command is:

cp *filename* *Directory1/Directory2/newfilename* ⓡ

To interpret: *filename* is a file in the current directory; *Directory1* is a directory one level below the current directory; *Directory2* is one level below *Directory1*; and *newfilename* is the name the copy of the file should have in its new home. (*Whew!*) You do not need to use the title *newfilename* for this new file, however. It can just be *filename* because it is in a different directory.

(5) ___ To see if *experience1* was properly copied and transported to its new home, move directly from your Home directory into your *Cabinet* directory by entering the command:

cd   *Study/Cabinet*   ®

(6) ___ Now type:

ls   ®

And there it is, your file named *experience2*.

(7) ___ To return to your Home directory type:

cd   ®

(8) **Finishing the Construction:** To demonstrate some of the wonders of UNIX we ask you to create two more directories.

(9) ___ Find the *Kitchen* directory on Figure C and note its location directly below your Home directory. At the moment, this directory does not exist. First make certain you are in your Home directory (type **cd**). Second, create the *Kitchen* directory by entering the command:

mkdir   *Kitchen*   ®

(10) ___ Now enter the command:

ls   ®

Your new directory *Kitchen* should be among the files and directories listed.

Figure C

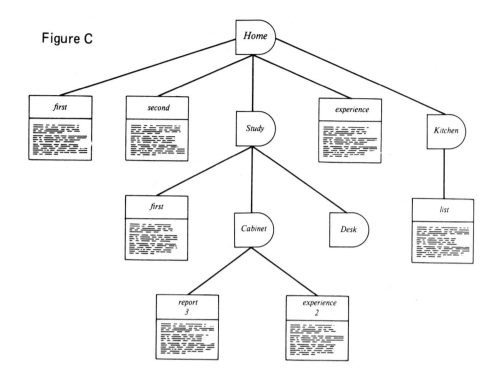

(11) ___ Move into this new directory with the command:

cd *Kitchen* ®

(12) ___ Create a file named *list* in your Kitchen directory.

vi *list* ®

(13) ___ Enter a few lines of text (perhaps the contents of a shopping list, e.g. *eggs, milk, bread, Cheetos*), then write this file into the memory of UNIX and return to the Shell with the **ZZ** command.

Now you have a file named *list* in your *Kitchen* directory which is located within your Home directory.

(14) ___ To move back to your Home directory enter the command:

cd ®

(15) The directory hierarchy you are building is now almost complete. Refer to Figure C. Note that, under the *Study* directory, you need to make one more directory—a *Desk* directory. To create the Desk directory, first move into the *Study* directory by entering the command:

cd *Study*   ®

(Of course you have to go into the Study to get into the Desk.)

(16) ___ You are now located in the *Study* directory. To create a *Desk* directory enter the command:

mkdir *Desk*   ®

(17) ___ Now enter the command:

ls -F   ®
    ↑ space

Your new directory *Desk* should be listed.

(18) ___ Move into the new directory *Desk* by entering

cd *Desk*   ®

(19) ___ Create a file *bills* in the *Desk* directory and list a few items in it. Put the file into storage (**ZZ**) and return to the Shell.

(20) ___ Leave the *Desk* directory and return to your Home directory.

cd   ®

Congratulations. Your directory hierarchy is now complete!

(21) **The Second Review:** Another chance to consider the material covered in this Module.

  (a) What command moves you from the Home directory to a directory *Education* which is located below *Proposals*, which is itself located below Home? _____

(b) From the Home directory what command would allow you to edit a file *kirby* in the *Proposals* directory? _____

(c) From the Home directory how could you create a directory *Rejected* inside the *Proposals* directory? _____

(d) How could you copy a file *hardyck* from the Home directory into the *Education* directory? _____

Answers: (a) **cd** *Proposals/Education*   (b) **vi** *Proposals/kirby*
(c) first enter **cd** *Proposals* then enter **mkdir** *Rejected*
(d) **cp** *hardyck*   *Proposals/Education*

Feeling a Bit Lost?

(1) **Where Am I?** A Shell command exists that can be very useful when you get lost within directories. First type **cd** to insure that you are in your Home directory.

___ From your Home directory enter the command

pwd   ®

which stands for **p***rint* **w***orking* **d***irectory*. In this instance you are located in your Home directory, so the pathname of your Home directory should appear on your screen. Note that the name of your Home directory is the last word listed and is the same as your *login* name. On almost any UNIX system (that can accommodate the visual editor) the name of your Home directory (your login name) will be preceded by a / character. Depending on how your UNIX system is configured, your login may also be preceded by the name of the machine on which your account is located (this is called your "system name"). Whatever precedes your login name is part of the pathname to your Home directory (this is how the person in charge of your system could locate your account). The pathname will be explained more fully in the following section.

(2) ___ Let's use a full pathname to move into your *Cabinet* directory. Enter the command:

cd *Study/Cabinet*   ®

Recall that commands of this form move you directly through multiple levels of directories. It should have moved you from your Home directory through the *Study* directly into the *Cabinet* directory.

(3) ___ Again enter the command:

pwd   ®

This time the full pathname of the *Cabinet* directory should be displayed. This pathname should begin with the pathname of your Home directory followed by */Study/Cabinet.* This is the full pathname of the *Cabinet* directory.

When you finish working on a file in some deep dark directory and you are presented with a Shell prompt, you can easily forget where you are. "Great, I'm in the Shell, but that doesn't tell me what directory I am in." The **pwd** command results in the Shell telling you the full pathname of your current directory. Lost no more.

___ Return to your Home directory (type **cd**).

(4) **Where Is that File?** Remember the good old days when life was simple and you always knew where your files were located? (You only had one directory, so there was no place to hide.) You now know that the **ls** command only lists the names of files located in your current directory. What if you want to find a file but can't remember just which directory you tucked it into?

(5) Assume you forgot what directory the file *list* was put in. If you want to find the file named *list* you should enter the following command from the Shell in your Home directory:

find ~ -name *list* **-print**   ®
↑ ↑ space   ↑   ↑

To find the file *report3* you would enter:

find ~ -name *report3* **-print**   ®

(The **find** command is almost as awkward to use as it is useful.) The second sequence above translates roughly as follows: "Find the file named *report3* and print its full pathname." The ~ indicates that the search for *report3* should begin with your Home directory and descend into the depths of your directory hierarchy from that point.

Using Special Characters to Move Between Directories

Look at Figure C as you consider the following statement: While we have discussed how to move into directories located *below* the current directory and how to move from a sub-directory *back* to your Home directory, we have said nothing about moving between two subdirectories located on different branches of a directory tree (from *Cabinet* to *Kitchen*, for example). The special characters we are about to introduce allow you to perform moves of this kind.

(1) **Dot and Dot-Dot** (*Samuel Morse would have been proud*): You should now be located in your *Cabinet* directory. To insure that this is indeed the case type the **cd** command to return Home, and then:

cd Study/Cabinet   ®

(You will soon learn how to accomplish these two command sequences in one act.)

(2) ___ Enter the command:

ls -a   ®

(The **ls** command with a **-a** option.) Your listing should look something like this:

.   ..   experience2

You know what *experience2* is [you created *experience2* in Step (4) of the prior section] but what about those dots?

(3) We can look into files with the **page** (or **more**) command. Let's try **page** on the dot file and try to figure out what it is. Type:

page .   ®

You should receive a message stating:

*** .: *directory* ***

___ Okay, let's see what **..** (dot-dot) contains. Type:

page .. ®

Another directory. So these mysterious beasties are directories. Hmmmm . . . .

(4) ___ Try to move into your **.** (dot) directory using the command:

cd . ®

O.K. That worked. You are now in the dot directory, but what or where is that? We know that we can ask for help when lost in the directory maze by entering **pwd**, so type:

pwd ®

The full pathname of your directory, *Cabinet*, should appear on the screen. But you have been in the Cabinet directory all along.

The single dot (**.**) is actually the name UNIX uses to refer to your current directory. Regardless of your current working directory, UNIX will use a dot (**.**) to "point to" your current position in its directory hierarchy.

(5) But what about the double-dot (**..**) directory? To move into the dot-dot directory, try:

cd .. ®

(6) What is the name of the **..** directory you have just entered? Let's ask UNIX by entering:

pwd ®

The pathname of your *Study* directory is displayed. *Study* is one level *above* the *Cabinet* directory where you were located. The command **cd ..** has moved you *one level above* your *Cabinet* directory.

This demonstrates that UNIX treats .. (dot-dot) as the name for whatever directory is located one level *above* your current directory. (Called the *parent* directory in Unijargon). At any directory level you can type **cd ..** and you are moved into the next higher (parent) directory.

(7) To move back into your *Cabinet* directory enter the command:

cd *Cabinet* ®

Summary: It is possible to move both directions in your directory hierarchy. The command **cd** *Sub-Directory* moves you down one level, and **cd ..** moves you up one level. Additionally, ~ and **cd** take you to the Home directory, regardless of where you are.

(8) **Using .. . and** ~ with Pathnames: Now that you know how UNIX treats these special characters, the next step is to use them with pathnames.

A question: what pathname would you use to move directly from your current directory (*Cabinet*) into the *Desk* directory?

Examine Figure C carefully. To go from the *Cabinet* directory to the *Desk* directory, you must go up through the *Study* directory and then down to the *Desk* directory (got that?!). Because *Study* is directly above your current directory *Cabinet,* it is the dot-dot .. directory.

___ Enter the command:

cd *../Desk* ®

which says, "go up one directory, and then from there, change directories to *Desk.*" You are now in the *Desk* directory.

A question: If you were in the *Study* directory and wanted to be in the *Kitchen* what command would you enter?

Answer: **cd** ../Kitchen

(9) How would you move from *Desk* to the *Kitchen* directory? Remember, *Kitchen* exists one level below your *Home* directory.

___ You know that ~ is UNIX talk for *Home* directory. Enter the command:

cd ~/*Kitchen* ®

which means: go *Home* (~), and then from there, change directories (**cd**) to *Kitchen*.

(10) ___ After you have entered the above command, list the contents of the directory to be sure you are in the *Kitchen*. Enter:

ls ®

OK, the name of the file containing your shopping *list* appears. You must be in the *Kitchen*. If in doubt, try the **pwd** command. (Be advised that Col. Mustard, with the lead pipe, and Miss Scarlett, with a candlestick, are also in the Kitchen.)

(11) **Action at a Distance:** What if you wanted to move your file *list* from this, your *Kitchen* directory, into your *Desk* directory? Using the full pathname of *Desk* will allow you to make such a transfer. Find both *Kitchen* and *Desk* directories on Figure C. The file *list* must be transported from the *Kitchen* directory, to Home, down to the *Study* directory, and then down to the *Desk* directory. From this *Kitchen* directory the set of directions for that move is:

mv *list* ~/*Study*/*Desk* ®

(12) To see whether the *list* file was relocated into your *Desk* directory type:

ls ~/*Study*/*Desk* ®

Your *list* file should appear along with the file *bills* that you created in the *Desk* several steps back.

(13) How can you visually edit the file *list* without moving from your current location in *Kitchen*? No problem. The long arm of UNIX allows you to edit *list* by entering:

vi *~/Study/Desk/list*   ®

Insert whatever items now occur to you (perhaps *large bottle of aspirin*) then press **ZZ** and return to the Shell. While you were editing a file residing in your *Desk* directory, you remained in your *Kitchen* directory.

(14) **Summary:** The **cd** command makes possible three kinds of motion within a directory tree. You can move: (1) downward to directories located below your current directory, through the use of regular directory or pathnames; (2) up toward your Home directory through the use of the **..** and the ~ special characters; or (3) you can move across to parallel directories using a combination of the above two methods. There exists no direct way of moving between two sub-directories below the same parent directory without going up through the parent directory and then down to the subdirectory of interest.

(15) **Final Review Time:**

(a)   What Shell command can you enter to identify your current directory? _____

(b)   What Shell command sequence would locate the lost *atlantis* file? _____

(c)   What command moves you "up" one directory, regardless of what directory you are in? _____

(d)   You are in a directory located five levels below the Home directory. You want to move to the *Marilyn* directory which is just one level below Home. What command would you enter? _____

(e)   Assume that directories *Jerry* and *Rick* have the same parent directory. How would you move from *Jerry* to *Rick*?
_____

Answers: (a) **pwd**   (b) **find** ~0 **-name** *atlantis* **-print**   (c) **cd** ..
(d) **cd** *~/Marilyn*   (e) **cd** *../Rick*

Module Sixteen
Account Management Activities

Introduction

As a person increases the number and complexity of files in a UNIX account, the need to identify the contents of files from the Shell, set limits on file removal, locate files, and otherwise manage files becomes apparent. The focus of this Module is on commands that will accomplish such tasks and on setting up your account to customize the way UNIX responds to you.

Prerequisites

Before beginning this Module you should be able to:

(1) Create and edit files; and

(2) Use the Shell commands which have been introduced in prior Modules (in particular, the **rm**, **mv**, **ls**, and **cp** commands).

Objectives

After finishing this Module you will be able to:

(1) Use a *filename expansion character* ∗ (also known as a *wild card* character) to simplify your file management activities;

(2) Employ several new Shell commands (**alias**, **echo**, **grep**, **clear**, **crypt**, **pack**, **unpack**, and **set**) that can be used to affect whole files; and

(3) Edit the contents of your "account management" files.

Procedure

These procedure steps are presented in three sections. The first introduces the special Shell character * and several new commands useful in account management. The second section demonstrates how you can *set* your account *environment* to meet your own needs. The final section briefly introduces the role of dot (.) files (*.login .reminder* and *.logout*) in account management.

Identifying, Scrambling, and Packing Files

or

How to Go on a UNIX Vacation

(1) **Identifying the Contents of a File:** In prior Modules you used the *slash-search* command (*/word*) to find occurrences of *word* within the file you were editing. With the Shell command **grep** you can *simultaneously* search several files for each occurrence of some word or pattern.

___ From the Shell type:

> **grep** |*fun*| |*experience*| ®

All instances of the word *fun* present in your file *experience* will be located and displayed on the screen. If *fun* was not part of your *experience* you will simply be greeted by a Shell prompt. (UNIX will not show its disappointment that you've not enjoyed your experience.) The **grep** command can be very useful if you forget in which file you entered a word or phrase.

The **grep** command used above had two arguments: *fun* and *experience*. The first argument to the **grep** command is the word to be looked for (*fun*), the second argument specifies the file(s) to be searched (in this case the file named *experience*).

Locating Phrases: In general, the command line is:

> **grep** |*target word*| |*filename*| ®

When using the **grep** command to search for a *phrase* instead of a single word in a file, the *'target phrase'* must be enclosed within single quotes ('). For example, the Shell command line:

grep *'elephant nose' zoolife* ®

will locate each instance of *elephant nose* in the file *zoolife*.

___ Select two files for the **grep** command to wander through. Then select a phrase (2 or 3 words) you'd like located. Enter:

grep `'target phrase'` `file1` `file2` ®

(2) **The Filename Expansion Character:** Module Seven noted that the **ls** command can be used with a filename as an argument. While this is not of great value in itself, the use of a *filename expansion character* in connection with this command line can increase its usefulness.

___ Type:

ls *f*★ ®

The ★ (asterisk, usually located above one of the number keys) is known as the *filename expansion character* and, when entered as part of a Shell command line, *matches any characters* (it is the *etc.* symbol for characters in a filename). Thus, the **ls** *f*★ command line should cause the Shell to list all of your filenames that start with a lower case *f* followed by any other characters. Likewise, the command **ls** *exp*★ will generate a listing of all files starting with the letters "exp" (such as *experience, expunge,* or *exponent*).

___ Enter a listing command such as:

ls *exp*★ ®

The ★ is often used when you forget the exact filename. For instance, if you had a file named either psychology or psychologist, entering the command **ls** *psycholo*★ should list the proper filename.

(3) **Using the ★ with Other Shell Commands:** When the expansion character is used alone (**ls** ★) it "matches" all filenames. This ability is useful with **grep** as well as other Shell commands.

___ Select a word which is probably in only one or two of your files. From the Shell enter the following command line.

grep |*word*| ∗   ®

This command line will locate all instances of the target *word* in any of the files located in your *current* directory only.

You have used the filename expansion character (∗) in connection with the **ls** and **grep** commands. This expansion character can also be used with other Shell commands. For instance (and this is only an example—**DO NOT DO THIS!!**), the Shell command **rm** ∗ instantly removes ALL files in your current directory. Quietly, with no fanfare, your files are sent to that great information dump in the sky. Sick is the resulting feeling. Try to avoid it.

(4) **Scrambling a File:** If for any reason you want to hide a file's contents from potential snoopers who share your account the **crypt** command is just the thing for you. The **crypt** program uses a four to eight character password or *key* (which you supply) to scramble the characters in your file. You use the same *key* to decrypt the selected file when you want to print or modify it.

For instance, the following will use the word *hidden* as the encryption key for encrypting the file *experience*. The encrypted contents will be placed into a new file named *rohwer:*

crypt *hidden* < *experience* > *rohwer*   ®

In general, file encryption takes place as the result of entering the following command:

crypt |*key*| < |*filename*| > |*newname*| ®

The **crypt** command causes the encryption, and *key* is the "password" you select for both encryption and decryption. The < tells **crypt** that the name of the file *to be encrypted* follows (take input from following file). The > instructs **crypt** to place the output of the encryption program (the encrypted file) into a new file *newname.*

___ Pick one of your files for "encryption," select a "password" (any word of 4-8 characters in length will do), and encrypt the file.

___ Interested in seeing what an encrypted file looks like? Use the **page** command to view the contents of your encrypted file.

(5) At this point the nonencrypted version of this file still exists as *filename*. You might want to remove this file for now so that its contents exist only in encrypted form.

___ Enter the command:

rm $\boxed{\textit{filename}}$ ®

(6) **Unscrambling a File:** When you want to work with the encrypted file again you must use the same password or *key* and have the file "uncrypted." For instance, to un**crypt** the file *rohwer,* and recreate your old file *experience*, the following command would be entered:

crypt *hidden* < *rohwer* > *experience*   ®

In general to "uncrypt" a file (*newname*) and have the original *filename* back again, the following Shell command line is entered:

crypt $\boxed{\textit{key}}$ < $\boxed{\textit{newname}}$ > $\boxed{\textit{filename}}$ ®

(7) ___ If you make changes to the file and then wish to re-encrypt it just enter the command:

crypt $\boxed{\textit{key}}$ < $\boxed{\textit{filename}}$ >! $\boxed{\textit{newname}}$ ®

The **!** after the > instructs the Shell to overwrite the old encrypted version of your file with the new encrypted version. (Don't forget that the new nonencrypted version still exists as *filename*; you may want to remove it.)

The Pack and Compact Commands: At many locations each UNIX account is allotted only so much disk space for the storage of files. With a modest amount of effort you can approach your storage limit in a short time. UNIX offers two methods for reducing the disk space occupied by your files: **pack** and **compact.** The **pack** and **compact** commands have a similar effect, yet are used on different UNIX systems. You should first try **pack,** and if it does not work, try **compact.**

(8) ___ Select a file for packing and enter the Shell command:

pack [*filename*]   ®

If you received the note *Command not found* when you entered the **pack** command, try the **compact** command:

compact [*filename*]   ®

List the contents of your current directory when the Shell prompt reappears. If the **pack** procedure works on your system the file *filename* will now appear as *filename.P* (With **compact** the file will be *filename.C*). The file is compressed and so occupies less disk space. *A file cannot be edited or printed while packed (or compacted).*

(9) **Time to Unpack:** The commands to reverse the **pack** or **compact** processes are, respectively, **unpack** and **uncompact**.

___ Select the appropriate command for your location and unpack (uncompact) your packed (compacted) file:

unpack [*filename*.**P**]   ®

(10) **The Alias Command:** The Shell command **alias** is, unfortunately, only available on UNIX systems that use the C Shell. This means that if you have a prompt other than the % you are probably unable to utilize this resource.

(11) ___ To discover whether the **alias** command is available to you, enter:

alias *p* **page**   ®

(12) ___ If the Shell responds "*alias: Command not found*" this command is not available for you and you should proceed to the next step of this section.

___ If you are greeted by a Shell prompt—and no nasty message appears—the letter **p** is now all you have to enter for the **page** command. The letter **p** is the Shell *alias* or *synonym* for the **page** command.

___ Select a *filename* and enter the command line:

p $\boxed{filename}$ ®

The Shell command **alias** allows you to *substitute* a few letters or a short word for a single Shell command or complete Shell command line. Awkward command lines or those you use regularly can be replaced with an alias of a few characters in length.

All aliases set from the Shell take effect from the time they are entered until you logout. Whenever you log back in you must reenter the alias to have it take effect. (Yes, it is possible to make such aliases more permanent features of your account and have them transcend logging out, but that is accomplished with modification of the *.login* file, a topic we will come to shortly.)

(13) **Using an Alias for a Command with an Option:** Another convenience afforded to you by the **alias** command is the ability to replace a command name with the command plus an option.

Note how each of the *aliases* used thus far were *only one word* long. There were no spaces in the strings of characters. A string of more than one word can be *aliased* by enclosing the string in single quotes.

___ Enter the command (leave one space between the **rm** and the **-i** option):

alias *rm* ´*rm* *-i*´ ®

The **-i** option for the **rm** command was introduced in Module Six. It causes the Shell to question your attempts to remove files before it removes them.

(14) **Note: Only if you successfully entered the alias in the previous step should you attempt the following.** The *alias* was successfully entered if you received *only* the Shell prompt upon entering the **alias rm ´rm -i´** command—and not a message indicating "*Command not found.*"

___ Select one of your *practice* files and enter the command:

rm $\boxed{filename}$ ®

278   *Account Management*

Because you have aliased the **rm** command to include the **-i** option your attempt to remove *filename* will be questioned. If you answer **y**, it will be removed. If you do not want the file removed, press the ® key.

(15) **Reading Arguments into an Alias:** Wouldn't it be nice to be able to alias long command lines (for example, the Shell command line **nroff -ms** *filename* | **page**)? To do this you need some mechanism for getting the *filename* you want to use into the middle of an alias.

___ Enter the following alias:

alias *format* ´**nroff -ms** \!* | **page**´   ®

The \!* tells the Shell to: (a) expect an argument (in this case a *filename* to the word *format*) when it is used as a Shell command; and (b) to replace itself with that argument in the command line.

(16) ___ To see this process in action enter the command:

format $\boxed{filename}$ ®

(17) **Clearing the Screen:** You can ask UNIX to clear the screen at any point while in the Shell Mode.

___ Enter the command:

clear

You will soon learn how this command can help during your logging out procedure.

(18) **The Echo Command:** The **echo** command may *at first* appear useless. This is not the case, however.

___ From the Shell type the command:

echo *hello*   ®

When used as a Shell command **echo** simply prints its argument (the word or words that follow it). When echoing multiple words they must be placed within 'single quotes.' While the fun of being at an electronic echo point is short lived, this command is actually quite useful when placed within your *.login* file (which, conveniently, is discussed in the final section of this Module).

(19) **A Brief Review:** Consider the following questions:

(a) What Shell command line will search for the word *bonehead* in all of your files? _____

(b) What will the **rm *** Shell command line accomplish?

_____

(c) What Shell command line will encrypt the file named *sharks* using the keyword *minnows* and place this new material in a file called *flounder?* _____

(d) What Shell command lines will pack (or compact) the file named *tolman?* _____

(e) Explain the following Shell command line: *alias lo logout*

_____

Answers: (a) **grep** *bonehead* *   (b) Remove all files in current directory
(c) **crypt** *minnows* < *sharks* > *flounder*   (d) **pack** *tolman* or **compact** *tolman*
(e) *lo* may now be used *in place of* the Shell Command **logout**

On Your Mark, Get Set, Go!

(1) **The Set Command:** You can determine something about how your *account environment* is currently *set up* with the **set** command.

___ From the Shell enter:

set   ®

You will be treated to a listing of the variables in your account that have been *set* for you by whom ever at your location distributes accounts. The **set** command with no arguments simply prints a list of the variables that have been *set* in your account. For now just glance through this list; the meanings of some of these settings will be explained later in this section.

(2) **The Set Noclobber Command:** You may have been lucky enough in your UNIX experience to have avoided accidentally vaporizing a file through the misuse of the > (redirect) command introduced in Module Six. Most of us have at one time or another redirected the output from a Shell program into an existing file and as a result lost the file. Helpfully, a command is available to keep us from our own unintentional destructive actions.

___ Enter the Shell command:

set noclobber

Once you have entered this command from the Shell you will be advised that the file already exists whenever you attempt to overwrite an existing file with the > command.

(3) ___ After you have entered the Shell command **set noclobber**, select one of your *practice* files and attempt to overwrite it with the following command (make certain you select a *practice* file, because if the **set noclobber** doesn't work you will *zap* your file):

spell ⌞*file1*⌟ **>** ⌞*file2*⌟ ®

(4) **The Set Ignoreeof Command:** You can normally logout of UNIX by pressing the **CTRL-D** keys. The problem with this command is that **CTRL-D** is also used at other times as the *end of file* marker (when sending electronic mail, for instance). Should you accidentally press **CTRL-D** a second time, you will logout. To avoid this you can enter the Shell command:

set ignoreeof

UNIX will no longer accept **CTRL-D** to mean *logout*.

___ Enter this Shell command, then attempt **CTRL-D**. You will now need to type the word *logout* to logout. (**ignoreeof** → **ignore** *end of f ile*)

Now that you have used the **set** command, it may be helpful to take a closer look at how it works. The *things* that are controlled by the **set** command (e.g. **ignoreeof** and **noclobber**) are known as *Shell variables*. The Shell variables that have been introduced in this Module have only two possible values—they are either *set* or *not set*.

(5) **Setting Numbers in the Editing Environment:** In addition to Shell variables, some versions of UNIX also support the setting of variables controlling your editor environment. In Module Thirteen we described how this can be done from within the Command Mode of the visual editor.

___ At various points in these Modules we have referred to the presence of line numbers which can appear during an editing session along the left of your screen. You can request these numbers (which are not a part of your file and exist only as a convenience) while in the visual editor Command Mode. From the Command Mode enter:

:set number   ®

(The numbers can be turned off by entering **:set nonumber** from the Command Mode.) The problem with setting the numbers from the editor is that the effect of having numbers appear on your screen while editing will last only until you finish editing the current file. (The temporary effect is an aspect of any of the settings made from within the visual editor.) Once you return to the Shell and begin editing a different file you will have to repeat the **:set number** command.

(6) **Setting the Edit Environment from the Shell:** Fortunately there is a Shell command which also places numbers in your editing environment so that they will be present for all files you edit in a given *session*. Numbers are included in all files that you edit until you logout from your account.

___ Enter the Shell command:

setenv EXINIT ′set number′   ®

Call up a file for editing and note the presence of the line numbers.

Yes, it is possible to set the environment of your account so that **number** and **noclobber** take effect every time you log on. At long last, we introduce . . .

The Reclusive Dot (.) Files

Whenever you have called for listings of the files in your account (with the **ls** command) you have seen the names of the files you created. There are one or more other files in your account that are not normally listed, however. These files have the names *.reminder*, *.login*, and *.logout*, and govern how your account operates. They are called "dot reminder", "dot login" and "dot logout" because each file's name begins with a dot or period.

UNIX has adopted the curious habit of making any file or directory name starting with a *dot* (.) invisible to normal listing. This feature is used in the naming of all files which relate to housekeeping tasks. You either currently possess or, if they have not been created for you, can create and use some of these files.

(1) ___ To find out what dot files you currently possess you can use a *modified list* command. The **ls** command with the **-a** option calls forth a *complete* list of *all* the files in your current directory and— assuming you are in your Home directory—this includes the dot files.

___ Enter the command:

ls -a ®
↑ space

Do the files *.login* *.logout* and *.reminder* (the . and .. filenames were introduced in Module Fifteen) appear along with the rest of your "regular" files? While the presence of the *.login* file is certain, the others may or may not exist. Please do not feel deprived if these others do not appear. We will soon show you what functions they perform and suggest items you may wish to enter as text into each.

(2) **The .reminder File:** If there is any text in the *.reminder* file it is displayed on the screen when you logon to your account, before the first Shell prompt is presented. The *.reminder* file is a "convenience" file in which you can place notes to yourself (or the other users of your UNIX account).

___ From the Shell call up the *.reminder* file for visual editing. There may or may not already be material in this file: delete this text if you wish. Go ahead and write yourself a brief note, prefacing it with some eye-catching design. Just enter the Append Mode and type away like any other file. Perhaps you would like to enter something like the following seven lines.

****
This is your UNIX .reminder file speaking.
Earlier you created the alias "format" for "nroff piped to page".
I await your next request.
(But you have to speak my language
or I won't understand.)
%%%%%%%%%%%%$$$$$$$$$$$$$$$$$$$$$

(3) ___ Once you have entered a few lines, save the file in the memory of UNIX and return to the Shell (**ZZ**). When you next logon you will be greeted by this message. If you can't wait to see your message you should logout and then log back in. The following procedures will wait for you to return.

(4) **The .login File:** All UNIX accounts are established with what is called a *.login* file. This is principally a *housekeeping* file containing various Shell commands which control the management of your particular account. The contents of a *.login* file can vary tremendously, due in part to the configuration of the UNIX system on which you are working and your individual preferences. As an example, we will present part of our *.login* file. You have met most of these commands in the prior section of this Module as Shell commands. Note: Lines beginning with a # are only comments describing the function of the following command line. Because they begin with a # they are ignored by UNIX. They are included in the file to help the owner of the account recall what the immediately following command line does.

> *# the cp command will not copy over an existing file*
> **alias cp ´cp -i´**
> *# the mv command will not write over an existing file*
> **alias mv ´mv -i´**
> *# the rm command will question your action*
> **alias rm ´rm -i´**
> *# the "word" print will format and lpr a file*
> **alias print ´nroff -ms \!* | lpr &´**

```
# the "word" lo will log you out
alias lo logout
# protects files from being clobbered by >
set noclobber
# CTRL-D will not log you out; must use logout
set ignoreeof
# puts line numbers in your editing environment
setenv EXINIT 'set number'
# greeted upon logging on
echo 'Welcome Back'
```

Why Bother? You can see there is a wide variety of Shell commands that can be appended to the contents of your *.login* file. What is the advantage in entering these commands into your *.login* file instead of just entering them from the Shell as you did in the previous section of this Module? With the method employed in the last section (entering each command from the Shell) the commands are "remembered" by the Shell only *until you logout* from that session. By placing these commands in your *.login* file you can overcome UNIX's short term memory problem. Whenever you login the Shell commands that are in your *.login* file are "read" and "executed" by UNIX as though they were typed (in the usual manner) from the Shell. The contents of the *.login* file are flash cards for the Shell.

In the next procedure step you will have an opportunity to insert any of the above commands that look interesting into your *.login* file.

(5) **Altering the .login File:** Your *.login* file can be edited like any other file in your account.

___ Call up your *.login* file for visual editing with the **vi** *.login* ® command.

The contents of this file should now be displayed on the screen. You will probably not understand what several of the lines present in this file mean. Do not distress, as they exist only to manage your account and you do not need to learn about them until you are interested. *DO NOT, however, alter or delete any lines in this file unless you have a very good idea what you are doing.* Without the contents of this file your account will be severely crippled.

(6) ___ Since the *.login* file is designed to serve the needs of each UNIX user, you can place within it those environment altering commands or aliases for Shell commands which are most helpful to you. What are some of the processes which you seem to perform regularly and which require more typing than you care to do? How about *logging out?* A simple process, certainly, but one that can be made alternately *more efficient* or *more creative.*

(7) ___ Place an alias for the word *logout* in your *.login* file (perhaps use the sequence **alias** *lo* **logout** or **alias** *bye* **logout**).

(8) **Aliasing the Find Command:** The following *alias* will simplify your use of the **find** command introduced in Module Fifteen. By entering the following command line in your *.login* file you will be able to use the alias **where** instead of the long **find** command.

alias *where* ´**find** ˜ **-name** \!* **-print**´

To use the alias to locate *filename*, you enter the following Shell command line:

where *filename* ®

Clearly it is more convenient to enter: **where** *experience*, than to type the entire **find** command line.

(9) ___ Insert any of the commands introduced in the previous procedural section (and/or any of the commands presented in the previous example that strike your fancy) into your *.login* file. You have already created an alias for **logout**. Do you want to **set noclobber** in the *.login* file?

(10) ___ When you have appended one or more Shell commands to your *.login* file, send the file back to the UNIX central electronic storehouse and return to the Shell.

(11) **Having the .login Read Immediately:** The Shell has been programmed to read the contents of your *.login* file only when you first logon to your account. It will not re-read it unless told to do so. Thus, right now UNIX does not know about your additions.

To use these *aliases* or *sets* during your current editing session you must tell UNIX to re-read your *.login* file (so it can "learn" about these new lines). To do this enter the command:

source *.login* ®

When the Shell prompt re-appears you will then be able to use whatever aliases you entered into the *.login* file.

(12) **The .logout File:** You possess an additional housekeeping file: a *.logout* file. This file is not nearly as much fun as your *.login* or *.reminder* files, but it can be useful. The principal use of the *.logout* file is to let you know you have successfully logged out.

___ Call up your *.logout* file for visual editing. Place the following six lines of text into this file:

> **# clear screen if possible**
> **clear**
> **# display statement on screen**
> **echo 'Hate to see you go'**
> **# check background for processes**
> **chkps -iv**

The last entry (**chkps -iv**) asks the Shell to check for any back-grounded processes still running. This command is described in Module Seventeen: *Backgrounding a Process*, and is only available on some systems.

(13) ___ Return to the Shell. The contents of your *.logout* file will be read and followed by UNIX upon your logging out.

(14) ___ Use one of your new **aliases** created in procedure step 7 to logout from your UNIX account.

Upon logging out the Shell will read the contents of your *.logout* file and the following actions will take place:

(a) Any processes running in the background will be noted by **chkps -iv** and you will be given an opportunity to terminate each. Press ® and the process will continue; type *kill* and the process will terminate;

(b) The display screen will go blank; and

(c) A note appears stating *Hate to see you go.*

You have now completed the procedure section of this Module. The next time you log into your UNIX account the note to yourself (stored in the *.reminder* file) and your *echo message* (stored in your *.login* file) should appear. If you'd like to check for their presence, go ahead and login.

(15) **A Review of Commands:**

(a) What Shell command will stop the Shell from overwriting an existing file when you use the redirect > symbol?

_____

(b) What editor Command Mode command will have numbers displayed when you edit a particular file? _____

(c) What Shell command will remove the editing numbers?

_____

(d) What Shell command will include numbers for any files that you edit in one session (until you logoff)? _____

(e) How could you have numbers appear in every file every time you logon to your account? _____

(f) What command produces a listing of all files in your Home directory, including the dot files? _____

(g) How could you have the word **format** interpreted by the Shell to mean **nroff -ms** [*whatever file you enter*] as an argument to **format**, and have the output sent to the **page** command?

_____

Answers: (a) **set noclobber**   (b) **set number**   (c) **set nonumber**
(d) **setenv EXINIT 'set number'**   (e) add **setenv EXINIT 'set number'** to the *.login* file. (f) **ls -a**   (g) enter **alias** *format* **'nroff -ms \!* | page'** into the *.login* file.

Module Seventeen
Backgrounding a Process

Introduction

At various places in this book we have mentioned the concept of running a job in the background. *Backgrounding a process* refers to having a current Shell process (**nroff**, **lpr**, etc.) run in such a way that the terminal is free to accept other Shell commands. You are then able to work on one task while UNIX quietly completes a different Shell command sequence. This Module presents an introduction to the commands that affect background processes.

Prerequisites

Before starting this Module you should have completed the exercises through Module Ten. In particular, make sure you are familiar with the **&** backgrounding character introduced in Module Six.

Objectives

After completing this Module you should be able to:

(1) Execute a Shell command sequence while you simultaneously work on some other UNIX task;

(2) Monitor jobs or processes that are running in the background; and

(3) Terminate jobs or processes that are running in the background.

Procedure

The procedure steps for this Module are presented in three sections. The first section deals with running jobs in the background. The second section discusses how processes currently running in the background can be stopped and re-started (a feature available on BSD 4.0, 4.1, and 4.2 UNIX versions only). The final section introduces the **batch** command—a cheaper way to run a job in the background.

Running a Shell Command Sequence in the Background

(1) Log onto your UNIX account. Select one of your larger text files for the exercises in this Procedure Section. A file with 300 to 400 lines would be ideal.

(2) **The Ampersand:** The **&** character was introduced in Module Six. This creature allows you to background a Shell command line.

___ To further explore how this command works enter the command sequence:

nroff   -ms   [*filename*] | lpr &   ®

Appending an ampersand to any Shell command line places the process into the background (where it is quietly but efficiently executed), and returns control of the terminal to you. (Kind of reminds us of the old tv series *Outer Limits.*)

You can then attend to other activities, without first having to wait for UNIX to complete your requested command sequence. Most versions of UNIX will inform you when the process is complete by writing a brief message on your screen. At some locations you may need to periodically check whether the process has been completed.

(3) **Waiting for Godot:** The simplest way to check on whether or not the background job is completed is to use the **wait** command. Enter the Shell command:

wait   ®

If the job sent into the background has not been completed, this command will cause UNIX to pause until the backgrounded job is complete. Using the **wait** command returns UNIX to the state it would have been in if you had not sent the job into the background.

If you get bored waiting for the process to finish or want to continue with another UNIX task press the **DELETE** key. This will delete the **wait** process, allowing the job to slip quietly back into the background.

(4) **Performing a Process Status Check:** While UNIX is attending to a Shell Command sequence such as the one you entered in Step Two, type the following Shell command:

ps   ®

You should receive a message which appears similar to the following:

PID	TT	STAT	TIME	COMMAND
12581	ia	R	:02	ps
12438	id	R	:46	nroff -ms experience

The **ps** command stands for **p**rocess **s**tatus and can be used at any time to report all processes submitted from your account.

If the formatter is particularly speedy (or if you sent a short file) the process status may not show that you are backgrounding an *nroff* process (as the process may have already finished). If this happens, submit a longer file to be formatted using the **&** to put the process in the background, then retype the **ps** command.

Note the **PID** number assigned to your backgrounded process. **PID** means *Process IDentification*: this is the "job number" assigned by UNIX to the command listed under the heading *Command*. The other headings are not of interest at this time.

(5) **Killing a Backgrounded Process:** You can terminate a backgrounded process with the **kill** command. For example, to kill the Shell process identified as *12438* in the above sample process status check, you would enter the sequence **kill** *12438*.

Enter the following Shell command sequence

kill PID ®

where PID is the process number found for your background job when you entered the **ps** command in the prior step. UNIX will abandon (kill) the Shell process associated with that number. Note: if the job is already completed, it cannot be killed.

(6) **Quiz Number One:**

(a) What command would cause UNIX to background the process of locating misspelled words in the file named *samneric* and put these words in a file named *spellsam?* _____

(b) What command can be used to see if the spell process initiated in question (a) above is completed? _____

(c) How could you tell UNIX you've changed your mind about the Shell process initiated in question (a) above and don't wish to have the process completed? _____

Answers: (a) **spell** *samneric* > *spellsam* **&**   (b) **ps**   (c) **kill** PID

Stopping and Re-Starting Jobs
(Available Only on Some Versions)

(1) **Stopping a Foreground Process:** Some UNIX systems will allow you to temporarily stop whatever process you are working on. In effect the process is placed in a state of suspended animation, while you are moved back into the Shell Mode (microprocessor cryogenics).

(2) ___ Call up one of your practice files for visual editing. Once the first several lines of the file are displayed, type (hold down CTRL and at the same time press the **Z** key once):

CTRL-Z ®

You should receive a note indicating *Stopped* and a Shell prompt should now appear. If those two events do not take place, your system probably does not have these features, and you should proceed to the next section: *Running Jobs through Batch.*

If you have stopped the job and are presented with a Shell prompt you can perform any Shell activity you desire—your stopped process will silently await your return. Perform some modest Shell command action (perhaps look up the spelling of all words beginning with the letters *uni*). Leave your file in suspended animation for another moment—you'll soon learn how to re-call it.

(3) **Checking the Background for Processes:** The **ps** command will report all processes running on your UNIX account. Most UNIX systems that support the **CTRL-Z** command also offer an alternative to the **ps** command for checking on stopped or backgrounded processes.

___ From the Shell enter:

jobs ®

A list of *backgrounded* or *stopped* processes will be displayed for your edification. The **jobs** command is the quickest way to discover these processes (much quicker but less thorough than the **ps** command).

(4) **Pulling a Stopped or Backgrounded Process into the Foreground:** Any Shell command sequence which has been backgrounded or stopped can be brought back into the foreground.

___ The process you stopped a few moments ago (with the **CTRL-Z** command) is still in suspended animation (you just checked with the **jobs** command). It can be brought into the *foreground* with the following command:

fg ®

Backgrounding a Process 293

Voilà! Your backgrounded editing process reappears, and you may continue work. Write the file onto the disk and return to the Shell with the **ZZ** command.

Warning: The following sequence of events is dangerous:

(a)   Begin editing a file;

(b)   Make some changes to it;

(c)   Stop work on the file with the **CTRL-Z** command, and perform some Shell task (such as look up the spelling of a word);

(d)   Forgetting that the buffer copy of the file was placed in limbo, again enter the **vi** *filename* command and thus call up a new buffer copy of the file [as it was before you began this editing session in step (a)]; then

(e)   Start editing this second version of the file.

At this point, in addition to the disk copy, you would have two temporary copies of your file, one in the background and one in the foreground. Both copies are now different from the original disk copy and different from each other. If you write one file onto the disk, and then write the other, the second will overwrite the first, resulting in the loss of the editing performed on the first copy. *Be certain to go back to files that are stopped rather than call up new versions of the file.*

The backgrounding of editing processes is especially useful when you need to look up the spelling of a word or if you want go into some other file to write out a portion for inclusion in the present file. Just remember to bring the file back into the foreground rather than starting over with a new edit command.

(5)   **Killing a Backgrounded Process with chkps:** As you now know, one of the uses of a process status check is to discover the process number assigned to your command so that you can kill that process. On most UNIX systems that support the **CTRL-Z**, **fg**, and **jobs** commands these two actions can be accomplished in one easy step.

___ From the Shell enter the command line:

chkps   -iv   ®

This command will individually list all processes currently in the background. You will be asked whether you would like to terminate any of the processes. If you want the job killed, enter *yes* (or *y*) and press the ⑧ key. If you want the process to continue, simply press ⑧ . This Shell command sequence is a useful addition to your *.logout* file, as it will detect any unwanted processes which might continue to use computer time after you logoff. For this reason, the **chkps** command is noted in Module Sixteen: *Account Management.*

(6) **Review:**

    (a)   If you are editing a file named *rhett* and need to know how to spell the word *butler*, how could you find the word using the *spell* command, without ending your editing session?

    _____

    (b)   Once you had the correct spelling, how would you return to editing the file *rhett*? _____

    (c)   What Shell command could you use to see if the file *rhett* is stopped and in suspended animation? _____

    (d)   What Shell command identifies all backgrounded jobs and permits you to decide whether each should be continued?

    _____

Answers: (a) First type **CTRL-Z**, then **look** *but*   (b) **fg**   (c) **jobs** or **ps**
(d) **chkps -iv**

Running Jobs Through Batch

While UNIX is designed primarily as an interactive operating system it is possible to run jobs through the UNIX *batch* facility. Each *batch* job is held by the system until UNIX has the resources necessary to complete the job at one time. This contrasts with *interactive* jobs, which are worked on in a piecemeal fashion. Although *batch* processing is usually slower then interactive processing, it does offer the advantage of allowing you to specify certain limits to the job that cannot be done with interactive jobs (e.g., run at night when costs go down or exit job if it takes longer then a specified amount of cpu time). In addition, *batch* is often considerably cheaper (and easier on the system) then running jobs interactively or in the background.

Batch jobs can be run with a wide variety of options. We will present only the basic process. Additional information is available from the on-line *UNIX Programmers' Manual*.

Running a Batch Job: The *batch* facility is accessed from the Shell. Running a *batch* job is a two step process: (1) the Shell command line(s) that you want followed (these are the same command lines you would submit from the Shell if you were running the job interactively) are entered into a file; (2) the file containing the Shell commands is then sent to the *batch* processor, where the commands are executed.

For instance, assume you have a text file named *report2* that you want to format. The steps necessary to *batch* this *nroff* job would be:

(a)   First create a "script" file containing the Shell command line to be submitted to *batch* (in this instance, the command line would be **nroff -ms** *report2* | **lpr**); and

(b)   Then submit the *script* file to batch by entering the appropriate Shell command line (e.g., **batch** *scriptfile*).

This general process is described in the following steps.

(1)   **Creating a Script File:** The *script* file in this example is easily created. Just place the command(s) you would normally use *from the Shell* into a file.

___   Use the visual editor to create a new file called *script* which will contain only the following Shell Command line:

      nroff -ms $\boxed{\textit{filename}}$ > $\boxed{\textit{nfile}}$

In this command sequence *filename* is the name of a file in your account that you would like formatted. The filename *nfile* is the name you would like given to the formatted version of this file. (Programmers can replace this line with the Shell command sequence necessary to compile a program.)

(2) **Submitting the Job:** The following Shell command sequence will ask UNIX to process your *batch* job (i.e., have the command(s) you entered into your *script* file obeyed):

batch *script* ®

The file named *script* is sent to be *batch* processed. In response, *batch* will do two things:

(a) Tell you the jobname being assigned to this job, such as *scrip17429*, and

(b) Create two files in your account: *batch.err* and *batch.out.*

Note the assigned jobname (such as *scrip17429*) as you will use it in the next Procedure Step.

The process of having jobs run through *batch* involves at least two files: one file consists only of the Shell command(s) which instruct the Shell to perform one or more specific processes, and the other file(s) is the file *to-be-worked-on.* The file containing Shell command line(s) and the to-be-worked-on file(s) are not the same file.

(3) **A General Nroff Script File:** It can be awkward having to go into the *script* file and change the name of the to-be-formatted file every time you want to *batch* (or botch) a formatting job. Much more useful is a script file that permits you to specify the to-be-formatted file *as you give the* **batch** *command.*

To create such a general script file you should replace the present line in your *script* file with the following line:

nroff -ms $1 > $2

With the **nroff -ms $1 > $2** line in your *script* file, you could use the following Shell command sequence to *batch* process the file *oldfile*:

batch *script oldfile newfile* ®

The file *oldfile* will be formatted and the output placed in a file named *newfile*.

The **$1** and **$2** are symbols interpreted by the Shell to mean: replace these characters with the first and second arguments that follow the name of the script file in the **batch** Shell command line. Consider another example: with the above Shell command sequence in a file named *script,* the Shell command sequence

batch *script experience n.exper* ®

will have *batch* format the file named *experience* and place this material into a file named *n.exper*. (Note: *Arguments* are discussed in Module Sixteen: *Account Management.*)

(4) **Checking the Batch Que:** In case you forget the batch job name assigned to your job or wish to otherwise check on the status of your batch job you may enter the following Shell command:

batq ®

UNIX will inform you of the status of your *batch* job (along with any others being processed) whenever you enter the **batq** Shell command.

(5) **Removing a Batch Job:** Occasionally you may send a job to *batch* and then realize that the job was not really ready for the requested processing. Jobs sent, but not processed, can be cancelled (removed from the *batch* que). All you need is the jobname assigned to the *batch* job (such as *scrip17429*) and the following command.

To remove the job *scrip17429*, you would enter the following Shell command:

batrm **-j** *scrip17429* ®

In general, to remove a batch job you use the following command sequence

batrm **-j** $\boxed{jobname}$ ®

where jobname is the name that *batch* assigned to your job.

(6) **Additional Commands:** Two additional Shell commands should be noted:

    (a) **batman**, which summons forth an overweight and poorly conditioned middle-aged man who dresses funny and drives a very unusual car which closely resembles a 1963 Cadillac, and

    (b) **robin**, which will do all that **batman** will do, but with much less self-confidence.

(7) **A Final Review:**

    (a) What Shell command sequence would you place within the script file named *script* to have files formatted by *nroff -ms* and sent to the line printer? _____

    (b) What Shell command line would you use to have the file *experience* formatted and printed using the batch script file named *script* created in question (a)?

_____

Answers: (a) **nroff -ms $1 | lpr**   (b) **batch** *script experience*

Background Command Summary

(Most Versions With Berkeley Enhancements)

Command	Function
&	Place Shell command sequence in the background. You are given a Shell prompt.
wait	Pause until backgrounded job is complete
ps	Perform a process status check. List processes :that belong to you (your terminal).
ps -g	Perform a process status check. List all processes that belong to your account.
kill #	Kill named process number #.
kill -9 #	Nuke named process number #.
batch	Execute a Shell script as a batch job.
batq	Check the batch que.
batrm	Remove a job from the batch que.

(BSD 4.0, 4.1, 4.2 Only)

Command	Function
CTRL-Z	Stop a process. Immediately place into Shell.
jobs	List all jobs currently stopped or running in the background.
fg	Bring a backgrounded or stopped job into the foreground.
chkps -iv	Perform a process status check. Will prompt for a process kill command (not available on BSD 4.2).

Module Eighteen
Parts and Wholes

Introduction

When writing a long or complicated paper, we usually focus on the development of only one part at a time. For instance, we may complete the problem statement or summary, and leave the remainder of the text alone. It is a waste of computer resources to have the entire paper formatted and printed whenever we want to examine only the part under construction. Conveniently, UNIX allows us to both separate files into smaller (and more easily edited) parts as well as join files together to make larger files. Additionally, it is possible to have Shell commands function on several separate files as if they were a single file.

Prerequisites

This Module will be most useful if you:

(1) Have completed Modules One through Ten;

(2) Have line numbers displayed next to each line when you edit a file (see the section on **setenv EXINIT** in Module Sixteen: *Account Management*);

(3) Have the Shell command **set noclobber** in your *.login* file (see Module Sixteen); and

(4) Have reviewed the process of working with directories as discussed in Module Fifteen: *The UNIX Directory Structure*.

Objectives

Upon completion of this Module you will be able to:

(1) Create new files which contain blocks of text drawn from the file you are currently editing;

(2) Add text from another file to the file you are currently editing;

(3) Create a file containing the contents of several files;

(4) Use several special Shell characters to perform various Shell functions (e.g. format and print text or compile and execute programs on several files with one command line); and

(5) Use several new *nroff* options to format selected parts of a file or files that are sections of a larger paper.

Procedure

The procedural steps in this Module are presented in four sections. The first section reviews a method of breaking a file into separate parts while working in an editor Command Mode. The second section reviews several methods of joining files together from within an editor Command Mode. A new Shell procedure that accomplishes a similar task in a different way is also introduced. The third section illustrates how you can use *filename expansion characters* to perform Shell functions on several files simultaneously. The final section presents *nroff* Shell command options which can be used in the production of a paper or text.

Separating a File into Component Parts

(1) **Writing Out Text:** To write out a block of text from your current file to a new file you need two pieces of information: (1) the line numbers of the first and last lines of the text you want to write out, and (2) a new filename for this material.

As an example suppose you are visually editing the file *letter.mom* and wish to save the first seven lines of text (perhaps as an introduction to your next bi-annual letter) as a separate file (to be titled *mom.start*). From *vi* Command Mode you would type:

:1,7 **w** *mom.start*   ®

The lines specified by the line address (*1, 7*) would be copied and written into a new file. The text would then exist in two places—in the file you are currently editing, and in a new file *mom.start*. If you did not want this text in your *letter.mom* file, you would need to delete it.

(2) Various forms of the **write** command are summarized below:

Command	Function
:1,6 **w** *newfile*	Creates *newfile* copying text lines 1 to 6
:1,6 **w** *>>* *oldfile*	Appends copy of lines 1 to 6 to end of *oldfile*
:1,6 **w!** *oldfile*	Overwrites (replaces) *oldfile* with contents of lines 1 to 6

Note: These are visual editor commands. To use these commands from the *ex* line editor you would drop the colon (:).

Joining Files Together from within an Editor

Two methods exist for joining files together while working in an editor Command Mode.

(1) **Writing out Text:** The *:1,6* **w** *>>* *oldfile* form of the *write* command reviewed above can be used to take part of one file and append it to another.

(2) **Reading in Text:** To read another file into the one you are editing, you need two pieces of information: (1) the *name* of the file containing the material you wish to copy into your current file, and (2) the *location* (line number) in your current file *after* which you want this new material to appear.

Suppose you are visual editing a file named *letter.mom* and wish to send her a copy of the poem you created for your English Composition course. This poem is contained in the *poem* file. From *vi* Command Mode (while editing the *letter.mom* file) you would type the following:

$$:8 \textbf{ read} \quad poem \qquad ®$$

A copy of the file *poem* would be read into *letter.mom* immediately following line 8. Once you *read in* this material it becomes a part of your current file and may be treated like the rest of the text. A copy was made of the originating file, and it is left unchanged.

Joining Files Together From the Shell

(3) **Copying Two Files to Create a Third:** In an earlier Module you met the Shell **cat** command as one way of viewing files (the fly-by, catch-me-if-you-can approach). Additionally, **cat** allows you to merge the contents of two or more files. **Cat** (which stands for *concatenate,* a word which few people recognize and even fewer can pronounce) is an excellent tool for the task of combining files.

To have the file *poem* combined with the file *letter.mom* into a new *poem.letter* file enter the Shell command sequence:

$$\textbf{cat} \quad poem \; letter.mom \; > \; poem.letter \qquad ®$$

The sequence to use this command in general is:

$$\textbf{cat} \; \boxed{file1} \quad \boxed{file2} \; > \; \boxed{file3} \quad ®$$

where *file1* and *file2* are the files to be combined, the > is the "larger than" right arrowhead (the *redirect* symbol), and *file3* is the name selected for a new file to receive the contents of files 1 and 2. Note: The contents of each file is not affected. The original *file1* and *file2* will still exist, while a new *file3* has been created to hold a copy of both *file1* and *file2*.

(4) **Beware!!!** Do not use the name of an existing file to receive files concatenated with a single arrow head (as demonstrated in the two examples in Step 3). At best you will be prohibited from executing the command, and at worst the existing file will be lost. If

your *.login* file *does not* contain the Shell command **noclobber** the following will occur: The **cat** command's first action is to empty the file following the > of its contents (if it has any). Thus, trying to **cat** one file into another using a single arrow head will result in the loss of one of the files. In this manner, the following **cat** command sequence *would be disastrous*:

cat *paper1 paper2* > *paper1* ⓡ

In this instance **cat** would first empty the file *paper1* then copy *paper2* into the empty *paper1*, leaving you without the first part of your paper.

(5) The **cat** sequence can be used to concatenate any number of files. Thus, the sequence

cat *file1 file2 file3 file4 file5* > *megafile* ⓡ

will create an enormous file (*megafile*) with copies of the contents of *file*1 to *file5*.

(6) **Combining Two Files:** It is also possible to **cat** one file directly onto the end of another, without affecting the second. The Shell command line

cat   *poem* >> *letter.mom* ⓡ

will append a copy of the *poem* file at the end of the file *letter.mom*.

The double arrowhead >> is interpreted to mean, "add the contents of the first file to whatever is in the second, without first deleting the second."

Due to the ease with which you can combine files, it is often a good idea to break a large file down into smaller and more easily managed files. These smaller files can be edited and revised separately. Whenever you want them re-assembled you can put them back together with the **cat** command.

(7) Before proceeding to the following review, log onto your account and try the following:

(a) Select two files and **cat** them together into a new third file.

(b) Visually edit the file you just married and give the two portions a divorce, using the **:w** command.

(c) From the Shell add one file to another with the command line **cat** *file1* >> *file2*.

(8) **Review Number One:** Consider the following questions:

(a) What *vi* command would you enter to place lines 1 to 33 of your current file in a new file named *debby.sue*?

———————————————————

(b) What *vi* command will replace the contents of an existing file named *schubert* with lines 29-200 of your current file?

———————————————————

(c) What *vi* command will append lines 36 through 74 of your current file onto the end of the file named *rick*?

———————————————————

(d) What *vi* command will *read in* the content of the file named *magoo* at line 40 of your current file? ——————————————

(e) What Shell command sequence would create a new file named *tortie* holding the contents of files named *sarah* and *peter*?

———————————————————

Answers: (a) :1,33 **w** *debby.sue*   (b) :29,200 **w!** *schubert*   (c) :36,74 **w** >> *rick*
(d) :40 **read** *magoo*   (e) **cat** *sarah peter* > *tortie*

File Name Expansion Characters

(1) The following lines are an example listing of the filenames in one of our directories:

mod1	mod5	mod9	smod1	tmod4
mod2	mod6	modindex	smod2	vi-summary
mod3	mod7	nmod1	tmod4	
mod4	mod8	nmod2	tmod4	

This group of file names will be used to demonstrate the role of file name expansion characters in performing various Shell functions.

All these files contain text relating to the Modules. For instance, *mod1* contains Module One, *mod2* contains Module Two, *modind* contains an index to the Modules, *smod1* contains a list of words misspelled in Module One, *vi-summary* is the table of *vi* commands, and *tmod4* contains a section of Module Four written out for testing a complex formatting command sequence. (Not to worry—you won't be quizzed on this material!)

(2) **Bracketed Filenames:** Sequential numbers or letters placed within brackets have a special meaning to the Shell. For instance, the Shell will understand the notation *mod[1-9]* to mean "act on all files from *mod1* through *mod9*." You can also bracket individual (non-sequential) filenames. For example, *mod[13569]* will be interpreted to mean "act on *mod1, mod3, mod5, mod6,* and *mod9.*"

Note that the characters enclosed in brackets are not separated by a space or comma, nor is there a space between the brackets and the rootname (here, *mod*).

(3) Suppose we wanted to list the files in this directory that contained an entire Module. The Shell command

ls *mod[1-9]*   ®

will list the names of the files containing entire Modules:

mod1 mod2 mod3 mod4 mod5
mod6 mod7 mod8 mod9

(4) ___ Create four short files using the same root in their filenames (for instance, call them *root1, root2, root3,* and *root4*). Each file should be very short. After all are created, use the brackets to list the files:

ls *root[#-#]*   ®

where *root* is the root you used for your filenames, and *#-#* are the alphabetical or numerical sequential labels.

Using file name expansion characters with the **ls** command is no big deal it itself. It is a good way to test what files will be accessed when you use these characters to perform a more dramatic Shell action, however. This is demonstrated in the following step.

(5) **Format and Line Print Files:** You can use a filename expansion character to sequentially format and print several files. For example, should we chose to format and print Modules One through Four we would enter this Shell Command sequence:

nroff -ms *mod[1-4]* | **lpr**   ®

Files *mod1* through *mod4* would then be formatted and printed together. *Page numbering will be continuous.*

(6) **Matching Any Set of Characters (∗):** The command

ls *mod∗*   ®

would yield this list of file names:

mod1   mod2   mod3   mod4 mod5
mod6   mod7   mod8   mod9 modindex

The ∗ matches *any one or more characters.* Thus the Shell command **ls** *m∗* would list all filenames (regardless of length) beginning with the letter *m.* The Shell command **ls** *∗m* would list all filenames (regardless of length) ending with the letter *m.*

(7) **Matching a Single Character:** The command

?mod2   ®

will generate this list of file names:

smod2   nmod2

The **?** matches any *single* character. As another example, the Shell command

ls *mod?*   ®

would list all filenames of four characters length beginning with the letters *mod.*

Your effectiveness with the commands introduced in this Module can be increased if you will name the component files of a large project *filename1 filename2 filename3 filename4 filename5* where *filename* is the *same root name* (the above examples have used the "word" *mod*). This root name obviously should have specific meaning to you. It could, for example, be the topic of your paper or series of programs.

(8) **Review Number Two:** Consider the following questions:

    (a)   What Shell command sequence will format the files named *manic1, manic2, manic3,* and *manic4?* _____

    (b)   What Shell command sequence will format the files named *apaper, bpaper, dpaper,* and *tpaper?* _____

    (c)   What files will be formatted with the following Shell command sequence: **nroff** *city[1-3]* _____

    (d)   What filenames could be listed with the **ls** *tree** command? _____

    (e)   What filenames could be listed with the following command: **ls** *?head** _____

Answers: (a) **nroff** *manic[1-4]*   (b) **nroff** *[abdt]paper*   (c) *city1 city2 city3* (d) all filenames beginning with the word *tree*   (e) all filenames beginning with any character followed by the word *head* and finishing with any other character(s).

Summary Table of Filename Expansion Characters

Character	Function
*	matches any string of characters
?	matches any single character
[ ]	matches any characters enclosed in brackets
[-]	matches any sequential range of characters

Several options are available to structure how *nroff* prepares the final copy of your paper. Options can be used to specify that only part of your paper is to be formatted. For instance, only page 9 would be printed using the following **nroff** command:

nroff -o9 $\boxed{\textit{filename}}$ | **lpr**   ®

The option (minus sign, lower case o, 9) must immediately follow the *nroff* command separated by a space.

If you want a file to be given page numbers starting with page ten, another option is available to you **(-n10)**. This is very convenient if the file is actually the second section of a paper and the first nine page section has already been formatted.

Each option is inserted into the **nroff** Shell Command line which formats and prints your paper. The presence of an option is indicated to UNIX by the inclusion of a single minus sign (-) followed *immediately* by the name of the option. You can use more than one option (for instance both the option to limit output to specified pages and the option to halt after every so many pages). However, all options must appear between **nroff** and the *filename*, and there must be a space *before* each minus (-) sign in the command line.

The general Shell command line for indicating a *nroff* option is:

nroff $\boxed{\textit{-option}}$ $\boxed{\textit{filename}}$ | **lpr**   ®

A Table of *Selected Nroff Options* follows as the last page of this Module. Additional options exist and can be learned through accessing the on-line *UNIX Programmer's Manual* with the **man** *nroff* command.

Selected Nroff Options

Option	Function
-o#	(minus lowercase o) Limits output to only those pages indicated by the # provided. For example, pages 3 through 5 only would be indicated as -o3-5 . You could ask for all pages up to page 6 with the notation -o-6 . You could ask for all pages after page 4 with the notation -o4- (*minus, lower case o, 4, minus*).
-n#	Numbers the first page of text # . For example, the option -n14 would cause the first page of your paper to sport page number 14, with the second page as 15.
-s#	Halts output every # pages. The option -s1 is useful in nroff if you are producing your finished paper on a typewriter-like printer and wish to hand feed individual sheets of high quality paper. Output resumes when you press **SPACEBAR**. Usually **-s** without an argument is set to be one page.

Module Nineteen
Phototypesetting with Troff & Troff -ms

Introduction

The UNIX *troff* text processing system interprets formatting commands in files to produce typeset quality output, such as the text of this book. The content of this Module is intended as an *introduction* to typesetting. For a more detailed examination of the topic consult the *Nroff/Troff User's Manual* and *A Troff Tutorial*, available from Bell Laboratories or your favorite computer science bookstore.

Prerequisites

You will be able to use this Module once you:

(1) Have mastered the use of formatting instructions (Modules Five and Nine);

(2) Are acquainted with advanced Shell commands (Module Six); and

(3) Have access to a phototypesetter on your UNIX system.

Objectives

Upon completion of this Module you should be able to:

(1) Use *troff* or *troff -ms* formatting instructions to specify the basic type size and style desired when typesetting a document;

(2) Determine type size and style for section headings and specific words or characters within a document;

(3) Utilize special *troff* characters.

Procedure

The procedure section of this Module contains four parts. The first section provides an overview of the *troff* text formatter. Section two introduces specific *troff* requests. The third section describes how *troff* keeps track of such variables as point size and line length. The final section considers how to use *troff* with the *-ms* macros.

The troff Text Formatter

troff is a text formatter just as is *nroff*. The *troff* system interprets the commands embedded in a file to format text for a photo-typesetter in the same way that *nroff* is used to format text for a line printer or terminal. When preparing a document for photo-typesetting you employ the same basic formatting instructions that you have already used with *nroff* to specify paragraphs, spaces, indents, and centered text. In addition to the *nroff* formatting options you have already used to produce typewriter-like print, the phototypesetter has the ability to vary the size of type (*point size*), and style of type (fonts: **Bold**, Roman, and *Italic*) used in the printing of the formatted text.

If you include *troff* instructions in a file, that file can still be sent to *nroff* to be formatted for a line printer. In most cases the line printer cannot accommodate your type changing requests, so *nroff* simply ignores them. The *troff* system parallels the *nroff* system—both are text formatters. *troff* is not a preprocessor to *nroff* (as are *tbl* and *neqn*). You do not send a file first to one and then the other—you select one *or* the other.

Determining Type Characteristics

This first section will illustrate how to determine point size and font of output using *troff* commands without the use of the *-ms* macro package.

(1) **Point Size:** The size of the typeface used in printing a document is measured in *points*. Most of the text in this book is set in 11 point type. A point is 1/72 of an inch: thus, six point type is 1/12 inch high, while thirty-six point type is ½ inch high.

Point Sizes Available on troff

The point sizes usually available on *troff* are:

6 point type: Six point type is of little use, except in advertisements for eye doctors. 12345#$%&

7 point type: Seven point type is not much of an improvement .12345!#$%&

8 point type: Eight points is a dull basketball quarter. 12345!#$%&

9 point type: Nine point type is often used as book type, but is hard to read for many people. 12345!#$%&

10 point type: When in the course of human events, it becomes necessary for 12345!#$%&

11 point type: When in the course of human events, it becomes necessary 12345!#$%&

12 point type: When in the human events course it became necessary 12345!#$%&

14 point type: The course was a necessary human event. 12345!#$%&

16 point type: The necessary human events course 12345!#$%&

18 point type: Human events are a necessary course. 12345!#$%&

20 point type: A humane, necessary course. 12345!#$%&

22 point type: Necessity, thy name is course. 12345!#$%&

24 point type: Are coarse human events necessary? 12345!#$%&

28 point type: Hopefully not. 12345!#$%&

36 point type: We hope. 12345!#$%&

(2) **Unspecified Point Size:** The default point size setting for most *troff* systems is:

9 point type, which is the point size of this line; or
10 point type, which was specified for this line.

Unless you specify a different value, the formatted text will be in the *default* point size.

(3) **Specifying Point Size:** To specify a different point size for some portion of text, you must include a *troff* instruction as the line in your file *immediately preceding* the line or lines of text you want formatted in a new point size. For example, if the following lines are included in a file, the **.ps 14** will be read as a point size request and the lines which follow will be set in 14 point type.

.ps*14*
This is the beginning of text set at 14 point type.
All text will be printed in 14 point type until
a new instruction for some different point size is included.
.ps*11*
This is the first line of type in the eleven point size.

The formatted typeset output will be:

This is the beginning of text set at 14 point type. All text will be printed in 14 point type until a new instruction for some different point size is included. This is the first line of type in the eleven point size.

To change point size you place the command **.ps** $\boxed{number}$ as the line preceding the text you want set in $\boxed{number}$ point size type. The change begins with the next line of the file. Whole lines are set in specified type sizes when you use the **.ps** $\boxed{number}$ command.

When using *troff*, point size commands are *one-way* commands. Once you specify the point size, all text will be set in that size until you instruct otherwise. (If you find that your point size specifications are mysteriously cancelled at the start of each new paragraph you are probably using the *-ms* macros. Be certain to read the *-ms macros* section of this Module.)

(4) **Changing Point Size Within a Line:** You do not have to limit yourself to specifying the text point size for entire lines of your file. Should you need to make a change within a specific line (or even within a word) you place a \s $\boxed{number}$ in front of the character *in the line* where the change is to occur.

For example, consider:

this dis\s16play of te\s11xt

When formatted, this appears as:

this display of text.

In the previous paragraph we played around with the point size in the words: "within a line or even a word." The following text line—with embedded commands—was used to format that line:

. . . within a line (or e\s14*ve*\s11*n*
wi\s11*t*\s14*hi*\s11*n*\s11
a w\s14*o*\s16*rd*\s11*) you place . . . .*

(5) **Vertical Spacing:** In music, the notes which are played are essential—but so is the silence between the notes. In setting the type for a printed page, the white space between lines of type is as important as the size of the type used. This book is set with a vertical spacing of 13 point, because the text is 11 point. The vertical spacing of *troff* output can be changed. For instance, by including the instruction:

.vs 9

in the text the amount of space between lines is reduced. The net effect is to put the type close together and make it difficult to read. Usually the vertical spacing is set to be two points larger than the size of the type selected for the text.

To change the vertical spacing include the command:

.vs $\boxed{number}$

Font Selection for Text

The phototypesetter usually offers 3 or 4 separate text fonts, such as Times Roman (the standard or default typeface), **Times Boldface**, *Times Italic*, plus a special character font which includes Greek letters, mathematical symbols and other gems. As is the case with point size changes, font changes can occur either between lines or **within** a *line* (or *word*).

(6) **Italics:** The *troff* command to change *font* to I*talics* is:

.ft I

When the **.ft I** command is placed alone on a line in the text, all lines which follow are set in I*talics*. The **.ft** command is a one-way command. It remains in force until a new font specification is entered.

For instance:

> It is easy to change fonts when typesetting.
> **.ft I**
> This text will be set in Italics.
> In fact all text will be in Italics
> until a new font is selected.
> **.ft R**
> After another font specification command
> is entered,
> the text is set in the new font.

When the file is formatted the resulting output is:

> It is easy to change fonts when typesetting. *This text will be set in Italics. In fact all text will be in Italics until a new font is selected.* After another font specification command is entered, the text is set in the new font.

(7) **Boldface:** Likewise, to set type in **Boldface** employ the *nroff* one-way command

.ft B

(8) **Roman:** To change the type used to **R**oman, the command is:

.ft R

The following example demonstrates all three fonts:

> .ft B
> Here I feel bold,
> .ft I
> here Italic,
> .ft R
> here Roman.

The following formatted sentence reflects these various moods:

> **Here I feel bold,** *here Italic,* here Roman.

(9) **Changing Fonts within a Line:** To change fonts in the middle of a word or sentence, enter one of the following commands ahead of the characters you want set in a particular type:

\fI for *Italic*,

\fB for **Bold**, and

\fR for Roman.

Place the change font instruction immediately preceding whatever character is to be set in the new font.

For instance, the following line in a file

\fBdis\fIease\fR

produces the formatted: **dis***ease*. To interpret the example, the \fB instructs the formatter to shift to Bold type. It then sets **d i s** in Bold type. The \fI changes the font to Italics, thus the letters *e a s e* are set in Italics. The last \fR merely resets the font to Roman for whatever follows.

Another example:

\fBantidis\fIestablish\fRmentar\fBian\fIism\fR

appears as:

antidis*establish*mentar**ian***ism*

Note: When using *troff* without the *-ms* macros a font change will remain in effect until you specify a new font.

(10) **Underlining and Boxes:** *troff* does **not** interpret the *nroff* command .ul to mean underline the next line of text. Rather, it will *italicize the next line of text.* Text may be underlined with *troff*, but it is a somewhat complicated task. Additionally, boxes can be drawn around words or blocks of text using *troff* commands. It is also a difficult task. If you have the *-ms* macros available to you it is much easier to use the boxing and underlining capabilities of that macro package. If you would like to learn how to draw lines or format boxes using *troff* commands alone, refer to the *Nroff/Troff User's Manual.*

(1) **One-Way troff Requests:** *troff* keeps track of the specific line length, point size, font, and several other one-way commands which determine the formatting of your text. Every time it starts formatting a line of text, *troff* checks its memory for the specified point size, font, line length, etc. *troff* begins with a "default" value for each of the variables (10 point type, Roman font etc.) which it will use until you specify otherwise.

Troff Requests and Default Values		
Input Command	**Default**	**What it Governs**
.ps #	10 point	Point size
.ss #	12/36em	Size of space character
.ft *F*	Roman	Type font used
.pl #	11 inches	Page length
.po #	0 inches	Page offset printed
.vs #	12 point	Vertical spacing
.ll #	6.5 inches	Line length

Note on Table of Troff Requests and Default Values: The # symbol is never used in the commands. You substitute an appropriate value in inches (3.5i), points (38p), centimeters (11c), picas (22P), or Em's (3m) for the #. The *F* is the appropriate Font: **B,R,** or **I**. When you are using *troff* without the *-ms* macros, the values you set for any of these variables will remain in force until you specify new values. They are ordinary one-way commands.

When you enter a font, point size or line length instruction, (**.ps** *12*, **.ll** *7.5i*, or **.ft B**) *troff* stores the information in its memory. Then, when *troff* checks for the latest instruction as it begins formatting the next line in your file, it finds the new specifications for font, point size or line length. It will then use the new instructions as it formats the line.

(2) **Special troff Characters:** One of the more useful aspects of typesetters is their ability to print characters not available on a typewriter. A sample of some interesting characters available with *troff* is presented in the following Table of Special Font Characters.

Special Font Characters			
Input	**Character**	**Input**	**Character**
\(sc	§	\(+-	±
\(aa	´	\(cu	∪
\(ga	`	\(ib	⊆
\(*a	α	\(if	∞
\(*b	β	\(is	∫
\(*g	γ	\(pt	∝
\(*D	Δ	\(es	∅
\(*H	Θ	\(br	|
\(*S	Σ	\(rh	☞
\(*W	Ω	\(lh	☜
\(->	→	\(ci	○
\(<-	←	\(ct	¢
\(ua	↑	\(bu	●
\(da	↓	\(14	¼
\(dg	†	\(12	½

Note on Table of Special Font Characters: Each of the characters listed can be used by including the input code as a "word" in the text where you want the character placed. The point size of these creatures has been changed to 12 to better highlight their appearance.

For example, the following line in a file:

It is as easy as \ (*a \ (*b \ (*g .

produces the following formatted line of text:

It is as easy as α β γ .

A more complete list of the special font characters is contained in the *Nroff/Troff User's Manual.*

(3) **Obtaining Output:** Because the *troff* system is a text formatter just like the *nroff* system, you send a file to the *troff* formatter (for phototypesetting) *instead of* the *nroff* formatter (for typewriter quality output). You will normally use a Shell command similar to the following to send your file to the phototypesetter:

troff [*filename*]   ®

If there is a queuing system at your location you might use:

troff -Q [*filename*]   ®

(4) **File Length for Typesetting:** Most phototypesetting machines have a maximum page length to the files which can be printed. A maximum length of 35 feet (about 35 pages) is not unusual. Before sending a file that is longer than several pages, be sure to inquire about the page length maximum in effect at your location. You may wish to discuss submitting longer jobs or breaking a long file into smaller parts with the *typeset operator.* (Note: typeset operators are in fact real, flesh-and-blood, genuine people.)

Using troff with the -ms Macros to Determine Type Characteristics

The most important difference between typesetting with *troff* alone and *troff -ms* is the way the variables such as point size and type font are handled. When you set the point size using *troff*, the size specified remains in effect until you specify a new one. This is not the case with *-ms*.

(1) **Paragraph Resets:** If you set the point size with a **.ps 16** command (a *troff* command) you would expect *all* of the text from that point on to be set in 16 point type. This is in fact how *troff* alone will respond. With *troff -ms*, however, only the text between the **.ps** instruction and the *next paragraph* macro will be in the requested (16 point) type size.

As soon as an *-ms* paragraph macro is encountered, the point size will be reset to the size stipulated in the *-ms number register* associated with point size. We have noted in several places how the *-ms* paragraph macros have a lot of unexpected effects written into them (this topic is considered in some detail in Modules Nine: *Advanced Formatting* and Twenty: *Macro Construction*). The font, type size, and a host of other page management variables are reset to the values in the appropriate number registers every time you invoke one of the *-ms* paragraph macros. For instance, in the case where the **.ps16** point size command is included in the file, the text will be set in 16 point type, until the next paragraph macro is encountered, where the point size is reset to the default 10 point (unless you have specified otherwise).

Every time an *-ms* paragraph macro is encountered, the formatter checks the *number register* named **PS** to see what point size is specified. Unless you have stipulated otherwise, the **.nr PS** register is set for 10 point type. After the formatter checks the register, it sets the type in 10 point. If you want a different *default* point size, you must adjust the number register to another value (such as 12 point). This way every time a paragraph calls for resetting the point size the value you set will be read.

To set a document in 12 point type you must change the point size number register to read "12 point." To do so include the following command as one of the first lines in a file:

.nr PS *12*

With this command the *number* r*egister* is now set at P*oint* S*ize 12*. Whenever the paragraph macros reset the point size they will reset to the value of 12 point.

(2) **Changing Default Values:** The *troff -ms* formatting process begins with deciding upon the basic page and type size characteristics of your paper. You then enter instructions for the appropriate

number registers, and place this material at the beginning of the file. For example, suppose you want lines to be 5 inches long (for 7 inch paper with one inch margins) and a 9 inch page length, set in 11 point type with vertical spacing of 13 point. You would enter the following commands at the top of your file:

> **.nr LL** *5i*
> **.nr PS** *11*
> **.nr VS** *13*
> **.pl** *9i*

Note that the page length control is the *nroff* instruction **.pl** and not an *-ms* number register. There is no *-ms* number register associated with page length. Page length is a one-way *nroff* command which is not reset by *-ms* paragraph macros.

Summary of -ms Number Registers		
Register	**Function**	**Default**
LL	Line length of text	6 inches
PO	Page offset	0 inches
FL	Line length of footnotes	5.5 inches
PI	Paragraph indentation	5 spaces
QI	Indentation of .QP paragraphs	5 spaces
HM	Header margin	1 inch
FM	Footer margin	1 inch
PD	Vertical offset of paragraphs	1v in *nroff* 0.3v in *troff*
PS	Point size of printout	10
VS	Vertical spacing	12

(3) **Boxes Around Text:** The *-ms* macros provide an easy way to box one or more words of text in your file. To box a single word you use the command **.BX** *word* with the word placed next to the command. For example, the following text in your file:

> *being drawn around the word*
> **.BX** *school*
> *(perhaps reflecting*
> *the school yard.)*

will result in a box being drawn around the word school (perhaps reflecting the school yard).

To box two or more words—or even entire paragraphs—you use the **.B1** and **.B2** commands. Place the text block within the commands **.B1** (to begin the box) and **.B2** (to end the box). The *-ms* macros will respond with a box of text.

> **.B1**
> *These lines of text in a file*
> *will be boxed.*
> *Note that the box commands*
> *precede and follow the to-be-boxed*
> *text.*
> **.B2**

These lines of text in a file will be boxed. Note that the box commands precede and follow the to-be-boxed text.

(4) **Underlining Text:** The *-ms* macro package will allow you to underline text. You must *individually* underline each word, however. The command **.UL** word will underline one word at a time. To underline several words, you need to use the **.UL** word command for each *word*. This means that

> **.UL** *each*
> **.UL** *word*
> **.UL** *must*
> **.UL** *be*
> **.UL** *individually*
> **.UL** *underlined.*

The above display illustrates the fact that, with the *-ms* macros, <u>each</u> <u>word</u> <u>must</u> <u>be</u> <u>individually</u> <u>underlined</u>.

This completes the introduction to phototypesetting with *troff* and *troff-ms*. Additional information is available in the *Nroff/Troff User's Manual* and *A Troff Tutorial*, produced by Bell Labs.

The developer for typesetting.

Module Twenty
Macro Construction

Introduction

In Module Five you used *nroff* formatting commands (also called *nroff requests*) to instruct *nroff* about how to format your text file. Module Nine described the *-ms* macro commands (also referred to as *macro calls*) which allow you to format your work with greater ease than is possible with *nroff* requests alone. Module Nineteen introduced the requests used to specify how *troff* should format more eloquent output for production on the phototypesetter. This Module illustrates how the *-ms* macros have been constructed from *nroff* requests. This information will start you on the road to understanding how to build your own macros to meet your individual needs.

Prerequisites

Before starting this Module you should be able to:

(1) Use *nroff* requests (Module Five) and the *-ms* macros (Module Nine) to have your file formatted; and

(2) Use *troff* requests (Module Nineteen) to perform fancy formatting feats (suggested only for section two of this Module).

Objectives

After completing this Module you should be able to:

(1) Describe the differences between an *nroff* request and a macro call;

(2) Access macros and macro packages in several different ways;

(3) Build basic macros tailored to fit your own needs; and

(4) Determine the compatibility of *nroff* requests, the *-ms* macros and your own home-made macros based on the internal workings of the *-ms* macro package.

Procedure

This procedure section is divided into five parts. The first section presents several simple home-made macros and demonstrates how macros are built by bundling *nroff* requests. The second section describes how UNIX accesses macros. The workings of a fairly complex macro are illustrated in the third section. The fourth section examines how *nroff* fills text lines and determines *exactly* when commands are followed. The final section presents a look inside a simplified segment of the *-ms* macro package to illustrate how it works.

An Important Review

Recall that an *nroff* request (such as **.ul**) is an instruction to the *nroff* formatter about how your file is to be formatted. Macros (like those that make up the *-ms* macro package) are collections or bundles of *nroff* requests that can be called into action (hence the term *macro call*) with a single command (such as **.PP**). The *-ms* macro package is a set of macros designed to work together when used to format a file.

The *-ms* macros were created to make your formatting tasks easier. There may be instances, however, where your needs are not met by these pre-packaged formatting commands. The ability to create your own macros which will then perform complex, repetitious, or boring formatting tasks (and thereby saving you time and energy) can be quite helpful.

Home-Made Macros

(1) ___ Log onto your UNIX account.

(2) ___ When the Shell prompt appears type:

vi *context* ®

This new file (*context*) will be the practice file used in this Module's exercises.

(3) ___ Enter three paragraphs of text into your new file. Make each paragraph 3 or 4 sentences in length, and write about anything you wish. Begin each new paragraph with the appropriate *-ms* paragraph macro call (**.IP, .LP, .PP, .QP,** or **.XP**).

(4) **A Centered Heading Using nroff Requests:** How about placing a centered title above the material in paragraph two? This is accomplished with the following four lines of text.

___ Place these four lines after paragraph one and before the paragraph formatting macro for paragraph two:

```
.sp
.ce
.ul
Paragraph Two
```

The above four lines of text will space down, center, and underline the words comprising the centered title. In this case the centered title will be *Paragraph Two*. If you want some other title, replace the line *Paragraph Two* with whatever text you want.

(5) ___ When all four lines are entered, use the **ZZ** commands to write the buffer version of the file and return to the Shell.

(6) ___ Enter the Shell command line

nroff -ms *context* | **page** ®

to have a formatted version of *context* displayed on the screen. Paragraph two should appear with a centered title above it.

The four lines necessary to create the centered title required only a modest amount of work on your part. But what if you had a file which required 26 centered titles? One option would be to retype (or yank and put) the four lines all 26 times—a somewhat tedious task. This is where a *home-made macro* can do some of the work for you.

(7) **Your First Home-Made Macro:**

___ Move to the first line in your file and open a new line above with the **O** command. At the top of your file, enter the following 6 lines exactly as they appear here:

> **.de** *Ct*
> **.sp**
> **.ne** *4.1v*
> **.ce**
> **.ul**
> **..**

These six lines are interpreted as follows:

.de *Ct*   Indicates to *nroff* that the following lines, up to the next line containing only two dots (..), define (**.de** → de*fine*) the macro **Ct**. The **Ct** was chosen to remind us of *Cen*tered **t** *itle*.

.sp   Spaces down one line;

.ne *4.1v*   Requests *nroff* to make sure that at least four lines are available on this page: if not go on to the next page;

.ce   Centers the next line of text;

.ul   Underlines the next line of text; finally

..   Concludes this macro.

These six lines from **.de** *Ct* to **..** taken together define the macro *Ct*. Now whenever you have need of a centered title in this file the macro **.Ct** can be used.

The **.Ct** is entered into a file just as you would any other *-ms* macro call. The **Ct** macro calls for the centering and underlining of the next line in the file. Thus you first enter the macro call, then on the next line enter the text for a centered title.

(8) ___ Return to your *context* file. At the moment you have a series of *nroff* requests preceding the text for centered titles. (You entered them in Procedure Step 4.)

___ Position the cursor between the first two paragraphs and delete the *nroff requests* **.sp**, **.ce**, and **.ul** which are located just before the text for the centered title.

___ In place of those *nroff* requests enter the new macro call **.Ct** on a line by itself.

___ Repeat this procedure for each centered title you placed in the file. Your file should now contain the 6 lines defining the **Ct** macro followed by the three paragraphs originally written. Additionally there should be one or more **.Ct** macro calls preceding the text for centered titles. For instance, if the centered titles are *Paragraph Two* and *Paragraph Three*, your input file should appear something like the following:

> Macro Definitions
> **.LP**
> Some text that will be paragraph one.
> **.Ct**
> *Paragraph Two*
> **.PP**
> Some text that will be another paragraph.
> **.Ct**
> *Paragraph Three*
> More text.

(9) ___ When finished, write this file and return to the Shell (with the **ZZ** command).

(10) ___ To view the formatting effects of your new macro type:

nroff -ms context | page   ®

As the formatted version of your file is displayed on the screen note how the **Ct** macro acted on your paper (automatically spaced down, centered, and underlined each centered title). (Note: Some terminals are unable to properly display underlining on the screen. Your printed text can be appropriately underlined, even though on the screen it may appear incorrect.)

(11) **How nroff Uses Macros to Format:** The process of employing a macro definition and a subsequent macro call is quite complex:

(a) The macro definition must first be read by *nroff*;

(b) When *nroff* encounters a call for this macro in your file it internally replaces the call with the *nroff* requests which comprise the macro into the file at the same location;

(c) The *nroff* requests (that make up the macro and have been inserted) are interpreted and followed; and

(d) Your text then reflects the effects of this new macro.

In the case of the **Ct** macro this process translates as:

(a) *Nroff* will first read the 6 lines defining the **Ct** macro (which are located at the top of the file) and store this information for later use;

(b) When *nroff* encounters a .**Ct** macro call in your file it interprets it to mean "insert the *nroff* requests located inside the macro definition named **Ct** at this point;"

(c) Then *nroff* spaces down one vertical line (.**sp**), makes certain that there are 4.1 vertical spaces available (.**ne**), centers (.**ce**) and underlines (.**ul**) the next input line in your file; and voilà

(d) The very next line in your file (following the .**Ct** macro call) appears as a centered title.

You have completed and used your first home-made macro. Obviously macros of this type can be of great assistance. It is important to remember that a macro defined at the start of a file can be used anywhere in that file, but only within that one file.

(12) **Naming Home-Made Macros:** We named the macro **Ct** employing one upper case and one lower case letter. This "mixed case" convention is followed in naming home-made macros to avoid confusion with -*ms* (all upper case) and *nroff* (all lower case) formatting commands.

(13) **Creating a Macro File:** Suppose you needed to use your **Ct** macro in several files? You could re-type the 6 definition lines which make up the **Ct** macro at the top of each file (a tedious and somewhat tacky choice) or you could create a permanent macro file and

place the 6 lines in it. This macro file can then be processed along with whatever file you are formatting, so that your macros will be effective in any file you select.

___ From the Shell type:

vi *mac* ®

The file *mac* will be the name of your new file for *mac*ros.

___ Insert the six lines comprising the **Ct** macro definition into your *mac* file:

```
.de Ct
.sp
.ne 4.1v
.ce
.ul
..
```

When finished, write this new file and return to the Shell with the **ZZ** command.

___ Call up your *context* file for visual editing and remove the **Ct** macro definition contained in the first six lines of the file. When finished, write the file and return to the Shell.

Before investigating how to get *nroff* to use the macros located in the *mac* file, it would be useful to examine how *-ms* works.

(14) **The -ms Macros:** In using the *-ms* macro package you place calls to various *-ms* macros (such as **.PP**) in the body of your paper.

What causes *nroff* to read the *-ms* macro definitions [analogous to Step 11(a) above]? This reading occurs before the process of formatting your paper is begun, and is initiated with the Shell command line (**nroff -ms** *filename* | **lpr**). By placing the **-ms** option *after* the command **nroff** and *before* the name of the to-be-formatted file you cause *nroff* to read the *-ms* macro package definitions *before* it reads your file. The *-ms* macro package file contains the definitions of each of the *-ms* macros (for instance **.PP**). This information permits *nroff* to interpret the *-ms* macro calls placed within the body of your file.

To bring our discussion back to the current situation: How do you ask UNIX to read your *mac* file before formatting *context*? In a way similar to how *-ms* is read by the formatter *before* the file is read.

___ Enter the Shell command line:

nroff -ms *mac context* | **page**   ®

The file *mac* will now be read after the *-ms* macro package and before the file *context*. In the above command line *nroff* reads the file containing the *-ms* macros, then it reads the macro definition contained in your *mac* file. While formatting the file *context*, *nroff* refers to the definition of **Ct** as well as other *-ms* macro definitions when each macro is called for in the trailing *context* file.

Did your macro definition and call work? If not, check to make sure you entered the commands exactly as demonstrated.

(15) **Quote Paragraphs:** The *-ms* quote paragraph call **.QP** brings the left and right margins in, but leaves the text spacing unchanged. Writers usually prefer to have quoted paragraphs single spaced. The following macro will do just that.

___ Append the following 11 lines to the end of your *mac* file:

```
.de Qs
.sp
.ls 1
.in  +10m
.ll  −10m
..
.de Qe
.ls 2    \"assumes  double spacing is wanted
.in  −10m
.ll  +10m
..
```

These 11 lines define *two* quote paragraph macros and demonstrate how one-way macros are defined. The **Qs** (*Quote start*) macro will:

(a) Skip one space (**.sp**);

(b) Set the line spacing to single space (**.ls** *1*); and

(c) move both the left (**.in** *+10m*) and right margins (**.ll** *−10m*) in ten ems (an em is a spacing unit used by *nroff* and *troff*).

The **Qe** (*Quote end*) macro is needed to reset the line spacing to double spacing and to restore the original left and right margins. You may find use for these two modest macros in simplifying your formatting chores.

(16) **Using the Quote Paragraph Macro:** Call up your *context* file for visual editing. With the following two additions, the second paragraph will appear formatted as a quote paragraph:

    (a)   Replace the *-ms* paragraph macro used to format the second paragraph with a **.Qs** (place a **.Qs** before the first line of text in the second paragraph); and

    (b)   Place a **.Qe** after the last line of that paragraph—before the next paragraph macro.

(17) ___ Now employ the Shell command line:

nroff -ms *mac context* | **page**   ®

Your text file will be formatted and you can see the effects of the new quote paragraph macro.

Accessing Macros

Thus far you have been introduced to two methods of accessing macros:

    (a)   You can place the macro definitions *within* the file (as was done in the earliest exercises in this Module). This method is the procedure of choice in the case of special purpose macros that are only used in one text file; or

    (b)   You can place the macro definitions in a separate file and have that file read during the nroff process (for example, **nroff** *mac context* | **page**). This second method is most similar to how the *-ms* macros are accessed.

A third method of accessing your own macros will now be presented.

(1) **The Nroff Source Command:** If you regularly employ a self-designed macro package, there is an *nroff* request that will both save you time and impress your friends.

(2) ___ Call up your *context* file for visual editing. Insert the following as the *first line* of the file

.so *mac*

where *mac* is the name of the file containing your macro definitions. This command instructs *nroff*—during the formatting process—to place the *mac* file at the beginning of your *context* file (to **so**urce in the *mac* file). It has the identical action as naming the *mac* file in the *nroff* Shell command line. After inserting this line write the *context* file and return to the Shell.

(3) ___ Now use the command

nroff -ms *context* | **page** ®

to have your text file formatted. Notice how you do not need to include *mac* in the Shell command line. Your *mac* file will be read by *nroff* because of the **so**urce command, located on line 1 of your *context* file.

Rethink—Remember Time:

(a) What *nroff* command indicates the beginning of a new macro named **Xy** ? _____

(b) What command indicates the conclusion of a macro definition? _____

(c) Where would the definition for a macro be placed to have it available only for use anywhere in the file named *david.waas*?
_____

(d) Suppose a set of home-made macros is in a file named *my-macros*. What Shell command would have a file named *lillian* formatted using only these home-made macros and *nroff*?
_____

(e) What formatting command—located as the first line of a file—will have *nroff* access the macro definitions located in the file named *my-macros*? _____

(f) Suppose the **.so** *my-macros* command is the first line of a file named *kenny-joyce*. What Shell command line will have the *kenny-joyce* file formatted using only the *my-macros* and *nroff*?
_____

Answers: (a) **.de** *Xy*   (b) **..**   (c) at beginning of file *david.waas*
(d) **nroff** *my-macros lillian*   *(e)* **.so** *my-macros*   *(f)* **nroff** *kenny-joyce*

The Workings of a Complex Macro

Arguments Within Macros: Frankly, it is very easy to get into arguments with macros—but avoid it. They always win.

(1) The following macro will leave a specified amount of blank space in your file for you to insert a figure or diagram. It will *automatically* label the space *Figure 1* the first time the macro is used, *Figure 2* the second time, and *Figure 3* the third time it is used, etc. Such high powered antics are possible because macros accept arguments.

___ Append the following 8 line **F*i*gure** macro to your *mac* file:

```
.nr Fg 0
.de Fg
.ul
.ce
.nr Fg \\n(Fg+1
Figure \\n(Fg
.sp \\$1
..
```

When finished, use the **ZZ** command to save the changes made to this file and return to the Shell. (The workings of this gem will be explained shortly).

(2) To leave space for two figures in your text, append these 12 lines to the end of your *context* file. (The commands should be entered exactly as are presented here; the text can be changed to suit your interests):

```
.sp
```
The following figure illustrates the effect of practice time on learning.
```
.Fg 3.5i
```
Clearly, when a person actually practices the commands they are remembered more easily than

when the person attempts to just read the book.
.sp 2
If the preceding figure didn't convince you,
this one certainly will.
.Fg 2.5i
which concludes (or precludes?) our argument.

___ Use the usual **ZZ** command to write the file and return to the Shell.

(3)   ___ Because the **.so** *mac* command is the first line in the context file, you can enter the command:

nroff -ms   *context* | **page**   ®

Examine the results of your figure macros. When you feel comfortable using these macros read on and discover *why* they work.

Behind the Lines in the Macro War: The remainder of this Module explores aspects of *nroff* and macro construction which are rather technical. Freak not—it is not necessary to master every detail in the explanations of how macros work until you begin seriously writing your own macros. For now you should read through it to obtain an overview of how the break, no break, backslash, and title line commands work. You can give this material a second (and third) reading later on.

(4)   **Interpreting the .Fg Macro:** You were introduced in Module Nine to the role of *number registers* in the formatting process. The *-ms* macros use number registers to control overall formatting tasks such as line length and page offset. Number registers are also used internally, by *nroff*, to keep track of many things including the current page number. As you read the following line-by-line description of the **.Fg** macro note how number registers were used.

The process of using macros begins with creating their definitions and then including the definitions either at the beginning of the text file or in a separate file consisting of macros. In either case *nroff* must read the macro definitions *before* it reads the text file. In the initial reading, *nroff* reads the file line by line, starting from the first line. All definitions of macros are transferred to *nroff* internal memory. Also any commands *not* inside the macro definition are performed in this initial pass through. (For instance, number registers can be set to specific values in this first reading.)

Later, when *nroff* is formatting the text, *nroff* will find calls for the macros in the text file (for instance **.Fg** *3.5i*). At that point *nroff* locates the definition of the macro in its memory and executes those requests.

Annotation of Requests in the **Fg** *Macro*

.nr *Fg 0*
A number register is named *Fg* and is set to the value zero. This number register request must appear *outside* the macro definition (which begins with the next line: **.de** *Fg*), so that the number register *Fg* can be set to zero before the macro is called during formatting. It is read (and executed) by *nroff* only during *nroff*'s first pass through the macro. Because this number register command is located outside of the macro definition, it is not read when the macro is called (with the **.Fg** command) during the actual formatting of your paper. When **Fg** is called, only the lines between the **.de** *Fg* and the trailing **..** are read.

.de *Fg*
This begins the definition of the *Fg* macro.

.ul
Underline the next line of text.

.ce
Center the next line of text.

.nr *Fg* \\n(*Fg+1*
The **.nr** *Fg* translates as "set the number register *Fg* to whatever value follows the space character in this line." If this line were **.nr** *Fg 5*, the number register would be set to *5*. However, what follows the *Fg* is not a number but directions as to where the formatter can locate the needed number. (We are beginning a short game of Hide and Go Seek.)

The \\n(means that the value the formatter needs (to set the *Fg* number register) is not here either, but is stored in a number register, whose name follows these symbols.

The **Fg+1** identifies the number register, (namely itself, **Fg**) but the **+1** stipulates "read the present value in **Fg**, then add 1 to it." Thus, whatever value is in **Fg** will be increased by one unit and then put back in **Fg**. Thus the numbers ascribed to each figure by the **Fg** macro will advance by one each time the macro is called.

Figure \\n(Fg

When the first **Fg** macro call is located in your file, the word *Figure* and the number held in the **Fg** register are printed. The \\n(Fg prints the current value of the **Fg** register (*1* the first time the macro is called, *2* the second time, etc.). Because the two prior requests in the macro definition (**.ce** and **.ul**) have been read, this line is centered and underlined (Italics in *troff*). This line results in *Figure 1* the first time the macro is called, *Figure 2* the second, etc.

.sp \\$1

This last line of the macro definition provides the space for the figure in the formatted output. If this line were **.sp** *5i*, five inches would always be left in the output for the figure. Instead, \\$1 space is called for. When *nroff* reads a request followed by a \\$1 it interprets this to mean "insert the first argument to the macro call here." You determined the amount of space when you attached the argument to the **.Fg** macro call. You entered the command **.Fg** *3.5* for Figure 1 in your file [in step (2)] and the resulting Figure 1 had 3.5 inches of space in the output.

The *3.5* is the *argument* for the **.Fg** macro call. That argument is *read into* the macro because of the \\$1 request on this line. When you put the macro call for the figure macro in your text file [step (2)] you followed the first call with *3.5i* and the second call with *2.5i*. Each time *nroff* processes the macro call (whenever it appears in your file) it inserts the number you entered following the **Fg** in place of the **$1**. This gives you *3.5* inches of blank space for the first figure and *2.5* inches of space for the second.

..   Ends the definition of the *.Fg* macro.

(5) **The Mystery of the Double Backslashes:** The characters that cause *nroff* to *read in* the first argument to your **.Fg** macro are **$1**. Note that references to both number registers (**n**(*Fg*)) and arguments (**$1**) within an *nroff* request begin with two backslashes (\\). Why is one needed, let alone two??

To the *nroff* command interpreter, the \ is the *escape* character. The purpose of the *nroff* escape character is to tell *nroff* to accept what follows as a command and not text. (This is the same role the [ESC] key plays within the visual editor.)

When *nroff* comes to a \ it removes it and interprets the following characters as a command, *unless* the next character is also a \, which it then leaves alone.

Commands which have double backslashes are contained within macro definitions. If only one backslash were used, *nroff* would remove the backslash, interpret the command that followed and act upon it. As a result, *nroff* would interpret and try to act on the commands *inside* macros during its first pass through the macro — although in this first pass *nroff* is to only read the macro definitions and store them for use when called.

The second backslash is necessary to "conceal" the rest of the request from *nroff* when the macro definition is first read.

For example, without the two backslashes in the line .sp **$1**, *nroff* would immediately act on the instructions. It would expect an argument to appear, though none would be provided. After all, this is *nroff's* first exposure to the macro, and is intended only to inform *nroff* of the existence of the macros and their definitions. You do not want *nroff* to act on the macro instructions until after it begins formatting the text of your file. During the first reading of the macro file *nroff* removes the first \, then finding another, moves on quietly. Later when *nroff* returns to the macro to execute it (as the result of a macro call) there will be only one backslash left. This time through the backslash is removed, and the command is exposed and followed.

Summary: The role of the second backslash is to "conceal" the rest of the request from *nroff* when the macro definition is first read. This first backslash is "peeled off" at the time the macro is initially read so that the rest of the request can be interpreted and acted on when the macro is actually *used*. This leaves a single backslash to identify this as a command when the macro call is processed during the formatting of your paper.

(6) **A Note of Caution:** The macros introduced in this Module were carefully designed to work with the *-ms* macro package. Be aware that not all home-made macros will be compatible with the *-ms* macro package. The source of most problems is the way *-ms* uses internal number registers. The *-ms* paragraph macros reset various number register values in a multitude of strange ways. Unless you understand and anticipate their actions, your macros may not work as you expect.

For example, the **.RS** macro call resets a number register that controls the left indent level. All *-ms* paragraph macros check this number register to determine the current indent level. This is why you can include one or more paragraphs between the **.RS** and the **.RE** and each paragraph will appear appropriately positioned on the page. Your home-made paragraph macros—unless given explicit instructions—do not access this register. Thus, they will be unaffected by a preceding **.RS** command. This means your home-made paragraph macro may not format text with the desired left margin.

If you want to use home-made macros in conjunction with the *-ms* macros (or whatever macro package you employ) it is advisable to test the compatibility of your home-made macros with the macro package you use. This notion of compatibility will become clearer once you complete the final sections of this Module.

A Look Inside Nroff

(1) **The Break Command:** It is sometimes necessary to make sure that *nroff* starts a new line at some point in your text. For example, you might want to produce output something like:

> For most people, *nroff* can be very frustrating. Although it is a very powerful formatter, it is difficult to learn for the following reasons:
> (a) There is a large variety of very specific commands which affect each other in strange ways, and
> (b) The effects of commands are not immediately observable.

The above output was produced with the following input lines:

> *For most people,*
> *.I nroff*
> *can be very frustrating.*
> *Although it is a very powerful formatter,*
> *it is difficult to learn*
> *for the following reasons:*
> *.br*
> *(a) There is a large variety*
> *of very specific commands*
> *which affect each other in strange ways, and*
> *.br*
> *(b) The effects of commands are*
> *not immediately observable.*

The **br***eak* (**.br**) command requests that a new output line be started. The last line of text *before* the break appears is entered but not adjusted to meet the right margin. Even though there is still room in the output line for more words, the line will be printed as it is. The text will not be adjusted to stretch from the left to the right margin by adding additional spaces.

Note that a **.sp** command will accomplish the same effect while also skipping a vertical space.

(2) **Filling and the Break Function:** As mentioned in Module Five, *filling* is the process of joining short input lines together to create output lines of approximately equal length. How does *nroff* perform this function?

(a) Starting with the first text line in a file, *nroff* collects this line and places it in its internal memory.

(b) Next *nroff* enters as many of the words from this input line as will fit onto the first output line. Usually all of the words from the first input line will fit on the first output line (because we all type short lines, right?!).

(c) *Nroff* then reads the next input line. If it contains text, *nroff* uses the text to continue filling the first output line. Soon the first output line contains as many words as can fit. At this point there are frequently several words from the last collected input line left over. There is no room to include them in the current output line. It is full.

(d) In this case, *nroff* stores these words in memory and reads the next input line.

(e) If this line contains more text, it is added to the words already in memory, and *nroff* starts filling the next output line.

(f) If, however, *nroff* encounters a format command as the next input line it must decide what to do with the text left over from the last input line (or lines) which it has stored in its memory.

There are two possibilities.

   (i) *Nroff* could enter the remaining text on the next output line and then perform the command function (i.e. if *nroff* encounters the **.sp** command, it could print the remaining text, then skip a line), or

   (ii) *Nroff* could first perform the command function (enter a blank line), while holding the remaining text in its memory. Then after performing the command, *nroff* could collect the next text input line, add it to the text it had remaining when it encountered the **.sp**, and begin the process of filling the next output line.

The possibility noted as (i) above is what actually happens when *nroff* encounters a command that causes a *break* to occur. The remaining text is entered as an output line, then the **.sp** is executed. In addition to the **.br** command itself, the **.bp**, **.sp**, **.ce**, **.in**, **.ti**, **.nf**, and **.fi** commands all normally cause a momentary *break* in the filling process to occur.

The second choice (ii) is the "no break" condition.

(3) **The Two Control Characters:** In Module Five you were informed that the dot (.) character—when it is the first character on a line—lets *nroff* know that a command follows. In this role the dot is a *control character*. The dot is actually one of two possible control characters. The other control character is the apostrophe ('). The apostrophe is the *no break control character*. As a result, **.sp** will cause a break, while **'sp** will not.

(4) **A Demonstration of Breaking and Filling:** The *nroff* requests **bp**, **sp**, **ce**, **in**, **ti**, **nf**, and **fi** can all be preceded by the apostrophe as well as the dot. With the **'** control character they do not cause a break. Consider the following twelve input lines. They will be formatted twice—first with the **sp** request using the usual dot (.) control character, and a second time with the no break (') character:

> *What is a break?*
> *These examples should help illustrate*
> *this nroff function*
> *that is often confusing,*
> *but also very important.*
> **.sp**
> *Let's try a few tests of the break function,*
> *using the old familiar space command (* **sp** *)*
> *with both*
> *the break and no break control characters*
> *to see what happens.*

This input produces the following output:

> *What is a break? These examples should help illustrate this nroff function that is often confusing, but also very important.*
>
> *Let's try a few tests of the break function, using the old familiar space command (* **sp** *) with both the break and no break control characters to see what happens.*

The same input, but with the **.sp** replaced by a **'sp**, produces a different output:

> *What is a break? These examples should help illustrate this nroff*
>
> *function that is often confusing, but also very important. Let's try a few tests of the break function, using the old familiar space command (* **sp** *) with both the break and no break control characters to see what happens.*

Note that the use of a **.sp** causes the space to occur directly after the word *important* (the last word preceding the command) and, in addition, causes a break in the filling process. The ´**sp**, however, does not cause a break in the filling process. *Nroff* filled and justified the first output line and had the words *function that is often confusing, but also very important* in memory, when it encountered the ´**sp** *nroff* request. Because ´**sp** is a no break command the words in memory were not entered as a partial line but kept in memory as the space (blank line) was entered. After the blank line was in place *nroff* collected another input line, added the text to the words already held in memory, and constructed the next output line. Thus the words *function that is . . . very important* begin the next line *after* the space.

(5) **The nroff Three Part Title Line Request:** It is possible to have the formatter include three part title lines in a file. For example, if the following input line was included in a file:

> .tl ´*Winston*´*Wogowon*´*Butler*´

The resulting output upon formatting would be:

Winston   Wogowon   Butler

The following *nroff* request, placed anywhere in your file will produce a three part title line:

> .tl ´*Word 1*´*Word 2*´*Word 3*´

Word 1 will be placed on the left, *Word 2* in the center and *Word 3* placed against the right margin.

The four apostrophes separate the title line into three parts. What ever is placed between the first two apostrophes will be placed on the left. The string of characters between the second and third apostrophes will be placed in the center, and text entered between the third and forth apostrophes will be formatted on the right.

A Look Inside Several -ms Like Macros

(1) **Top and Bottom of Page:** In Module Five you were introduced to the (**.pl**) page length command. At that time you were informed that although you can specify the page length, *nroff* is unable to do

anything at the top and bottom of pages without the help of macros. Module Nine introduced the **.nr HM** and **.nr FM** number registers and the **.ds LH, .ds CH, .ds RH, .ds LF, .ds CF** and **.ds RF** string definitions. These commands affect various registers and can be used with the *-ms* macros to produce header and footer margins and title lines.

This section introduces the way headers and footers operate. Included is an example of how you can instruct *nroff* to create top and bottom margins (complete with title lines) using your own home-made macros. This example also illustrates how string definitions can be used with your own macros in much the same way as they are used with the *-ms* macros.

(2) ___ Begin a new practice file which we will call *pages*. This file needs to contain at least 100 lines of text, *with no formatting commands.* If you do not have such a file you can copy one of your existing files, remove all formatting commands from it, and finally increase its length using the **:1,$ copy $** command. Once the file is at least 100 lines long and void of formatting commands, you should enter the twelve lines comprising the **he** and **fo** macros exactly as they appear here *at the top of the file.* [Note: the | character used in line six (**'sp** | *1i*) is the pipe character.]

The following *nroff* requests will (a) Define the page header macro **he** to include space and a three part title line, (b) Define the page footer macro **fo** to include a space and a three part title line, and (c) Set a "trap" to call the header macro into action at the top of each page and the footer at the bottom.

```
.wh 0 he
.wh -1i fo
.de he
'sp .5i
.tl '\\*(lh'\\*(ch'\\*(rh'
'sp |1i
..
.de fo
'sp .5i
.tl '\\*(lf'\\*(cf'\\*(rf'
'bp
..
```

These twelve lines will have the following meaning to *nroff*:

.wh *0 he*

This request tells *nroff* to perform a specific function when (**wh***en*) a particular position on a page is reached (sometimes called setting a *trap*).

The **.wh** request is used with two arguments. The first argument (in this case *0*) indicates the position on a page where *nroff* is supposed to act. (The *0* position is the top of the page.) The second argument (*he*) must be a call for a macro that specifies *what to do* at that position (when the *0* position on each page is reached). The fact that this second argument must be a macro call—and not an *nroff* request—is significant; it is the reason why you cannot instruct *nroff* about what to do at the top and bottom of pages without using macros.

.wh *-1i fo*

This **.wh** request instructs *nroff* to call the **fo** (**fo***oter*) macro at the *-1i* page position. The *-1i* position is one inch up from the bottom of the page. Any position specified with a minus (-) number is a relative position based on the page length. The *-1i* position on a three inch page is two inches from the top, while on a ten inch page this position would be nine inches from the top.

.de *he*

This begins the definition of the **he***ader* macro that will be called at the top of every page. This automatic calling was specified with the **.wh** *0 he* request.

`'sp .5i`

The first action of the **he**ader macro will be to space down one half of an inch. The *no break control character* is used so that text remaining in *nroff's* internal memory will be printed after the `'sp` action is performed, not before. Thus it avoids having a break before the top of each new page. The text is carried into the body of the next page.

`.tl '\\*(lh'\\*(ch'\\*(rh'`

This is a title line. Because this title line is included in a header macro that is called at the top of every page it will produce the same header on all pages.

To make this macro useful beyond a single paper the particular phrases to be placed in each position have not been specified. Instead, characters such as `\\*(lh` in the left title position are included. The `\\*(` informs *nroff* that:

(a) A two character name for a string follows (*.lh*);

(b) Somewhere else in the file the two character string is defined (such as **.ds** *lh Authors' Pets*); and

(c) The two character name should be replaced by the string definition (*Authors' Pets* will replace the *lh*).

`'sp |1i`

This *nroff* request again uses the no break control character to avoid causing a break before the top of each new page. The | symbol can be used with any *nroff* request that includes a numeric value. It is known as the *absolute position indicator* and, in this

	case, informs *nroff* to space down to the position *one inch from the top of the page* (instead of spacing down one inch from *the current position* on the page).
..	This indicates the end of the *he* definition.
.de *fo*	This line begins the definition of the **fo**oter macro which, in response to the **.wh** -*1i fo* request, will be called whenever *nroff* reaches a position one inch from the bottom of every page.
´**sp** .*5i*	The first action of the **fo** macro is to space down a half of an inch.
.tl ´*(lf´*(cf´*(rf´	A title line will be placed at this position on the page. The title line will consist of up to three parts: a left, center, and right footer. To be included in one of its three fields a string of characters must be specified as a string definition. Such string definitions are placed following the macro definitions in your file.
´**bp**	The final action of the footer macro is to cause a page break to occur after the title line is printed. Notice that the no break control character is used.
..	This ends the definition of the **fo** macro.

(3) **Using String Definitions With Your Own Macros:** At this point you can use the **.ds** request to specify strings to be used in your header and footer title lines in much the same way as you do with the -*ms* macros.

___ Enter something like the following requests in your *pages* file (place the following requests *before* any text but *after* your macro definitions):

.**ds lh**   *left header*
.**ds ch**   *center header*
.**ds rh**   *right header*
.**ds lf**   *left footer*
.**ds cf**   *center footer*
.**ds rf**   *right footer*

(4)   **Testing the Page Control Macros:** At this time you may want to test your new page control macros.

___ You can send your file to be formatted with the following Shell command (do *not* include the **-ms** flag in your command line):

nroff |*filename*| | **page**   ®

(5)   **The Strange Paragraph Reset Macro:** If you regularly use the *-ms* macro package (or read the material in Module Nine describing these beasties) you have probably discovered that the paragraph macros do a lot more than format paragraphs. In fact, all paragraph macro calls in the *-ms* system not only do what you expect (in the way of indentation and spacing) but also call a series of *nroff* requests that look something like the following .**RT** macro:

```
.de RT
.sp
.ne 1.1
.in 0
.ul 0
.ce 0
.ft R
.ll \\n(LL
.ps \\n(PS
.vs \\n(VS
..
```

The .**RT** macro is known as the **R**ese**T** macro and is called by all *-ms* paragraph macros. It turns off underlining (.**ul 0**) and centering (**.ce 0**), resets the font to Roman (**.ft R**), and resets the line length (**.ll** \\n(**LL**), point size (**.ps** \\n(**PS**), and the vertical spacing (**.vs** \\n(**VS**) to the values stored in the **LL**, **PS**, and **VS** number registers. This is why a **.ul** request will have no effect if placed *before* a *-ms* paragraph macro call. The *-ms* paragraph macro will *turn off* the *nroff* request for underlining even though you have just set it to underline.

Similarly, a change in the number register which controls the point size (**.nr PS**) request does not take immediate effect but must wait until after the next paragraph macro call. The change to the number register will not be read by *nroff* until it encounters the next paragraph macro. This is the reason why you must place a *-ms* paragraph macro call at the beginning of your file, after any number register requests that you use. That paragraph macro is necessary as it will establish the *-ms* defaults for these number registers. It is the initializing macro.

(6) **Viewing the -ms Macros:** For those of you who are interested, the *-ms* macro package is contained in a file with the following full path name: */usr/lib/tmac/tmac.s*

___ To view this file enter the command:

vi */usr/lib/tmac/tmac.s*   ®

If that command sequence does not work enter the command:

whereis *tmac.s*   ®

Use the full pathname returned by the **whereis** command to visit the lair of the *-ms* macro package.

Spend some time browsing through the *-ms* macros, and see if you can interpret how some of the commands actually perform their functions.

The quiz which follows concludes your introduction to the complex topic of macros. You may want to return to this Module after you have completed the remaining material in this book and give it a second reading. As you now know, the internal workings of macros decide how your formatted paper will appear. Your ability to select the appropriate macro—and occasionally construct your own when the necessary command does not exist—can make your formatting experiences both more effective and more satisfying.

A Final Quiz:

(a) Describe the effect of the following *nroff* request:

> **.tl ´jerry´and´meredith´**

_____

(b) Consider a file named *test*, which contains the following six lines:

> **.de Hi**
> **.ce**
> **\$1**
> **..**
> **.Hi** *there*
> *How are you?*

If this file was sent to *nroff* to be formatted, what would the resulting output look like?

_____

(c) What effect will the command **´br** have if entered in a text file?

_____

(d) Suppose you placed the following *nroff* request at the top of a text file. What effect will it have on the resulting formatted output?

> **.wh -1 bp**

_____

Answers: (a) A three part title line will appear with the word *jerry* on the left, *and* in the middle, and *meredith* against the right margin. (b) The word "there" would not appear in the output, due to the presence of a \$1 instead of \\$1 in the macro definition; the line "How are you?" would be centered. (c) Nothing, as the break command with the no break control character will have no net effect. (d) Nothing, as only macros can be used as arguments to the **.wh** request.

New nroff Requests

Command	Function
.de $\boxed{XX}$	Begins macro de*finition*. Replace *XX* with two character macro name.
..	Ends macro definition.
.so $\boxed{file}$	File named *file*, containing macro definitions, will be **so***urced* into current file.
.tl ´$\boxed{1}$´ $\boxed{2}$´ $\boxed{3}$´	Prints a three part t*it*le line.
\n($\boxed{XX}$	Reads in value stored in *XX* **n***umber* register. Replace *XX* with two character number register name.
*($\boxed{XX}$	Reads in string stored in *XX* string register. Replace *XX* with two character string register name.
\$1	Reads in first argument to macro call.
|	Absolute position indicator.
´	No break control character.

Module Twenty-One
Utility Programs

Introduction

Through the first twenty Modules you have seen how UNIX can be used to create and edit files, locate spelling errors, organize a directory system, communicate with other users, and line print or typeset all kinds of files. The remaining Modules will describe in some detail how UNIX can format form letters, tables of contents, tables, equations, and maintain a bibliography. The final Module briefly introduces several additional UNIX resources which can assist with your editing, programming, or writing tasks.

What more can UNIX do? Quite a bit, actually. In this Module you will meet programs which will locate files, compare two files to see if they are the same, translate specific characters in a file into other characters, and sort lines alphabetically. And these are but a few of its various capabilities.

Prerequisites

To utilize the information in this Module you should be able to spell "utility" and use the information presented in the first eight Modules of this book. Module Five is optional, while Modules Fifteen (*The UNIX Directory Structure*) and Twenty-Two (*Commands, Files and Directories*) are recommended.

355

Objectives

Upon completion of this Module you should be able to:

(1) Automatically remove all formatting commands from a file;

(2) Sort a file according to an alphabetic or numeric rule;

(3) Translate all occurrences of a string or range of characters into a new string or range of characters;

(4) Remove all redundant lines from a file;

(5) Compare two files and find lines that are unique to either file or common to both;

(6) Combine the above actions into useful "pipelines."

Procedure

This Module will introduce several new programs useful for text processing. The format used to describe these utility programs will differ from the approach used in other Modules, and will be similar to that used in the *UNIX Programmer's Manual*. The final section will present an example of how these programs can be joined together to accomplish a complicated task.

deroff

NAME (and function)

deroff — remove nroff, troff, tbl and eqn commands

SYNOPSIS (how command is entered; brackets identify options)

deroff [**-w**] *filename*

DESCRIPTION

The Shell command

deroff |*filename*| ®

will output to the terminal a copy of *filename*, minus all formatting instructions.

To have the output listed not by lines but in single words, use the Shell command:

deroff -w [*filename*]   ®

PROBLEMS

deroff does not always remove subtle formatting constructs.

sort

NAME (and function)

sort − sort a file

SYNOPSIS (how command is entered; brackets identify options)

sort [**-o -d -f -r**] [**+pos1**] [**−pos2**] *filename*

DESCRIPTION

The **sort** program will alphabetically and/or numerically sort lines of a file. In its basic form (if no **+pos1** or **−pos2** is specified) **sort** arranges the lines of a file in alphabetic and numeric order by comparing the first character of each line in a file. For example, the following is the contents of a file named *test:*

> *.nr PO 2i*
> *.LP*
> *This is a*
> *file to be sorted*
> *by the sort routine.*
> *.nf*
> *11223*
> *12133*
> *13100*
> *13101*
> *.fi*

The following **sort** Shell sequence would sort the above text and have the resulting output displayed on the terminal:

sort *test*   ®

The resulting sorted material would look like:

> *.LP*
> *.fi*
> *.nf*
> *.nr PO 2i*
> *11223*
> *12133*
> *13100*
> *13101*
> *This is a*
> *by the sort routine.*
> *file to be sorted*

Note the sorting order: symbols were listed first (periods), then numbers, followed by upper and then lower case letters.

Changes in the sorting routine are possible. The following will sort the file named *test* and place the output into a file named *output*:

sort -o [output] [test] ®

The **-o** option tells **sort** to direct its output to the file named as an argument to the option (*output*) instead of directing its output to the standard output. This command will accomplish the same result as:

sort [test] > [output] ®

To sort only those lines beginning with a letter, digit, or blank (**d**ictionary order) you would use the command line:

sort -d [filename]   ®

Whatever lines do not begin with a letter, digit, or blank will be placed at the bottom of the output. Thus the special characters, *nroff* requests, and macro calls would be removed from the sorting and placed as residue at the end.

If both upper and lower case letters should be sorted together (**f***olded* together), use:

sort -f ⬚*filename*⬚   ®

The order of sorting can be **r***eversed* (so that the line which would normally be sorted as the first line would instead be sorted last) by:

sort -r ⬚*filename*⬚   ®

In addition, the file(s) need not be sorted based upon the first character in each line. Most lines of text or numeric data can be considered as being composed of separate fields. A field is defined as a group of characters separated by white space (a word, a number, a series of letters, etc.). Thus the following line can be considered as consisting of six fields:

Name B. Fido Nerfball Age 47

The word *Name* is the first field, *B.* is the second, *Fido* is the third, and *Nerfball* is the fourth field. The word *Age* is the fifth field, and the number *47* is the sixth. Suppose you had a hundred line file with each line containing the same five fields of information (one line for each individual). You could sort the file according to last name (4th field) with the command:

sort +3 ⬚*filename*⬚   ®

The **+3** tells sort to skip the first three fields and thus base the sort on the fourth and following fields. If you wanted the sort to be based *only* on the fourth field you would use the command:

sort +3 −5 ⬚*filename*⬚   ®

This command translates as, "base the sort on the field(s) following the third field and preceding the fifth field (the fourth field)."

PROBLEMS

sort only sorts lines. It cannot easily sort records consisting of multiple lines based on a field in only one of the lines of the record.

SEE ALSO

deroff, **uniq**, **comp**

tr

NAME (and function)

tr − translate input characters

SYNOPSIS (how command is entered; brackets identify options)

tr [**-c -d -s**] [*string1*] [*string2*] *filename*

DESCRIPTION

With the **tr** command you can translate one string of characters into another. The hyphen (-) can be used to specify a range of characters. For example the command

$$\text{\textbf{tr}} \ \textit{A-Z} \ \textit{a-z} \ \boxed{\textit{filename}} \qquad \circledR$$
↑ space ↑

will translate all uppercase characters to lowercase.

SEE ALSO

sed

uniq

NAME (and function)

uniq − remove redundant lines from a file

SYNOPSIS (how command is entered; brackets identify options)

uniq [**-u -q**] *filename*

DESCRIPTION

Often when sorting or making an index you wind up with a file in which there are duplicate lines. The **uniq** program will assist in situations where there are several copies of identical lines. Note: duplicate lines must be adjacent when using **uniq**. If duplicate lines are not adjacent you should first **sort** the file and then use **uniq** to deal with duplicate lines.

To produce an output of single copies of all lines (in which the second copy of any line is deleted) use the following Shell command. Output will consist of one copy of all unique lines and one copy of all duplicated lines:

uniq [filename]   ®

The Shell command

uniq -u [filename]   ®

will examine *filename* and print all lines that appear in the file only one time (**u***nique* lines only). Output consists only of one copy of unique lines. Duplicate lines are ignored.

Additionally, the command:

uniq -q [filename]   ®

will examine *filename* and find only those lines that are *repeated* (duplicate lines only). It will then print a single copy of each line, no matter how often it was repeated in the file. Output consists of no copy of all unique lines and one copy of all duplicated lines.

SEE ALSO

sort, **comm**

comm

NAME (and function)

comm − compare two files

SYNOPSIS (how command is entered; brackets identify options)

comm [**- 123**] *file1 file2*

DESCRIPTION

The **comm** program compares two files, line by line and separates the lines into three categories:

(1)   Lines found in *file1* but not in *file2*

(2)   Lines found in *file2* but not in *file1,* and

(3)   Lines found in both files.

The Shell command:

$$\textbf{comm} \quad \boxed{\textit{file1}} \quad \boxed{\textit{file2}} \quad ®$$

will perform the separation and then print all three categories.

To suppress the printing of lines found in *file1* and not *file2* include the number **1** as a flag in the command sequence:

$$\textbf{comm -1} \quad \boxed{\textit{file1}} \quad \boxed{\textit{file2}} \quad ®$$

This will result in the printing of those lines found in *file2* only or in both files. Those lines found only in *file1* will not be printed.

To list only those lines common to both files, use the **-12** flag in the command sequence:

$$\textbf{comm -12} \quad \boxed{\textit{file1}} \quad \boxed{\textit{file2}} \quad ®$$

With the **-23** flag the **comm** command will produce a list of lines in *file1* (for instance the names of all students who are in a doctoral program) not in *file2* (names of all students whose registrations were blocked). The resulting list are those names in *file1* not in *file2* (students who are in the program but whose registrations were not blocked). Such a list would be created by:

$$\textbf{comm -23} \quad \boxed{\textit{file1}} \quad \boxed{\textit{file2}} \quad ®$$

SEE ALSO

sort, deroff, uniq, comp, diff

An Example of the Wonders of Piping

Not for Plumbers Only

The five utility programs introduced in this Module can be used together to transform a text file complete with formatting commands into a relatively short list of "unusual words."

The final step in this process is to compare a list of words consisting of every word found in one of your files with a list of common English words. This second list of common English words exists on most UNIX systems in a file with the full path name */usr/lib/eign*. The **comm** command introduced in this Module is used to compare the two files and identify all words found in one file but not in the other. Certain constraints must be met, however, before the two files can be effectively compared with the **comm** command: (a) Both files must be sorted in ascending sequence; (b) Every word in each file should be on a line by itself; (c) Every word in each file can occur only once; and (d) Because **comm** will treat a word beginning with a capital letter as different from the same word not capitalized, all characters must be translated into lower case.

(1) The actions necessary to meet these constraints can all be performed within a single Shell command line. It is easier—and for many purposes more useful—to perform these actions in two steps, however. For these reasons, we will first illustrate the two-step method and then present the one-step method.

(2) **Preparing the File of Common English Words:** Before this file (*/usr/lib/eign*) can be compared to one of your files it must be sorted into ascending sequence. This is done with the following command sequence:

$$\textbf{sort} \quad /usr/lib/eign \; > \; common \qquad ®$$

This command line will create a sorted copy of the */usr/lib/eign* file (containing the one-hundred and fifty most common English words) and place this new *common* file into your current directory. (Later on this file can be expanded as you discover other frequently used words. Don't forget to resort your *common* file after making additions, however.)

(3) **Preparing Your Text File:** Before your text file can be compared to your new *common* file several actions must occur. The file must be stripped of all formatting commands, and each word must appear on a line by itself. The words must be sorted into ascending sequence, all characters translated into lower case, and all redundant words must be removed.

___ The following command line will perform all these actions and do the actual comparison. (An explanation of each step follows the command line, but attempt to decipher it yourself first):

deroff -w *filename* | **tr** *A-Z a-z* | **sort** | **uniq** | **comm -23** - *common* > *unusual*

All formatting commands in *filename* are first removed by **droff**, which will then put the remaining words on individual lines (**-w**). The output from **deroff** will be passed on to **tr**, which will convert all upper-case letters to lower-case. (This step is required by the **uniq** program.) This material is passed to **sort** which will put these words into alphabetical order. The output of the **sort** program is passed to **uniq**, which will discard all redundant lines (words) and then hand its output to **comm**. The **comm** command then compares this output (or input, depending on your point of view) to the file named *common* which contains a sorted list of the 150 most common English words. The output from **comm** (the words in *filename* that are not among the 150 most common English words) will be placed in a file called *unusual*. Whew!!

The file named *unusual* will contain a list of the words in *filename* which were not in the UNIX list of very common English words. Such a list could be used to create a glossary or index (and was in fact how the index to this book was generated).

(4) **The One-Step Method:** The above two-step procedure can be consolidated into a single step by using the semi-colon (;) character. This special Shell character is used to separate two command lines to be performed in sequence.

If two command lines are separated by a ; the first will be completed before the second one begins. For example, consider the following Shell command line:

sort *otherfile* > *tempfile*;**comm -23** *file tempfile*

Here, **sort** will first **sort** the file named *otherfile* and place the output into a file name *tempfile*. Once this process is complete, **comm** will then compare *file* to *tempfile*.

This procedure has one potential drawback. You are left with a *tempfile* that you may never again use. You can avoid this problem through the use of two additional UNIX features. The first involves the use of the UNIX **temp**orary directory. The full path name of this directory is */tmp*. The */tmp* directory is publicly accessible and is periodically cleaned out by the "powers that be." Thus, it is a convenient place to deposit a file that is of only temporary use.

The second feature is the **$$** symbol. It can be used to assign a unique name to a temporary file. The command line

sort *filename* > */tmp/***$$**

will **sort** *filename* and place the output into a file with a numerical name in the */tmp* directory. (For those who are interested, this number is the process ID of the parent Shell.)

(5) With this as an introduction, you are now ready for the grand finale. The following Shell command line puts all these UNIX features to work and accomplishes our task all in one step. (Note: We display the command line as two lines, owing to the length of the sequence. This is, however, one continuous command line. Do not press ® until the entire command has been typed):

sort */usr/lib/eign* > */tmp/***$$**; **deroff -w** *filename* | **tr** *A-Z a-z* |
sort | **uniq** | **comm -23 -** */tmp/***$$** > *newname* ®

Module Twenty-Two
Commands, Files, and Directories:
or
Paths, Bins, and Yellow Brick Modes

Introduction

We have stated in prior Modules that UNIX stores information in files. In practice UNIX treats everything as a file, even your terminal. This is truly a remarkable feature, and one that allows you to tie together (in conjunction with the *pipe* | and the standard input and output) Shell commands in an infinite number of combinations. This ability is what makes UNIX so flexible and powerful.

You have created and worked with your own files, but what about the commands that allow you to go about your UNIX tasks (**vi**, **nroff**, **cp**, **page**, and **lpr**, to name but a few)? They also exist in files. We would like to guide you into their lair—the UNIX storage bins. This trek will allow for a discussion of how it is that a file (like the one named **page**) can act upon another file (as occurs when you enter the command **page** *filename*).

Prerequisites

To use this Module you should have completed the material in Modules One through Eight (Five optional), Fifteen: *The UNIX Directory Structure* (essential), and Sixteen: *Account Management.*

Objectives

Upon completion of this Module you will be able to:

(1) Use file permissions and modes to make a file executable (able to perform a function); and

(2) Describe how directories, bins, and search paths affect your interactions with UNIX.

Procedure

These procedure steps are presented in two sections. The first section explores modes, permissions, owners, and executable Shell scripts. Section two takes you on a tour of the UNIX command storage bins and discusses how the Shell "locates" a command.

Modes, Permissions, Owners, and Executable Shell Scripts

You need to begin the exercises in this Module from your Home directory. To insure that you are Home type:

> cd   ®

Module Fifteen: *The UNIX Directory Structure* discusses the concept of the Home directory.

(1) **Creating an Executable File:** An executable file begins life the same as any other file. Begin a new file by entering the command:

> **vi** *facts*   ®

(2) ___ Place the following six lines in this *facts* file:

> **echo**
> **echo** *'My current directory is:'*
> **pwd**
> **echo**
> **echo** *'The files in this directory are:'*
> **ls**

(3) ___ When finished, write the file into the memory of the Beast and return to the Shell.

(4) ___ From the Shell type:

facts   ®

What happened? You receive a note stating:

facts: Permission denied.

This note lets you know that the Shell tried to execute the file *facts* but found that it did not have "permission" to execute it. The file at this point is not *executable.*

So what is the nature of this beast called an executable file? Well, the Shell program **page** is a good example of an executable file. The Shell can apply the contents of the **page** file to almost any file that you have created, resulting in the specified file being displayed on the screen. The line editor **ex** is also an executable file.

If a file is executable, the Shell has been given permission to perform the actions specified within the file.

As far as UNIX is concerned the file *facts* is still only a plain, ordinary, non-executable file. This will soon change . . . .

(5) **File Permissions:** List the filenames in your Home directory. From the Shell enter the command (lower case l, s, space, minus sign, lower case l):

ls -l   ®

space ↑

The Shell command **ls -l** will give you a *long listing* of the files located in your current directory. Among other things, this long listing will include the permissions attached to your files.

Something like the following should be displayed on your screen:

total 9

```
drwx------  2  login   544  Nov 13  17:04    Study
-rw-------  1  login  6100  Oct 12  11:32    second
-rw-------  1  login  1452  Sep  7  11:58  experience
-rw-------  1  login  1064  Sep  2  21:14     first
-rw-------  1  login    93  Dec 19  10:32     facts
```

Each line is the long listing for one file or directory in your current directory. Each long listing consists of several parts.

(a)   The first part is 10 characters long (*drwx------*) or (*-rw-------*) and specifies the "permissions" (known also as the *file mode*) attached to each file. We will refer to this portion as the *permissions field*.

(b)   The second part of the listing is a number (*1* or *2*) which identifies the number of links attached to the file and is of no concern for the moment.

(c)   The third part of the long listing is the login of the owner of the file (in this case we have just entered the word *login*).

(d)   The fourth portion of the listing is the length of the file in bytes.

(e)   The date the file was last altered is displayed as the fifth part of the listing; and

(f)   The last entry is the file's name.

Information Fields in a Long Listing

drwx------	*2*	*login*	*544*	*Nov 13 17:04*	*Study*
Permission Fields	# of Links	File's Owner	size in bytes	Date of Last Modification	Filename

For the moment the important feature is the permissions field: the 10 characters on the left of each line. Each of the 10 positions has a particular significance.

The first position indicates whether the listing is for a file, a directory, or some other UNIX beast. A **d** for directory, or - for *not* a directory (i.e., a file), will most often appear in this position. The first character in the permissions field (− in the case of the file *facts*) indicates that *facts* is not a directory. The file *Study* is a directory, as evidenced by the **d** in the first position of the permissions field.

The next nine characters can be considered as three fields of three characters each. For now we need only concern ourselves with the first of these three fields following the directory character. These three characters determine what you (the owner of the file or directory) can do with it.

If the first of these three positions is filled with an **r** the owner has **r**ead permission and can view the contents of the file. A — (minus sign) indicates that the owner does *not* have read permission.

If the second of these three positions is a **w** the owner has **w**rite permission and can make changes in the file. A minus sign in this position would indicate that the owner would not have write permission.

The third position indicates whether the file can be executed. An **x** indicates that the owner has *execute* permission; a minus sign means that the file does not have execute permission.

In summary, the presence of a **r**, **w**, or **x** in a permission field indicates that the associated permission is granted; a — indicates that this permission is not granted.

For now let's interpret the permissions field associated with the file named *facts*. The line -rw------- indicates that it is not a directory (a - in first position) and that the owner (you) has both read and write, but not execute permission (**rw-** in positions 2-4).

Execute permission means that the file is a Shell script or a compiled program and that it has permission to perform its function. (An executable directory allows you to look for files in it.) Whenever you create a file it automatically has read and write—but not execute—permission. To add execute permission to a file you must change its *mode*.

(6) **Filemodes:** You will now change the mode of *facts* to make it executable. Type:

chmod   *700 facts*   ®

The command **chmod** stands for **ch**ange **mod**e. The number *700* gives the owner read, write, and execute permission for the file. The *700* can also be considered to have three fields (7 0 0). Again, we are only concerned here with the first field (the number *7*), because this field determines what the owner can do with the file.

The number seven in the first field is actually a "composite" number (sum) constructed from the following "primitives:"

(a) 1 grants execute permission
(b) 2 grants write permission
(c) 4 grants read permission.

These primitives can be added together to grant any combination of permissions.

The basic permissions for the file's owner are:

000 grants no permissions
100 grants execute permission only
200 grants write permission only
400 grants read permission only

The sum of 100 + 200 + 400 = 700 would mean that read, write and execute permissions would all be granted.

Additionally, 300 grants execute and write permissions (100 + 200); and 500 grants read and execute permissions (100 + 400). The permission of 600 grants read and write permissions (200 + 400). These mode changing codes relate to permissions *to the owner of the file.* These three numbers (1, 2, and 4) can be used to express the eight possible states involving combinations of these three binary conditions (yes or no for execute, write, and read permissions). As a point of interest, no other combination of three single-digit numbers yields this continuous and unique scale for binary combinations.

(7) ___ To check on whether the command sequence **chmod** *700 facts* affected the filemode of *facts* enter the command:

ls -l facts   ®

Note the presence of the letter *x* in the position third from the left in the permissions section. This *x* tells you that *facts* is now executable. So what does this do for you?

(8) ___ Type:

facts   ®

This time you are treated to the display of the name of your current working directory, along with a listing of all files in your current directory. This information is the result of the two Shell commands placed within your *facts* file. No big deal (although it beats a poke in the eye with a sharp stick), but it illustrates how any file containing Shell commands can be made executable: the owner must change its filemode to 700.

With a filemode of 700 a file becomes, in effect, a Shell command. You can execute the contents of the file by simply typing its name.

(9) **A Second Executable File:** As another example, you can create an executable file which will cause the Shell to first change directories to a specified sub directory and then start the process of visually editing a file in that directory.

(10) ___ Make sure you are in your Home directory. Once there you should create a file named *go* containing only the following 2 lines. (Substitute the name of one of your sub directories for *directory* and the name of a file located in that directory for *filename*):

> **cd** *directory*
> **vi** *filename*

___ Return to the Shell and change the mode of the *go* file to 700. Then from the Shell type:

> **go**   ®

If all went according to plan you should be moved to the specified *directory* and *filename* should present itself for visual editing.

(11) **Creating a Bin:** You may wish later to create additional (and hopefully more interesting) executable files. It is useful to create a directory (bin) to hold all of your executable files. Let's do this now. From within your Home directory type:

> **mkdir** *Bin*   ®

(12) ___ Next relocate *facts* into your *Bin* directory. Use the following command sequence:

> **mv facts** *Bin*   ®

(13) ___ Once again enter the command:

facts ®

The Shell replies "facts: Command not found" because it does not know where to look for the new **facts** command. In the next section of this Module you will learn how to include your own *Bin* in the search path followed by the Shell when looking for executable files.

Uses of Executable Files: The two example executable files presented here were designed to allow you to practice constructing files and changing their modes. In fact the tasks which these two files accomplished are more efficiently handled with the **alias** command. Executable files are normally used for more complex tasks not easily solved by an **alias** command.

(14) **Yes, Another Quick Review:**

(a) What command gives you a long listing of your filenames, including the permissions attached to each file? _____

(b) What permissions are granted to a file with the following permissions field (-r-x------)? _____

(c) What command would you use to change a file's permissions to include read, write, and execute permission for the owner of the file (include the mode number)? _____

(d) What would the permissions field for a file look like after you had changed its mode to include read, write, and execute permission? _____

Answers: (a) **ls -l**   (b) read and execute but not write permissions
(c) **chmod 700** *filename* (d) -rwx------

UNIX Commands, Storage Bins, and Search Paths

(1) ___ Log onto your UNIX account. If already logged on, make sure you are located in your Home directory. Type:

cd ®

(2) In Module Fifteen you learned that .. (dot dot) is the UNIX name for the directory located *immediately above* your current directory. Ever wonder who or what exists above your Home directory? Here's your chance to find out. Type:

cd ..   ®

You are now located one level *above* your Home directory. (Take several deep breaths—the air is pretty thin at these elevations.)

(3) ___ To determine the contents of your current working directory (now one level above your Home directory) type:

ls   ®

The *logins* of the other users of your UNIX system should be displayed. Your *login* will be found among the list.

(4) **Root:** You will need to use a UNIX "special character" for the next directory move. Type:

cd /   ®
     space ↑

The / is the UNIX name for the "root" directory (in addition to being the character used to separate directory and filenames when you use a full path name). *Root* is, curiously, located in the UNIX penthouse. All files and directories are located below *root.*

(5) ___ What files exist in the / (*root*) directory? Type:

ls   ®

The list of filenames probably does not look too exciting. One of the names listed should be the *usr* directory, however.

(6) ___ Change directories to the *usr* directory. Type:

cd *usr*   ®

(7) ___ List the contents of the *usr* directory with the **ls** command. Anything look familiar? If you are a UCBerkeley-type, your attention may be drawn to the directory named *ucb*.

(8) ___ To explore the contents of the *ucb* directory. Type:

cd *ucb* ®

(9) ___ List the filenames in this directory.

(10) Recognize any files? The names of Shell commands used to work with UNIX should now appear. (We told you this was pretty heady stuff.)

___ If the directory **ucb** *did not* appear, type:

cd *bin* ®

The *ucb* (or *ucb/bin*) directory is one of the UNIX directories containing the files that are Shell commands. The directories which hold UNIX Shell commands are referred to (in UniJargon) as *bins*. The only difference between a bin and a garden variety directory is that bins contain executable files. The term *bin* is derived from the fact that most of the executable files stored in these UNIX system directories are in a *bin*ary format.

(11) ___ To find out what a binary file looks like enter the command:

page ex ®

You should receive a note indicating:

ex: Permission Denied

The commands stored in the *ucb* directory are contained in files that are *executable* but not *readable*. Although you can *use* these commands you cannot *view* the files that contain them (this is part of the UNIX security system).

(12) ___ For the next activity you need to be located in your Home directory. To insure that you are there enter the **cd** command.

(13) **Discovering Your Search Path:** You now know that most UNIX commands are actually executable files stored in directories (known as bins). The bins that the Shell searches and the order in

which they are searched is determined by the setting of the Shell variable named *path*. The **set** command (introduced in Module Sixteen) is used to control the search path in the same way it is used to set the Shell variables *ignoreeof* and *noclobber*.

___ From the Shell enter the command:

set   ®

Recall that the **set** command, used without arguments, will list the settings of the Shell variables attendant to your account (see Module Sixteen). Your list should look something like the following:

```
argv ()
cwd  /pbjmpb/Book/Minis
history    25
home       /pbjmpb
ignoreeof
noclobber
path (. /usr/ucb /bin /usr/bin)
shell /bin/csh
status     0
term f100
user  pbjmpb
```

The *ignoreeof* and *noclobber* variables should be familiar. For now note the information that follows the word "path," as this is how your search path is currently set. When you enter almost any command (some exceptions are **alias**, **set**, and **cd**), the Shell will start its search for an executable file with that name in the first directory listed in your search path. For example, suppose you type the Shell command **facts** (the name of the executable file you created earlier in this Module). The Shell will begin looking in the current directory (.). If a file with that name (**facts**) is not found in the current directory, the Shell will next check the **/usr/ucb** bin. If still unsatisfied, the Shell goes to the **/bin** bin. The last stop is **/usr/bin**. Each of these bin names is preceded by a / because they are all located one or more levels below the root (/) directory. Finally, if the Shell cannot find the command in any of these locations (and it would not find **facts** with this search path) you will be greeted by the now familiar reply, "*Command not found.*"

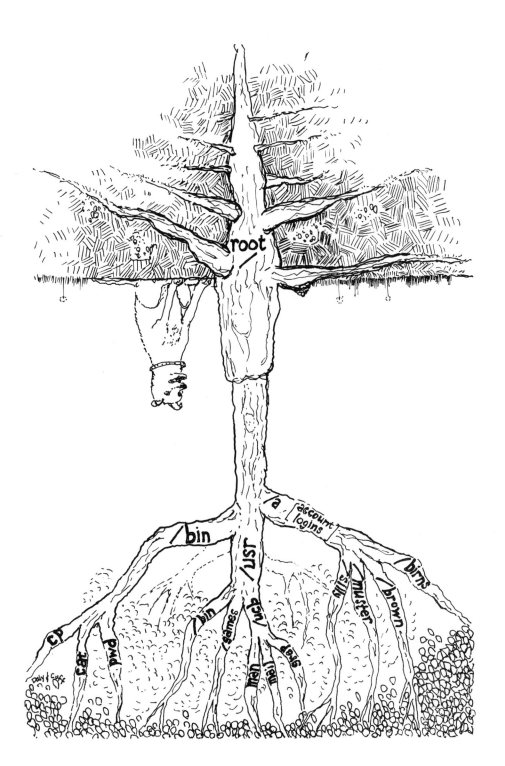

377

On most UNIX systems a command can exist in several different forms, each in a file with the same name, but located in different bins. These forms will be the command as it evolved over different versions of UNIX. (The process of storing different files with identical names in separate directories was discussed in Module Fifteen.) The most commonly used bins for BSD UNIX are: **/usr/ucb**, **/bin**, and **/usr/bin**.

The order in which bins are searched is very important, because the Shell discontinues its search upon locating the first instance of an executable file with the right name. It does not matter, to the Shell, if that filename also exists further down the path. It does, however, matter to you. The search order can determine which executable file is found (and therefore used by you).

(14) **Setting Your Path:** Remember the file *facts* located in your *Bin* directory? An easy way to advise the Shell about executable files located in your *Bin* is to set your *search path* to include a trip through *Bin*. Go ahead and advise the Shell of the existence of your *Bin* directory with the following Shell command sequence:

set path = (. /usr/ucb /bin /usr/bin ˜/Bin)
↑ *space*   ↑   ↑   ↑

Note: If you make a mistake in specifying your path the Shell may be unable to find any Shell commands. Should this happen you will receive the "*Command not found*" message upon typing in your Shell commands. Fear not—you need only logout and log back in again. Order will be automatically restored to your search path.

(15) ___ Now type the command

facts   ®

Did the Shell locate and execute the commands contained within this executable file? If not, carefully reset your search path and attempt this step a second time.

(16) The sequence you entered in procedure step 14 has only a temporary effect—the Shell will forget about your *Bin* bin when you log out. You can permanently remind the Shell by inserting the above line in your *.login* file.

Double Warning: If you err in entering the following text into your *.login* file, you will continue to receive the *"Command not found"* message to your Shell commands. Logging out and back in again will not help. You will have successfully piloted your search path into a *black hole,* and you will need to perform the following three steps to escape from this situation: (a) Reset your path from the Shell (Enter from the Shell the **set path** command sequence noted in Step 14 above); (b) Re-edit your *.login* file to include the correct path; and (c) Again enter the **source** *.login* command.

(a) Call up your *.login* (*dot login*) file for visual editing. Once it appears on the screen find the line beginning with the words *set path.*

(b) *Carefully* append the following characters at the end of your search path (inside the right paren):

$$\tilde{}/Bin$$

Without these characters added to your path it will look similar to this:

> **set path = (. /usr/ucb /bin /usr/bin)**

With these characters added to your path it will look similar to this:

> **set path = (. /usr/ucb /bin /usr/bin *~/Bin*)**

(c) Return to the Shell and type the **source** *.login* Shell command.

Note: If the *set path* line does not appear in your *.login* file just insert the following line somewhere in the *.login* file:

> **set path = (. /usr/ucb /bin /usr/bin *~/Bin*)**
>   ↑ *space*   ↑   ↑   ↑

(17) **More on File Permissions and Modes:** As you now know, the permissions attached to files and directories determine *who* can do *what* with each file or directory. We have already discussed the role of the first four positions in a permission field: the first character indicates whether the file is a directory, and the next three characters indicate what the owner of a file can do with it. The second set of three characters determine the same permissions

(read, write, and execute) for users in the *file owner's group*. Just who belongs to a group can be specified by the owner: see the *UNIX Programmer's Manual* entry for **newgrp**. The final set of characters represent the permissions granted to everyone else (others).

In most cases these three permission groups (owner, group, others) will have the following meanings to you:

(a) The *owner's* permissions will determine what you can do with the files you create;

(b) *Group* permissions will determine what people in your group can do with files. For instance, files containing Shell commands (such as the **ex** file—containing the line editor—that you attempted to view earlier in the Module), are executable but not readable to members of the file owners (root) group (everyone with an account on the UNIX system you are on); and

(c) *Others'* permissions will determine what other users can do with the files you create. Normally this will be nothing, although you can specify otherwise.

If the topic of permissions interests you you might return to the root directory and explore some more. Try doing a long listing in several of the bins and interpreting the information supplied to you. In other words, spend a few moments and "get lost," but do report back.

(18) Additional information about *bins* and *modes* is available in the *UNIX Programmer's Manual*. To access this material enter the Shell commands:

apropos modes   ®

or

apropos bins   ®

(19) **A Final Quick Review:** Consider these questions:

(a) What Shell command will move you directly to the root directory? _____

(b) What command would you use to reset your path from the Shell? _____

(c) What three steps would you take to reset your path by modifying your *.login* file?

(1) _____

(2) _____

(3) _____

Answers: (a) **cd /** (b) **set path = (new path)** (c) (1) **vi** *.login*
(2) append "**set path = (new path)**" (3) **source** *.login*

Module Twenty-Three
Form Letters

Introduction

Multiple copies of a form letter can easily be generated on UNIX. This process requires only that you learn a few additional commands.

Prerequisites

Before starting this Module you should be able to:
(1)   Use the visual editor; and
(2)   Use both *nroff* and *-ms* macro commands to format text.

Objectives

Upon completion of this Module you should be able to produce multiple copies of a form letter.

Procedure

When producing form letters you create two files: the first contains the basic form letter, complete with blanks to be filled in later; the second contains the list of whatever text (names, addresses) should be inserted in the blanks of the form letter.

(1) ___ Log onto your UNIX account and when the Shell prompt is presented use the visual editor to start a new file called *letter*.

(2) **An *Nroff* Request for Reading Input:** Insert the following five lines in this new file:

> **.LP**
> *Dear*
> **.rd**
> **.PP**
> *How's it going*

The **.rd** command stands for **read**, and lets *nroff* know that this part of your letter is to be filled in later. The next file you create will contain a list of names that will be inserted where the **.rd** is located.

(3) ___ Use the **ZZ** command to store this file and return to the Shell.

(4) ___ Use the visual editor to create another new file called *list*.

(5) **Contents of the Input File:**
Insert the following line in this new file:

> *Helen*

This line is the name to be used to fill in the blank in the form letter.

(6) ___ Use the **ZZ** command to store this file and return to the Shell.

(7) **The Shell Command Line to Read Input:** From the Shell enter the command:

> **nroff -ms** *letter* < *list* | **page**   ®

This command tells UNIX to format the *letter* file. The *list* file will be used to supply the input to fill in the blank space in *letter* (where the **.rd** command appears). The whole mess is then sent to **page** and should appear on your screen. (Refer back to the section

Module Seven entitled *Standard Input and Output* for a discussion of the use of the < symbol to *redirect* input from a file to the *standard input.*)

(8) **Multiple Copies Through Looping:** With the **.rd** request you can produce a single form letter. The following command requests *nroff* to *loop* through your form *letter*, thereby producing multiple copies.

___ Use the visual editor to call up your *letter* file. Insert the following line at the end of this file:

    .nx *letter*

The **.nx** instruction is an *nroff* command that stands for **n**e*xt*. In this case it tells *nroff* that after *letter* has been formatted it should look for a file called *letter* and start formatting it. Since *letter* is the same file *nroff* just finished formatting the **.nx** command puts *nroff* into a loop. As soon as it finishes formatting *letter* it again starts formatting *letter*. In the following procedure step you will add another entry to your *list* file so that you can create two copies of your form letter, each addressing a different person.

(9) Use the **ZZ** command to store *letter* and return to the Shell.

(10) Call up your *list* file for visual editing.

(11) **Multiple Entries to a List File:** Edit your *list* file so that it looks *exactly* like the following five lines. Don't forget the blank lines between the three entries, as they are essential:

    Helen

    Bill

    .ex

When finished return to the Shell with the **ZZ** command.

The first (*Helen*) and third (*Bill*) lines are names to be used to fill in the form letter (where the **.rd** command is positioned). The second and fourth lines are blank lines that instruct *nroff* to return to the form letter and continue formatting its contents. The **.ex** is an *nroff* request that stands for **ex***it*, and is the break that tells *nroff* to stop looping. This command is crucial. Without it *nroff* will continue to loop through your form letter. The process will not terminate until you press the ⌷DEL⌷ key (if the process is running in the foreground) or kill the process (if it is running in the background). The section of Module Seventeen entitled *Running a Shell Command Sequence in the Background* explains how to kill a backgrounded process.

(12) **Check Point:** At this point your file named *letter* should look like this:

> **.LP**
> *Dear*
> **.rd**
> **.PP**
> *How's it going*
> **.nx** *letter*

And your file named *list* should look like this:

> *Helen*
>
> *Bill*
>
> **.ex**

(13) ___ From the Shell enter the command sequence:

> **nroff -ms** *letter* < *list* | **page**   ®

(14) ___ As you read the following refer to the above displays of what your pre-formatted files should look like. We will offer an explanation of what each instruction will cause *nroff* to do. The Shell command sequence initiated in Step 13 tells UNIX to send the file called *letter* to *nroff* and to use *list* as the source of input for each **.rd** command. When *nroff* comes to the first **.rd** it will look for the file named *list* to supply the input to fill in the blank. *Nroff* will insert the name *Helen* into the letter at the point of the **.rd**

command, and upon reaching a blank line in the *list* file returns to formatting the contents of *letter*. When *nroff* reaches the **.nx** *letter* line in the *letter* file it will start the entire process over again except that the next time it reads a **.rd** command it will use the next line from *list* (in this case it will ignore *Helen* and use *Bill*). The whole mess is again sent to **page** and should appear on your screen.

(15) **Multiple .rd Commands in a Form Letter:** It is possible to include more then one **.rd** request in a form letter.

___ Use the visual editor to edit your file called *letter*. Insert an additional **.rd** request just before the **.nx** *letter* command (which should be the last line of this file).

(16) ___ Use the **ZZ** command to store this file and return to the Shell.

(17) ___ Call up your *list* file for visual editing. Edit this file so that it looks exactly like the following. Again: don't forget the blank lines; they are essential:

Helen

in Yucatan?

Bill

in Maui?

.ex

The first (*Helen*) and third (*in Yucatan?*) lines will be used to supply the input to the first and second **.rd** commands in the *letter* file. The fifth (*Bill*) and seventh (*in Maui?*) lines will be used by *nroff* in the same way during the second pass through your form letter. The second, fourth, six, and eighth lines are blank lines that tell *nroff* to return to the form letter and continue formatting its contents. Finally, you will recall that the **.ex** is an *nroff* command that stands for *exit*. This command tells *nroff* to stop cycling through your form letter.

(18) **Check Point:** At this point your file named *letter* should look like this:

```
.LP
Dear
.rd
.PP
How's it going
.rd
.nx  letter
```

And your file named *list* should look like this:

```
Helen

in Mexico?

Bill

in Maui?

.ex
```

(19) ___ Again, from the Shell enter the command sequence:

nroff -ms *letter* < *list* | **page**   ®

A line printed copy of your letters can be produced with this command sequence:

nroff -ms *letter* < *list* | **lpr**   ®

You now possess experience using the basic formatting commands necessary to produce a form letter. There are some additional points you should consider, however.

Some Hints on More Complex Letters

(1) **Output on Separate Pages:** By inserting a **.bp** as the next to last command in your form letter file (*letter* in this example) you can have each copy of your form letter printed on a separate page. For example, a **.bp** positioned appropriately in your *letter* file would appear as follows:

> **.LP**
> *Dear*
> **.rd**
> **.PP**
> *How's it going*
> **.rd**
> **.bp**
> **.nx** *letter*

(2) **Text Blocks:** You can use the *list* file to supply multiple lines of input (a text block) for each **.rd** request in the form letter file. Just don't put blank lines within such a block of text and make sure this block is followed by a blank line. If you follow these rules your text block will be read into the letter. For example, your *list* file with a text block would appear:

> *Helen Clifton*
>
> *Helen*
>
> *in Yucatan?*
> *Hope you are enjoying the pyramids.*
>
> *Bill Tuthill*
>
> *Bill*
>
> *in Maui?*
> *The volcanos must be putting on quite a show.*
> *Enjoy them while you can.*
>
> **.ex**

(3) **One-Way Formatting Commands:** If you use any one-way formatting command at the end of your form letter (perhaps a **.in #** command to indent the closing) make sure you give the return command before the **.nx** *letter* line. For example, your *letter* file with an indented closing would appear:

```
.ds CH
.ND
.LP
.rd
.sp 2
.LP
Dear
.rd
.PP
How's it going
.rd
.sp
.in 20
Sincerely yours,
.sp
UNIX
.in 0
.bp
.nx letter
```

The output that would be generated by this example is presented on the following page. The actual output would consist of each letter on a separate page. They are presented here on a single page for economy of space.

Two Questions: Consider the information presented in this Module as you answer the following questions.

(a) What redirect symbol is used to get *nroff* to read input from a file through the standard input? _____

(b) What *nroff* request stops the looping initiated by the **.nx** *filename* request? _____

Answers: (a) <   (b) .ex

Helen Clifton

Dear Helen

   How's it going in Yucatan? Hope you are enjoying the
pyramids.

                    Sincerely yours,

                    UNIX

Bill Tuthill

Dear Bill

   How's it going in Maui? The volcanos must be putting on
quite a show. Enjoy them while you can.

                    Sincerely yours,

                    UNIX

Form Letter Summary

Shell Command Line

Command	Function
nroff -ms *form* < *list*	Formats the file *form*, reading input for the **.rd** requests from the file *list*.

Nroff Requests

.rd	Asks *nroff* to take input from standard input. Used to read text into a file.
.nx *list*	Causes *nroff* to start formatting *list*. May be used to loop through *list* additional times.
.ex	Exits from *nroff*. When placed at end of *list* file it discontinues the looping process.

Module Twenty-Four

Special Formatting Topics:

A Title Page, Table of Contents, & Index

Introduction

This Module presents the formatting command sequences necessary to produce a title page, table of contents, and an index. The title page format instructions will serve as basic examples of simple cover sheets and can be customized to meet your own individual needs.

Prerequisites

To format the basic title page you should be able to use *nroff* commands to format text. To prepare the *-ms* macro title page or table of contents/index you need to be able to use the *-ms* commands to format text.

Objectives

After completing this Module you will be able to:

(a) Prepare a wide variety of title pages using *nroff* requests with or without the *-ms* macros;

(b) generate a table of contents and index for your paper or project.

Procedure

These procedure steps are in four sections. The first describes how to format a title page using *nroff* requests; the second illustrates how to employ *-ms* macros. Section Three illustrates how to create a table of contents and the fourth section describes how an index can be formatted.

The set of title page commands is placed at the *beginning* of a file (which is usually where you want the title page to appear), *after* any number register, string definition, or initializing commands have been entered.

Two title page formatting approaches will be presented. The first employs only *nroff* commands, while the second uses *nroff* plus *-ms* macros.

A Title Page Using nroff Requests

You can create your own title page through the selective use of *nroff* formatting commands. A generic title page of this type is presented here, which you can modify to meet your needs. The command sequence used to prepare the title page is presented, along with notations describing each command. A sample, unformatted title page follows, with commands and text as entered into the file. A sample title page, formatted according to these commands, is then included. Modifications of the basic title page are easily made allowing you to customize the formatting.

The Title Page Input File:

```
\&
.sp 1.5i
.ce 8
Hermeneutical Homemaking
.sp 8
B. Fido Nerfball
.sp
University of California, Berkeley
.sp 3
Fred Flintstone
.sp
Bedrock School of Mining
.sp 1i
This research was made possible through a grant
.sp
from the Oil Foundation
.ce 0
.bp 1
The text of the paper follows here.
```

Interpreting the Input File: An annotation of the *nroff* commands used in the input file displayed above will now be presented:

\&	Places an invisible character at the top of the page, which gives the formatter something to measure from if you want the first text spaced down the page. If you do not include the printing of this nonprinting character, the initial **.sp** *nroff* request will be ignored.
.sp 1.5i	Space down the page 1.5 inches.
.ce 8	Tells *nroff* to center the next 8 lines of text. The number 8 is arbitrary—you may select any large number.

Hermeneutical Homemaking	Title of Paper.
.sp8	Space down the page 8 lines.
B. Fido Nerfball	Author Information.
.sp2	Space down the page 2 lines.
UC Berkeley	Author's Institutional Affiliation.
.sp 3	Space down 3 lines.
Fred Flintstone	Second Author's name
.sp	Space down 1 line.
Bedrock School of Mining	Second Author's Affiliation.
.sp 1i	Space down one inch.
Other Information	This may include a project title, professor's name, a course number, or whatever. You may insert additional spaces and notations as necessary.
.ce 0	Tells *nroff* to "center no more lines."
.bp 1	Break page. New page will begin with page number 1.

Changing the Generic Title Page: The variations to this theme are, of course, endless. You can change the vertical spacing of items, center some entries and not center others, include other information. . . .

The commands used in this section are described in the *Command Summary Section* at the end of the book. In addition, Module Five offers a more thorough description of each command.

The keys to successful title page formatting are the \& which allow you to format from the top of the formatted page, and the **.bp 1** which begins the next page at page one. If those two commands are included in the file, whatever you do in between is up to you. (Try not to have the called for spaces add up to more than one page.)

Hermeneutical Homemaking

B. Fido Nerfball

University of California, Berkeley

Fred Flintstone

Bedrock School of Mining

This research was made possible through a grant

from the Oil Foundation

Using the nroff Title Page in a -ms File: If you are using the *nroff* title page format in a file that uses the *-ms* macros, you may need to add the following to your file:

(a) An initializing macro such as **.LP** on a line *before* the **\&** command.

(b) A **.ND** (for **N**o **D**ate) command following the initializing paragraph command to suppress the printing of today's date as the center footer. (If you want the date on pages within the body of the text, add the command **.DA** to your file *just before* the **.bp 1** command.)

A Title Page Using the -ms Macros

A series of specific *-ms* macros can be used in place of *nroff* requests to construct a title page. The command sequences placed within a file to prepare a title page will first be shown. Notations describing each command follow. A sample title page, formatted according to these commands, has not been included. Rather, you are encouraged to create your own.

The Input File:

```
.RP
.TL
Hermeneutical Homemaking
.AU
B. Fido Nerfball
.AI
University of California, Berkeley
.AU
Fred Flintstone
.AI
Bedrock Mining College
.AB
This article offers an ethnographic look at the daily
existence of Wilma Flintstone and her associates at
the Bedrock Retirement Facility, circa 2 Million B.C.
.AE
As with any research purporting to examine prehistoric
life, one must first consult 1960's era American cartoons . . . .
```

Interpreting the Input File: The following annotation of the *-ms* macro commands used in the above input file explains the function of each command. Following the annotation is a list of important constraints on the use of the commands.

COMMAND	FUNCTION
.RP	Requests a separate cover sheet (optional).
.TL	Tells UNIX that the next line(s) of text will be the title (must appear).
Place the Title Information Here	
.AU	The name(s) of the author(s) follow on the next line(s). Type the names in exactly as you would like them presented.
Place the Author Information Here	
.AI	The author's institution appears on the next line(s).
Place the Institution Information Here	
.AB	An abstract of the paper follows until the **.AE** command appears (optional).
Place the Abstract Text Here	
.AE	Marks end of abstract (must appear if the **.AB** is used).
Begin the Text of Your Paper	

Notes on the -ms Title Page: The above commands follow specific conventions that result in different outputs:

(a) With the **.RP** command included in the file, the *title* and *author's institution* will appear in two places: on the title page and *also* on page 1 of the paper. Without the **.RP** command a separate cover page will not be prepared. The title page material will instead appear on page one with the text immediately following.

(b) The command **.RP no** used in place of the **.RP** will suppress the printing of the information on page one.

(c) The abstract will appear under a centered heading *Abstract* when the **.AB** request is included. To suppress this heading use the **.AB no** in place of the **.AB** request.

(d) The commands related to *author* (**.AU**) and *institution* (**.AI**) may be repeated if there are several authors from different institutions (as demonstrated in the above example).

Creating a Table of Contents

When creating a major paper, there are two ways to collect and enter the list of entries which become the table of contents:

(a) You may produce a draft of the paper, identify the pages that each major section landed on, and then enter each of the entries into a separate section of your paper or,

(b) You may ask *nroff* to collect the entries from within the text itself, noting the appropriate pages.

Each of these approaches is explained below.

Creating a Basic Table of Contents: The *-ms* system of macros includes a specific command to inform the formatter that an entry is the beginning of a Table of Contents. There is another command to identify intervening entries, and another for indicating the last entry. The input file on the top of the next page uses **-ms** macros. An explanation of each macro call follows.

The Input File:

```
.XS 1
Phenomenological Issues
.XA 16
You, Me, and Phenomenology
.XA 25
Tree-Frog Consciousness
.XA 32 5
Mocha Almond Fudge
.XA 40
Suicide Brings on Changes
.XA 52 0
Finale-Husserl at Play
.XE
.PX
```

Interpreting the Input File: An annotation of the command lines included above follows:

.XS 1

Is used to identify the first Table of Contents entry. The number which follows (here, the number *1*) indicates the page number of the first topic item (here, page 1 for *Phenomenological Issues*).

Phenomenological Issues

.XA 16

Next topic item will follow, and the *16* is the page number of that item.

You, Me, and Phenomenology

.XA 25

Next topic item will follow, and the *25* is the page number of that item.

Tree-Frog Consciousness

.XA 32 5

Next topic item will follow, and the *32* is the page number of that item. The number *5* tells *nroff* to indent this item 5 spaces to the right. The indentation will remain until you inform *nroff* to return to 0 indentation (which follows).

Mocha Almond Fudge

.XA 40   Next topic item will follow, and the *40* is the page number of that item.

Suicide Brings on Changes

.XA 52 0   Next topic item will follow, and the *52* is the page number of that item. The number *0* tells UNIX to indent this item 0 spaces to the right (i.e., return the left margin to its normal, non-indented position).

Finale-Husserl at Play

.XE   Marks the last entry of the Table of Contents. This command must appear.

.PX   Tells *nroff* to print this material as a Table of Contents when the paper is formatted. This command must appear.

The Formatted Table of Contents: When the above input file is sent to the formatter with the Shell command line **nroff -ms** *filename*, the following results:

Table of Contents

Collecting Entries from within the Text: The entries for the Table of Contents do not have to appear together as a set in the file (as was the case in the previous example). Instead, they may appear within the text of your paper *on the pages they refer to.* UNIX can be instructed to collect the entries and *assign the appropriate page numbers* for your table of contents. The Table of Contents generated in this way will appear identical to the one created in the prior example.

An example of this alternate approach would be the following portion of a file.

```
        . . . and he spoke as the Leader of the Pack.
.sp
.ce
Mocha Almond Fudge
.XS
Mocha Almond Fudge
.XE
.sp
This brings us into historical realism and  . . . .
```

The **.XS** and **.XE** are entered into the text file wherever sections are located that you want included in the contents. In this case, *Mocha Almond Fudge* is a section title. Right after the section title is entered, an entry for the Table of Contents is included. The **.XS** and **.XE** surrounding the second *Mocha Almond Fudge* in the file will cause *Mocha Almond Fudge* to be an entry in the Table of Contents. You can not enter a page number for the entry because you do not know what page the entry will fall on during formatting. The formatter will enter the appropriate page number for the entry after the formatting is completed.

Informing the Formatter: When generating a Table of Contents using the above approach you must include a **.TC** command at the end of your file, so UNIX knows to collect your topics and assemble a Table of Contents. The **.PX** command, which is included when you enter the Table as a unit, is not employed when the formatter collects the entries.

Creating an Index

The procedures employed in having the formatter create a Table of Contents can be used to create an Index. The process is the same; make all entries in the file using the **.XS** and **.XE** commands.

The **.TC** will have the formatter collect all the entries and prepare them as a *Table of Contents*. Since this is to be an Index, you will need change the name of this list to *Index*.

Module Twenty-Five
Bibliographies and Footnotes:
The REFER Program

Introduction

> *I don't mind writing the paper, but I can't stand typing the*
> *bibliography . . . underline this, put in periods, commas*
> *. . . does the date go before the city? Then there are the*
> *footnotes. Yuk.*

If the above statement reflects your attitude toward bibliographies,
then the UNIX *refer* bibliographic formatting package is for you.
Refer first prompts you for the necessary information, then formats and alphabetizes your bibliography while you sit back and
smile. In addition, when formatting a paper it will appropriately
place footnotes at the bottoms of pages or at the end of the paper,
given just part of a citation.

Prerequisites

Bibliographic entries and modification call for basic editing and
UNIX system knowledge. Specifically:

(1) You should be able to edit text using the visual editor; and

(2) Because this Module consists largely of creating a bibliography, you will need to have available either a series of 10 or more books and articles or their bibliographic citations (title, author, date, journal, etc.).

Objectives

Upon completion of this Module you should be able to:

(1) Use the *refer* package to format a bibliography, including annotations;

(2) Have your bibliography printed both with and without the annotations;

(3) Correct citation entries in the bibliography;

(4) Alter the prompts that *refer* presents to meet your own needs; and

(5) Use *refer* to create properly formatted footnotes in a written work.

Procedure

The procedures will consist of seven sections. The first section discusses the use of the *refer* prompts to enter citation information into a file named *database*. Section two describes how to edit the citations. Formatting and getting a copy of a bibliography is covered in section three. Section four considers the entire *refer* prompt field and describes how to create your own prompt list. Entering bibliographies without abstracts is explained in section five. Section six discusses how to cite references in papers using the *refer* system. The final section contains a sample bibliography.

Using Prompts to Create a Basic Bibliography

(1) ___ Log onto your UNIX account. When the Shell prompt appears enter the command (Note: the ® means *press the* **RETURN** *key*):

addbib |*database*| ®

If the *refer* pre-processing package is available on your system the query

Instructions?

will be displayed on the screen. Answer by typing:

yes ®

(2) The **addbib** *database* command you just entered initiates the *refer* process and is in two parts:

 (a) **addbib** is the Shell command that tells UNIX that you want to enter bibliographic information using the *refer* package, and

 (b) *database* is the name of the file in which the information will be placed. While you can name the file whatever you want we will refer to it as *database*.

(3) Instructions will now be presented on the screen. Go ahead and read through them, but don't worry if everything is not clear. The instructions will be covered in some detail in the next few pages.

On this first pass through the *addbib* process we suggest you *not* enter the information from an actual reference citation, but rather make up quick answers to each query. You will have a chance to enter a real citation in a moment.

(4) The prompt *Author* should appear on the screen. Type an author's name, such as your own, or

Sigmund Freud

After you have entered the author's name, press ® .

Enter the name in normal order (i.e., don't enter surname first). When the file is formatted your bibliographic entries will be alphabetized by the first author's surname. The output will then be printed surname first, resulting in: *Freud, Sigmund*

(5) Pressing the ® key indicates you have finished entering the author's name. The *Author* prompt then disappears and the request for *Title* is displayed on the screen.

(6) ___ Enter a *title* such as:

Psychoanalysis and the Couch

Press ⑧ and the *Title* prompt gives way to *Journal*.

(7) ___ Continue through the prompts, answering those that you want, leaving others blank until you get to *Abstract*. After each entry press ⑧ to move to the next prompt.

(8) ___ When the prompt *Abstract* appears, start entering comments about the mythical book you are citing. Since abstracts are invariably longer than one line, *refer* is designed so that the ⑧ key now works in the normal fashion, opening up a new line for text and *not* shifting to the next prompt. You can enter several lines of comments in the *Abstract* field.

How do you let *refer* know you are finished making comments, since ⑧ is acting in its normal way? When you have completed the abstract you enter the command:

CTRL-D

(While holding down the CTRL key, press the **d** key one time.)

(9) ___ The prompt *Continue?* should appear on the screen. You have two choices:

(a) If you are finished entering citations and want to return to the Shell type *no* or *quit*;

(b) If you want to continue adding citations, you can start with a new *Author* prompt by pressing the ⑧ key.

(10) You have now worked through the fundamental process of entering bibliographic information using the *refer* system. There are several things to keep in mind while entering citations into *refer*:

(a) **Mistakes:** Don't worry about mistakes, as they can easily be edited later;

(b) **Irrelevant Prompt Fields:** Simply pass over (with a ⑧) those fields which do not pertain to your citation, and they will be ignored when the formatting takes place;

(c) **Multiple Authors:** When dealing with multiple authors, enter the name of the first individual, then press Ⓡ which will call up the *Title* prompt. Instead of typing the title, enter the *minus sign* (−) and then press Ⓡ . This procedure will bring up another *Author* prompt. The names of several authors can be entered in this fashion.

(d) **Lengthy Titles:** Titles are often too long to fit on one line. Because of this users will often enter most of a title and, seeing that the cursor is near the right edge of the screen, press Ⓡ . They then find themselves facing the next prompt instead of a new line to finish entering the title. If an entry is too long for one line (such as a long title of an article) enter a backslash (\) *as the last character in the line before pressing the* Ⓡ *key.* The cursor will move to the start of a new line, but (because of the backslash) that line will be considered part of the previous line.

(e) **Terminating a Citation:** If while you are entering a citation you must quit (or you have totally messed it up) just pass through the remaining prompt fields by pressing the Ⓡ until you reach the *Abstract:* prompt. The CTRL-D will bring up the prompt: *Continue?* At that point you can either bail out or start a new cycle with a new *Author* prompt. Later, when you edit the file, you can remove any aborted partial citations.

(11) To learn how to edit, format, and print the bibliography you will need several citations entered into your *database* file. Use the *refer* prompts to enter the information for at least four published works. Use journal articles or books, but avoid articles written by one author and located in a book edited by someone else, as we'll get to that later.

Editing the File

(1) When you have entered your last abstract and have been presented with the *Continue?* prompt, enter the command:

vi

This permits visual editing of your *database* file. You can only enter the visual editor when *addbib* presents the *Continue?* query.

(2) ___ Once you have entered the visual editor, examine the file. It should look similar to the *database* file located at the end of this Module. Note that the citation information begins with %A %T %J etc., and the abstract material is at the end of each citation.

The %A and %T characters which begin each line are the *refer codes* placed in the file by *refer* to identify each *Author*, *Title*, or other data field. Your first complete entry should look something like:

%A Sigmund Freud
%T Psychoanalysis and the Couch
%J The Vienna Circle
%D 1897
%V 2
%X Brief account of criteria for selection
of couch for office: not too hard, nor sleep inducing.

When the *addbib* program prompts you with *Author,* it places the %A in the file, followed on the same line by whatever you type, until you press ® . The interactive process of incorporating the prompt with the data you enter is how each field (*Title, Journal, Date*) is created.

Because you entered **vi** when you were presented with the *Continue?* prompt, you can now visually edit *database* as you would any file. The visual editor may be used to correct spelling errors, modify each abstract, or delete aborted citations.

Notice that there is a blank line between each full citation. The blank line is used by *refer* to keep all the information concerning one citation together. *Do not delete these blank lines. They are essential.*

___ When finished editing the file be certain all the prompt abbreviations (such as %A or %T) and the blank lines are still in their proper places.

(3) ___ Remove the first citation (your mythical article by *Freud*) and make any other corrections you wish. When you are finished editing, type **ZZ**. The **ZZ** command does not take you back to the Shell, but rather to the *Continue?* prompt in *refer*. At this point you can press ® to continue adding reference citations, or enter **no** to return to the Shell.

Returning to the File: When you type **no** in response to the *Continue?* prompt you are returned to the Shell, and the *database* file is written onto the disk for permanent storage. What if you want to add more citations to the file? You simply type **addbib** *database*. When you use **addbib** with an already existing file, the new citations are appended to the end of the file.

Formatting and Producing a Copy of the Bibliography

When you entered the command **addbib** *database* you started the process of creating a file called *database* into which all bibliographic entries were made. The *database* file is placed in your UNIX account (just like any other file) and can be formatted and line printed.

(1) **A Screen Display:** To get the file *database* properly formatted and displayed on the screen enter:

> **sortbib** ⟨*database*⟩ | **roffbib** | **page**   ®

(2) **Line Printed Copy:** To send a formatted copy of the bibliography to the line printer enter:

> **sortbib** ⟨*database*⟩ | **roffbib** | **lpr**   ®

(3) **Without Annotations:** If you want the bibliography printed out without the annotations a **-x** option is included with the **roffbib** command:

> **sortbib** ⟨*database*⟩ | **roffbib** **-x** | **lpr**   ®

(4) **With Page Offset:** If you want the bibliography printed with a one inch page offset (a larger left margin), a **-rO1i** option (minus, lower case r, upper case O, one, eye) is included with the **roffbib** command:

> **sortbib** ⟨*database*⟩ | **roffbib** **-rO1i** | **lpr**   ®

Explanation of Commands: The command lines just presented can be interpreted as follows:

(a) The **sortbib** sorts the entries in the file *database* by author (and by date);

(b) The file is next sent to **roffbib** which converts the %A %T %J prompts into specific formatting instructions and then formats the file.

(c) Finally, depending upon what you specify, the file is sent either to the screen (default) or the line printer.

Use of Fields Not Included in the Prompts

(1) The *addbib* program does not prompt you with all the possible fields. For instance, if a citation is an article in a book edited by someone else, you are not prompted for *Editor?*, although that prompt does exist. The following is a complete list of fields that the *roffbib* program recognizes:

%A Author's name
%B Title of book in which article is located
%C City where published
%D Date of publication
%E Editor of book which contains the article being cited
%G Government order number
%H Header commentary which is printed above citation
%I Publisher (Issuer;"P" is taken by "page number")
%J Name of journal
%K Keywords used to locate reference
%N Number of issue within the volume
%O Other information or commentary
%P Page number(s)
%Q Corporate or foreign author (name is not reversed)
%R Report number
%S Series title, if book is one part of such a series
%T Title of book or article
%V Volume of the periodical
%X Abstract

(2) There are three ways to include fields in your file *database* which are not in the prompts that *refer* automatically provides you:

(a) *Entering Additional Fields from vi*: You can place additional field identifiers and field information directly into the file using the visual editor. First type the usual **vi** *database* Shell command sequence. Next, enter the appropriate *refer* code (such as **%E**) followed by a space and the necessary information. The order that you include these fields is not important; *refer* will place all information in an established order. Be sure to include a blank line between citations.

(b) *Entering Additional Fields Using addbib*: When you have typed all the information for one of the prompts (such as *Title?*) enter a backslash as the *last* character. Then press the ® key. For instance:

Title: *Psychoanalysis and the Couch*\ ®

Instead of a new prompt, you will be presented with a new line. Enter the refer code and appropriate information. Then press **RETURN**. The next prompt will now be presented.

(c) *Entering Additional Fields by Changing the Prompts*: The third way to use the other *refer* codes is to change the prompts presented you to include the set you want. This approach will next be discussed.

(3) **Changing the Prompts:** If you wish to have *addbib* provide additional prompts (such as **%E** for *Editor of a book*), or if you want to eliminate those which you do not use, you must set up your own prompt list.

To have *addbib* present only those prompts *that you select* you must create a file named *prompts* which will include the screen prompts you want displayed along with the associated *refer* codes (**%A %B %R %S** or whatever). Each line of the *prompt* file must contain the following:

(a) The prompt itself is positioned against the left margin;

(b) A single TAB character follows each prompt; and

(c) The *refer* code (drawn from the list above) is the final entry on the line.

Each subsequent line will also include a prompt and its *refer* code, separated by a TAB .

Note: TAB means *Press the* TAB key. (If you do not have a TAB key on your terminal, press **CTRL-I**.) With each TAB the cursor may or may not move, and no character will appear on the screen. Because the invisible TAB character can be confusing, it is possible to have a character appear on the screen to indicate where you entered each TAB character.

From the Command Mode of the visual editor, enter the following command (don't forget the colon):

:set list

Your TAB will now appear as the ^I character.

When you want the TAB characters to no longer appear in the terminal output, enter the command:

:set nolist

(4) The *prompt* file which would result in *all fields prompted* would look like the following display.

Contents of File Named "Prompts"

Author? TAB %A
Corporate or Foreign Author? TAB %Q
Article/Book Title? TAB %T
Edited Book Title? TAB %B
Journal? TAB %J
Edited by? TAB %E
Title of Series? TAB %S
Volume? TAB %V
Number? TAB %N
Report Number? TAB %R
Page(s)? TAB %P
Publisher? TAB %I
City? TAB %C
Date? TAB %D

Government Order Number [TAB] %G
Header Commentary? [TAB] %H
Other? [TAB] %O
Keywords? [TAB] %K
Abstract? [TAB] %X

(5) Once you have established a *prompt* file in your account, it is activated (whenever you want to enter citation information) with the following Shell Command:

addbib -p [prompts] [database]   ®
       ↑ space

The **-p** *prompts* included in the above command line instructs *addbib* to use the prompts listed in the *prompts* file in your current directory, rather than the standard set.

(6) When the time comes to sort, format, and print your *database* file, the sorting (**sortbib**), formatting (**roffbib**), and printing (**lpr**) commands are the same as described earlier. They are not affected by the method you use to create the *database* file.

Entering Bibliographies without Abstracts

You may want to enter bibliographic information without entering abstract comments. The *Abstract?* prompt will not be presented if you include the **-a** option with the **addbib** command:

addbib -a [database]   ®
    space ↑

All prompts will now be used except *Abstract:*.

Citing References in Papers

(1) **Incorporating Footnotes:** The *refer* pre-processor not only creates bibliographies which can be appended to a paper, but also takes care of the messy job of footnoting.

For example,[1] the footnote at the bottom of this page was produced by including the following lines in this file:

> *For example,*
> .[
> **Tuthill 1982**
> .]
> *the footnote at the bottom of this page was . . .*

You do not have to include the entire citation at this point in your text; just enough to let *refer* identify which reference you want (the name of the lead author and the date will usually be enough to allow *refer* to access the correct citation).

Obtaining Formatted Footnotes

(2) The default option in *refer* is to have footnotes numbered and placed at the bottom of the page.

(3) **Page Bottom Footnotes**: When it is time to format and print a file and you want the footnotes placed at the bottom of the page, use the following Shell command sequence:

refer -p ⟨*database*⟩ ⟨*filename*⟩ **| nroff -ms | lpr** ®

Here *database* is the file of citations and *filename* is the text file that has the footnote calls embedded in the text. (The **-p** indicates that you are using the *database* in your current directory—your **p***rivate* database—instead of the system database.)

(4) **Listed Footnotes**: The *refer* package will also place footnoted references together at the end of a chapter, instead of at the bottom of each page. The Shell command sequence line which formats and prints your paper in this form includes the **-e** option:

refer -e -p ⟨*database*⟩ ⟨*filename*⟩ **| nroff -ms | lpr** ®

---

[1] Bill Tuthill, *Refer-A Bibliographic System,* University of California, Berkeley, California, 1982. Computing Services.

With the **-e** option footnotes will not be placed on each page, but wherever in the text you place the following three lines:

.[

$LIST$

.]

(5) **Bracketed Citations:** Social Science citations such as this one [Tuthill, 1982] are also possible in place of superscript numbered footnotes. You enter the same footnote marker:

.[

partial citation

.]

in the text in the same manner, but use a different Shell command to format the paper. The Shell command line which formats your paper must include the **-l** ("*minus ell*") flag:

refer -l -p `database` `filename` | **nroff -ms** | **lpr**   ®

↑ ↑ *space*

With the **-l** option the senior author's name and publication date are bracketed at the appropriate text locations.

(6) **Use with Other Pre-Processors**: If you are using more than one pre-processor (perhaps *tbl* and *neqn*) for a paper, the correct Shell Command sequence would be:

refer -p `database` `filename` | **tbl** | **neqn** | **nroff -ms**   ®

Modification of the Programs

The format of the bibliography produced with the *refer* package is useful for most paper and report writing activities. It does not, however, comply with the specific style requirements of many publications (such as the *APA Style Manual* published by the American Psychological Association). It may be necessary for you to modify how the *refer* and *roffbib* programs punctuate and order the elements of the bibliographic citations. Although such modifications are beyond the scope of this edition, the interested reader is *refer*red to the *Tuthill* monograph footnoted on the prior page. This is an excellent source of information about the *refer* pre-processing package and describes how to modify these programs.

A Sample Bibliography

The following list of citation information is the contents of the *database* file which was used to produce the bibliography located at the end of this Module:

```
%A Joel Kies
%A Bill Tuthill
%T UNIX Text Formatting Using the -ms Macros
%I Computing Services, University of California
%C Berkeley, California
%D 1983
%K software document preparation
%X All commands and conventions of -ms are explained
for use with the Berkeley system, including table of
contents and other fancy features.

%A Bill Tuthill
%T Refer—A Bibliographic System
%I University of California
%C Berkeley, California
%D 1982
%O Computing Services
%X The most complete source of information about the
refer program.  A must if you intend to use refer extensively.

%A Brian W. Kerninghan
%A Dennis M. Ritchie
%T The C Programming Language
%I Prentice-Hall
%C Englewood Cliffs, New Jersey
%D 1978
%K software
%X This is the classic handbook for programmers
who work in the C language.  The rules of the
game are carefully explained.
%A Joseph F. Ossanna
%T Nroff/Troff User's Manual
%I Bell Laboratories
%C Murray Hill, New Jersey
%D 1976
```

%K software document preparation
%X All the specifics of nroff and troff are included
in careful detail, including options, arguments etc.

%A Neil Postman
%A Charles Weingartner
%T Teaching as a Subversive Activity
%I Dell Publishing Company
%C New York
%D 1969
%X The classic book for anyone interested in teaching,
if assisting people to learn to think is of interest.

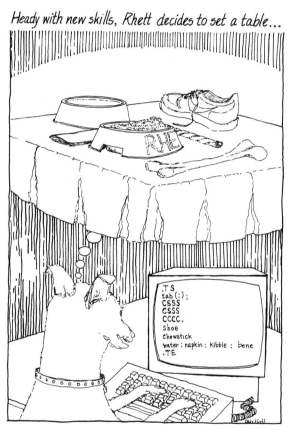

Heady with new skills, Rhett decides to set a table...

The bibliography on the next page results when the above *database*
file is sent to the sorter and formatter with the following command
line:

sortbib $\boxed{database}$ | **roffbib** | **lpr** ®

BIBLIOGRAPHY

Kerninghan, Brian W. and Dennis M. Ritchie, *The C Programming Language,* Prentice-Hall, Englewood Cliffs, New Jersey, 1978.

    This is the classic handbook for programmers who work in the C language. The rules of the game are carefully explained.

Kies, Joel and Bill Tuthill, *UNIX Text Formatting Using the -ms Macros,* Computing Services, University of California, Berkeley, California, 1983.

    All commands and conventions of -ms are explained for use with the Berkeley system, including table of contents and other fancy features.

Ossanna, Joseph F., *Nroff/Troff User's Manual,* Bell Laboratories, Murray Hill, New Jersey, 1976.

    All the specifics of nroff and troff are included in careful detail, including options, arguments etc.

Postman, Neil and Charles Weingartner, *Teaching as a Subversive Activity,* Dell Publishing Company, New York, 1969.

    The classic book for anyone interested in teaching, if assisting people to learn to think is of interest.

Tuthill, Bill, *Refer-A Bibliographic System,* University of California, Berkeley, California, 1982. Computing Services.

    The most complete source of information about the refer program. A must if you intend to use refer extensively.

Module Twenty-Six
Setting Tables: A Busboy's Nightmare
The TBL Pre-Processor

Introduction

Text processing often requires that information be presented in columns or tables. Merely the thought of having to tediously count the needed spaces, divide by 2, center, backspace, etc., is enough to convince all but the most determined writer to seek some alternate way to present the information. Fortunately UNIX contains *tbl* to help with this task.

Prerequisites

In writing this section, we assume that you are able to:

(1) Use the visual editor to add and change text in a file;

(2) Use the basic *nroff* commands to center lines, underline words, and skip lines; and

(3) Use Shell commands to format a file and send that file to the line printer.

Objectives

Upon completion of this Module you should be able to:

(1) Properly format multicolumn tables which contain numbers, words or text entries.

(2) Systematically troubleshoot when tables do not work as planned.

Procedure

The following introduction to table formatting starts with a two column format and, by adding commands, demonstrates some of the more complex forms which are possible.

These procedure steps are grouped into four sections. The first section presents instructions for formatting a simple two column table. Section two describes how to send a file containing a table to the formatter. The third section builds upon the simple table by adding more columns and different kinds of data. The last section includes examples of boxes and the use of different sizes of type.

A Table for Two, Please

An Example Table: The following two column display was produced using the UNIX *tbl* program. This table will serve as the starting point for the more complex tables to be presented in later sections of this Module. An explanation of the commands used to produce this table follows.

Table A

Equipment	Cost
Hammer	14.95
Radial Arm Saw	389.50
Tool Box	39.50
Electric Sander	69.95
Work Bench	179.
Gasoline Chain Saw	166.80

How Tables are Formatted: Tables are formatted by giving specific instructions as to how each *row* and *column* are to be presented. Columns are the vertical, *up and down* units in a table; rows the horizontal, *across* units.

For example, in *Table A* the two *columns* are:

Column One   *Column Two*

Equipment	Cost
Hammer	14.95
Radial Arm Saw	389.50
Tool Box	39.50
Electric Sander	69.95
Work Bench	179.
Gasoline Chain Saw	166.80

A *row* is "sliced" horizontally. The first row of *Table A* is:

Equipment   Cost

and the second row is:

Hammer   14.95

For *tbl* and *nroff* to be able to format the display of a table you must provide specific instructions as well as the data to be entered. For *all* tables you must indicate:

(a) The number of columns of information the table will contain (in *Table A* there are two columns);

(b) How the information in each column is to be displayed (i.e., whether each entry should be centered in the column, pushed against a left or right column margin, or, if the information is numbers, adjusted relative to a decimal point); and

(c) The actual information (data) you want placed in each column.

Using the TAB **Key:** The directions for *Table A* using the TAB were entered as follows:

```
.TS
c c
l n.
Equipment   Cost
.sp
Hammer      14.95
Radial Arm Saw      389.50
Tool Box   39.50
Electric Sander      69.95
Work Bench         179.
Gasoline Chain Saw         166.80
.TE
```

What is tricky with this example is that in looking at the above display you would never know the TAB key was used to separate the entries for each row into two columns. For instance, there is a TAB entered between **Hammer** and **14.95** in the first row of data. There usually is no apparent symbol. (A TAB character tends to be quite secretive.) This is due in part to the fact that the TAB key does *not* adjust your screen display in the same way as the TAB key on a typewriter affects the typed page.

Defining a TAB **Character:** Because the TAB key can be very confusing to use when setting tables (and is almost impossible to demonstrate here) we recommend defining some other character which *will* show up on the screen to separate column entries. The following table instructions produce the exact same *Table A* seen above, only the plus sign (**+**) is defined as the separation character. In this example the separation character can be seen embedded in the instructions.

```
.TS                    Instructions for Table A Using the Plus Sign
tab (+) ;
c c
l n.
Equipment+Cost
.sp
Hammer+14.95
Radial Arm Saw+389.50
Tool Box+39.50
Electric Sander+69.95
Work Bench+179.
Gasoline Chain Saw+166.80
.TE
```

(1) ___ Log onto your UNIX account. Select one of your *practice* files (such as the musty *first* file) to use with these exercises. As you read through the following examples, enter the format instructions at some interesting point in your file.

In entering the tables into your file, you should follow the format instructions that we present. You could easily change the data to whatever content amuses you, however.

Explanation of Instructions for Table A

This section will describe the function of each of the above Table Format instructions used in setting *Table A*, beginning with the first command line. As you read the following, examine the effect of each command on the formatted *Table A*.

.TS   Indicates that a **T**able **S**tarts with the next line of text. It is a one-way command and is paired with the **T**able **E**nd (.TE) command (which must be the **last** command in the table). The entire unit, from .TS to .TE, can be located in a separate file or placed in a text file at the exact location where you want the formatted table to appear.

tab(+); Informs the *tbl* program formatter that you will use a plus sign character (**+**) instead of a TAB to separate the column entries in the input line. *Without this line the program will look for* TAB *characters.* The semicolon (;) at the end of this line indicates that the options are concluded and that the actual column layout instructions will follow. The semicolon *must* appear if any options are selected.

c c Instructs *tbl* concerning how you want data entries placed in the first *row* of the table, namely that:

(a) there are two symbols, therefore the table is to be formatted in two columns,

(b) the first entry for the first column should be c*entered* (**c**) and,

(c) the first entry for the second column should also be c*entered* (**c**). (These entries will in fact be the column heads.)

l n. Indicates how the data in the second row is to be formatted. The first entry is to be placed against the left (**l**) margin of the first column. The second entry is to be one number (**n**) arranged in the second column so the decimal points are aligned. The *period* must be included at the *end* of whichever is the last line of table formatting commands. The period indicates that the formatting instructions are over and that the data to be included in the table will start on the next line. *Without the period, the table is not set, and no dinner will be served.* Failure to include the period is the most common table formatting error.

Data The actual table information is then entered, line by line, with a plus sign (**+**) separating the column entries. The data entry for the first row of the table is:

Equipment+Cost

The formatter reads the **+** sign as *move on to the next column.* Thus, in the formatted output, **Equipment** will be in the first column, and **Cost** in the second.

When the first line of the table has been entered the **RETURN** ⓡ key is pressed. The next line is then typed, followed by the next, until all the data has been entered. Each row is a separate line in your file. These remaining lines would look like the following:

Hammer+14.95
Radial Arm Saw+389.50
Tool Box+39.50
Electric Sander+69.95
Work Bench+179.
Gasoline Chain Saw+166.80

.TE   When the entire table has been entered you must indicate the conclusion with the **.TE** command.

Relationship Between Instruction Line and Data Line: Look back at the instructions for *Table A.* The first line of the format instructions (**c c**) and the first line of the data (**Equipment+Cost**) are *both* needed in order to format the first *row* of the table. The formatting instruction consists of two characters, **c c** which indicates that there will be two columns. The fact that the first character is a **c** indicates that the first piece of information is to be centered in the first column. The scond **c** indicates that the data for the second column should also be centered. The first line of data provides the two pieces of information needed for the first row. They are separated by a plus sign (**+**).

The second line of instructions and the second line of data— *together*—provide both the data and format instructions for the second row in the formatted table. In this row, the first entry for the first column is to be formatted left, and the second column entry lined up by its decimal point. The last instruction line (**l n.**) is then used with all remaining data lines to format all remaining rows in the table.

Having a Table Formatted

A General Process Comment: The formatting commands and the table information are both entered into a file *just like all other content and formatting commands.* The only difference is that if a file contains a table, it must first be sent to the *tbl* pre-formatter *before* it is sent to the regular *nroff* (or *nroff -ms*, if you use the *-ms* macros) formatter.

(1) A copy of the formatted table can be displayed on your terminal screen by entering the Shell command line:

tbl [*filename*] | **nroff** | **page**   ®

(2) To produce a line printed copy of the table, enter the Shell command line:

tbl [*filename*] | **nroff** | **lpr**   ®

(3) The *tbl* pre-formatter is a *pre-processing program* that takes your table instructions and converts them into commands that the *nroff* format program can understand. Once *tbl* is finished, the output must be sent (with the pipe | command) to *nroff* (or *nroff -ms*) where the table is finally formatted.

Setting A Different Table
Would Amy Vanderbilt Approve?

There are innumerable variations to the ways tables may be set. A table can be centered on the page or spread out to full page width; entries can be placed differently in the layout; several columns can be created; entries can span columns; and text can be included in addition to words or numbers. Each of these will be demonstrated by making changes in the command structure of the sample *Table A* you have already examined.

(1) **Locating a Table on a Page:** *Table A* was printed against the left margin of the page. Additional choices exist, however.

The following set of instructions produces a formatted *Table B*, which is *centered* on the page:

```
.TS                           Instructions for Table B
tab (+) center;
c c
l n.
Equipment+Cost
.sp
Hammer+14.95
Radial Arm Saw+389.50
Tool Box+39.50
Electric Sander+69.95
Work Bench+179.
Gasoline Chain Saw+166.80
.TE
```

The above instructions result in the following centered *Table B:*

Equipment	Cost
Hammer	14.95
Radial Arm Saw	389.50
Tool Box	39.50
Electric Sander	69.95
Work Bench	179.
Gasoline Chain Saw	166.80

Notice that the only difference between the instructions for *Table A* and *Table B* is the inclusion of the word *center* inserted between the **tab** (+) and the semicolon on the second line. Without the *center* instruction, *tbl* defaults to placing the table against the left margin, as it did in *Table A*.

(2) The table can be expanded to the full width of the page by replacing *center* with the word *expand*.

___ Try first centering and then expanding the table you have been making.

428   *The TBL Program*

(3) **Center, Right, Left, and Number Data Placement:** In the preceding examples the column headings were centered over the column, the items (first column) were placed against the left margin, and prices (second column) were lined up according to the decimal points.

We can just as easily instruct *tbl* to format the table with both the headings and the content pushed to the right margins. This is effected with the following set of formatting instructions for *Table C*:

```
.TS                          Instructions for Table C
tab(+) center;
r r
r r.
Equipment+Cost
.sp
Hammer+14.95
Radial Arm Saw+389.50
Tool Box+39.50
Electric Sander+69.95
Work Bench+179.
Gasoline Chain Saw+166.80
.TE
```

The formatted and centered *Table C* appears as follows:

Equipment	Cost
Hammer	14.95
Radial Arm Saw	389.50
Tool Box	39.50
Electric Sander	69.95
Work Bench	179.
Gasoline Chain Saw	166.80

(4) The only differences between the instructions for *Table C* and *Table B* are the two **r r** lines (lines 3 and 4) which appear in *Table C*, replacing the **c c** and **l n** formatting instructions. Each set of instructions contains 2 characters, corresponding to the 2

columns in each table. The **r** calls for the column entry to be placed against the *right* edge, while **c** formats to the **c***enter*, **l** against the **l***eft* edge, and **n** adjusts **n***umbers* according to decimal points in the respective columns.

___ Try various combinations of the column entry instructions **n**, **r**, **l**, and **c**.

(5) **Headings:** Often it is useful to have a table entry act as a title or as a sub-heading. This requires that the title be written (*spanned*) across more than one column. Try the following instructions for *Table D*:

```
.TS                          Instructions for Table D
tab(+) center;
c s
c s
c c
l n.
Table D
.sp 2
House Building Equipment
.sp
Equipment+Cost
.sp
Hammer+14.95
Radial Arm Saw+389.50
Tool Box+39.50
Electric Sander+69.95
Work Bench+179.
Gasoline Chain Saw+166.80
.TE
```

The above instructions produced the following headings in *Table D*:

Table D

House Building Equipment

Equipment	Cost
Hammer	14.95
Radial Arm Saw	389.50
Tool Box	39.50
Electric Sander	69.95
Work Bench	179.
Gasoline Chain Saw	166.80

The **c s** command entered for rows one and two means **c***enter* and **s***pan*. Thus, the entry is spanned across both columns of the table.

Table Entry Command Summary

The options for specifying placement of table entries are:

Option	Function
r	Places the entries against the right edge of the column.
l	Places the entries against the left edge of the column.
c	Places the entries in the center of the column.
n	Adjusts all entries so that the decimal points are lined up.
s	Spans the previous entry across this column.

(6) ___ Try using each of the Table Entry Commands to vary the placement of the headings and data in your table. When finished go ahead and eat lunch—you deserve to eat from a table (considering how many you have set). There is more to come. . . .

Waiter, a Table for Four, Please

(7) Multicolumn tables are created by: (1) changing the instructions to indicate the number of desired columns to be used as well as how you want the information placed in them, and (2) including the needed table data.

Table E demonstrates how to create a four columned table. The formatted *Table E* follows on the next page.

```
.TS                              Instructions for Table E
tab(+) center;
c s s s
c s s s
c c c c
l n l r.
Table E
.sp 2
House Building Equipment For Sale
.sp
Equipment+Cost+Color+Condition
.sp
Hammer+14.95+brown+Beat up
Radial Arm Saw+389.50+blue+New
Tool Box+39.50+green+Fair
Electric Sander+69.95+mauve+Untouched
Work Bench+179.+grey+Bad news
Gasoline Chain Saw+166.80+red+Trouble
.TE
```

Table E

House Building Equipment For Sale

Equipment	Cost	Color	Condition
Hammer	14.95	brown	Beat up
Radial Arm Saw	389.50	blue	New
Tool Box	39.50	green	Fair
Electric Sander	69.95	mauve	Untouched
Work Bench	179.	grey	Bad news
Gasoline Chain Saw	166.80	red	Trouble

How Instructions Resulted in Table E

(a) The fact that each instruction line has four characters in it (such as **c s s s**) means that there will be four columns;

(b) The first line of instructions tells how the first row of the table should be formatted: **c s s s** means *center the first (and only) data entry across all four columns;*

The first instruction corresponds with the first line of data: **Table E**. Therefore, **Table E** is centered across all four columns.

(c) The second instruction line (**c s s s**) also calls for one entry to be spanned across all four columns: **House Building Equipment For Sale**.

(d) The third instruction (**c c c c**) calls for centering of information in **each** of four columns. Therefore in the third data line there must be four entries separated by the *plus* **+** character: **Equipment**, **Cost**, **Color**, and **Condition**; and

(e) The fourth line of instructions (**l n l r.**) tells the computer how to format each of the remaining rows: **l**eft, **n**umber, **l**eft and **r**ight. Because all of the remaining rows of data will follow this format, the instruction line does not have to be repeated. The period (.) *must* follow the last character in this line.

(8) In constructing a table it may be necessary to change the format after some of the data are entered. Perhaps a sub-heading or related but different data must be entered. For instance, assume the house building equipment in our example is available at two different times. The following table could convey that information.

```
.TS                            Instructions for Table F
tab(+) center;
c s s s
c s s s
c c c c
l n l r.
Table F
.sp 2
House Building Equipment For Sale
.sp
Equipment+Cost+Color+Condition
.sp
Hammer+14.95+brown+Beat up
Radial Arm Saw+389.50+blue+New
Tool Box+39.50+green+Fair
.T&
c s s s
l n l r.
.sp
Available After June 30
.sp
Electric Sander+69.95+mauve+Untouched
Work Bench+179.+grey+Bad news
Gasoline Chain Saw+166.80+red+Trouble
Truck+1200+white+200K miles
.TE
```

The resulting table—with format instructions changed in the middle—follows:

Table F

House Building Equipment For Sale

Equipment	Cost	Color	Condition
Hammer	14.95	brown	Beat up
Radial Arm Saw	389.50	blue	New
Tool Box	39.50	green	Fair

Available After June 30

Equipment	Cost	Color	Condition
Electric Sander	69.95	mauve	Untouched
Work Bench	179.	grey	Bad news
Gasoline Chain Saw	166.80	red	Trouble
Truck	1200	white	200K miles

The initial format commands for *Table F* are the same as for *Table E*. The fourth line specifies how the table data should be placed (**l n l r**). All of the data lines will be formatted following that specification, *until the .T& command is encountered.* Following the **.T&** additional format commands and then new data can be entered. The result is that you can format a table, enter data, alter the format of a table, enter more data, alter the format, and again enter more data.

___ Try creating your own table in which the format changes during mid-course.

Using Text for Entries

(9) In addition to numbers and a few words, tables can have entries which are entire blocks of text. The following example demonstrates the use of the blocked text option of the table program.

```
.TS
tab (+) center;
c s
c s
c c
l lw (3i).
Table G
.sp 2
Housebuilding Equipment for Sale
.sp
Equipment+Comments
.sp
Hammer+T{
This is a standard 20 oz. nail whomper, well used in
construction of two houses.
T}
Radial Arm Saw+T{
An extremely useful tool, can change blade direction for
wide variety of cutting angles.
T}
Tool Box +T{
Standard carpenter's multi level
carry everything, find nothing tool box.
T}
Electric Sander+T{
Vibrate your eyes out, fill your lungs with dust, blast your
ears ordinary sander.
T}
Work Bench+T{
Wood, 3 ft by 6 ft 8 drawer, one vise butcher shop.
T}
Gasoline Chain Saw+T{
Been through two forest fires and four friends' fireplace supplies.
T}
.TE
```

The table generated with these format instructions is presented on the next page.

Table G

Housebuilding Equipment for Sale

Equipment	Comments
Hammer	This is a standard 20 oz. nail whomper, well used in construction of two houses.
Radial Arm Saw	An extremely useful tool, can change blade direction for wide variety of cutting angles.
Tool Box	Standard carpenter's multi level carry everything, find nothing tool box.
Electric Sander	Vibrate your eyes out, fill your lungs with dust, blast your ears ordinary sander.
Work Bench	Wood, 3 ft by 6 ft 8 drawer, one vise butcher shop.
Gasoline Chain Saw	Been through two forest fires and four friends' fireplace supplies.

When using text blocks in a table you need to remember four things:

(a) The width of a text block is stated in the instruction section of the table. You use the notation **w(#)** where the **#** number can be in inches, picas, points, centimeters, or toothbrushes. In *Table G* this instruction line reads **l lw(3i).**, indicating that the second column will have a **w**idth of **3 i**nches.

(b) The **T{** is placed after the TAB character and indicates that a text block will follow;

(c) The text begins on the next line; and

(d) The **T}** is placed on the next line after the end the text block.

"Spanning" Information Across Rows

Tables are seldom as neat and tidy as those we have presented so far. The following example demonstrates how to center an entry across two rows.

```
.TS
tab (+) center;
c s s s
c s s s
c c c c
l n c n.
Table H
.sp
Students in Braucher Elementary School
.sp
Teacher+Grade+Gender+Number
McKinney+6+Boys+13
\^+\^+Girls+18
Forbes+7+Boys+16
\^+\^+Girls+15
Place+8+Boys+17
\^+\^+Girls+15
.TE
```

The above commands produce the following *Table H*:

Table H

Students in Braucher Elementary School

Teacher	Grade	Gender	Number
McKinney	6	Boys	13
		Girls	18
Forbes	7	Boys	16
		Girls	15
Place	8	Boys	17
		Girls	15

Note the placement of the \^ commands in the data field. They instruct the formatter (1) not to place any new element in that position, but instead to (2) *pull down* the information from the row above so that it is *horizontally* centered across both rows. Thus, *McKinney* and *6* appear appropriately at the middle of the two rows (*Boys* and *Girls*).

You can format even fancier tables if you have access to a photo-typesetter. Consider the following several examples.

Allbox: The **allbox** in the options line of the instructions results in the centered *Table I* with each data item individually boxed:

```
.TS                        Instructions for Table I
tab (+) allbox center;
c c
l n.
Equipment+Cost
.sp
Hammer+14.95
Radial Arm Saw+389.50
Tool Box+39.50
Electric Sander+69.95
Work Bench+179.
Gasoline Chain Saw+166.80
.TE
```

Table I

Equipment	Cost
Hammer	14.95
Radial Arm Saw	389.50
Tool Box	39.50
Electric Sander	69.95
Work Bench	179.
Gasoline Chain Saw	166.80

Box: The **allbox** option can be replaced with **box**, which will produce a single box around the entire table. This is demonstrated in *Table J*, presented on the following page.

```
.TS
tab (+) box center;
c c
l n.
Equipment+Cost
.sp
Hammer+14.95
Radial Arm Saw+389.50
Tool Box+39.50
Electric Sander+69.95
Work Bench+179.
Gasoline Chain Saw+166.80
.TE
```

The **box** in the options line of the instructions results in the following boxed display.

Table J

Equipment	Cost
Hammer	14.95
Radial Arm Saw	389.50
Tool Box	39.50
Electric Sander	69.95
Work Bench	179.
Gasoline Chain Saw	166.80

Vertical and Horizontal Line Placement: It is also possible to specify where vertical and horizontal lines should be included *inside* a basic box table. This is demonstrated in the following *Table K*, which appears on the next page. The instructions necessary to produce the table are presented first, with the finished formatted table following.

```
.TS
tab (+) center box;
c s s s
c s s s
c c c c
l ‖ n | c n.
Table K
.sp
Students in Braucher Elementary School
.sp
=
Teacher+Grade+Gender+Number

_
Cavette+6+Boys+13
\^+\^+_+_
\^+\^+Girls+18

_
Forbes+7+Boys+16
\^+\^+_+_
\^+\^+Girls+15

_
Koettel+8+Boys+17
\^+\^+_+_
\^+\^+Girls+15
.TE
```

Table K			
Students in Braucher Elementary School			
Teacher	Grade	Gender	Number
Cavette	6	Boys	13
		Girls	18
Forbes	7	Boys	16
		Girls	15
Koettel	8	Boys	17
		Girls	15

The pipe | placed within the format instructions calls for a single vertical line, while a double pipe ‖ produces a double line. The underscore _ in the data requests a single horizontal line (note that this underscore is not a *minus sign, hyphen,* or *dash*); and an equal sign = results in a double horizontal line.

Changing Type Characteristics

The phototypesetter allows you to change font types or point size of your printed output. Font type can be affected with the following line in your format instructions:

cfB s s s

The **cfB s s s** instruction reads c*enter* and s*pan* the data across all four columns, and *change* f*ont* to **B***oldface*. Point size can be affected with the following line in your format instructions:

cp14 s s s

The **cp14 s s s** instruction reads c*enter* and s*pan* the data across all four columns, and *change* **p***oint size* to 14.

Finally, both font type and point size can be affected with the following li. .n your format instructions:

cfBp14 s s s

The **cfBp14 s s s** instruction reads c*enter* and s*pan* the data across all four columns, *change* f*ont* type to **B***oldface*, and *change* **p***oint size* to 14. The effects of changing font type and point size are demonstrated in *Table L*, which follows on the next page.

Reference Material: With the material contained in this Module your table settings should please even the most demanding diner. Should you require additional help—and good help is so hard to find these days—you might look at a pamphlet available from Bell Labs entitled *Tbl—A Program to Format Tables*.

```
.TS
tab (+) center box;
cfBp12 s s s
cp16 s s s
cfBp12 cp12 cp12 cp12
l ‖ n | c n.
Table L
.sp
Students in Pat Lloyd Elementary School
.sp
=
Teacher+Grade+Gender+Number

McKinney+6+Boys+13
\ˆ+\ˆ+_+_
\ˆ+\ˆ+Girls+18

Calhoun+7+Boys+16
\ˆ+\ˆ+_+_
\ˆ+\ˆ+Girls+15

Place+8+Boys+17
\ˆ+\ˆ+_+_
\ˆ+\ˆ+Girls+15
.TE
```

Table L			
Students in Pat Lloyd Elementary School			
Teacher	**Grade**	**Gender**	**Number**
McKinney	6	Boys	13
		Girls	18
Calhoun	7	Boys	16
		Girls	15
Place	8	Boys	17
		Girls	15

Table Formatting Summary

Shell Commands

Command	Function
tbl $\boxed{file1}$ | **nroff -ms**	Sends *file1* to be formatted; results will be displayed on screen.
tbl $\boxed{file1}$| **nroff -ms** | **lpr**	Sends *file1* to be formatted and sends the formatted version to the line printer.
tbl $\boxed{file1}$ | **troff -ms** **−Q**	Sends *file1* to be formatted and sends the formatted version to the phototypesetter.

Formatting Commands

.TS	Notifies *nroff* that a table follows.
.TE	Notifies *nroff* to return to normal formatting.

Table Commands

l	left justify
c	center
r	right justify
n	number
s	span

Module Twenty-Seven
Equalizing Equations
The EQN Pre-Processor

Introduction

Mathematical equations employing symbols and characters foreign to typewriters are usually hand-drawn for inclusion in papers and reports. With the text preformatters *eqn* and *neqn* you can have UNIX format extremely complex equations—regardless of whether they make any sense—allowing you to include equations in your written work or reports.

Prerequisites

Before working on this Module, you should be able to:

(1) Employ the visual editor to add text to a file; and

(2) Use *nroff*, *troff*, and *-ms* macro commands to have files formatted and printed.

Objectives

After completion of this Module you should be able to:

(1) Write instructions necessary to properly format a wide variety of mathematical equations;

(2)   Have equations numbered, centered as figures, or included in the body of text; and

(3)   Make use of *eqn* reference materials to solve more complicated equation formatting problems.

Procedure

UNIX will format mathematical equations including a very wide variety of mathematical symbols—providing you include the proper instructions. Although this process is designed primarily for use with more versatile output devices (such as a phototypesetter or terminals with graphics capabilities), basic equations employing only keyboard characters can be displayed on a terminal of modest intelligence or a standard line printer.

This Module is in two sections. In the first, simple equations that can be displayed on most terminals will be employed to illustrate the general formatting processes. The second section will demonstrate several more complex examples which you will probably not be able to view on your terminal. Normally you will need to use a typesetter or similar device to properly format these equations. (See Module Nineteen: *Phototypesetting with Troff* for more information about typesetting.)

Single Line Equations

(1)   **Basic Formatting Steps:** Log onto your UNIX account. When the Shell prompt is presented start a new file called *eqn.example.*

(2)   Enter the following two lines in the file:

.PP
This file is an example file for equations.

Then enter the following three lines:

.EQ
6 times 5 = 30
.EN

The **.EQ** is a *one-way* command that tells the pre-formatter an equation will begin with the next line. The conclusion of the equation specifications is marked with a **.EN** instruction. As with all formatting commands, the **.EQ** and **.EN** must be on lines by themselves and must start with periods. Whatever is typed on lines between the two commands will be formatted as an equation.

(3) **Formatting Files that Include Equations:** To have the terminal display your *eqn.example* file with its formatted equation, you should return to the Shell and enter the following:

neqn | *eqn.example* | | **nroff -ms** | **page** ®

The resulting equation should appear centered on your screen as:

$$6 \times 5 = 30$$

(4) The *neqn* program is a preformatter for *nroff* with the *-ms* macro formatting package. It translates your equation instructions into specific commands that can be formatted by *nroff*. Thus the file must first be sent to **neqn** and then piped to **nroff**. (In the above example, the formatters replace the word *times* with a multiplication sign, and then properly center and space the equation.)

The *neqn* preformatting package is designed to do the best possible job of formatting equations for terminals and line printers, given the constraints of available characters and full line spacing on most terminals.

"But I could just type 6x5=30 without ever invoking the preformatter," you say. True, but the keyboard characters and spacing capabilities of most terminals would make the following equation a tad difficult:

$$t = \frac{\overline{X}_E - \overline{X}_C}{\sqrt{S_X^2 \left(\frac{1}{n_1} + \frac{1}{n_2} \right)}} = 1.96$$

Although terminal display of such equations is seldom possible, you will soon be able to enter commands to have UNIX produce monsters like this one on a typesetter.

When the final output is to be produced on a typesetter (and not a line printer or your terminal screen) you enter the identical formatting commands in your text, *but a different preformatter is employed.* The *troff* preformatter is named *eqn*, while *neqn* is the *nroff* preformatter. The *eqn* preformatter interprets the same formatting commands, but in a way to take advantage of the wide range of symbols and spacing capabilities provided by a typesetting machine.

When *neqn* interprets the formatting commands, it uses the keyboard symbols to approximate as well as possible the mathematical symbols requested. As could be expected, the *neqn* interpretation of the formatting commands as printed on line printers and terminals is often less than satisfactory.

(5) **Placement on the Page:** If you employ the *-ms* macro package with either *nroff* or *troff*, equations are centered on a page unless you instruct otherwise. To have the equation placed next to the left margin of the text, replace the **.EQ** with **.EQ L** (as in the following instructions):

> **.EQ L**
> **5 times 6 = 30**
> **.EN**

The resulting equation appears at the left margin:

$5 \times 6 = 30$

(6) Equations can be indented from the left margin much like paragraphs. To have the equation indented, use the starting command **.EQ I** (**I** → **I**ndent) followed by the content of the equation. For example:

> **.EQ I**
> **5 times 6 = 30**
> **.EN**

The product, upon formatting, is in an indented equation:

$5 \times 6 = 30$

(7) **Identification:** Equations can also be numbered or labeled. Consider:

.EQ (Equation-A-)
5 times 6 = 30
.EN

The above set of instructions produces the following labeled equation:

$$5 \times 6 = 30 \qquad\qquad \text{(Equation-A-)}$$

(8) Note that there are no spaces in the label. The formatter is programmed to accept only one "word." If you do want a space character in a label (such as "Equation A") you must specify the space with a backslash and zero \0 such as:

.EQ (Equation\0A)
5 times 6 = 30
.EN

The equation with a space in the label appears:

$$5 \times 6 = 30 \qquad\qquad \text{(Equation A)}$$

(9) **Inclusion within a Line of Text:** The process of placing equations within a line of text text is slightly more complicated. First, the formatter must be informed of the symbol you are using in the text to indicate where an equation is to be included. Then it must be given equation formatting instructions. For instance, dollar signs can be used as an equation delimiter if the following three lines are entered in a file:

.EQ
delim $$
.EN

Once the formatter reads to the above lines it will then treat *as equation instructions* all text located between two dollar signs, even if they are in the middle of a line. This process makes it possible to place equations in the middle of a line of text. The following line in a file:

Simple equations such as $5 times 6 = 30 $ can be included.

will appear formatted as:

Simple equations such as 5×6=30 can be included.

What if you need to use a $ for its normal purposes? You must have the delimiter turned off. To do so you enter:

.EQ
delim off
.EN

Advanced Equations Using Mathematical Symbols

The following examples will not look very satisfactory on most terminals. You should enter them into your file, then send them to the *eqn* preformatter, and then to *troff* *-ms* for formatting and phototypesetting. The usual command to do this will be:

eqn $\boxed{\textit{filename}}$ | **troff** **-ms**   ®

If you are not familiar with the *troff* text processor see Module Nineteen: *Phototypesetting with Troff.*

(1) **Available Symbols:** Table 1 presents a list of symbols available on *eqn*. They are approximated as closely as possible by *neqn* for line printers and terminals.

(2) **Use of the Diacritical Marks:** Quite often an equation requires that a vector, bar, underline, and other diacritical mark be placed on top or below letters or symbols. The commands which create these effects are **bar, dot, dotdot, dyad, hat, tilde, vec,** and **under.** The selected command, if placed *after* any letter, symbol, or word

Table 1

Symbols Available with eqn

Mathematical Symbols

Input	Results
approx	≈
cdot	·
del	∇
grad	∇
half	½
inf	∞
int	∫
inter	∩
nothing	
partial	∂
prime	′
prod	∏
sqrt	√
sum	Σ
times	×
union	∪
->	→
<-	←
<=	≤
>=	≥
<<	≪
>>	≫
+-	±
!=	≠
==	≡
,...,	, . . . ,
x bar	$\bar{x}$
x under	$\underline{x}$
x dot	$\dot{x}$
x dotdot	$\ddot{x}$
x hat	$\hat{x}$
x tilde	$\tilde{x}$
x vec	$\vec{x}$
x dyad	$\overleftrightarrow{x}$

Greek Letters

Input	Results
DELTA	Δ
GAMMA	Γ
LAMBDA	Λ
OMEGA	Ω
PHI	Φ
PI	Π
PSI	Ψ
SIGMA	Σ
THETA	Θ
UPSILON	Υ
XI	Ξ
alpha	α
beta	β
chi	χ
delta	δ
epsilon	ε
eta	η
gamma	γ
iota	ι
kappa	κ
lambda	λ
mu	μ
nu	ν
omega	ω
omicron	o
pi	π
psi	ψ
rho	ρ
sigma	σ
tau	τ
theta	θ
upsilon	υ
xi	ξ
zeta	ζ

in the formatting instructions, will position the mark appropriately in the output. This is demonstrated in the next equation.

```
.EQ
x hat +
Y dyad -
OMEGA under times
word vec +
A tilde +
y dotdot
.EN
```

The above material produces symbols with diacritical marks:

$$\hat{x} + \overline{Y} - \underline{\Omega} \times \overrightarrow{word} + \tilde{A} + \ddot{y}$$

(3) **Greek Letters:** A wide range of equations is possible using the mathematical symbols, Greek letters, and words. Consider:

```
.EQ
union 24 apples + dough + spices -> 4 PI
.EN
```

The above instructions—when properly baked by the formatter—produce:

$$\bigcup 24 apples + dough + spices \rightarrow 4\Pi$$

Of course, a corollary is:

```
.EQ
int 4 PI + 4 people -> approx 4 SIGMA I K people
.EN
```

$$\int 4\Pi + 4 people \rightarrow \approx 4\Sigma IK people$$

(4) **Spacing and Lines:** Before we enter more complicated equations it is necessary to describe how the *eqn* and *neqn* preformatters handle spaces between words, characters, and lines.

(a) Spaces are used to delineate the "pieces" of an equation. For instance:

```
.EQ
5 OMEGA times 6 = sum x dot + LAMBDA
.EN
```

is formatted as:

$$5\Omega \times 6 = \sum \dot{x} + \Lambda$$

If some of the spaces are not included:

```
.EQ
5OMEGA times 6 = sumx dot + LAMBDA
.EN
```

the formatted equation comes out looking quite different:

$$5OMEGA \times 6 = su\dot{m}x + \Lambda$$

When the formatter comes to *5OMEGA* it does not recognize the string of characters as code for any symbol, so the string is printed out as is. Likewise, because *sumx* is not in its repertoire, the *sumx* is printed. Then *eqn* follows the **dot** instruction by placing a dot over *sumx*.

Summary: Spaces are essential for the formatter to recognize each part of instructions.

(b) Extra spaces are ignored:

```
.EQ
5  OMEGA    times 6 =   sum   x dot + LAMBDA
.EN
```

is formatted with proper spacing:

$$5\Omega \times 6 = \sum \dot{x} + \Lambda$$

(c) Use the tilde ˜ if you want extra space included within an equation. For instance:

```
.EQ
5 ˜ OMEGA ˜ times ˜ 6 ˜ = ˜ sum x dot ˜ ˜ +
˜ ˜ LAMBDA
.EN
```

produces a spaced equation:

$$5 \ \Omega \times 6 = \sum \dot{x} \ + \ \Lambda$$

Notice the differences in spacing between the equations as formatted in (b) and (c).

(d) In the example of diacritical marks (procedure step 2) each element was placed on a separate line, yet the output appeared as one "equation." That is possible because the formatter treats spaces between words and the ends of lines simply as the "edge" of symbols. Thus one equation can be entered on several lines in a file. To offer another example,

```
.EQ
5 OMEGA times 6
=
sum x dot
+
LAMBDA
.EN
```

continues to produce:

$$5\Omega \times 6 = \sum \dot{x} + \Lambda$$

This multi-line input property of *eqn* is especially useful when trying to keep your formatting wits about you.

Yet More Complicated Equations

This section will introduce single element examples of more difficult to format equations. The first seven steps describe how to effect changes in vertical spacing, such as:

$$\frac{6x}{3}$$

Later steps demonstrate how to bracket elements which go together in more complex examples:

$$\frac{6(x+3)}{\sqrt{3+e^{\cos\alpha}}}$$

(5) **Exponents:** To have an exponent or **sup**erscript added to a number, letter or symbol, the **sup** instruction is used. For instance:

```
.EQ
A  sup  2  +  B  sup  2  =  C  sup  2
.EN
```

produces a superscripted equation:

$$A^2 + B^2 = C^2$$

(6) **Subscripts:** Likewise, **sub**scripts are formatted with the **sub** instruction. For example:

```
.EQ
X  sub  3  +  Y  sub  j  -  Z  sub  ii  +  R  sub  alpha
.EN
```

Upon formatting, the above instruction produces a subscripted equation:

$$X_3 + Y_j - Z_{ii} + R_\alpha$$

(7) **Subscripts and Superscripts:** If you want *both* a subscript and a superscript on the *same* symbol, the **sub**script must *precede* the **sup**erscript instruction (alphabetical order). For instance,

```
.EQ
Y sub a sup 2 +
 X sub b sup alpha  =
 Z sub garbage sup 3
.EN
```

is the instructions for sub and superscripted symbols:

$$Y_a^2 + X_b^\alpha = Z_{garbage}^3$$

Reversing the order of **sup** and **sub** results in a very different output.

```
.EQ
Y sup 2 sub a +
 X sup alpha sub b  =
 Z sup 3 sub garbage
.EN
```

produces the following equation with subscripts on the superscripts:

$$Y^{2a} + X^{\alpha b} = Z^{3garbage}$$

(8) **Fractions:** The magic instruction to format fractions is **over**. Consider:

```
.EQ
30 PI over 6 = 5 PI
.EN
```

will produce:

$$30\frac{\Pi}{6} = 5\Pi$$

(9) **Limits:** Statistical or mathematical equations may require the use of limits on symbols such as: $\int$ $\sum$ $\prod$ etc. For example:

> .EQ
> Y = int from 0 to 1 x ˜ dx
> ˜ + ˜ sum from 1 to inf N ˜ − ˜ 1
> .EN

The following limited equation is produced:

$$Y = \int_0^1 x \ dx + \sum_1^\infty N - 1$$

The instruction **from** identifies the lower limit and **to** identifies the upper.

(10) **Brackets, Braces, Parentheses, and Bars:** Equations often require large parentheses around whole sections of symbols. The instructions **left** and **right** when associated with brackets { }, parentheses ( ), braces [ ], and bars (the *pipe*) | | will cause the formatter to include an appropriately large symbol in the output. For instance:

> .EQ
> left (
> A over 6
> right) ˜ + ˜
> left {
> 3 over sqrt b
> right } ˜ - ˜
> left |
> x dotdot over y sub alpha
> right |
> ˜ = ˜ PSI
> .EN

The above instructions produce:

$$\left[\frac{A}{6} \right] + \left\{ \frac{3}{\sqrt{b}} \right\} - \left| \frac{\ddot{x}}{y_\alpha} \right| = \Psi$$

(11) **Grouping Parts of Equations:** What you have learned thus far will permit you to format a wide variety of equations. Problems arise, however, when it is necessary to use several elements following a format instruction (such as **over** or **sup**). Consider:

$$e^{\cos \alpha + t}$$

This looks like a simple figure to format. The first solution that most people try is:

> **.EQ**
> **e sup cos ˜ alpha ˜ + ˜ t**
> **.EN**

But the computer does not know that all of *cos, alpha,* and $+ t$ are to be placed as the exponent. In fact, it is programmed to superscript *only* the next symbol. As a result, the formatter produces an errant:

$$e^{\cos} \alpha + t$$

The way to avoid such surprises is to bracket symbols that go together. You must use, of all things, brackets $\{\ \}$.

For instance, the format instructions:

> **.EQ**
> **e sup {cos ˜ alpha ˜ + ˜ t}**
> **.EN**

uses brackets to enclose those elements that are all to be placed in the exponent. The resulting output is appropriately superscripted:

$$e^{\cos \alpha + t}$$

The brackets used in this section are for communicating with the formatter. In the previous section you were introduced to brackets *which were printed in the formatted equation* to assist the reader. The difference is in the instructions **left** and **right**. If the bracket is used without **left** or **right**, it will be read by the formatter only as identifying those elements which stay together, and then the bracket is discarded. If the **left** or **right** command precedes the bracket, the formatter will include the appropriately sized bracket in the final output.

(12) **Examples of Complex Equations Using Brackets:** Each of the following equations includes brackets that identify entire sections of the equations which need to be treated as units. Any complex group of symbols, letters, and numbers, *if surrounded by brackets,* can be used where just one symbol normally would be used. Variations of the previous examples are:

```
.EQ (Example\0A)
{6 (x + 3)}
over
{sqrt {3 + x bar}}
.EN
```

$$\frac{6(x+3)}{\sqrt{3+\bar{x}}}$$

(Example A)

```
.EQ (Example\0B)
{6 {(x + 3)}} over
{sqrt {3 + e sup {cos alpha}}}
.EN
```

$$\frac{6(x+3)}{\sqrt{3+e^{\cos\alpha}}}$$

(Example B)

```
.EQ (Example\0C)
Y~ =~ int from { alpha , 1} to { delta , 3}
B sub {alpha sub 1}
+ C sub {beta sub 2}
+ D sub {delta sub 3}
- {x + y + z} bar
.EN
```

$$Y = \int_{\alpha,1}^{\delta,3} B_{\alpha_1} + C_{\beta_2} + D_{\delta_3} - \overline{x+y+z}$$

(Example C)

eqn   459

.EQ (Example\0D)
Y ~ ~ = ~ ~ 2 pi int from 1 to inf
{{ sin {(omega t + 6)}}
over
{3 alpha}}
~ dt
.EN

$$Y \ = \ 2\pi \int_{1}^{\infty} \frac{\sin(\omega t + 6)}{3\alpha} \ dt \qquad \text{(Example D)}$$

.EQ (Example\0E)
t ~ = ~
{X bar sub E
~ _ ~
X bar sub C}
over
{sqrt {S sub X sup 2 ~
left (1 over {n sub 1} ~ + ~ 1 over {n sub 2} right) }}
~ = ~ 1.96
.EN

$$t = \frac{\bar{X}_E - \bar{X}_C}{\sqrt{S_X^2 \ (\frac{1}{n_1} + \frac{1}{n_2})}} = 1.96 \qquad \text{(Example E)}$$

.EQ (Example\0F)
Y ~ ~ = ~ ~
sum from {i = 0} to {i = inf }
{ OMEGA + 3.7} over
sqrt {alpha sub 1 + beta sub 1}
.EN

$$Y \ = \ \sum_{i=0}^{i=\infty} \frac{\Omega + 3.7}{\sqrt{\alpha_1 + \beta_1}} \qquad \text{(Example F)}$$

```
.EQ (Example\0G)
sigma sup 2 ~ = ~
1 over k sup 2 ~
sum  from  i=1 to  k  ~
left  (
1 over n tilde sub i
~ + ~ delta sup 2
over { 2m sub i }
right )
.EN
```

$$\sigma^2 \; = \; \frac{1}{k^2} \sum_{i=1}^{k} \left[\frac{1}{\tilde{n}_i} + \frac{\delta^2}{2m_i} \right]$$
(Example G)

```
.EQ (Ex.\0H)
{left [ { {xi sup 2 + nu sup 2 }
over
sqrt 6 } over x sup 2
right ] }
sup 3 ~ = ~
left [ {6 sqrt {3 z times OMEGA}}
over
Z sub nonsense right ]
~ - 41
~ +- psi hat
~ times ~
left (
{ a + b + c } bar
right )
.EN
```

$$\left[\frac{\frac{\xi^2+\nu^2}{\sqrt{6}}}{x^2} \right]^3 = \left[\frac{6\sqrt{3z \times \Omega}}{Z_{nonsense}} \right] -41 \; \pm \hat{\psi} \; \times \left[\overline{a+b+c} \right]$$
(Ex. H)

(13) **Arranging Several Symbols in a Display:** Vertical arrays of symbols or numbers can be formatted with the **pile** command. An example of this effect begins the next page.

The following instructions are interpreted to produce an equation containing a vertical array:

```
.EQ
OMEGA ˜ ˜ = ˜ ˜ left [
pile {1 above 2 above 3 above 4}
˜ ˜
pile {W above X above Y above Z}
right ]
.EN
```

$$\Omega \;=\; \begin{bmatrix} 1 & W \\ 2 & X \\ 3 & Y \\ 4 & Z \end{bmatrix}$$

The next example shows how the "piles" can be left or right justified by using the **lpile** and **rpile** commands. Note the difference in placement of elements between the two columns in the formatted version. The alpha is against the left of the first column; the beta to the right in the second.

```
.EQ
OMEGA
˜ ˜ = ˜ ˜
left [
lpile {alpha above {2.78 over A} above {x + y} above
 4 LAMBDA}
right ]
˜ ˜ + ˜ ˜
left [
rpile {beta above 5.32 above {a + b} above PSI}
right ]
.EN
```

$$\Omega \;=\; \begin{bmatrix} \alpha \\ \dfrac{2.78}{A} \\ x+y \\ 4\Lambda \end{bmatrix} \;+\; \begin{bmatrix} \beta \\ 5.32 \\ a+b \\ \Psi \end{bmatrix}$$

(14) Matrices: The **pile** command formats each column independently. If you have an array of elements that vary in height in different columns, **pile** will result in different columns being spaced differently. The command **matrix** will look at *all* columns and then make spacing decisions based on all entries in the matrix. The major requirement is that there be the same number of elements in all columns. An example:

```
.EQ
OMEGA ~ ~ = ~ ~ left [{
matrix {
ccol {alpha above  {2.78 over A }
above {x + y} above {4 LAMBDA }}
ccol {beta above 5.32 above {a + b} above PSI}
}
} right ]
.EN
```

$$\Omega \;=\; \left[\begin{matrix} \alpha & \beta \\ \dfrac{2.78}{A} & 5.32 \\ x+y & a+b \\ 4\Lambda & \Psi \end{matrix} \right.$$

The instruction **ccol** results in the matrix elements being *centered* in each column. The alternatives are **lcol** and **rcol**, which place the elements at the left and right of columns, respectively. Another example (and the formatted equation):

```
.EQ
Y ~ ~ = ~ ~
matrix {
lcol { X sub alpha above {153 + 2z} above .09 t}
ccol { Y sub beta above {186 - 5n} above 1.3 s}
rcol { Z sub gamma above {264 + 3s} above 80 g}
}
.EN
```

$$Y \;=\; \begin{matrix} X_\alpha & Y_\beta & Z_\gamma \\ 153+2z & 186-5n & 264+3s \\ .09t & 1.3s & 80g \end{matrix}$$

(15) **Type Size and Font Selection:** Point size and type font can be specified for individual characters in an equation or for all characters. For any specific character the point size of the type can be specified by the instruction **size** ⟨N⟩ where **N** is a point size from 6 to 36. Here you see a 36 point Omega and 6 point "D":

```
.EQ
size 36 OMEGA ~ = ~ left [
pile { A above B above C above size 6 D }
right ]
.EN
```

$$\Omega = \begin{bmatrix} A \\ B \\ C \\ {\scriptstyle D} \end{bmatrix}$$

Note that only the Ω was affected by the 36 point type size specification. The formatter reverted back to standard (11 point) type for all symbols, until it encountered the next point size change command. The D was then specified to be in 6 point type.

In addition to point sizes, the fonts can be specified by: **roman, italic, bold** and **fat**. The **fat** specification makes the letter or symbol slightly "heavier" in whatever font is in use. For instance, these instructions result in different fonts for each column:

```
.EQ
size 36 OMEGA ~ = ~ left [
pile {
italic {A + 14 r sup 2}
above bold {B - 12 c sup alpha}
above roman {C + 43 d sub j }
above fat {D times 78 del sup 2 }}
right ]
.EN
```

$$\Omega = \begin{bmatrix} A+14r^2 \\ \mathbf{B-12c^\alpha} \\ C+43d_j \\ D\times78\nabla^2 \end{bmatrix}$$

(16) **Changing the Exact Location of Symbols:** If you are unhappy with the exact placement of characters in the formatted equations in the first copy of your output it is possible to "fine tune" the placement of symbols. When we saw that the Ω in the above equation was not centered relative to the equal sign, we modified the format instructions as follows:

```
.EQ
down 60
size 36 OMEGA ~ = ~ left [
pile {
italic {A + 14 r sup 2}
above bold {B − 12 c sup alpha}
above roman {C + 43 d sub j }
above fat {D times 78 del sup 2 }}
right ]
.EN
```

The resulting formatted display has the Omega properly placed:

$$\Omega = \begin{bmatrix} A+14r^2 \\ B-12c^\alpha \\ C+43d_j \\ D\times78\nabla^2 \end{bmatrix}$$

The **down** $\boxed{Number}$ command affects only the next symbol or bracketed unit. In this case the instructions **down 60** call for the omega to be moved down 60 one hundredths of an "em." Since an "em" is about the size of the letter m in whatever type is being employed (in this case 36 point), the Ω is lined up with the equals sign.

In addition, the commands **up** $\boxed{Number}$, **back** $\boxed{Number}$, and **fwd** $\boxed{Number}$ will re-position the immediately following symbol.

(17) **Global Font or Point Size Changes:** The *eqn* formatter will type all equations in 10 point type unless you specify otherwise. You can at any point instruct the formatter to employ a different basic point size (or type font), which will be used until you specify another. (For more information on this process see the *number registers* section Module Nineteen: *Phototypesetting with Troff.*)

The global command to affect the point size of the equation—but not the surrounding text—is **gsize** $\boxed{Number}$. The command **gfont** $\boxed{Font}$ is used to specify the font (where $\boxed{Font}$ is *Italic*, **Bold**, or Roman). For instance:

```
.EQ
gsize 14
gfont italic
omega == int from here to eternity
LAMBDA GAMMA EPSILON
.EN
```

produces an italic, point size 14 equation:

$$\omega \equiv \int_{here}^{eternity} \Lambda\Gamma\mathrm{E}$$

Changes in point size and font remain in effect until a new one is specified. The size and font may be changed as often as the author sees fit. These changes affect only the equation and not the surrounding text.

Obtaining Output:

Typeset: If the output is to be typeset, the Shell execution command is:

$$\textbf{eqn}\ \ \boxed{\textit{filename}}\,|\ \textbf{troff -ms -Q}\qquad ®$$

Line Printed: If the output is to be sent to a line printer, the Shell execution command is:

$$\textbf{neqn}\ \ \boxed{\textit{filename}}\,|\ \textbf{nroff -ms} \,|\ \textbf{lpr}\qquad ®$$

Using tbl with eqn: If tables are also included in the file, the *tbl* preformatter should *precede* the *eqn* process:

$$\textbf{tbl}\ \ \boxed{\textit{filename}}\,|\ \textbf{eqn} \,|\ \textbf{troff -ms -Q}\qquad ®$$

Using refer and tbl with eqn: If tables, references, and equations are included in a file, the proper order for using all three preprocessers is:

refer -p *database* $\boxed{\textit{filename}}$ | **tbl** | **eqn** | **troff** **-ms** **-Q**   ®

Note: Three of the above Shell Command sequences include a **-Q** for placement of the job in the *troff* queue. If your installation uses some other *troff* queue procedure, remove the **-Q** and substitute the proper argument.

Detecting eqn Format Problems: UNIX maintains a program which will check your equations for formatting errors. Before you have a paper containing sophisticated equations formatted you might want to let **checkeq** review your work. The program isn't foolproof, but it can be of some help pointing out possible trouble spots.

The Shell command line to use **checkeq** is:

checkeq $\boxed{\textit{filename}}$ | **page**   ®

Additional Reference Material: Two pamphlets in wide distribution are:

(a) *TBL—A Program to Format Tables*, by Lesk, published by Bell Laboratories, and

(b) *Typesetting Mathematics—User's Guide*, by Kernighan and Cherry, published by Bell Laboratories.

Module Twenty-Eight
Troubleshooting

Introduction

Problems encountered while using UNIX are both frustrating and not uncommon, owing in part to the complexity and power of the system (and the vagaries and moods of any electronic beast). This cannot be a comprehensive section, due to the incredible variety of errors possible with the UNIX system. We have, however, attempted to address the more common problems encountered by us and the many UNIX users with whom we have worked.

Prerequisites

Before using this Module you should have encountered a problem (so, what else is new?).

Objectives

After reading the diagnostic section of this Module you should, in many cases, be able to locate the appropriate remedy for your problem in the second part of the Module (or have some idea as to where to start).

Procedure

The procedure section of this Module is presented in five parts. The first section is designed to help you diagnose your problem. This material should be read carefully, as it will direct you to the appropriate location(s) in the Module where the remedy to your problem may reside. The remaining four sections include descriptions of the most common problems we have encountered and our suggested solutions. These problem-remedy paragraphs are presented in four major groupings:

> *I - Problems Logging On;*
>
> *II - Unexpected Formatted Output;*
>
> *III - Shell Problems and Error Messages;* and
>
> *IV - Editing Problems.*

Each of these groupings begins with an index to the problems it addresses. The diagnostic section will refer you to the appropriate solution section.

The section entitled *Resetting Your Terminal Type* referred to in earlier Modules is part (H) of section *IV - Editing Problems.*

Diagnosing the Problem

When working with UNIX you know you've got a problem when something unexpected happens (why did that funny message appear on my screen while I was editing this file?) or when you accidently do something resulting in an expected, but undesirable outcome (why did I delete the first thousand lines from the report I just finished editing?). To begin diagnosing your problem you should consider in which category your problem falls:

(1) **Problems Logging On:** If you are experiencing difficulty logging on to the system, proceed directly to the first problem-remedy section of this Module entitled *Problems Logging On.*

(2) **Unexpected Formatted Text Output:** If your problem is with unexpected output of formatted text proceed to the second problem-remedy section: *Unexpected Formatted Output.*

(3) **Shell or Editor Problem:** The other unexpected or undesirable events covered in this Module can be classified as occurring either while you are interacting with the Shell or with an editor.

If you know you were interacting with the Shell when your problem occurred proceed to the third problem-remedy section of this Module entitled *Shell Problems and Error Messages*.

If you were in an editor Mode when the troublesome event(s) occurred proceed to the final problem-remedy section: *Editing Problems*.

If you are not sure where you were when the trouble began continue to procedure step (4), which follows.

(4) **Where Am I?** When you are lost within UNIX the |DEL| or |RUB| key can be your light through the darkness.

___ If you are still logged on you should press the |DEL| or |RUB| key.

If nothing happens you are probably no longer in communication with UNIX. This means that either your keyboard has locked up, or the system has crashed or that you have in some other way been disconnected from the system. In this case we can offer little assistance and suggest you locate an experienced user near by or talk to whoever administers your local system. (As software types we can only offer the time honored response, "*Hey, what can I say? That's a hardware problem.*")

If you were in communication with UNIX when you pressed the |DEL| or |RUB| key one of three things probably happened:

(a) *The terminal "beeped".* You are in the visual editor. If you were in Command Mode, you were left there and the beep sounded. If you were in Append Mode you were moved to Command Mode and the beep sounded. (The |DEL| key works like the |ESC| key, in that it moves you to Command Mode if you were in Append. It will, however, cause the terminal to beep regardless of which mode you were in.)

(b) *The word "Interrupt" appeared on the screen.* You are in the line editor. If you were in the Append Mode, you have been moved to Command. If you were in Command Mode, you remain there.

(c) *A question mark appeared on the screen.* You were in a Shell process. By pressing the $\boxed{\text{DEL}}$ key you ended the process (killed it) and are presented with another Shell prompt.

At this time you should know were you are and have two choices about how to proceed. If you feel like your problem is solved — and have no need for further information — then continue with your work. If you desire to know more about the troublesome event you should examine the index of the appropriate problem-remedy section of this Module and read the related information.

Organization of Problem-Remedy Sections: Each of the following problem areas is divided into symptom categories (*A,B,C*, etc.). Each symptom has listed under it one or more possible causes. The proposed remedies (identified with a ●) are placed below each of the symptoms.

Section I - Problems Logging On

INDEX

(A) **No Cursor**

(B) **Strange Characters Appear on the Screen**

(C) **Cannot Get Logged In**

(D) **No Login Banner**

PROBLEMS and REMEDIES

(A) **No Cursor**

(1) *Brightness turned down, or terminal is not on, not plugged in, or in need of repair.*

● Make sure the brightness is turned up, switch is on, the terminal is plugged in, and you have given it 15 seconds to warm up. If still no cursor appears, try another terminal and report the problem.

(B) Strange Characters Appear on the Screen

(1) *Switch settings of terminal are wrong.*

- Try a different terminal.
- Examine a similar terminal for proper settings.

(2) *Terminal is receiving noise from line or modem.*

- Try a different terminal.
- Logoff (hangup phone and/or turn off the modem). Logon a second time.
- Report problem for service.

(C) Cannot Get Logged In

(1) *Error made in entering either the login or password.*

- Carefully enter each "word," leaving no spaces between the characters in your login and password. There probably are no upper case letters or spaces in either (upper vs. lower case is critical).

(2) *The system does not recognize either the password or login.*

- First be sure you are correctly entering the "words." Then check with the system administrator to be certain that you have an exact copy of a working password and account login.

(D) No Login Banner

(1) *Dead connection with UNIX central.*

- Try another terminal.
- See if anyone else is logged into your system.
- Call the system administrator.

(2) *System went down.*

- Scream, cry, go play tennis; see system administrator.

Section II - Unexpected Formatted Output

Many formatting problems can be identified in advance of actually formatting the file by employing the check nr*off* program. From the Shell enter **checknr** *filename* to locate potential problems. See Module Nine for more information about the **checknr** program.

INDEX

(A) **No Output**

(B) **Margin Is Not Where It Should Be**

(C) **Extra Underlining**

(D) **Text Is Not Filled**

(E) **Missing Text**

PROBLEMS and REMEDIES

(A) **No Output**

(1) *Entered incorrect command line.*

- Make certain the Shell command contains all the proper pieces, that it has the appropriate arguments (each separated by a space), and that the command line calls for the right *filename.*

(2) *Logged out before job was finished.*

- Unless your account is set up to continue work after logging out you should not do so until all processes are completed. Module Seventeen: *Backgrounding a Process* describes how this can be done.

(3) *File contains unbalanced .FS, .DS, .KS, etc.*

- Do you have a *Table Start* without a *Table End* or a *Keep Start* without a *Keep End*? Pairing these commands is essential. Check that you have not forgotten to match each **.FS**, **.DS**, or **.KS** with a matching **.FE**, **.DE**, or **.KE**.

(B) Margin Is Not Where It Should Be

(1) *File has unbalanced indent requests.*

- Check that for each **.RS** there is a **.RE** to return the margin to its original position.

(2) *File includes mixed .RS and .in formatting commands.*

- These commands do not access the same number registers. Thus, indenting can quickly become fouled up when both are used. For this reason you should stick with one or the other.

(3) *Error in specification of margin.*

- The units you use are critical. For instance, **.in** *5* will indent five spaces, while **.in** *5i* indents five inches. To the formatter, **.in** *5P* (pica) does not equal **.in** *5p* (points).

(C) Extra Underlining

(1) *An unbalanced one-way underline command used.*

- You probably began underlining with the **.I** command. You must return to non-underlining status with the **.R** command. (When using *nroff* both the **.B** and **.I** result in underlining.) In addition, section headers are underlined if you use the *-ms* macros.

(D) Text Is Not Filled

(1) *Unbalanced nroff requests.*

- You probably inserted a **.nf** to isolate a block of unfilled text, and did not include the matching **.fi** command.

(2) *Text does not begin at left margin.*

- A line of text which does not begin at the left margin will result in a blank space in the formatted text. Check that all lines in your file begin at the left margin.

(E) Missing Text

(1) *A text line begins with period or apostrophe.*

- An input line beginning with a period or apostrophe is considered by the formatter to be a formatting instruction *and not text.* Make certain that the missing text is not on a line beginning with a period or apostrophe.

(2) *Illegal text is included on a formatting command line.*

- Although a few formatting commands take text as arguments (**.IP** *(A)* for instance), most do not. Any text placed on a line with most formatting requests will be ignored. For instance, this input line would not print:

.ul *distinguished scholars Pulos and Chang*

Section III - Shell Problems and Error Messages

INDEX

(A) **Messages Appear on the Screen**

(B) **Where's My Prompt?**

(C) **Lost in a Directory**

PROBLEMS and REMEDIES

(A) **Messages Appear on the Screen**

(1) *Command not found.*

- Usually means the command name was misspelled.

(2) *Cannot open filename.*

- Usually means the *filename* you included in a command line is not in your current directory, or you incorrectly typed the *filename.*

(3) *Broken Pipe.*

- You probably deleted the job while it was being executed. Try reissuing the Shell Command (or, if wealthy, call a plumber). May also occur if the Shell must break a process for any reason (for example, if you route a formatting job into an already existing *filename*).

(4) *Stopped.*

- If a note reading *Stopped* appears at the bottom of the screen, along with the Shell prompt, press these keys:

fg   ®

(The source of your problem was pressing of the CTRL-Z key, which places a process into the background and gives you a Shell prompt. The command **fg** means *foreground,* and pulls this backgrounded process into the foreground.)

(5) *There are Stopped Jobs.*

- Will occur when attempting to logout and you have put a job into the background (with the CTRL-Z command). See (4) above.

(6) *Permission denied.*

- Usually indicates you forgot to include the command in the command line. You probably entered a *filename* alone rather than a Shell command followed by a *filename.*

- The file you specified does not have execute permission. You must change the mode of a file to 700 for it to be executed. See Module Twenty-Two: *Commands, Files, and Directories.*

(7) *Core dumped.*

- A Shell process was abnormally terminated. A file named core, containing an image of core at the time of termination, is added to your home directory. You may remove this *core* file and suffer no ill effects.

(8) *Usage: . . .*

- Indicates incorrect use of Shell command (i.e., too few or too many arguments). For example, if you use **cp** with only one *filename* in the command line you will get a message something like the following:

Usage: cp f1 f2; or cp [-r] f1 . . . fn d2

Attempt to decipher the cryptic message or, if you know how to use the command (and just made a typing error), ignore it and enter the correct command line.

(9) *No match.*

 • You were probably using a filename expansion character to locate a file. No *filename* exists in the current directory that fits the expanded file name as you specified it. See Module Sixteen: *Account Management Activities.*

(B) **Where's My Prompt?**

(1) *Stuck in a Shell process.*

 • If you entered a Shell process (such as **Mail** or **write**) you will remain there until you end it. Try using a CTRL-D. (See Module Fourteen: *Communicating with Others* for assistance with **Mail** and **write**.)

 • Other Shell commands can have a similar effect. If you entered **vi** without specifying a *filename*, the visual editor will be invoked. You will be in the Command Mode, and can return to the Shell by entering **:w** *filename* (to save the file material) and **ZZ**, or **:q!** (to trash it).

(C) **Lost in a Directory**

(1) *Do not remember which directory you are in.*

 • Enter **pwd** to discover your current "working directory."

(2) *Want to return to Home directory.*

 • Enter the **cd** Shell command and you will be placed in your Home directory.

Section IV - Editing Problems

INDEX

(A) **Deleted Wrong Text from File**

(B) **Made a Complete Mess of File**

(C) **Display Went Blank**

(D) **Display Is a Word Salad**

(E) **Messages on Screen**

(F) **Strange Characters on Screen**

(G) **Numbers and Text Crammed Together**

(H) **Arrow Keys Don't Work Correctly (Resetting Your Terminal Type)**

(I) **Cursor Skips Lines**

PROBLEMS and SOLUTIONS

(A) Deleted Wrong Text from File

(1) *And you have not entered another command since accidentally removing the text.*

- Press the **u** key one time. This **u***ndo* command undoes the last modification to the file.

(2) *You deleted the text several steps back and* **u** *does not retrieve it.*

- The visual editor saves the last nine (9) text deletions in buffers numbered 1 to 9. To access these buffers type "#**p** (double quotes, [1-9], **p**). If the desired text does not appear, type **u** (for undo), and then press the period (.) key. You can repeat this procedure (**u.u.u.**) until the desired text appears. See Module Thirteen: *Truly Advanced Visual Editing.*

(3) *Error was too far back for numbered buffers.*

- You have a choice: If you would rather go back to how the file was *before* you began this editing session (or last typed the :**w** command) you can return to the Shell without writing the present version onto the permanent memory. To perform this action you:

  (a) First press the ESC key;

  (b) Second type :**q!** and you will return to the Shell, with work of that editing session vaporized.

(B) Made a Complete Mess of File

(1) *May be caused by a variety of reasons.*

- See (A) 3 directly above.

(C) **Display Went Blank**

(1) *You pressed* CTRL-Z *and stopped the process.*

- See *Section III - Shell Problems* paragraph A (4) *Stopped.*

(D) **Display Is a Word Salad**

(1) *May be caused by a variety of reasons.*

- From the Command Mode press these keys

z-   ®

(Z minus → clear and redraw the screen).

(2) *Your terminal needs to be reset.*

- If your screen *regularly* fouls up during an editing session (one common problem is text in your file cramming up against the line numbers displayed on the screen) try the following:

Place yourself in the Shell, type

reset   ®

and then again attempt to visually edit a file.

(E) **Messages on Screen**

(1) *Could be a note about completed process or a write message from another user.*

- See *Section III - Shell Problems* for a description of various screen messages.

- If it is a message from another user, you might want to write back. See Module Fourteen: *Communicating with Others.*

- If you are staring at a message from UNIX and just want to get rid of it, enter **z-** to redraw the screen.

(F) **Strange Characters on Screen**

(1) *Screen displays characters such as* ^H ˄J K˄L.

- You probably tried to move the cursor (using the arrow keys) while in the Append Mode. These are the control characters associated with those keys. Press $\boxed{\text{ESC}}$ to move into the Command Mode. Remove the control characters, and continue your work.

(G) Numbers and Text Crammed Together

(1) *Momentary power outage or other terminal disruption.*

- If there was a power failure—or you momentarily turned the terminal off—the text may be jammed against the editing numbers.

Enter:

reset

(H) Arrow Keys Don't Work Correctly (Resetting Your Terminal Type)

(1) *Login error.*

- You probably made an error in informing UNIX of the type of terminal you are using. To give yourself a second chance enter the command (don't forget the dot in *.login*):

source *. login*

This command will, among other things, tell UNIX to ask you once again what type of terminal you are using. Refer to the section *Accessing the UNIX System* in Module Two for help with this step.

(I) Cursor Skips Lines

(1) *You did not use ⑧ at the end of each line.*

- What *appears* to be a discrete line of text is in fact a *continuation* of the prior line(s). A single very long line is occupying two or more screen lines. You probably noticed while entering the text that the cursor automatically returned to the left side of the screen; thus you did not press the ⑧ key. The resulting several lines of screen text are in fact only one line to the editor. Place the cursor on a space between two words, press **r** and the ⑧ key, and the line will be divided into two lines.

Module Twenty-Nine
Where to Now?

Introduction

Congratulations! You have reached the last Module in this book. So far, you have been using the features of the UNIX operating system that we identified as most important for text processing and program writing. There are several other, more complex features also available on most UNIX systems which this final Module will briefly introduce. References will be provided for more thorough investigation.

Prerequisites

Before starting this Module you should have completed Modules One through Twelve.

Objectives

Upon completion of this Module you will have introductory knowledge (and be able to access the appropriate documentation to learn more) about the following UNIX programs and resources:

(1) *Sed*, a stream editor similar in command syntax to the *ex* line editor;

(2) *Awk*, a pattern scanning language;

(3) *Shell programming*, a method used to create powerful Shell scripts;

(4) *C-Language*, the programming language in which UNIX is written;

(5) *Ingres*, a data-base management system available on some UNIX systems;

(6) *ISP* and *S*, interactive statistical packages; and

(7) *Writers' Workbench*, a collection of programs designed to increase the overall effectiveness of written work (particularly helpful with technical writing).

Procedures

This procedure section is presented in seven parts. In each section you will be provided with a brief description of a selected UNIX resource. Several of the descriptions include examples. You may wish to try out the examples presented, but this is not essential for understanding.

Sed, the Stream Editor

Sed is an editor which performs many of the same functions as the *ex* line editor, but in a different manner. The line editor, *ex* applies the first command of a series to all lines in the file. Then the second command is applied to all lines, etc. *Sed*, which is a stream editor, works in the opposite way. It applies all specified commands to one line of text, then it applies all commands to the next line of text, etc.

The *Sed* editor is most useful when included in a series of "piped" Shell commands, because it performs its functions on the standard input and routes its output to the standard output (the standard input and output were described in Module Seven).

For example, the following command sequence will format the file named *test*, remove all blank lines from the input, and send this abridged text to the **page** command:

nroff -ms *test* | **sed** ´/^$/d´ | **page**   ®

Note how *sed* uses a command syntax very similar to the *ex* editor language (in this instance the special editor characters ^ and $).

Documentation: Sed—A Non-interactive Text Editor, from Bell Laboratories.

Awk, the Pattern Scanner

Awk is a pattern scanning language. It is very useful for performing more complex searches than are possible with the *ex* or *sed* editors. In addition, *awk* can be used to write simple programs which do not require detailed specifications.

For example, the following procedures could be used to select from a large file all individuals taller than 70" who wear shoes larger than a size eleven:

(a) Create a file (referred to here as *data*) containing the pertinent data:

name	height	shoe
Paul-Johnston	*71*	*10*
Harold-Atkins	*72*	*12*
H-Dan-Smith	*73*	*10*
Lyle-Strand	*70*	*10*
Walter-Mitchell	*73*	*9*

Each of the above lines contains three pieces of data. In this example each record is on a line by itself and each datum is separated from the others by blank spaces.

(b) Create a second file (here called *program*) containing the *awk* program:

{if ($2>=70 && $3>=11) print $1 }

This line translates as, "find the record(s) that have a second field (data point) greater than or equal to 70 (**$2>=70**) and (**&&**) a third field greater than or equal to 11 (**$3>=11**) For these cases print the first field (**print $1**)."

(c) Enter the command that instructs the Shell to execute the *awk* program contained in the file *program* on the data contained in the file *data*:

awk -f *program data*   ®

In our example this *Awk* program would display the following results on your screen:

Harold-Atkins

Documentation: Awk—A Pattern Scanning and Processing Language, from Bell Laboratories.

Shell Programming

Shell programming lies somewhere in the gray area between using pre-packaged software and actual programming. It offers a method for adding programming control structures (e.g. *if statements*) and setting variables in order to create powerful Shell scripts.

For example, the following Shell program would cause the Shell to evaluate whether or not a file contained any tables and would format the file according to this evaluation. (The program must be placed into a file and made executable. Module Twenty-Two: *Commands, Files, and Directories* describes Shell scripts and executable files.)

(a) Place the following lines holding the Shell program into a file (here called *check*):

```
# to avoid petes dilemma
foreach file ($argv)
        set a=(`grep -s TS $file`)
        if ($status == 0) then
                tbl $file | nroff -ms | lpr
        else
                nroff -ms $file | lpr
        endif
end
```

(b) Select a file to be formatted and enter the Shell command sequence:

check [*filename*]   ®

Documentation: An Introduction to the UNIX Shell, by Steve Bourne, from Bell Laboratories, and *An Introduction to the C Shell*, by William Joy, UC Berkeley Computing Services.

C-Language

UNIX is programmed in the C language. This makes it appropriate to consider writing your own C programs to supplement those already available to you as UNIX commands. Before rushing off to write a C program, however, be quite certain that you could not accomplish the intended task by using Shell commands (including *awk* and/or Shell scripts) already available on the system.

The following C program requires a four line file and, once compiled and executed, simply prints the phrase "hi there":

```
main()
{
    printf("hi there\n");
}
```

Note, however, that the same task is more easily accomplished with the Shell command:

echo ´ *hi there* ´   ®

Documentation: The C Programming Language, Kernighan & Ritchie, Prentice-Hall Publishers, and *UNIX Programming*, Kernighan & Ritchie, Bell Laboratories.

Ingres

Ingres is a data base management system available on some versions of UNIX. It is useful for maintaining and updating large databases which require frequent report generation.

Documentation: A Tutorial on Ingres and *Creating and Maintaining a Database using Ingres*, both by E. Epstein, Electronics Research Laboratory, College of Engineering, U.C. Berkeley.

ISP and *S*

ISP and *S* are both interactive statistical packages. *ISP* is distributed by the University of California at Berkeley, and *S* is distributed by Bell Laboratories. Each can perform many common statistical analyses—including multiple regression and T-tests—in a highly interactive manner. Of the two packages *ISP* is more easily learned and so makes a very useful instructional tool. *S* offers a more powerful and sophisticated system.

Documentation: ISP is described in *A Tutorial Introduction to Berkeley ISP*, from UC Berkeley Computing Services; *S* is described in *S—A Language and System for Data Analysis*, from Bell Laboratories.

Writers' Workbench

Writers' Workbench is a collection of programs designed to help you improve your writing. The package can be used to identify, and in some cases correct, grammatical, spelling, and stylistic problems in your written work. There are over twenty programs within the Writers' Workbench package.

In most instances you access a program by typing (from the Shell) the name of the program followed by the *filename* you want to have acted upon. A list of several of these programs and the functions they perform is presented on the next page.

Selected Writers' Workbench Programs

Command	Function
findbe [*file*]	Identifies all forms of verb *to be* in *file*.
org [*file*]	Prints text structure of *file*.
diction [*file*]	Identifies troublesome syntax in *file*.
splitrules	Explains split infinitives.
suggest [*words*]	Suggests alternatives to *words*.
style [*file*]	Analyzes surface characteristics of *file*.
topic [*file*]	Locates frequent noun phrases in *file*.
proofr [*file*]	Invokes several *Workbench* programs which check spelling, punctuation, double words, syntax, and split infinitives.
punctrules	Displays rules enforced in the **proofr** program.
sexist [*file*]	Identifies sexist phrases in *file*.

Shell Command Summary

Special Characters

Command	Function
|	Routes standard output from a prior Shell command to the next Shell command (Pipe).
>	Routes standard output from a prior Shell command to a specified file.
>&	Routes both standard output and error from a prior Shell command into a specified file.
&	Causes Shell command line to run in the background when appended to end of command line.
;	Allows you to type several Shell commands on one line (each command is separated by the ;).
$$	Expands to process ID of current Shell. Useful for generating a unique filename. For example, **uniq** *file* > *file*.**$$**, results in a new file containing **uniq***ue* lines and named *file.somenumber*, where *somenumber* is the process ID of the parent Shell.
?	Matches any single character.
*	Matches any sequence of characters.

Shell Commands

Command	Function
alias $\boxed{x}$ $\boxed{command}$	Makes *x* an **alias** for a *command* line.
awk $\boxed{prog}$ $\boxed{file1}$	Executes an **awk** *prog*ram on *file1*. **awk** is a high level pattern scanning and numerical programming language very useful in data-base management.
batch $\boxed{scriptfile}$	Executes a **batch** *scriptfile*. Almost any job can be submitted to batch, which can normally run a job more cheaply then interactive work.
cal $\boxed{month}$ $\boxed{year}$	Prints a **cal**endar for the specified *year* (i.e., 1983). A *month* may be specified by a number (1-12) before the year.
cat $\boxed{file1}$ $\boxed{file2}$	*Con***cat***enates* file(s). By default, the concatenated file(s) will be displayed on your screen. Use > to redirect output to new file. If output is displayed on screen, press CTRL-S to halt scrolling.
cd $\boxed{directoryname}$	*C*hanges *d*irectory to *directoryname* (*directoryname* must be a subdirectory of current directory).
checkeqn $\boxed{file1}$	**check***s* *file1* (containing **eqn** constructs) for problematic **eqn** commands.
checknr $\boxed{file1}$	**check***s* *file1* for nonbalanced formatting constructs (**nr***off* and *-ms* commands).
chkps	**ch***ecks* **p***rocess* **s***tatus*. (Available only on some systems.)

Command	Function
chmod $\boxed{mode\#}$ $\boxed{file1}$	**ch**anges **mod**e of *file1* to *mode#* (which specifies the permissions attached to a file). Permissions are **r**ead, **w**rite, and ex*ecute* permission for owner, group members, and others (see Module Twenty-Two).
clear	**clear**s screen and places cursor at top.
col	Removes reverse line feeds from a text file. Often used as a filter when piping output from **tbl** to an output device that can't do reverse motion (i.e., line printer).
comm $\boxed{file1}$ $\boxed{file2}$	Selects or rejects words **comm**on to two sorted lists (*file1* and *file2*). Identifies words in one file and not the other or words found in both files.
compact $\boxed{file1}$	**compact**s *file1*. Reduces disk space occupied by file. **compact**ed version of *file1* will have .C appended to filename (*file1.C*). Must use **uncompact** before editing or otherwise using file (if this command does not work for you try **pack** and **unpack**).
cp $\boxed{file1}$ $\boxed{file2}$	Creates a second **c**o**p**y of *file1* called *file2*.
crypt	*En*crypt*s* and de**crypt**s a file (see Module Sixteen).
date	Displays the current **date** and time.
dc	**d**esk **c**alculator. Performs arithmetic calculations. Easy to use once you learn assembly language programming.
deroff $\boxed{file1}$	Removes formatting constructs from *file1* (**de** *n*roffs a file).
diction $\boxed{file1}$	Identifies problematic **diction** in *file1*.

Command	Function
dirs	Displays pathname of current directory: **dir**ec-tory s*tatus.* (Works faster than **pwd** but is only available on some systems.)
du	**d**isplays disk u*sage* in blocks. (Available only on some systems.)
echo [*string*]	Displays (**echo**es) *string* on screen.
eqn [*file1*]	Preformats all **eq**uation*s* in *file1.* Output should be piped to the *troff* formatter (use **neqn** as a preprocesser for *nroff* formatting).
fg	Recalls a backgrounded process into the **f**o*r-*g*round*; this process will become your current process. (Available only on some systems.)
find	**find**s *file* specified with **-n** option. Must use **-p** option to have full pathname of *file* **p**rinted (See Module Fifteen, *The* UNIX *Directory Structure*).
grep [*string*] [*file1*]	Locates all instances of *string* (a **g**lobal **r**egular **e**x*pression* or **p**att*ern*) in *file1.*
head [*file1*]	Displays first ten lines (**head**) of *file1.*
history	Reports **history** of last # number of Shell commands, where # is the number that history variable has been set to. (Available only with C Shell.)
jobs	Displays list of processes (**jobs**) currently *stopped* or running in the *background.*
kill #	**kill**s process number (#); **kill -9 #** will nuke process number (#).
logout	Ends communication with UNIX.

Command	Function
look $\boxed{string}$	**look**s in dictionary for words that match *string* and displays on screen this list of words.
lookbib $\boxed{database}$	**look**s through a **bib**liographic *database* file for references containing specified keywords.
lpr $\boxed{file1}$	Causes a copy of *file1* to be printed on the **l**ine **pr**inter.
ls	Displays a list of all files in your current directory.
mail $\boxed{login}$	Sends a message to *login*. End message with a CTRL-D (see **write**). When used without a *login* as an argument initiates a **mail** receiving session and displays a list of all messages sent to your UNIX account.
man $\boxed{command}$	Displays the UNIX **man**ual information about whatever *command* you specify.
mesg y or **n**	Permits other user to write **mes**ages to your terminal (and you to write them). Default value is **y**es (**n** for **n**o).
mkdir $\boxed{directory}$	**m**akes a new **dir**ectory named *directory*.
more $\boxed{file1}$	Displays *file1* one **more** window at a time. Similar to **page**.
mv $\boxed{file1}$ $\boxed{file2}$	**m**oves *file1* into *file2* (changes name of *file1* to *file2*).
neqn $\boxed{file1}$	Preformats all equations in *file1*. Output should be piped to the *nroff* formatter (use **eqn** as preprocesser for *troff* formatter).
nroff $\boxed{file1}$	Formats *file1* according to *nroff* commands embedded in the text (**n**ew **r**un **off**). Must use **nroff -ms** to format *file1* when -*ms* macro calls are embedded in the text.

Command	Function
pack [file1]	**pack**s file1. Reduces disk space occupied by file. **pack**ed version of *file1* will have **.P** appended to filename (*file1.P*). Must use **unpack** before editing or otherwise using file (if this command does not work try **compact** and **uncompact**).
page [file1]	Displays *file1* a **page** at a time (file can not be edited, only viewed). Similar to **more**.
passwd	Changes your **passw**o**rd**.
ps	Provides **p**rocess **s**tatus information (**ps -g** will provide more **g**lobal information).
pwd	Displays pathname of current directory (**p**rint **w**orking **d**irectory).
refer [file1]	Prepares *file1* containing **refer** bibliographic fields for formatting by a macro package (i.e., -*ms*).
reset	**reset**s terminal to a sensible state.
roffbib [file1]	Prints out fields from a bibliographic data base as endnotes instead of footnotes (as **refer** does). Generally used with **sortbib** as follows: **sortbib** *file1* | **roffbib**.
rev [file1]	**rev**erses all lines in *file1* (why? don't ask us, but it's great fun).
rm [file1]	**rm**oves *file1* (be careful!).
rmdir [directory]	**rm**oves **dir**ectory *directory*. (If *directory* contains files you must use **rm -r** *directory*.)
sed	**s**tream **ed**itor. Uses **ex**-like syntax. Most useful as a filter to modify information passing through a pipe.

Command	Function
set	With no arguments **set** displays variables that have been **set** for your account.
set noclobber	Prevents overwriting (**clobber***ing*) an existing file.
set ignoreeof	Prevents CTRL-D from logging you out of UNIX (**ignoreeof** → **ignore** *end of* **file**; CTRL-D is the UNIX "end of file" message).
sort *file1*	**sort***s file1* into *ascii* sequence.
sortbib *file1*	**sort***s* a **bib***liographic* data base (see **roffbib**).
source *file1*	Asks Shell to execute *file1* containing Shell commands (uses *file1* as **source** code for Shell). Most useful for requesting Shell to re-read your *.login* file.
spell *file1*	Compares **spell***ing* of all words in *file1* to words in UNIX dictionary and reports all those found in *file1* and not in dictionary.
stty	**S***ets* **t***erminal* **ty***pe* parameters.
tail *file1*	Displays last ten lines (**tail**) of *file1*.
tbl *file1*	Preformats all tables in *file1*. Output must then be piped to the *nroff* or *troff* formatter.
tee *file1*	**tee** is a pipe fitting. Catches output within a pipeline and puts a copy in *file1*. For example, **nroff** *textfile* | **tee** *ntext* | **lpr** will format *textfile* and place a copy of the formatted output in *ntext* while sending an additional copy to the l*ine***pr***inter*.
tr	**tr***anslates* some specified characters or range of characters from the standard input into a different set of characters and sends this translation to the standard output.

Command	Function
troff [*file1*]	Formats *file1* according to *troff* commands embedded in the text. Formatted version will be phototypeset (**t**ypeset **r**un **off**). Must use **troff -ms** to format *file1* when *-ms* macro calls are embedded in the text.
tset	**set**s **t**erminal erase, kill, and other special characters.
uniq [*file1*]	Removes redundant lines from *file1*, leaving only **uniq**ue lines.
vi [*file1*]	Starts a file or retrieves an existing file named *file1* for **vi**sual editing. Moves you into Command Mode. See summary section which follows on *Commands to Enter an Editor*.
wait	Causes Shell to **wait** until backgrounded Shell command is complete.
wc [*file1*]	Displays total number of lines, words, and characters in *file1* (**w**ord **c**ount). Very useful for high school English papers that "must be 500 words or longer."
whatis [*command*]	Displays synopsis line from manual for specified *command*. Tells **what** *command* **is** all about.
whereis [*command*]	Displays full pathname of specified command. Tells **where** *command* **is** located.
who	Presents a list of **who** is currently logged onto your UNIX system.
write [*login*]	Immediately **write**s to *login* while both of you are logged on (see **mail**); end session with a CTRL-D.

Commands to Enter an Editor

Command	Function
vi $\boxed{file1}$	Starts a file or retrieves an existing file named *file1* for **vi***sual* editing. Moves you into Command Mode.
vi +# $\boxed{file1}$	Puts you into the **vi***sual* editor Command Mode at line # in *file1*. If no # is specified, places cursor at last line of *file1*.
vi +/ $\boxed{word}$ $\boxed{file1}$	Moves you into the **vi***sual* editor Command Mode at first instance of word in *file1*.
vi	Creates a buffer for **vi***sual* editing. Material must be given filename (with **:w** *name*) to be saved when editing session terminated. Moves you into Command Mode.
ex $\boxed{file1}$	Starts a file or retrieves an existing file named *file1* for line editing. Moves you into the (**ex***tinct*) line editor Command Mode.

Visual Editor Command Summary

Cursor Moving Commands

Command	Function
←↓↑→	(h j k l) Moves cursor one line up/down or one space right or left.
0	(zero) Moves cursor to the beginning of line.
$	Moves cursor to the end of the current line.
42G	Goes to line 42 (or any number).
G	Goes to the last line in your file.
L	Positions cursor at Low point on the screen.
M	Positions cursor at Mid point on the screen.
H	Positions cursor at High point on the screen.
w	Moves cursor forward to the beginning of the next word in your file.
W	Moves cursor forward to the beginning of the next Word in your file, ignoring punctuation.
e	Moves cursor forward to the end of next word in your file.
b	Moves cursor backward to the beginning prior word in your file.
B	Moves cursor Backward to the beginning of prior word in your file, ignoring punctuation.

497

Command	Function
f $\boxed{b}$	Moves cursor *forward* through text to next *b*.
F $\boxed{b}$	Moves cursor backward through text to prior *b*.
t $\boxed{b}$	Moves cursor forward through text *to* next *b*.
T $\boxed{b}$	Moves cursor backward through text **T***o* prior *b*.
/ $\boxed{word}$	Moves cursor forward through text to next *word*.
? $\boxed{word}$	Moves cursor backward through text to prior *word*.
n	Repeats last **/** or **?** search: Moves cursor forward (or backward) through text to **n***ext* character or word.
N	Repeats last **/** or **?** search but reverses direction of search.
)	Moves cursor forward through text to beginning of next sentence.
(	Moves cursor backward through text to beginning of prior sentence.
}	Moves cursor forward through text to beginning of next paragraph.
{	Moves cursor backward through text to beginning of prior paragraph.
]]	Moves cursor forward through text to beginning of next section.
[[	Moves cursor backward through text to beginning of prior section.
''	(Two single quotes) Moves cursor to prior position in file.

Display Adjusting Commands

Command	Function
CTRL-D	Scrolls **d**own or moves on to more text in the file.
*12***CTRL-D**	Scrolls down or moves on to 12 more lines of text in the file.
CTRL-U	Scrolls **u**p or moves back to prior text.
CTRL-F	Goes **f**orward to next block or window of text.
CTRL-B	Goes **b**ack a window of text.
CTRL-E	Displays an additional line at bottom of screen.
CTRL-Y	Displays an additional line at top of screen.
z.	Redraws screen, with the current line in middle of the window.
z4.	Makes screen show only 4 lines of text. The number can be 1-23 (don't forget the period).
z-	Redraws screen, with the current line on bottom of the window.
z ®	Redraws screen; current line at top of window.
CTRL-R	Redraw screen.

Undo Commands

u	(lower case **u**) **u**ndoes the effect of the last text change command.
U	(Upper Case **U**) **U**ndoes all changes made to the current line.

Text Changing Commands

One-Way Commands

(Leave You In Append Mode
Until You Press ESCAPE)

Command	Function
a	Starts adding text one space to the *right* of the cursor (**a**ppend).
i	Starts adding text one space to the *left* of the cursor (**i**nsert).
o	**o**pens a line for text *below* the cursor line.
O	(Upper Case) **O**pens a line for text *above* the cursor line.
A	(Upper Case) Starts adding text at the end of the line (**A**ppend).
I	(Upper Case) Inserts text at the beginning of the line (**I**nsert).
cw	**c**hanges the one **w**ord to the right of the cursor.
s	(lower case) *substitutes* text for a single character.
S	(Upper Case) **S**ubstitutes text for an entire line.
cc	Substitutes text for an entire line (**cc**hanges; same as **S**).
C	Substitutes text for the rest of the line (**C**hanges from the cursor position forward).
R	**R**eplaces characters you type over with new characters (overlay type).

Text Changing Commands

Two-Way Commands

(*Return You To Command Mode*)

Command	Function
x	Erases the character under the cursor (**x** *out*).
X	Erases the character before the cursor.
xp	Transposes characters.
r $\boxed{b}$	**r***eplaces* the character under the cursor with the letter *b*.
dw	**d***eletes* from the cursor position forward to start of next **w***ord.*
db	**d***eletes* from cursor position backward to **begin-***ning* of previous word.
dd	Deletes the entire cursor line (**dd***eletes*).
D	**D***eletes* the rest of the line (from the cursor position forward).
*:1,26***d**	**d***eletes* lines 1 through 26 (you select the line numbers).
J	**J***oins* cursor line with the next line in your text.
<<	Shifts cursor line left one shiftwidth (distance of one **TAB**, normally 8 spaces).
>>	Shifts cursor line right one shiftwidth (distance of one **TAB**, normally 8 spaces).
.	(Dot) Repeats last text change command.

Text Relocation Commands

Command	Function
yy	Yanks the cursor line of text and places in unnamed buffer (**yy***anks*; same as **Y**).
*6***yy**	Yanks 6 lines and places in unnamed buffer (See *Put* command).
" $\boxed{a}$ **yy**	(Double quotes) Yanks cursor line of text and stores in *a* register (registers *a* to *z* available).
" $\boxed{c}$ *3***yy**	(Double quotes) Yanks 3 lines of text and stores in *c* register (registers *a* to *z* available).
" $\boxed{b}$ **dd**	(Double quotes) Deletes cursor line of text and stores in *b* register (**dd***eletes*; registers *a* to *z* available).
P	(Upper Case) **P***uts* text stored in unnamed register just above the cursor line (or before the cursor).
p	(lower case) **p***uts* the yanked or deleted text just below the cursor line (or after the cursor).
" $\boxed{a}$ **P**	(Double quotes) **P***uts* the text stored in register *a* just above the cursor line (or before the cursor).
" $\boxed{6}$ **p**	(Double quotes) **p***uts* the deleted text stored in register *6* just below the cursor line (or after the cursor). Note: last 9 text block deletions are automatically stored in registers 1 to 9.
:*1,26* **m** *82*	**m***oves* lines *1* through *26* to after line *82*.
:*1,26* **co** *82*	**co***pies* lines *1* through *26* and places after line *82*.
:**w** $\boxed{file1}$	**w***rites* current file to disk—names it *file1*.

Command	Function
:1,26 **w** [*file1*]	**w**rites lines 1 to 26 as new file—names it *file1*.
:1,26 **w** >> [*file1*]	Appends lines *1* to *26* to end of existing file *file1*.
:26 **r**ead [*file1*]	Places contents of *file1* into current file after line *26* (**r**eads in *file*).

Miscellaneous Additional Commands

:sh	Stops processing—places current file in background and moves to the **sh**ell (return to file with **CTRL-D**).
:!command	Temporary Shell escape. Insert whatever Shell *command* you wish. Output from command, if any, becomes part of current buffer.
Q	Moves from *vi* to the line editor Command Mode (Return to *vi* with **vi** command).
CTRL-G	Status check of current file: displays filename, percent of file edited, and cursor position in file.
CTRL-M	**RETURN** character: advances cursor one line.
CTRL-Z	Stops processing—places current file in background and moves to the Shell (return to the file with the **fg** Shell command). Note: Not available on some systems.
:map [$] [*abc*]	Creates own Command Mode command. You replace $ with any character (#1 for function key 1) and *abc* with any series of actions (remove with **:unmap $**).
:ab [*abc*] [*phrase*]	Establishes *abc* as **ab**breviation for *phrase* (remove with **:una** *abc*).

Quit Working on the File and
Return to Shell Commands

Command	Function
ZZ	Writes all changes made to the file during an editing session and returns to the Shell (the "I am finished working on this file" command).
:w ®	**w**rites all the changes made in a file and leaves you in the visual editor to continue working on the file.
:q! ®	**q**uits an editing session and returns you to Shell, but *does not write* changes made to file (the "can I start over" command).
:wq! ®	**w**rites all changes made in a file during an editing session, **q**uits and returns to the Shell.

Regular Characters for
Search and Substitutions

c	When placed at end of search it prompts you to **c**onfirm substitution. Enter **y** to execute substitution; press ® to cancel it.
d	When placed at end of search it **d**eletes pattern found.
g	When placed at the beginning of a search it addresses all lines in the file; at end of search it functions on all cases of pattern within specified lines. When used in both places it functions on all cases of pattern within current file (**g**lobal search).

Commands to Enter an Editor

Command | Function

vi $\boxed{file1}$ Starts a file or retrieves an existing file named *file1* for **vi**sual editing. Moves you into Command Mode.

vi +# $\boxed{file1}$ Puts you into the **vi**sual editor Command Mode at line # in *file1*. If no # is specified, places cursor at last line of *file1*.

vi +/ $\boxed{word}$ $\boxed{file1}$ Moves you into the **vi**sual editor Command Mode at first instance of *word* in *file1*.

vi   Creates a buffer for **vi**sual editing. Material must be given filename (with **:w** *name*) to be saved when editing session terminated. Moves you into Command Mode.

ex $\boxed{file1}$ Starts a file or retrieves an existing file named *file1* for line editing. Moves you into the (**ex**tinct) line editor Command Mode.

Special Characters in Append Mode

Command	Function
BACKSPACE	Backspaces one character.
DELETE	(**RUBOUT**) Interrupts Append Mode and places you in Command Mode.
ESC	**ESC**apes to Command Mode.
CTRL-H	Backspaces one character.
CTRL-I	**TAB** character (moves 8 spaces right).
CTRL-V	Allows input of a **SPACE**, **TAB**, or **RETURN** character.
CTRL-W	Backspaces one word.
\	Allows input of a **CTRL-H**, **BACKSPACE**, or @ character.
@	Erases all input on a line.

Summary of Text Operators

Affected Text	move to	delete	change	yank
lines	®	**dd**	**cc**	**yy**
word to right	**w**	**dw**	**cw**	**yw**
word to left	**b**	**db**	**cb**	**yb**
right to g	**t**g	**dt**g	**ct**g	**yt**g
left to g	**T**g	**dT**g	**cT**g	**yT**g
right including g	**f**g	**df**g	**cf**g	**yf**g
left including g	**F**g	**dF**g	**cF**g	**yF**g

Formatting Command Summary

Nroff/Troff Commands

Command	Function
.ad b	b*egins* **ad**j*usting* text (this is the default state).
.bp	Causes a temporary **b**r*eak* between **p**a*ges*; begins a new page of text. A number used as an argument becomes the page number of the new page (e.g., **.bp** *4*).
.br	Causes a **br**e*ak* in text filling; begins a new line of text.
.ce $\boxed{\#}$	**ce***nters* # number of lines.
.cu $\boxed{\#}$	*continuously* **u***nderlines* for next # number of lines; italicizes in *troff.*
.de $\boxed{XX}$	Begins a macro **de***finition*; replace *XX* with two character macro name. Use **..** to indicate end of macro definition.
.ds $\boxed{XX}$ $\boxed{string}$	**d***efines* **s***tring XX* as the specified *string*. (See \ (* in *Escape Sequences* section.)
.ex	**ex***its* from *nroff* or *troff.*
.fi	Resumes the **fi***lling* of input lines (default).
.ft $\boxed{X}$	Changes **f***ont* to *X* where *X* is either **B** for **Bold**, **I** for *Italic*, **R** for **R**oman, or **S** for Special Mathematical; default is Roman. Use \ **f***X* to change font within a line.

507

Command	Function
.hy	Starts **hy***phenation* (this is the default state).
.in #̲	**in***dents* left margin # number of spaces. [This is a one-way command; **.in 0** (zero) is the return command.]
.ll #̲	Sets **l***ine* **l***ength* to # number (default is 6 1/2 inches).
.ls #̲	(lower case l) Sets the **l***inespacing* of paper at # number (i.e., **.ls 2** double spaces). Single spacing is default state.
.lt #̲	Sets the **l***ength* of **t***itle* to # number (default is 6 1/2 inches).
.na	Leaves right edge jagged; **n***o* **a***djusting*. (This is a one-way command; **.ad b** returns to normal justification.)
.ne #̲	Checks if # number of output lines available; if not available a premature page break occurs (**ne***ed* # number of continuous lines).
.nf	**n***o* **f***ill*; Stops the filling process. (This is a one-way command; **.fi** returns to normal text filling.)
.nh	**n***o* **h***yphenate*; stops hyphenation.
.nm #̲	**n***um***bers** next # number of lines.
.nn	Stops numbering (**n***o* **n***umber*).
.nr *XX̲* *value̲*	Defines **n***umber* **r***egister XX* as the specified *value*.
.pl #̲	Sets **p***age* **l***ength* at # number (11 inch default).
.pn #̲	Sets **p***age* **n***umber* for next page at # number.

Command	Function
.po #̲	Sets **p**age **o**ffset to # number.
.ps #̲	Changes **p**oint **s**ize to # number (default is 10 point). Use \s# to change point size within a line.
.rd 𝑓𝑖𝑙𝑒	Causes input to be **rea**d from *file* if *file* specified. The standard input (usually your terminal) will be read if no file is specified (see *Form Letters* Module).
.so 𝑓𝑖𝑙𝑒	**so**urces in file named *file* (which may contain macro definitions) to current file.
.sp #̲	**sp**aces down # number distance.
.ss #̲	Changes **s**pace character **s**ize to # number; default is 12/36 em.
.ta #̲	Sets TAB to # number of characters; this distance can be a series of numbers, each indicating a separate TAB stop (default is 8 characters per TAB).
.ti #̲	**t**emporarily **i**ndents left margin # number of spaces (next output line only).
.tl ′ 1̲ ′ 2̲ ′ 3̲ ′	Prints a three part **ti**t**l**e line.
.ul #̲	**u**nder**l**ines next # number of lines; will italicize in *troff*.
.vs #̲	Changes **v**ertical **s**pacing to # number (default is 12 point).
.wh #̲ 𝑋𝑋̲	Calls macro *XX* **wh**en page position # is reached; also known as "setting a trap."

Escape Sequences Allowing Printing of Nroff/Troff Special Characters

(Special Mathematical Characters Available on Troff Described in *Phototypesetting* Module)

Command	Function
\ $\boxed{x}$	The backslash prevents interpretation of *x*.
\e	Allows printing of current e*scape* character.
\´	Prints an accute accent in *troff.*
\`	Prints a grave accent in *troff.*
\−	Prints a minus sign in *troff.*
\0	Creates an "unpaddable" space the width of a 0.
\ $\boxed{\text{SPACE}}$	Creates an "unpaddable" space in the current space size.
\\|	Creates an "unpaddable" space the width of 1/6 em.
\&	Deposits a non-printing character that occupies no space (zero width character).
\"	When placed at the beginning of line, masks line from formatter (allows comment in file).
\d	Shifts text **d**own 1/2 em in *troff*, 1/2 space in *nroff.*
\u	Shifts text **u**p 1/2 em in *troff*, 1/2 space in *nroff.*
\f $\boxed{X}$	Changes type **f**ont to *X* where **B** is **B**oldface, **I** is **I***talics*, **R** is **R**oman, and **S** is **S**pecial Mathematical font.

Command	Function
\h′ # ′	Shifts right # distance (**h**orizontal shift).
\l′ # ′	Draws a horizontal **l**ine # distance.
\L′ # ′	Draws a vertical **L**ine # distance.
\o′ xyz ′	**o**verstrikes characters *xyz*.
\p	Breaks filling and spreads out line (**p**ulls).
\r	**r**everses print direction 1 em in *troff*; reverse line-feed in *nroff*.
\n(XX	Causes value stored in *XX* **n**umber register to be read in (where *XX* is a two character name for a number register). See **.nr**.
*(XX	Causes string stored in *XX* string register to be read in (where *XX* is a two character name for a string register). See **.ds**.
\$1	Causes first argument to macro call to be read into a macro.

-ms Macro Commands

Paragraph Macros

Command	Function
.PP	Begins a standard, five space indented **P**ara-gra**P**h.
.LP	Begins a **L**eft block **P**aragraph (no indenting).
.IP	Begins an **I**ndented **P**aragraph (left margin of the entire paragraph is indented right 5 spaces).
.IP X	Begins a labeled **I**ndented **P**aragraph. Replace the *X* with numbers, letters or a word that you want placed to the left of your paragraph.

Command	Function
.IP $\boxed{X}$ $\boxed{\#}$	Begins a labeled **I**ndented **P**aragraph. Replace the *X* with numbers, letters or a word that you want placed to the left of your paragraph. Replace # with a number indicating indentation of paragraph.
.QP	Begins a **Q**uote **P**aragraph. Indent 5 spaces from both left and right margins. Automatic single line-spacing not provided.
.XP	Begins an e**X**dented **P**aragraph. The first line of the paragraph is at the left margin, while the remaining lines are indented.

Footnotes, Keeps, and Displays

.FS	**S**tarts a **F**ootnote: Text between an **.FS** and an **.FE** command is formatted as a footnote. Footnotes are not numbered. (Some systems will allow you to produce numbered footnotes. To do this you must also place these three characters "**" in the text where you wish the numbered footnote to appear.) (.FS is a one-way command; .FE is the return command.)
.FE	**E**nds a **F**ootnote: Returns to normal text layout.
.KS	**S**tarts a **K**eep: Text between a **.KS** and a **.KE** command is printed on a single page. If necessary a new page is started. (This is a one-way command; .KE is the return command.)
.KF	Begins a **F**loating **K**eep. If text will not fit on current page and a page break is required, text following the keep will be used to fill rest of page. (This is a one-way command; .KE is the return command.)
.KE	**E**nds the **K**eep: Returns to normal page layout.

Command	Function
.LG	Increases point size by two points (**La**r**G**er).
.SM	Decreases point size by two points (**SM**aller).
.NL	**N**orma**L** point size; resets point size to original value (the value of the **nr PS** number register).
.RS	Indents left margin of text to the value specified in the **.nr PI** register which has a default value of five spaces (**R**ight **S**tart). Can be repeated for additional indenting. (This is a one-way command; **.RE** is the return command.)
.RE	Moves left margin back five spaces (**R**ight **E**nd). (Number of **.RE** commands used must match number of **.RS** commands used.)
.DA	Provides today's **DA**te as center footer of paper. (This is the default condition.)
.DA date	Prints **DA**te as center footer of paper.
.ND	Suppresses printing of today's date as footer on paper (**N**o **D**ate).
.2C	Begins **2 C**olumn format of paper. Will automatically cause a page break. (This is a one-way command; **.1C** will return to single column output.)
.1C	Returns to **1 C**olumn output on a new page.
.MC #	Sets column width to # number characters. Will automatically cause a break page (**M**ulti-**C**olumn). (The number of columns is computed automatically, based upon line length.)

Command	Function
.AU	Centers following text line(s) as **AU**thor's name(s); *troff* sets name(s) in ten point italic type.
.AI	Centers A*uthor's* I*nstitution*; Use repeated **.AU** and **.AI** calls for multiple authors from different institutions.
.AB XXX	B*egins* A*bsract*, where *XXX* is the abstract's label. If nothing is entered for *XXX* the abstract will not be labeled. The abstract will be filled and adjusted to a line length of 5/6 the normal text line length.
.AE	E*nds* A*bstract*.

Other -ms Macros

Command	Function
.UL word	U*nder*L*ines* word. Only the one *word* on the line with the **.UL** command will be underlined.
.I	Begins underlining of text; will I*talicize* in *troff*. (This is a one-way command; **.R** returns to non-underlining in *nroff* and **R**oman type in *troff*.)
.B	B*olds* text, underlines in *nroff*. (This is a one-way command; **.R** returns to non-underlining in *nroff* and **R**oman type in *troff*.)
.R	Stops underlining text in *nroff*; will return to **R**oman type in *troff*.
.BX word	Draws a **B**o**X** around *word*.
.B1	Begins a block of text to be enclosed in a **B**ox.
.B2	Indicates end of passage to be enclosed by **B**ox.

Command	Function
.LG	Increases point size by two points (**La**r**G**er).
.SM	Decreases point size by two points (**SM**aller).
.NL	**N**orma**L** point size; resets point size to original value (the value of the **nr PS** number register).
.RS	Indents left margin of text five spaces (**R**ight **S**tart). Can be repeated for additional indenting. (This is a one-way command; **.RE** is the return command.)
.RE	Moves left margin back five spaces (**R**ight **E**nd). (Number of **.RE** commands used must match number of **.RS** commands used.)
.DA	Provides today's **DA**te as center footer of paper. (This is the default condition.)
.DA *date*	Prints **da**te as center footer of paper.
.ND	Suppresses printing of today's date as footer on paper (**N**o **D**ate).
.2C	Begins **2** **C**olumn format of paper. Will automatically cause a page break. (This is a one-way command; **.1C** will return to single column output.)
.1C	Returns to **1** **C**olumn output on a new page.
.MC *#*	Sets column width to # number characters. Will automatically cause a break page (**M**ulti-**C**olumn). (The number of columns is computed automatically, based upon line length.)

String Definition Commands

Command	Function
.ds LH $\boxed{X}$	*Left Header:* Puts X in top left corner of pages.
.ds CH $\boxed{X}$	*Center Header:* Puts X in top center position of all pages.
.ds RH $\boxed{X}$	*Right Header:* Puts X in upper right corner of all pages.
.ds LF $\boxed{X}$	*Left Footer:* Puts X in lower left corner of pages.
.ds CF $\boxed{X}$	*Center Footer:* Puts X in center bottom position of all pages.
.ds RF $\boxed{X}$	*Right Footer:* Puts X in lower right corner of all pages.

Note: the % symbol may be substituted for X in any of the above headers or footers, and page numbers will appear in that position.

Summary of -ms Number Registers

Register	Function	Default Value (for *nroff*)
.nr LL	*Line Length* of text	6 inches
.nr PO	*Page Offset*	0 inches
.nr FL	*Footnote Line* length	5.5 inches
.nr PI	*Paragraph Indentation*	5 spaces
.nr QI	*Quote* paragraph *Indentation*	5 spaces
.nr HM	*Header Margin*	1 inch
.nr FM	*Footer Margin*	1 inch
.nr PD	Between *Paragraph Distance*	1v
.nr PS	*Point Size*	10p
.nr VS	*Vertical Spacing*	12p

Distances may be indicated in inches, centimeters, em's, v's, or Picas; point size and vertical spacing is specified in points.

INDEX

518

526

QUICK ACCESS CHART [*]

	Character	Word	Line
Add	24, 129 a i I A o O	24, 129 a i I A o O	24, 129 a i I A o O
Change	47, 231 r s	48, 231 cw	49, 231 cc S
Copy		229, 231 yw	136, 229 yy, *:4* **co** *6*
Create	24, 129 a i I A o O	24, 129 a i I A o O	24, 129 a i I A o O
Delete	46 x	45, 230 dw	44, 231 dd
Find	15 */ b*	43 */ word*	125 *64*G
Insert	24, 129 i I	24, 129 i I	24, 129, 194 i I
Join			133 J
Move		231 dw & p	139, 231 dd & p, *:6* **m** *33*
Remove	46 x	45, 230 dw	44, 231 dd, *:6* **d**
Substitute	48, 130 s	48, 231 cw	49, 130 cc S

[*] Note: Page number appears in top row; command(s) appears in bottom row.

Paragraph	File	Directory	
24, 129 a i I A o O	23, 191 vi ex	172, 250 mkdir	**Add**
49, 231 7cc 6S	27, 107 ZZ & vi	250 cd	**Change**
136 5yy, :4, 6 co 9	84 cp		**Copy**
24, 129 a i I A o O	24, 191 vi ex	172, 251 mkdir	**Create**
44 6dd	85 rm	493 rmdir	**Delete**
226 { }	266, 286 find		**Find**
			Insert
	87, 304 cat		**Join**
139, 231 6dd & p, :3, 6m 8	85 mv		**Move**
44, 139 6dd, :2,5 d	85 rm	493 rmdir	**Remove**
49, 130 6cc 6S			**Substitute**

528

Map A

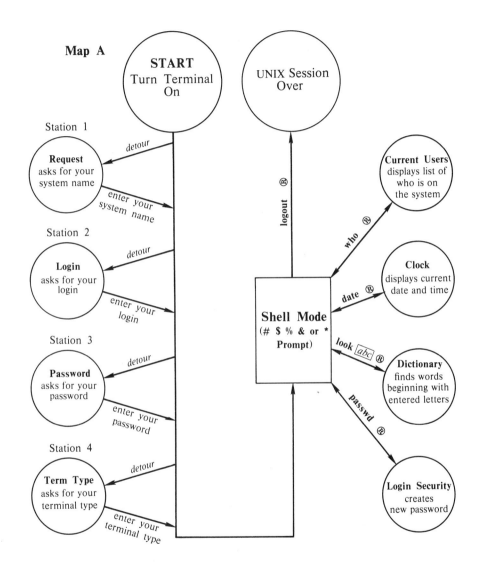

Map B

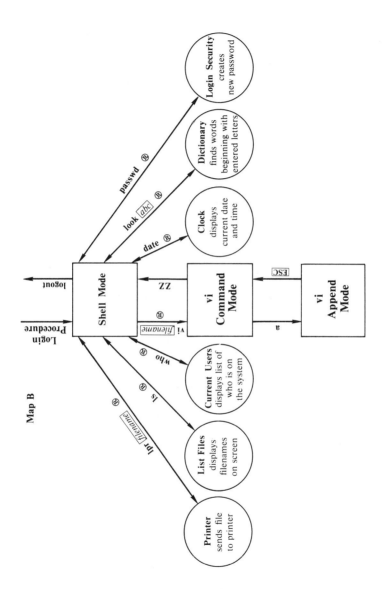

Login Security
creates
new password

Dictionary
finds words
beginning with
entered letters

Clock
displays
current date
and time

passwd ®

look abc ®

date ®

Shell Mode

logout

ZZ

vi
Command
Mode

ESC

Login
Procedure

®

vi filename

vi
Append
Mode

a

who ®

Current Users
displays list of
who is on
the system

ls ®

List Files
displays
filenames
on screen

lpr filename ®

Printer
sends file
to printer

Map C

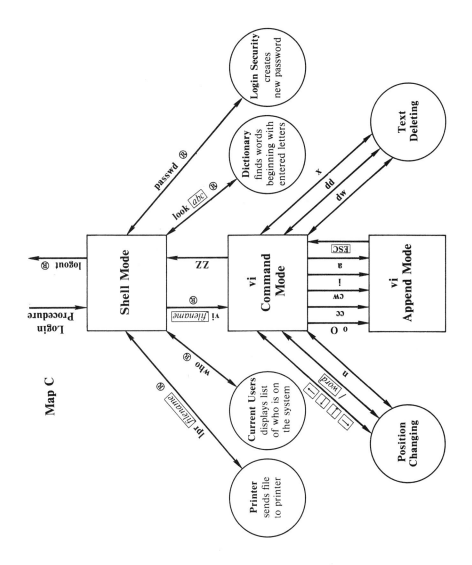

Login Procedure ® →

← logout ®

Shell Mode

vi Command Mode

vi Append Mode

passwd ®

Login Security
creates
new password

look [abc] ®

Dictionary
finds words
beginning with
entered letters

ZZ

vi [filename] ®

x

dd

dw

Text Deleting

ESC

a

i

cw

cc

O o

u

/ [word]

← ↑ ↓ →

Position Changing

who ®

Current Users
displays list
of who is on
the system

lpr [filename] ®

Printer
sends file
to printer

Map D

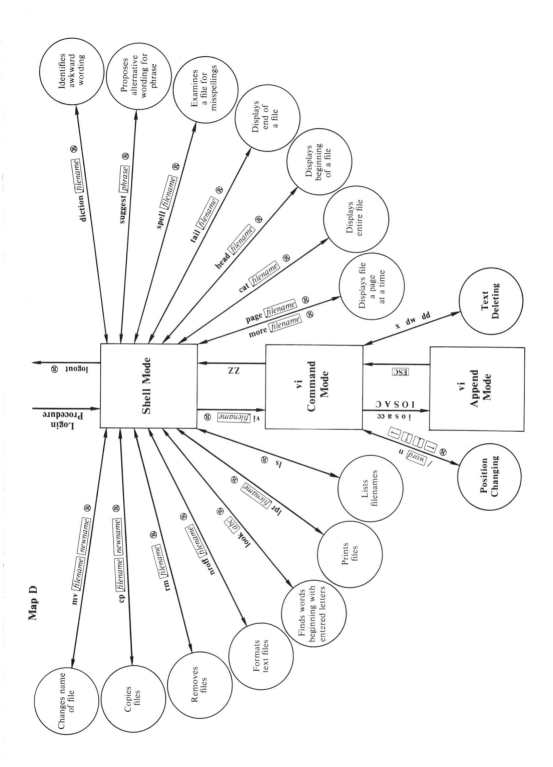

Identifies awkward wording

Proposes alternative wording for phrase

Examines a file for misspellings

Displays end of a file

Displays beginning of a file

Displays entire file

Displays file a page at a time

diction *filename* ®

suggest *phrase* ®

spell *filename* ®

tail *filename* ®

head *filename* ®

cat *filename* ®

page *filename* ®

more *filename* ®

logout ®

Login Procedure

Shell Mode

vi Command Mode

vi Append Mode

ZZ

vi *filename* ®

ESC

i o s a c c
I O S A C

Text Deleting

x   dw   dd

Position Changing

/ *word* ®
n

ls ®

lpr *filename* ®

look *abc* ®

nroff *filename* ®

rm *filename* ®

cp *filename* *newname* ®

mv *filename* *newname* ®

Lists filenames

Prints files

Finds words beginning with entered letters

Formats text files

Removes files

Copies files

Changes name of file

Map E

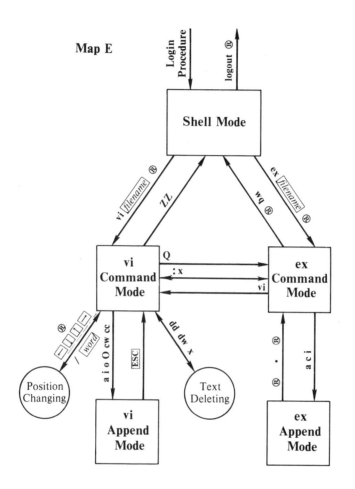